# The United States' Emergence as a Southeast Asian Power, 1940-1950

# The United States' Emergence as a Southeast Asian Power, 1940–1950

Gary R. Hess

Columbia University Press
New York  1987

Library of Congress Cataloging-in-Publication Data

Hess Gary R.
   The United States' emergence as a Southeast Asian
power, 1940–1950.

   Bibliography: p.
   Includes index.
   1. Asia, Southeastern—Foreign relations—United
States. 2. United States—Foreign relations—Asia,
Southeastern. I. Title.
DS525.9.U6H47   1987        (327.73059)        86-18861
ISBN 0-231-06190-0


Columbia University Press
New York   Guildford, Surrey
Copyright © 1987 Columbia University Press

Printed in the United States of America


This book is
Smyth-sewn.

Book design by J.S. Roberts

**To Ryan**

# Contents

# Preface

THIS STUDY TRACES the development of U.S. policy in Southeast Asia during the critical period beginning with the Japanese-American rivalry over the region in 1940–1941—when the United States sought to protect its own substantial interests in the region as well as those of the European colonial powers—and concluding with the outbreak of the Korean War in 1950. During that decade, the American interst in Southeast Asia increased substantially with the consistent objective of building close political and economic relations between the region and the Western nations, and, by 1949, with Japan as well. The extensive post-World War II planning, in which the State Department engaged from 1942 to 1945, sought to forestall anti-Western political movements and upheavals by providing for a peaceful, gradual transitition from European colonial rule to independence. After the war, the nationalist upheavals throughout Southeast Asia, particularly those in Indonesia and Indochina, forced the United States to make difficult choices between supporting the colonial policies of European allies or endorsing the nationalist aspirations of colonial peoples. With Communist leadership dominating the nationalist movement in Indochina and Communist influence strong elsewhere, especially in Burma and the Philippines, Southeast Asia appeared, by 1948–1949 as the Chinese Communist approached victory in their civil war struggle against the Kuomintang, to be especially vulnerable. The plans to rebuild the Japanese economy as a means of enhancing American interests in the Pacific also increased the importance of Southeast Asia for it could provide raw materials and markets for the Japanese. Thus, by the time of the Communist victory in China and the beginning of the Korean War, the United States had made plans to increase substantially its political, economic, and military commitments to the region.

This book began with an interest in World War II planning for postwar Southeast Asia, in particular the European colonial countries of Indochina, Indonesia, Burma, and Malaya. As the research progressed, it became increasingly evident that a broader regional study was called for, since American officials, from the time of the 1940–1941 crisis with Japan, began thinking of Southeast Asia in regional terms; the links between Japanese encroachments on Indochina and the status of the Netherlands East Indies and other areas of importance to the United States forced a change in political and strategic plans. As the war progressed, the regional approach was reflected in postwar planning. In particular, the assumption that the American experience in the Philippines provided a model for orderly training in self-government guided American anticolonial objectives. Also, the British-American differences over Thailand touched on colonial issues and highlighted the emerging American influence in that region. The decision to continue the study into the postwar period resulted from an interest in determining the extent to which wartime planning actually influenced later developments and from a conviction that, taken as a whole, the decade of the 1940s constituted an important unit of American policy in the region.

For the sake of consistency, I have referred throughout the book to Thailand, not Siam. Both were official titles of the country during the period under consideration; in 1939, the name was changed from Siam to Thailand and in 1946, Siam again became the official name. Since 1949, Thailand has been the official name.

I have been assisted by several agencies and individuals in this project. A fellowship from the National Endowment for the Humanities enabled me to devote six months to full-time research. In addition, grants-in-aid from the Eleanor Roosevelt Institute and the Harry S. Truman Library Institute facilitated travel to the Franklin D. Roosevelt Library and Truman Library respectively. The Faculty Researh Committee of Bowling Green State University provided support for several research trips to Washington, D.C., as well as to London. Gayle Morris, Sue Hayward Banchich, and Suzanne Carmichael provided vaulable help as student assistants. And Judy Gilbert typed the entire manuscript with efficiency, accuracy, and an unerring eye for problems.

A number of colleagues have taken the time to offer advice on various parts of the manuscript. From 1982 to 1984, I participated in a seminar on American-East Asian relations from 1931-1949 that Akira Iriye organized at the University of Chicago with funding provided by the Henry Luce Foundation. My seminar paper summarized the principal points of this book, and I benefitted immensely from the comments and suggestions of Warren Cohen, Sherman Cochran, Waldo Heinrichs (who also read part of the book manuscript), Robert Messer, Chihiro Hosoya, Luo Rangqu, K. Usui, Wang Xi, and of course, Akira Iriye. His support and encouragement have been especially helpful; and like all others working in the American-Asian area, I am indebted to his scholarship which has forced reconsideration of traditional ways of thinking. Besides the seminar participants, Frank Freidel, Melvyn Leffler, William Roger Louis, Robert McMahon, and Basil Rauch offered valuable advice. Their expertise on various aspects of this study proved exceptionally helpful. Finally, Russell Fifield, whose work on American-Southeast Asian relations has served as a model of scholarship and objectivity, graciously went beyond the expectations of a reader for the Columbia University Press and offered to meet with me and go over the manuscript in detail. I am indebted to each of these scholars, and I hope that the final work reflects the high quality of their advice.

My wife, Rose, has, as always, been supportive of my work, and has understood the need for absences to engage in research and the self-absorption which too often accompanies writing. My son, Ryan, too, has been encouraging, in countless ways that he will understand more fully some day.

Gary R. Hess

# The United States Emergence
## as a Southeast Asian Power, 1940-1950

# 1.

# The United States and the Colonial System in Southeast Asia

> The power that rules the Pacific . . . is the power that rules the world. And, with the Philippines, that power is and will forever be the American Republic.
>
> Senator Albert Beveridge

PRIOR TO WORLD War II, Southeast Asia—aside from the Philippines—was a region of negligible concern to American policymakers. With the exception of the colonial administrative responsibilities in the Philippines and the diplomatic relations with Thailand (the region's only independent nation), the United States dealt with Southeast Asia principally through the European nations which dominated the area: the preeminent British, with their empire encompassing Malaya and Burma; the French, with their control over the Indochina states; and the Dutch with their prize colonial posession, the Netherlands East Indies. The colonial system served American economic interests, especially by providing raw materials and offering modestly expanding investment opportunities. Politically, the United States took pride in its colonial record in the Philippines and in a record of substantial influence in Thailand. By the late 1930s, however, the stability of the colonial system began to be undermined by Japan's expansion. The preservation of the Western-dominated political and economic structure of Southeast Asia depended upon European military power, especially that of Great Britain. But even before war began in Europe, Britain's capability to influence Asian affairs was diminishing. As a result, with the outbreak of Sino-Japanese warfare in 1937, the United States faced the issue of whether American interests necessitated an enlarged military and political role in Southeast Asia and the Pacific generally.

## An Ambiguous Legacy: American Rule in the Philippines

While participating in the Western colonial system, the United States considered its record in the Philippines to be exceptional—an example of enlightened colonial policy. Americans took pride in introducing economic and social improvements, and in preparing Filipinos for independence. The Tydings-McDuffie Act of 1934 established the Philippine Commonwealth as a transitional government in anticipation of American withdrawl in 1946. The American administration of the Philippines had indeed brought many changes during the four decades since the Spanish-American War, but the imperial record also betrayed political and economic inconsistencies that would leave an ambiguous legacy.

From the early years of American dominance, control had rested on the "imperialism of suasion" which accommodated the interests, insofar as was possible, of the native elite. The sudden acquisition of the islands in 1898 gave the United States responsibility for a vast archipelago which had experienced, during the late nineteenth century, widespread discontent with the stultifying effects of Spanish administration. Various divisive forces fragmented the Philippine Revolution and its fledgling government headed by Emilio Aguinaldo. Yet it required the dispatch of two-thirds of the American army to suppress the "insurrection." Following that brutal antiguerrilla campaign, the maintenance of the American position in the Philippines depended upon cultivating Filipino support, which resulted in drawing the elite into political participation and appropriating the modernization and nation-building process to which the elite was committed. In deference to the interests of the elite, the United States ignored the need for far-reaching social reform and economic development. Although American policy accommodated its interests, the elite pressed for independence which became the issue that gave it a unity of purpose and enhanced its political dominance. By the 1920s, the independence issue had become central to the Philippine-American relationship.[1]

The Philippine elite and American officials shared an interest in the modernization of the islands. The United States brought especially far-reaching quantitative and substantive changes to the educational system. From a total of fewer than 7,000 students in 1898, enrollment in elementary, secondary and collegiate schools increased to 1, 237,000 by 1935–36 and to over 2,000,000 by 1940–41. Moreover, the educational process was thoroughly Americanized in content, language, and method. While the educational reforms had certain defects (including too little attention to higher education and a concentration of training at that level in only a few professions), they substantially increased the literacy rate and served as an agent of westernization. Likewise, the development of a system of public health, the improvement of communications and transportation, the monetization of the economy, and the stimulus to urbanization all facilitated the modernization process.[2]

The Tydings-McDuffie Act resolved the question of independence, but not the problems derived from the policy of accommodation. The inadequacy of the independence legislation resulted partly from the fact that its principal impetus came from agrarian interests and labor groups that sought to reduce Philippine competition. As critics warned at the time, independence was being granted in the wrong way and at the wrong time. The legislation provided no remedy for Philippine economic dependence on the United States and left the islands more vulnerable than ever to Japanese aggression.[3] The Commonwealth government had little time to deal with the central problems of a maldistribution of political power, uneven economic development, and military insecurity.

Economic dependency was the most intractable problem. Since the passage of the Underwood Tariff in 1913, which provided for reciprocal free trade between the mainland and the islands, the Philippine economy had been encouraged to produce and export sugar, hemp, and coconut oil into the American market and had, in turn, become dependent upon the import of consumer goods at the expense of the development of its own manufacturing. By 1930, the Philippines depended upon the United States for 79 percent of its exports and 63 percent of its imports. The Tydings-McDuffie Act provided for continued free trade until 1940 but with Philippine exports subject to quotas; there were no limits, however, on exports to the islands. As a result, Philippine dependence became even greater; by 1940, the United States was absorbing 83 percent of Philippine exports and providing 77 percent of the imports. Philippine labor remained heavily concentrated in agricultural production. In sum, neither the U. S. government nor the Philippine elite took advantage of the opportunity to parallel the planned political decolonization with steps leading to economic development.[4]

The commitment to independence, nonetheless, was a significant step in the development of Western relations with colonial Asia. The rapidity of decolonization after World War II has obscured the impact of the Tydings-McDuffie Act as the first firm promise of independence to a colonial people. The decision was made, as noted, for diverse reasons, and despite their nationalist rhetoric, Filipino leaders acknowledged the dangers of severance from the United States; indeed, in the late 1930s, some Filipinos and Americans contemplated the postponement of independence. Regardless of the motives and second thoughts, the American policy exerted wide influence. National-ists elsewhere in Asia were heartened. In the nearby East Indies, Indonesian leaders quickly raised the question of their indepen-dence from the Netherlands. The Dutch as well as the other Western powers were apprehensive about the implications of the American example for their own empires.[5]

The most serious shortcoming of American rule was the inability of the United States to defend the islands. For decades Philippine security had been recognized as precarious. War Plan Orange—the strategic plan for the contingency of war with Japan—anticipated that following an outbreak of hostilities, American forces would hold Manila Bay for as long as six mon-ths until they were reinforced when the United States would take the initiative in the Western Pacific. Throughout the 1920s and 1930s, that strategy seemed "literally an act of madness."[6] The War Department, which in any event was sparsely funded, never provided the support necessary for a stong garrison and naval base at Manila. Moreover, Japan's League of Nations mandate over the Marshall, Mariana, and Carolina islands, which she had taken from Germany in World War I, effectively prevented any relief of the Philippines. War Department officers acknowledged that in the event of war, the Philippines would be lost quickly. In recognition of the limits of American Power, War Plan Orange was modified. In 1935, the navy stipulated that the Marshall and Carolina islands would have to be captured and developed as bases before the Philippines could be relieved. And the following year, the mission of the Philippine garrison was reduced to holding just the entrances to Manila Bay. To go further and concede the American inability to defend the is-lands, however, risked alienating important groups in both the United States and the Philippines.[7]

General Douglas MacArthur set out to defend the inde-fensible. Following his tour of duty as U.S. Chief of Staff, MacArthur returned to the Philippines in 1935 as military adviser to Commonwealth President Manuel Quezon. The fol-lowing year Quezon named him Field Marshall of the Philippine army which, as MacArthur's Chief-of-Staff Dwight Eisenhower later noted, was "a virtually nonexisting army."[8] Undaunted, MacArthur envisioned a nation of citizen-soldiers, modeled on the example of Switzerland, who would be trained for the defense of the islands. A fleet of torpedo boats, air force fighters, and bombers would engage invaders in hit-and-run tactics. Officials in Washington criticized MacArthur's scheme; citizen-soldiers might be adequate to defend landlocked mountainous Switzerland, but not the Philippine archipelago. In Manila, Quezon initially supported MacArthur, but many leaders questioned whether the Commonwealth could absorb the cost of such a vast defense plan and maintained that defense remained an American responsibility until independence. Despite Mac-Arthur's optimistic pronouncements, the training program moved very slowly and lacked adequate supplies. The Philippine public showed little enthusiasm, and the recruits were typically malnourished and poorly educated. The number of registrants for national conscription declined sharply between 1936 and 1940, and those completing basic training never approached the annual objective of 40,000 men.

By that time Quezon had come to despair of defending the islands and, with other Filipinos, believed that neutralization offered the only means of avoiding defeat in the event of war between the United States and Japan. Much to the annoyance of MacArthur, Quezon championed early independence and neutralization of the islands.[9]

That alternative might well have served Philippine interests. When the Tydings–McDuffie Act was passed, some members of Congress and other observers urged immediate American withdrawal. More recently, it has been argued that while an independent Philippines would still have been overrun by the Japanese, the conquest, administration, and withdrawal would likely have been much less devastating than the Philippines experience from 1942 to 1945. Philippine cooperation with Japan—a necessity under any circumstances—would have lacked the element of U.S. disloyalty which was to cause tensions in the Philippine-American relationship at the end of the war. Clearly retention of responsibility for the Philippines should have been accompanied by a substantial naval and air buildup sufficient to deter a Japanese invasion. But in view of the isolationist mood of the 1930s, congressional reluctance to support the military, and the priority given to Europe, the prospects for adequate defense of the Philippines were almost nil. Hence, the most practical, if not the ideal, solution to America's imperial problems in the mid-1930s might have been immediate independence.[10]

## The United States and Thailand

Next to the Philippines among the Southeast Asian countries, the United States exerted the greatest influence in Thailand. American relations with Thailand dated to the early nineteenth century when Thailand was gradually ending its self-imposed isolation from the West. Commercial contacts began in 1818 and grew out of the China trade. As was the case in the development of treaty relations with China, the United States followed the British lead in Thailand. Agreements of 1833 opening the Thai market and of 1856 granting extraterritorial privileges and "most favored nation" commercial status were both modeled on earlier British-Thai treaties.

During the early twentieth century, the United States supported Thailand's determination to uphold its territorial integrity. Substantial territorial losses to the French in Indochina and the British in Malaya, and the extraterritorial privileges enjoyed by the Western powers, undermined Thailand's independence. In 1892 King Chulalongkorn established the practice of employing a foreign advisor, who was to come from a neutral country without territorial ambitions in Southeast Asia. For the first decade, a distinguished Belgian held the position of General Adviser, but beginning in 1902, a series of Americans, mostly graduates of Harvard Law School, were named to that important office. The appointments were coordinated by Harvard, the Department of State, and the Thai minister in Washington, subject to the approval of the King. The first two American advisers—Edward Strobel and Jens Westengard—strongly influenced Thailand's diplomatic development. In addition to advising the King on foreign affairs, the Americans served as Thai diplomatic agents and mediated in the frequent border disputes with neighboring countries.

U.S. policy after World War I strengthened Thailand's international position. Entering the war on the Allied side, Thailand was represented at the Paris Peace Conference and was given membership in the Assembly of the League of Nations. At Paris, President Woodrow Wilson championed Thailand's appeal for an end to its unequal treaties with the Western nations. In 1920 the United States took the lead in relinquishing extraterritoriality and restoring tariff autonomy. With the revised American treaty as a model, the Thai government in 1924 sent its American adviser, Francis B. Sayre, who was Wilson's son-in-law, on a mission to negotiate an end to the other unequal treaties. Within a year, Sayre negotiated revised treaties with the British, French and seven other Western nations, with the result that by 1927, Thailand had gained fiscal and judicial autonomy. For his achievement, Sayre was honored in Bangkok and later served as Thailand's representative on The Hague Permanent Court of Arbitration.[11]

During the 1930s Thai-American relations became strained as a result of internal and international factors which encouraged a strident Thai nationalism with anti-Western overtones. A coup d'etat in 1932 headed by army officers and civilian intellectuals established a constitutional monarchy in Bangkok. The revolution also led to a struggle between the army group headed by Pibul Songgram and the civilians led by Pridi Panamyong. The civilians were dominant until 1938, when Pibul gained the ascendancy and established a virtual dictatorship. Nationalization of the economy sought to reduce the influence of the resident Chinese (who constituted about one-sixth of the population) and foreign-owned companies, including the American-owned Standard Vacuum Oil Company. This reinvigorated nationalism called for regaining territories lost to the British and French. To reaffirm the connection with Thai peoples living outside, the nation's English name was officially changed to "Thailand." (The Thai considered the historic name "Siam" to be of foreign origin.)

Thailand's nationalism bore certain parallels to Japan's expansionism. American officials regarded Thailand as unnecessarily deferential to Japan, thus inviting Tokyo's influence. The United States and Thailand differed over Japan's takeover of Manchuria. In the Assembly of the League of Nations, Thailand was the only member to abstain in the vote on the Lytton Report condemning Japan's invasion. Thailand's silence on this issue, which ran counter to the counsel of the American adviser in Bangkok, was generally interpreted in both Tokyo and Washington as indicative of sympathy with Japan's ambitions. In reality, Thailand's abstention reflected principally its historic practice of upholding independence by not antagonizing a stronger nation. In the next few years, Japan cultivated Thailand's friendship and greatly extended its economic and cultural influence. Japan's share of Thailand's imports dramatically increased, with the result that by 1938 its share of that market nearly equalled that of Britain, which at the turn of the century had controlled 95 percent of Thailand's imports. Thai leaders looked to Japan for support in regaining their lost territories. While seeking to exploit once again a changing international situation to their nation's advantage, Thai leaders remained wary of Japan. By 1940, however, American officials had become skeptical about Thai protestations of determination to remain independent of Japan.[12]

## American Economic Expansion

The American economic stake in Southeast Asia, while not comparable to that in western Europe or the western hemisphere, was nonetheless important. The principal interest in the region was as a source of raw materials, especially rubber, tin, and oil. By the 1930s, Southeast Asia supplied about 90 percent of American crude rubber and 75 percent of its tin. During the interwar period, Southeast Asia provided between 9 percent and 14 percent of the total value of American imports. Trade with Southeast Asia had followed the worldwide trend of expansion for a decade after World War I, a sharp decline between 1930 and 1934, and then uneven resurgence after 1935. Aside from the Philippines, the region was not a lucrative market for American products; the value of exports generally ran about one-third of that of imports. By the end of the 1930s, however, Southeast Asian countries were absorbing a modestly higher percentage of American goods; from 1920 to 1934, Southeast Asian countries altogether imported products at levels comparable to China, but moved significantly ahead of China after 1935. (Tables 1.1 and 1.2 detail the patterns of 1920-1940 trade.)

The supply of raw materials provided the key economic link and led to mutual dependency, especially involving the United States with British Malaya and the Netherlands East Indies. Owing to American purchases of its rubber and tin, the Malayan economy became dependent upon the United States. The value of Malayan exports to the United States exceeded that of the Philippines throughout the 1920s and again after 1935, once a Depression-caused decline in rubber prices had been reversed. Indeed, the United States was Malaya's best customer, accounting for one-half to two-thirds of the rubber and tin exports. By the late 1930s, about 40 percent of Malayan exports were to the United States. Nowhere in Southeast Asia, however, was American trade more imbalanced, for the United States exported little to Malaya. American imports exceeded by ten to twenty times the value of exports to Malaya. The immense profits derived from the Malayan sales to America benefited the foreign-owned companies which ran the tin mines and rubber plantations. Since British capital dominated the investment in Malaya, American imports of rubber and tin meant that, from the perspective of Malayan nationalists, the

**Table 1.1.** U.S. Trade with Southeast Asia, 1922-1930 (in U.S. $ million)

| | Exports | | | | | Imports | | | | |
|---|---|---|---|---|---|---|---|---|---|---|
| | 1922-26[a] | 1927 | 1928 | 1929 | 1930 | 1922-26[a] | 1927 | 1928 | 1929 | 1930 |
| British Malaya | 9.3 | 13.6 | 11.8 | 14.6 | 9.6 | 218.6 | 277.8 | 204.4 | 239.2 | 144.0 |
| East Indies | 16.3 | 32.1 | 34.4 | 45.7 | 30.4 | 72.5 | 91.4 | 86.1 | 82.3 | 57.9 |
| French Indochina | 1.4 | 1.4 | 1.7 | 2.5 | 1.5 | .4 | .1 | b | b | .2 |
| Philippines | 56.4 | 69.5 | 79.8 | 85.5 | 64.9 | 90.4 | 116.6 | 115.6 | 125.8 | 109.4 |
| Total[c] | 84.6 | 118.5 | 130.3 | 151.5 | 108.8 | 382.3 | 485.9 | 406.4 | 447.8 | 311.9 |
| China[d] | 121.2 | 102.4 | 159.7 | 143.8 | 106.4 | 166.5 | 166.5 | 153.6 | 177.9 | 110.5 |
| Japan | 246.4 | 257.6 | 288.2 | 259.1 | 164.7 | 365.3 | 402.1 | 384.4 | 431.9 | 259.1 |
| Asian Total[e] | 505.2 | 559.6 | 654.5 | 643.2 | 447.9 | 1,099.4 | 1,256.8 | 1,168.9 | 1,280.3 | 856.6 |
| Southeast Asian % of Asia Total | 16.8% | 21.3% | 20.2% | 23.5% | 24.5% | 34.8% | 39.5% | 34.8% | 35.0% | 36.3% |
| Southeast Asian % of World Total | — | 1.8% | 2.1% | 2.8% | 2.9% | — | 11.6% | 9.9% | 11.1% | 10.2% |

SOURCE: U.S. Dept. of Commerce, Bureau of Census, *Historical Abstracts of the United States Colonial Times to 1970* (Washington: GPO, 1975), Series U317-U334, pp. 903-06; U.S. Department of Commerce, *Commerce Yearbook 1931*, 1:164-75.

[a]1922-26 data: annual averages of trade value for that five year period

[b]Less than $50,000

[c]Includes all Southeast Asian trade

[d]Includes Hong Kong

[e]Includes South Asia, Soviet Asia, and Western Asia (Aden, Arabia, Iraq, Palestine, Syria, Persia, Turkey)

**Table 1.2.** U.S. Share of International Trade of Southeast Asian Countries, 1931-1939

|  | IMPORTS from United States (in U.S. $ million)[a] (percent of total imports) | | | | | | | | |
|---|---|---|---|---|---|---|---|---|---|
|  | 1931 | 1932 | 1933 | 1934 | 1935 | 1936 | 1937 | 1938 | 1939 |
| Burma[b] | 1.7 | | | | | | 3.9 | 2.7 | 4.7 |
|  | 3.5% | | | | | | 4.4% | 3.6% | 5.8% |
| Indochina | | 1.3 | 1.3 | 1.3 | 1.4 | 2.1 | 2.1 | 2.8 | 2.5 |
|  | | 3.4% | 3.5% | 2.1% | 2.3% | 3.3% | 3.3% | 5.0% | 4.2% |
| Malaya | 6.1 | 2.9 | 2.1 | 4.9 | 5.2 | 5.5 | 9.2 | 9.8 | 9.4 |
|  | 2.5% | 1.9% | 1.6% | 2.0% | 1.9% | 1.9% | 2.3% | 3.1% | 2.9% |
| East Indies | 20.7 | 9.9 | 6.2 | 11.9 | 12.8 | 14.0 | 27.5 | 33.1 | 33.9 |
|  | 9.1% | 6.7% | 4.9% | 6.1% | 6.9% | 7.7% | 10.2% | 12.6% | 13.5% |
| Philippines | 62.1 | 51.2 | 35.1 | 32.6 | 54.4 | 61.5 | 63.3 | 90.4 | |
|  | 62.6% | 64.6% | 60.0% | 65.4% | 63.6% | 60.8% | 58.1% | 68.1% | |
| Thailand | 1.1 | .7 | .8 | 1.2 | 1.5 | 1.9 | 2.6 | 2.7 | |
|  | 3.2% | 2.4% | 2.2% | 2.7% | 3.0% | 3.8% | 5.1% | 4.1% | |

EXPORTS to United States
(in $ U.S. million)[a]
(% of total exports)

| | 1931 | 1932 | 1933 | 1934 | 1935 | 1936 | 1937 | 1938 | 1939 |
|---|---|---|---|---|---|---|---|---|---|
| Burma[b] | | | | | | | .4 | .3 | 1.7 |
| | | | | | | | 0.2% | 0.4% | 1.0% |
| Indochina | .2 | .1 | .3 | 2.5 | 3.6 | 6.4 | 7.1 | 7.2 | 10.7 |
| | 0.4% | 0.2% | 0.7% | 3.6% | 4.3% | 6.3% | 7.1% | 9.0% | 12.1% |
| Malaya | 70.7 | 29.2 | 48.1 | 111.3 | 122.1 | 172.2 | 231.2 | 97.3 | 165.6 |
| | 31.3% | 19.9% | 31.2% | 34.7% | 37.5% | 47.1% | 44.5% | 30.0% | 43.5% |
| East Indies | 35.3 | 26.4 | 22.0 | 37.5 | 43.1 | 61.1 | 97.9 | 49.1 | 78.4 |
| | 11.8% | 12.1% | 11.8% | 11.4% | 14.3% | 17.7% | 18.7% | 13.6% | 19.7% |
| Philippines | 83.4 | 87.6 | 73.6 | 55.1 | 75.0 | 107.5 | 120.7 | 89.4 | |
| | 80.2% | 92.0% | 89.0% | 89.0% | 83.7% | 78.7% | 79.8% | 77.2% | |
| Thailand | .2 | c | c | .2 | .1 | .3 | .5 | .2 | |
| | 0.3% | 0.1% | 0.1% | 0.2% | 0.2% | 0.4% | 0.7% | 0.3% | |

SOURCE: U. S. Department of Commerce, *Foreign Commerce Yearbook 1933*, pp. 260-86; *Foreign Commerce Yearbook 1935*, pp. 283-311; *Foreign Commerce Yearbook 1938*, pp. 314-25; *Foreign Commerce Yearbook 1939*, pp. 234-317; *Foreign Commerce Yearbook 1948*, pp. 421-534.

[a]through 1933 values in gold dollars

[b]Burma administered as part of India until April 1, 1937

[c]Thailand exports to U.S.: $48,000 in 1933 and $34,000 in 1934

United States shared with the British in the foreign exploitation of their country.

A similar pattern developed in the Netherlands East Indies, although the Americans did not share in that market as fully as they did in Malaya and the trade was more nearly balanced. Throughout the 1920s, the United States accounted for about one-half of the expanding East Indian rubber exports. With the resurgence of international trade in 1934, the United States again became the major outlet, accounting for about 40 percent of the total rubber exports. Throughout that decade, American trade with the East Indies steadily increased, with the result that by 1939, the United States accounted for nearly 20 percent of exports (only the mother country and Malaya were better customers) and was providing 13.5 percent of the imports.

American purchasing of rubber in Indochina in the 1930s led to a considerable increase in its exports to the United States. The American share of Indochina's exports increased from less than 1 percent in the early 1930s to 12.1 percent by 1939. While Indochina's export trade was heavily tied to France and other French colonies, the United States ranked behind Hong Kong as the best non-French customer for the country's products. Trade with Burma and Thailand remained insignificant.[13]

American private investment in Southeast Asia helped to stimulate the commercial relations. Throughout the early twentieth century, American firms, acting often with strong official support, moved aggressively into the colonial areas. During World War I, American rubber tire companies, responding to wartime demands, concentrated their investments in Malaya and the East Indies, thus reducing earlier dependence on British and Dutch interests for the crude rubber of the region. In the 1920s as the rubber companies expanded their Southeast Asian interests, the region also became important as part of a concerted worldwide search by American oil companies for new supplies; the steady success of this drive would steadily increase the American share of foreign oil products at the expense of the

British-Dutch group. By 1929, American investment in Southeast Asia (Philippines, Malaya, East Indies) totalled about $165 million, which constituted about 45 percent of the total American investment in Asia, and increased by another $20 million during the next decade (table 1.3).[14]

The most notable accomplishment of private investment was Jersey Standard's breaking of the Dutch monopoly on East Indies oil. Assisted by the State and Interior departments as well as congressional legislation directed toward countries that discriminated against American oil companies, Jersey Standard overcame the preferential treatment given by the Netherlands to the Royal-Dutch Oil Company. In 1922, the American firm discovered oil in commercial quantities and constructed a refinery near Palembarg. By 1926, Jersey Standard marketed its first East Indian refined oil and in 1933 it joined with Socony-Vacuum to produce, refine, and market their products in Asia and Africa. The resulting organization, known as Standard-Vacuum Oil Company (Stanvac), owned by the two leading American oil companies, expanded its Netherlands Indies interests. By 1939, Stanvac was producing 27 percent of the total Indies oil output. Another American company, California-Texaco, had also discovered oil there, but was not yet in production. The Stanvac refinery in the East Indies was one of only

**Table  1.3.** U.S. Direct Investments in East Asia: 1930, 1936, 1940 (in U.S. $ million)

|                | 1930  | 1936  | 1940 |
|----------------|-------|-------|------|
| China          | 129.8 | 90.6[a] | 46.1 |
| Japan          | 61.5  | 46.7  | 37.7 |
| Philippines    | 81.4  | 92.1  | 90.7 |
| East Indies    | 66.2  | 69.8  | 71.3 |
| British Malaya | 27.1  | 23.7  | 21.4 |

SOURCE: Mira Wilkins, "The Role of U.S. Business," p. 374.

[a]Part of this drop from the 1930 level was due to changes in valuation by compilers; part was due to currency depreciations.

three American refineries outside the Americas and western Europe.[15]

Stanvac, with its extensive marketing operations throughout East and Southeast Asia, constituted the largest single direct American enterprise in these regions. By 1941, Stanvac had $20.7 million invested in its production and refining operations in the East Indies and a total of $46.1 million in all of East and Southeast Asia. With its considerable stake in the Indies and its importance as a supplier of oil to Japan, Stanvac interests were directly affected by political changes. A process of Stanvac coordination with Royal Dutch Shell and the British and American governments, that began in the early 1930s, was intensified by the pressures resulting from the "China incident." Stanvac sought to protect its marketing outlets in China and Japan, but without permitting Japan to engage in stockpiling. As the East Indian oil fields came to be recognized as the ultimate target of Japanese expansion, Stanvac sought support from the American government and during the tensions of 1940–41, its representatives worked closely with the State, Navy, and Treasury departments in the formulation of American policy.[16]

## Anglo-American Interests and Japanese Expansion

As international tensions increased in the 1930s, the Western powers—especially Great Britain and the United States—reconsidered their Asian interests. The Japanese takeover of Manchuria in 1931–32 undermined the Washington Conference system of cooperation between the Japanese and Western powers and challenged the League of Nations structure of collective security. Upon entering the White House in 1933, President Franklin D. Roosevelt modestly strengthened the American position in the Pacific through a naval buildup; the decision to extend diplomatic recognition to the Soviet Union assumed, among other considerations, that Russian influence might counter Japan's expansion. Yet Roosevelt was restrained by the necessity to devote priority to the problems of the Depression and by the strength of isolationist sentiment in the country. The fragile East Asian interlude of peace was shattered by the Japanese assault upon northern China following the Marco Polo Bridge incident of July 1937. The resulting full-scale war between China and Japan threatened the economic and political position of the Western powers in China. Japan's early successes in the fighting raised questions about the security of Western interests throughout Asia.

British interests far surpassed those of the United States, but by the time of the outbreak of the Sino-Japanese War, British military power was in decline. Symbolic of the distinction between British and American interests was the fact that the Royal Dutch Shell Company investments in the Netherlands East Indies exceeded that of all American firms in both Japan and China. The vast British imperial lifeline—the immense investment and trade in China centering on the crown colony Hong Kong; the important resources of Malaya and Southeast Asia generally centering on Singapore; the dominions of New Zealand and Australia; and the very symbol of empire, the Raj in India—stretched across Asia to the Pacific. Yet like the Americans in their modest empire in the Philippines, British commitments, in the crisis-ridden world of the late 1930s, surpassed military capability.

Accordingly, an objective of British policy after July 1937 was to encourage Anglo-American collaboration in the stabilization of East Asia and the Pacific. The pursuit of the policy of appeasement toward Nazi Germany in 1937–1938 necessitated the avoidance of distracting tensions in Asia. Perhaps after an accommodation was reached with Hitler, the British would be able to deal forthrightly with the Japanese. British policymakers rejected appeasement as the appropriate policy toward Japan. Determined to uphold their preeminent position in Asia, British leaders dismissed any action which suggested weakness in dealing with Japan. Moreover, London feared that any hint of appeasing Japan would antagonize the United States, which identified more strongly with China's resistance to Japan's aggression. Finally, British policy toward Japan rested on optimism regarding China's capacity to withstand Japan's attack; Japan, it was foreseen, would become ensnarled in a frustrating war on the Asian mainland. As that sanguine view of China's endurance suggested, British leaders generally discounted Japan's military strength and its willingness to risk war with Britain or the United States.

While seeking an enlarged American political and military role in Asia, British officials distrusted the Americans. In view of its inconsistent history of involvement in world affairs, would the United States be a reliable ally? If Americans shared more responsibility, could they be controlled? Or would they expand their interests at Britain's expense? Would seeking an enlarged American naval presence in the Pacific encourage growth making it "second to none"?[17]

The United States, as the British anticipated, proved to be a reluctant and, in some ways, competitive, partner. Shortly after the Marco Polo Bridge incident, the State Department indicated that American policy would follow "parallel" lines but not joint action.[18] The United States ought not become, in the words of the department's chief of the European division, Jay Pierrepont Moffat, "the junior partner of Great Britain policing the world."[19] The worsening situation, however, necessitated some tentative steps toward cooperation and plans for an enlarged naval presence. Roosevelt groped for an alternative to the discredited system of collective security. His "quarantine the aggressors" speech of October 1937 vaguely suggested at least "parallel" measures, but seemingly failed to arouse public support for a more forthright American role in preserving international peace. In December, the Japanese attack on the U.S.S. *Panay* in the Yangtze River stirred considerable public indignation and made American officials more responsive to British overtures. Roosevelt approved joint naval talks which began in early 1938.[20]

The Anglo-American discussions signaled far-reaching naval cooperation and the ascendancy of American power in the Pacific. In the event of war with Japan, the two navies—British through Southeast Asia and the American in the Pacific—were to sever Japan's trade lines. In the accord developed from the Ingersoll-Phillips conversations, the Americans and the British implicitly assumed a division of responsibility with the American naval power concentrated in the Pacific, while the British maintained control of the Atlantic Ocean-Mediterranean Sea-Indian Ocean area. Accordingly, in the revised Orange Plan, completed just after the talks with the British, the Joint Army-Navy Board envisioned a more ambitious naval role than had been earlier planned for conflict with Japan. Army leaders still generally favored a defensive strategy in the Pacific. Since by this time, relief of the Philippines was no longer anticipated, the navy was to concentrate on cutting Japan's trade and prepare for an offensive across the western Pacific. This projection of American power found expression in the Vinson-Trammell Act of May 1938 providing for further expansion of the battleship and carrier fleets.

The Czechoslovakian crisis of the fall of 1938 forced American strategists to broaden their perspectives. War in the Pacific had been considered previously without reference to possible simultaneous conflict in Europe. As the British struggled to appease Hitler, and as the Germans and Japanese negotiated, the Joint Board produced in April 1939 the Rainbow War Plans which considered the various alternatives of war with more than one enemy. Naval leaders were attracted to Rainbow 2, which assumed support of the British and French in the Pacific and thus facililtated the broad mission defined in the Anglo-American conversations and the revised Orange Plan. The necessity of preventing Japanese access to the oil of the East Indies was an objective of the Rainbow 2 plan. It called for the Pacific Fleet to advance quickly from Hawaii to New Guinea, and through the Moluccas to the Java Sea, where in concert with the British, it would guard the Malay Barrier (Singapore to

Timor). While this program necessitated naval base construction and faced opposition from the Army, it illustrated how far American strategy had progressed within the two years following the beginning of the Sino-Japanese War. Denial of the resources of Southeast Asia to Japan had become a strategic contingency.[21]

Exactly how U.S. power would be used in the event of conflict remained uncertain as Europe drifted to war in 1939. Hitler's easy conquest of Poland followed by the "phony war" of the winter of 1939–40, coupled with the anticipation that the fighting, if it resumed, might be a repetition of the war of attrition of 1914–1918, permitted American leaders to delay deciding which of the Rainbow alternatives best served American capabilities and interests. Only the startling events of the spring of 1940—with their repercussions for Europe, America, and Asia—would force a clearer definition of American objectives.

# 2.

# The Rivalry of Japan and the United States Over Southeast Asia, 1940–1941

We of course do not want to be drawn into a war with Japan and we do not want to be drawn into any war anywhere. There is, however, very close connection between the hostilities which have been going on for three and a half years in the Far East and those which have been going on for sixteen months in eastern Europe and the Mediterranean. . . . We are faced with the danger of Japan's continuing her expansion in the Far East especially toward the south, while the European issue remains in the balance. If Japan, moving further southward, should gain possession of the region of the Netherlands East Indies and the Malay Peninsula, would not the chances of Germany's defeating Great Britain be increased and the chances of England's winning be decreased thereby?

Franklin D. Roosevelt to Francis B. Sayre,
December 31, 1940

THE INTERNATIONAL TENSIONS of 1940–1941 thrust the United States into the position of defending Western interests in Southeast Asia. The German invasion of the Low Countries and

France in the spring of 1940 forced an American reassessment of its interests in Europe and Asia. With the collapse of resistance in The Netherlands and France, the defense of Great Britain and of Southeast Asia became closely linked as the United States formulated its response to crises in Europe and Asia. French Indochina, the Dutch East Indies, the British colonies in Burma and Malaya, and independent Thailand and the Philippines, lay vulnerable to Japanese expansion. The status of Southeast Asia became the principal issue in Japanese-American relations. Neither side wanted war over Southeast Asia, but each regarded certain interests as non-negotiable. Those compelling considerations eventually led to conflict.

## The European War and the Redefinition of Japanese and American Policies

For Japan, the German advance through the Low Countries and France, and the vulnerability of Great Britain provided the opportunity to resolve the longstanding uncertainty over its position in Asia. Pan-Asianist doctrine, embodied in the New Order enunciated in late 1938, sought to build Asian resistance to Western imperialism while fostering regional cooperation and harmony. Japan began to develop intraregional trade with Manchukuo and the areas of China under its control known as the "yen bloc." Yet economic integration could provide only part of Japan's needs; dependency upon the United States and the European countries and their colonies left Japan vulnerable to international economic pressures. Militarily, Japan was frustrated by the unexpectedly prolonged warfare in China. And clashes with Russian troops along the Manchurian border in 1938 and again in 1939 not only raised the specter of a two-front war, but also revealed Soviet superiority in air power and armored units.

Events beyond Japan's control increasingly influenced Japan's policy. The pursuit of an alliance with Germany was based on the assumption that Hitler would defeat his European enemies and thus pave the way for Japan's exploitation of their colonies. Matsuoko Yosuke, who became Foreign Minister in July 1940, believed that settlement of the war in China and the establishment of the New Order in East Asia depended upon European developments. The Tripartite Pact of September 1940 tied Japan's destiny to Germany's military advantage in Europe.

While seeking to exploit Germany's strength, Matsuoko and other Japanese leaders redefined relations with the United States and the Soviet Union, the two Western powers not yet involved in the European war. Calculating that neither wanted to fight on two fronts and that to both European interests were paramount, Japan believed that the Americans and Soviets would be tolerant of its expansion. The need for an understanding with the Soviet Union led to the nonaggression pact of April 1941. Besides reducing tensions with Russia, that pact, in the view of Matsuoko, put additional pressure on the United States to accept the New Order. But Japanese policy from the spring of 1940 through mid-1941 continued on an indefinite course. Coercion implicit in the Axis alliance and the nonaggression pact was balanced by the pursuit of American goodwill.[1]

As the Japanese calculated, events in Europe made the United States anxious to avoid conflict in Asia, but that did not result in a willingness to accommodate the New Order. U.S. policy sought to uphold the status quo through diplomatic means and the use of economic pressures. Germany's conquests forced a resolution of uncertainties about American military strategy and resulted in a commitment to a Europe-first strategy. The war plans for severance of Japan's supply lines and a counteroffensive across the Pacific were abandoned. Britain's unexpected naval weakness in 1940 made impossible such an aggressive thrust of Anglo-American naval power in the Pacific. Thus even the naval leadership, which had traditionally urged firmness in the Pacific, reoriented its strategy and dispositions to the Atlantic and cautioned restraint in dealing with Japan.

War Plan D (or Dog, in military parlance)—which became the basis of the revised mililtary strategy—called for a defensive posture in the Pacific and efforts to avoid war with Japan.[2]

While the United States committed its resources to the survival of Great Britain, American interests also necessitated holding the line against Japanese encroachments in Southeast Asia. The British government as well as the surviving Dutch and French colonial regimes in the East Indies and Indochina, respectively, looked to the United States as the only power capable of resisting Japan. Upholding the Western access to Southeast Asia was dictated both by the American need for the region's resources and by the implications of their loss. Not only would Japan be strengthened, but Britain would be weakened. Increasingly American officials recognized that they were being drawn into support of the British Empire as a necessary component of the determination to assist Britain against Germany. As Roosevelt acknowledged, if the United States had an interest in Britain's survival, then it also had an interest in the survival of the British empire.

To compensate for the weakness of the Western position, the United States had to play for time in dealing with Japan. In late 1940 Roosevelt authorized $100 million credit and aircraft for China. This  was intended, in part, to tie Japan down in China and thus deter aggression to the south. Besides bolstering China's resistance, the United States also endeavored to restrain Japan by seeking its adherence to the principle of peaceful change. Within the State Department's Division of Far Eastern Affairs, this policy was rarely questioned. The dominant policymaker was Stanley K. Hornbeck, who had long experience on Asian affairs and was a recognized authority on East Asian international relations. To Hornbeck and those around him, the United States had to deal forthrightly with Japan in order to maintain the stability of East Asia.[3]

In responding to Japanese pressures on Southeast Asia, U.S. policy thus consistently held to the well-established American objective of an orderly international system based on adherence to the status quo and acceptance of only those political changes arrived at through peaceful and legitimate processes. In the previous decade, nonrecognition of the changes brought by Japanese aggression in Manchuria and northern China had reflected that principle, but it also had revealed the negligible effect of moral posturing without substantive economic or military support. In the face of Japanese pressures on Indochina in July 1940, Secretary of State Cordell Hull reiterated that position succinctly: "Our position in the maintenence of the status quo in French Indochina is a part of a general policy which this Government endeavors constantly and consistently to pursue of respect for the status quo except as changes may be brought about through orderly processes with due consideration for the rights and legitimate interests of all concerned."[4]

Thus the State Department urged non-accommodation with Japan and criticized any acts suggestive of appeasement. The tactic of endeavoring to strengthen Southeast Asia but without American commitment was summarized by Hull for the benefit of British and Australian officials: "We have encouraged countries like Indochina, just as we did the British, to delay and parley and hold out to the last minute against the Japanese demands, and that in all probability Japan would not dare make a military attack."[5]

As that statement suggested, American firmness in dealing with Japan assumed that Japan would not risk war with the United States. Officials in Washington calculated, at least until July 1941, that Japan's pursuit of the New Order would be cautious and nonprovocative.

## The Strategic Prize: Rivalry over the East Indies

The principal focus of the Western-Japanese tensions in Southeast Asia was the Dutch East Indies. Differences first surfaced even before the fall of the Netherlands. In February 1940, Japan requested various economic concessions, and at the time of the German invasion of Denmark and Norway in April, the Japanese Foreign Ministry issued a statement which implied a claim to special interests in the East Indies. On April 17, Hull publicly stated that any change in the status of the East Indies would affect many nations. Relying on the Washington Conference system as the basis for Asian stability, Hull pointedly called attention to the British, French, American, and Japanese pledge of 1922 to respect the rights of the Netherlands in its insular possessions. The German attack on the Netherlands on May 10 intensified the East Indian situation. Concerned that the British or French might takeover the islands and thus provide a pretext for Japanese intervention, the United States secured pledges from Britain and France not to occupy the East Indies. In early June, a defeated Netherlands government granted Japan's request for increased trade. As a follow-up to Hull's April warning, the Roosevelt administration decided to keep the U.S. fleet at Hawaii—a modest show of force principally intended to deter any Japanese advance on the East Indies.[6]

From June 1940 to December 1941, the East Indies stood as the strategic prize in the Pacific. The virtual end of trade with the Netherlands opened the market and materials of the islands, and the United States was the principal beneficiary. The strongly anti-Japanese colonial government of the East Indies sought to limit Japanese influence, but recognized that without Anglo-American support, it could not resist indefinitely. Repeatedly it sought assurances of intervention in the event of a Japanese attack; the British maintained that they could not act unilaterally and the United States withheld the long sought assurances of its military support until the eve of Pearl Harbor. In the meantime, the United States became dependent on the East Indies; a Department of State report of December 3, 1941, described the islands as the "arsenal of strategic raw materials for the democracies." Imports from the East Indies increased in value from about $80 million in 1939 to $241 million by 1941. The islands were providing about one-third of the rubber and one-eighth of the tin imports of the United States. In addition, the United States replaced the Netherlands as the principal supplier of manufactured goods, as American exports went from $35 million in value in 1939 to $124 million in 1941.

Japanese trade with the islands increased considerably following the 1940 concessions, but not at the rate of growth of the American trade. The value of Japanese exports, which had far surpassed those of the United States since 1931, was virtually equalled by the United States in 1940; the following year, American exports exceeded Japanese by 70 percent. American imports were six times greater than those of Japan in 1940, and seventeen times greater in 1941. Japan, however, remained dependent upon the East Indies for oil; the islands ranked behind only the United States as a source of oil imports.[7] This dependency increased the vulnerability of the East Indies. Any American embargo of Japanese trade invariably invited a Japanese move to secure the East Indian oil resources. As the Americans, British, and Japanese confronted the immediate questions centering on the status of Indochina and Thailand in 1940–1941, control of the East Indies always remained the overriding concern.

## The Crises over Indochina and Thailand, June 1940–June 1941

Japan's initial efforts to exploit the decline of Western authority in Southeast Asia brought a reluctant United States into a predominant position in the relations of Japan with the European imperial powers. Capitalizing on the collapse of France, Tokyo decided to cut off the southern supply routes to China. Accordingly, the Japanese pressured French authorities in Indochina to prevent transportation of military supplies from the port of Haiphong to Kunming, and the British to close the Burma Road and the frontier at Hong Kong. In Indochina, Governor-General George Catroux was inclined to resist, but only with assurances of assistance. At a meeting with the French ambassador on June 19, Undersecretary of State Sumner Welles advised that the

United States could provide no support. Behind Welles' statement was not only an inability to supply Indochina and the
desirability of avoiding complications in the Pacific, but uncertainty about the relationship of the United States with the new
government, headed by Marshal Philippe Pétain, which was
then negotiating an armistice with the Germans.

Likewise, the British sought American assistance before
responding to the Japanese demands. On June 27, Lord Lothian,
the British ambassador in Washington, presented a lengthy
aide-memoire to Hull which urged an American initiative to
uphold the status quo. The British maintained that the United
States should either exert economic pressure on Japan or undertake to reach a general settlement which would include Japanese
respect for the European possessions in Southeast Asia. The
next day Hull indicated that the United States could undertake
neither of those approaches, but he did encourage British efforts
to reach an agreement with Japan. Endeavoring to accommodate the Japanese without antagonizing the Chinese and the
Americans, the British proposed a three-month closing of the
Burma Road, with the understanding that during that period,
Britain, Japan, and China would undertake to reach a general
Asian settlement. The Japanese agreed to the British plan, and
the Burma Road was closed on July 18 to the transport of arms,
ammunition, gasoline, trucks, and railway material. Both Hull
and Secretary of War Henry Stimson reproached British officials
for suspending the Burma supply route, but privately it was acknowledged that the British had no choice.[8]

In addition to the pressures from Britain and France, the
Chinese and Dutch also called for an enlarged American role in
Southeast Asia. As French sovereignty in Indochina eroded, the
Chinese called for an unequivocal declaration of U.S. support for
the status quo.[9] The Governor-General of the Netherlands East
Indies appealed on economic and racial grounds for American
support. As his views were conveyed by the Netherlands minister in Washington, the Netherlands East Indies"must either
become absorbed in the East Asiatic economic bloc or be
retained as a source of wealth for the white race." While the

United States recognized the value of the East Indies as a source
of rubber and tin, it had not appreciated the potential of a
market for manufactured goods; by remaining in Dutch hands,
the islands "could be further developed in the interests of the
white race."[10]

The United States took half-measures to restrain Japan,
but without effect. In response to Japanese demands for a virtual
military occupation of northern Indochina and renewed French
appeals to Washington for support, Ambassador Joseph Grew
informed the Japanese on August 7 that the earlier U.S. position
on the Netherlands East Indies applied equally to Indochina.[11]
This gesture not only failed, as the French acceded to the
Japanese pressures, but the episode left bitterness in Franco-
American relations as American officials criticized the Pétain-
led collaborationist government at Vichy for dealing in secrecy
with the Axis while the French officials at Vichy justified their
actions by maintaining that Grew's representations had been
tardy and insufficient.[12]

As Japan solidified its position in Indochina, it began to
exert pressure on neighboring Thailand. For the United States,
the status of Thailand had many complications. As a matter of
principle, the threat to the only independent nation in the region
whose integrity had been upheld by the United States aroused
more concern than did the encroachments upon the European
colonies. The Thai government, however, had shown signs of
accommodating itself to Japan's emerging predominance. Moreover, it had raised old territorial issues with Indochina and
seemed to be capitalizing upon Indochina's weakness to secure
the return of territories lost to the French in the late nineteenth
and early twentieth centuries. Thailand's opportunism caused
considerable indignation among American officials. In particular, Hugh Grant, the minister in Bangkok, persistently
criticized Thai leaders and his reports influenced State department thinking. Hence, American officials questioned whether
Thailand deserved support. On the other hand, the British, who
had long played a predominant role in Thailand, were inclined
to sympathize with the Thai position. Thailand held consider-

able importance for the British position in Southeast Asia. Japanese control of the Kra peninsula would threaten Burma and by extension the Indian Ocean, as well as opening the back door to Singapore; Japanese influence in Bangkok would fore-shadow base agreements with the same effects. Hence, British policy sought, above all, to strengthen Thailand as the best means of preventing Japanese encroachment. This Anglo-American disagreement over the Pibul government's policies of 1940 marked the beginning of six years of differences over Thailand.

From the Thai perspective, its border claims and the manner of their resolution were misunderstood in the West, especailly the United States. Rather than being an opportunistic venture that only enhanced Japan's strength, Thai policy can be seen as a determined, but futile, effort to redress a longstanding grievance through direct negotiation which finally left no alter-native but to seek Japanese support. On June 12, 1940, Thai-land, in an effort to adjust to the changing international situation, signed nonaggression pacts with Great Britain, France, and Japan; the first two agreements included provisions for redressing the border disputes. The French minister in Bangkok and officials in Paris sympathized with Thailand's requests, but the French colonial administration in Indochina adamantly opposed any concessions. As Japanese pressure on Indochina increased and the French procrastinated on the boun-dary issues, Thailand became apprehensive that Indochina, including the disputed territories, would fall completely under Japanese control. In August 1940, Phibun sent Colonel Phrom Jothi on a diplomatic mission to Hanoi, but Vice Admiral Jean Decoux, who had replaced Catroux as governor-general of French Indochina, avoided the Thai official and refused to be drawn into discussions on the boundary questions. As a result of repeated French rebuffs and a sense that time was working against its interests, Bangkok thus gravitated to Tokyo for support.[13]

The United States undertook to discourage Thailand's move toward accomodation with Japan. In a meeting with Grant on August 17, Pibul set forth the boundary concerns and noted that the Jothi mission, which had gone on to Tokyo from Hanoi, would discuss the matter with the Japanese.[14] As the State Department reiterated its adherence to the principle of resolution of such problems through negotiations,[15] Grant warned his superiors in Washington that only substantial pressure from the United States and Britain could discourage Thailand from pressing its advantage with Indochina.[16] In an effort to force restraint, in mid-October the United States revoked licenses for the sale of ten bombers and six fighters to Thailand. Grant, however, maintained that such action would be insufficient— only a direct statement by the President or Secretary of State could reverse the drift toward Japan's orbit.[17] Officials in Washington rejected the call for a stronger stand. The minimal effort at restraining Thailand had, however, the effect of increasing Thai dependency upon Japan. To counter the canceled sale of American aircraft, Thailand purchased replacements from Japan.

By the end of 1940, French resistance to Thailand's demands had led to a state of undeclared war with widespread fighting along the Indochina-Thailand frontier. Japan offered to mediate the conflict, an act which officials in London and Washington believed would result in a settlement favorable to Thailand at the price of increased Japanese influence in that country. In responding to this development, the United States again was unwilling to undertake meaningful initiatives. In January 1941, the British proposed that the United States and Britain take quiet measures to resolve the Thai-French differences and thus forestall Japanese mediation; modest concessions by the French, it was believed, would satisfy Thailand.[18] The State Department, however, declined the British suggestions on the grounds that insecurity in Thailand and Indochina prevented a permanant settlement. Conversations between British embassy officials and Welles and political adviser Stanley Hornbeck underscored the important difference in British and American views: the State Department regarded Japanese influence in both countries as so substantial that negotiations would be of little value, whereas the Foreign Office sought to delay the Japanese absorption of Indochina as a means of bolstering anti-Japanese elements in Thailand.[19] The United States accordingly only urged restraint on both parties by reminding them that Japan would benefit from prolonged warfare.[20] The British continued to press for a more forthright position, seeking an American statement endorsing negotiations. Later, after the Japanese had gained the approval of Thailand and Indochina to mediate the dispute, British Ambassador Lord Halifax sought an American statement criticizing the Japanese role, but Hull demurred on the grounds that it would not be beneficial.[21]

The passive role of the United States not only disappointed the British, but it also caused further Franco-American antagonism. French authorities in Vichy and Washington took issue over the failure to provide Indochina with the war material that had been repeatedly requested since the previous summer. France's military frustrations against the Thais were, in effect, blamed on the United States.[22]

In the meantime, the negotiations under Japanese mediation proceeded in Toyko. Under the settlement announced on March 11, Thailand received extensive Laotian territory west of the Mekong River and about one-third of the territory of Cambodia.[23] The limited American effort to prevent the enhancement of Japan's position in Thailand had failed.

The Japanese influence in the Thailand-Indochina issue renewed pressures on the United States to react more forthrightly to the southern advance. As the negotiations progressed, American policy in Southeast Asia was repeatedly challenged. From Tokyo, Ambassador Joseph Grew warned the State Department that the stability of South and Southeast Asia was threatened; he foresaw the imminent collapse of morale in China and the East Indies.[24] Grew's position was reinforced by the arguments of Dutch officials in Batavia and London who sought, in addition to American arms, a clear indication to Tokyo that the United States would not tolerate further Japanese aggression. The British and Australian governments pressed for a similar American representation to Toyko.[25] While sharing the concerns expressed by these sources, officials in Washington continued to be restrained by American military weakness and the overriding priority given to the European war.

Moreover, it appeared in the spring of 1941 that the United States and Japan might be able to resolve their differences peacefully, an opportunity which the State Department fully pursued. Mediation of the Indochina-Thailand dispute was accompanied by various official signs and private initiatives suggestive of a less strident Japanese diplomacy which encouraged the beginning of extensive Japanese-American discussions on points of disagreement. Negotiations, at the very least, bought the Americans more time. On February 11, Admiral Nomura Kichisaburo, Japan's new ambassador, arrived in Washington, entrusted by his government with responsibility for improving the strained relations with the United States. Toward that end, he began discussions with Hull over a wide range of issues.[26]

At the same time, Japan remained committed to the extension of its influence in Southeast Asia. The Russo-Japanese nonaggression pact, signed in Moscow on April 13, facilitated concentration on the southern advance. The Liaison Conference of Military and Civilian leaders on April 16 reaffirmed the objective of enhancing Japan's position in Indochina, Thailand, and the Netherlands Indies, but on the assumption that political and economic means would be sufficient. War would be considered only in the event of intolerable U.S. economic pressures or "encirclement" by the United States, Great Britain, China, and the Netherlands Indies.[27]

As the Japanese-American discussions slowly progressed, policymakers in Washington remained concerned about the status of Thailand. During the spring of 1941, the British renewed their pressures for joint steps to preserve Thailand's independence and to prevent Japan from acquiring a monopoly on Thai tin and rubber. In response to an April 8 proposal for Anglo-American cooperation in extending to Thailand a development loan and providing supplies of oil, Hull informed Halifax that he had long been convinced that Thailand could not be saved from Japanese influence.[28] Hull's cavalier attitude antagonized the Foreign Office; in writing to Halifax on April 18, exasperated British Foreign Secretary Anthony Eden commented: "Until it is proved that the Thais are past praying for, we cannot afford to take a view at once so pessimistic and detached as Mr. Hull of the position in a country where our vital strategic interests are so much at stake, and where we are bound to make another effort to retrieve what we can of the ruins left by Japanese mediation."[29]

Reflecting Eden's determination, R. A. Butler, Undersecretary of State for Foreign Affairs, spoke on April 21 with American ambassador John Gilbert Winant about the British need for American cooperation in order to salvage some influence in Thailand. That same day, the British embassy in Washington urged that the United States join with the Netherlands and Britain in issuing a warning that any further Japanese southern advance would affect the security of all three powers. In addition, the British detailed their plans to prevent Japanese absorption of Thailand, but American financial support was vital. Again, Hull, reiterating his skepticism about Thailand, declined any joint statement.[30]

The American position on Thailand reflected not only a difference of opinion about the extent of Japanese influence and the disparity of British-American interests in the country, but a lingering criticism of British policy in Thailand. In particular, the State Department blamed the British for contributing to Thailand's precarious position, in that London had encouraged Bangkok to press its advantage with a vulnerable Indochina, which had led to the border warfare, Japanese mediation, and had enhanced Japanese influence and prestige in Thailand.[31] Moreover, Grant's reports emphasized that the British were essentially being coerced by the Thais who were threatening additional concessions to the Japanese; the American consul thus warned against being drawn into a trap which would benefit Japan.[32] Grant's profound cynicism of Thai leadership led him to discourage any American association with British policy.

"The fundamental fact in the matter," Grant cabled, "is that the Thai are ready to climb on the bandwagon with the winner in this war."[33]

Despite Grant's misgivings and after prolonged delay, the State Department on June 17 agreed to the essence of the British April 8 proposal. The United States was now prepared to purchase Thai rubber and tin, to consider granting a commodity credit of $3 million for the purchase of American goods as well as possibly providing a $3 million loan, and to recommend that oil interests participate in a program to supply limited quantities of petroleum products to Thailand.[34] Why did Hull reverse his earlier inclination to "write off" Thailand? In part, the American position resulted from British pressure and the recogntion that the Thailand question threatened a serious difference between the two nations. Perhaps more important was concern with the East Indies where the government was resisting Japanese pressures for substantial economic concessions. If the United States intended to encourage such resistance, it necessitated indications of support and, at the moment, Thailand was especially vulnerable to Japanese pressure. Moreover, it was reported that the Japanese were preparing to enhance and extend their position in Indochina, which would clearly place Thailand, unless somehow reinforced, under Japanese influence. Finally, the rubber and tin resources of Thailand were important strategically, and American interests necessitated some effort to prevent their full utilization by Japan and possibly Germany.[35]

## The Deterioration of Japanese-American Relations, July–December 1941

Developments in Asia continued to be shaped largely by events in Europe. Hitler's invasion of the Soviet Union on June 22 seemed to provide an opportunity for Japan to resolve its uncertain route to the New Order. To Japan's leaders, it appeared that expansion through peaceful means was failing as the officials in the Netherlands East Indies refused concessions, Thailand played off East against West, and the negotiations with the United States yielded no concessions. The German attack on Russia forced Japan to decide between the alternatives of advancing on Siberia or pressing the movement to the south. The northern advance, which would have violated the non-aggression pact with the Soviets, would have eliminated one of the two major obstacles to Japan's expansion. Preparations for such an attack, however, required several months; moreover, Japan's leaders anticipated an early Nazi victory, so perhaps the objective of minimizing Soviet power would be accomplished by the Germans. Thus, at a July 2 meeting of cabinet ministers and military leaders with the emperor, it was decided to advance into southern Indochina. The use of force in Southeast Asia was necessary "in order to consolidate the base of our national existence and self-defense." Preparations for a Russian campaign would also continue. While Anglo-American protests over Indochina were expected, Japanese leaders assumed that the move would not risk war.[36]

Japan's movement on Indochina contributed to the deterioration of Japanese-American relations and to an increasingly difficult American effort to reinforce the steadily weakening Western position, for Japanese hegemony over southern Indochina clearly would intimidate Thailand and the East Indies. Singapore would be within range of bombers based in Indochina. As the Japanese began pressing the Vichy government to permit a military occupation of southern Indochina, the United States urged delaying tactics,[37] but within two weeks French authorities at Vichy and Hanoi had granted Japan air and naval bases and the utilization of roads, railroads, airfields, and ports for military purposes. In Washington, officials desperately sought means of preventing the Japanese takeover, but approaches varied sharply. Hull suggested the "carrot" of promising expanded trade with the United States as part of a general settlement of the Pacific issues, while Maxwell Hamilton, chief of the Division of Far Eastern Affairs, urged the "stick" of threatening to curtail negotiations.[38]

The importance of the Japanese action brought Roosevelt fully into the formulation of the American response. While he had been preoccupied with the war in Europe and determining how the United States should react to the invasion of Russia, Roosevelt fully appreciated the importance of Japan's decision. He noted on July 1: "The Japs are having a real drag-down and knock-out fight among themselves . . . trying to decide which way they are going to jump—attack Russia, attack the South Seas (thus throwing in their lot definitely with Germany), or whether they will sit on the fence and be more friendly with us."[39]

At the same time, Roosevelt acknowledged the limits of American power in the Pacific: "It is terribly important for the control of the Atlantic for us to help keep peace in the Pacific. I simply have not got enough Navy to go around—and every little episode in the Pacific means fewer ships in the Atlantic."[40] Under these circumstances, Japan's threats on Indochina led Roosevelt to offer a "carrot" while preparing to use, if necessary, a "stick." Thus at a July 18 Cabinet meeting, Roosevelt worked out a program of economic sanctions (but not a total oil embargo) should Japan pursue its demands on Indochina.[41] This plan was balanced with a final effort at accommodation over Indochina. Roosevelt met with Ambassador Nomura on July 24 (three days after Vichy had assented to the Japanese demands and one day after Japan had pressed the issue with officials at Hanoi) and proposed the neutralization of Indochina. In return for the withdrawl of all Japanese forces, the United States would seek Chinese, British, and Dutch agreement to regard Indochina as a neutral country in which the existing French government would remain in control. Japan would be guaranteed an opportunity to acquire food supplies and raw materials in Indochina.[42] This inititative, which in any event offered less than the Japanese government believed necessary to secure its objectives, came too late. By the time of the Roosevelt-Nomura conversation, Japanese plans for occupying Indochina were fully operational, and on July 25 some 30,000 troops landed in southern Indochina.

In response, the United States applied its ultimate economic pressure. In a momentous step, Roosevelt issued an order freezing all Japanese funds, property, and assets in the United States. Shortly thereafter, the British and Dutch followed with economic sanctions which, together with the earlier American measures, constituted a virtual Western embargo. The American policy in practice, however, was more restrictive than Roosevelt had intended. Anxious to put pressure on the Japanese but not to goad them into aggression on the East Indies, Roosevelt wanted only limitations on oil exports, not a complete embargo; the freezing order gave him flexibility to increase, if necessary, the pressure on Japan. But during August while Roosevelt was meeting Winston Churchill at Placentia Bay, zealous officials in the State Department imposed a total embargo. When Roosevelt and Hull belatedly learned of that action, they could not risk modification for that would have suggested appeasement and indecision.[43]

The embargo reflected a stiffening of American policy in both Europe and Asia during the late summer and fall of 1941. The invasion of Russia lessened the German pressure on Britain and made likely Soviet-British-American cooperation against the Axis powers, provided, of course, that the Russian armies could withstand the German offensive. Roosevelt gradually led the United States into an undeclared naval war on the Atlantic and began Lend-Lease assistance to the Soviet Union. While still anxious to avoid war with Japan, Roosevelt followed the embargo with other measures that reinforced the American determination to support China and to prevent further advances in Southeast Asia. Lend-lease weapons and equipment were extended to China, and an "American Volunteer Group" of aviators and technicians were released for service in China. From the Philippines, MacArthur's pleas for weapons and equipment met with approval from military leaders who came to share his conviction that the islands could be defended. The reinforcement included B-17 bombers which were capable of striking invading forces at sea.[44] A certain buoyancy now characterized American planning; in October, a War Department report concluded that: "American air and ground units now available for dispatch to the Philippine islands in the near future have changed the entire picture in the Asiatic area."[45]

A legacy of the capitulation of Indochina was the extension of Franco-American suspicions and recriminations. At Vichy on August 1, Vice-Premier Jean Francois Darlan told Ambassador William Leahy, as Petain nodded occasional approval, that the United States had consistently acted too late to help the French withstand Japanese encroachments. Later in Washington, the French ambassador, in conversations with Hull and Assistant Secretary of State Adolph Berle, reiterated the long-standing Vichy grievance against the United States for failing to provide arms to Indochina. At the same time he sought assurances that Japanese-American negotiations would not result in the sacrificing of French interests in Indochina. Incredulous American officials were offended by such concerns inasmuch as they believed that the United States had done more than the Vichy government to uphold French sovereignty in Indochina.[46]

The most immediate consequence of the southern Indochina occupation was the intensification of the Japanese pressure on Thailand, which resulted in further differences between Americans and the British and Thais. The June 17 plan to wean Thailand from Japan by economic measures would have required considerable time to be effective. The Thais had made previous commitments to provide Japan with about two-thirds of its rubber production. In still another effort to hold the line, Welles informed Nomura on July 31 that the United States was prepared to extend the neutralization concept to Thailand. No one expected that gesture would be accepted, and like the Indochina neutralization suggestions, it was ignored by Japan.[47] As the Japanese consolidated their hold on Indochina, British and Thai officials pressed for assurances of U.S. support in the event of a Japanese attack. Hull, however, made assistance conditional on evidence of Thai resistance. The Thai minister in Washington affirmed that his government intended to resist aggression with force. Hull subsequently offered assurances that in such an eventuality, the United States would place Thailand in the same defense priority category as China.[48]

The Thai government, however, sought support in advance of Japanese aggression and on the question of the timing of American assistance, Thai-American collaboration foundered in late 1941. Immediate support was urged by Willys Peck, who in September replaced Grant as the American minister in Bangkok. Unlike his predecessor who had long ago assumed that the Japanese had such influence within the Bangkok government so as to foreclose any reorientation toward the West, Peck quickly advocated extensive economic and military assistance, especially the sale of aircraft. In the face of increased Japanese pressure, on October 15 the Thai government, with the strong backing of the British, requested that the United States provide airplanes.[49]

Within the State Department, military assistance was opposed. Hornbeck argued that the British and Thais were exaggerating the degree of Japanese intimidation and that the most effective means of preventing a Japanese attack was for the United States and Britain to make clear their determination to defend Thailand.[50] While Peck, the British embassy, and Thai government continued to press for military assistance, the State Department declined, suggesting that the British could provide the needed aircraft. The deterioration of Japanese-American relations undermined the inclination to support Thailand, for if war came to the Pacific, Thailand would be defenseless. On November 22, Hull decided that the United States, in view of needs elsewhere, could not provide arms and ammunition.[51]

As the tensions in Asia and the Pacific mounted, Peck warned on November 26 and December 3 of growing Thai disenchantment with Britain and the United States, but he maintained that pro-Western sympathies could still be cultivated. The Thai Foreign Office on December 4 appealed for guarantees of military assistance as the only means of reassuring those officials who had become skeptical of Western intentions and susceptible to the Japanese line that all European nations guaranteed British protection had come under German domination.[52] But by that time, Thailand was of little consequence to the United States.

Japan and the United States were on the verge of war. Under pressure from the embargo and other measures, Japan's leaders saw their nation confronting clear-cut alternatives. Since the United States—contrary to Japan's calculations—had refused to acquiesce in the southern Indochina advance, Japan's New Order could be pursued only at the risk of war with the United States and Britain. Or, Japan could retreat and thus accommodate the Western powers. On September 6, the Japanese cabinet and military leaders took steps to force the issue; talks with the United States were to continue, but if no satisfactory settlement could be obtained by mid-October, Japan would prepare for war. Time, Japanese as well as American leaders knew, was in America's favor. As the discussions in Washington failed to produce any American concessions on Japan's objectives in China or Southeast Asia, Japan's leaders come to believe that war was inevitable. General Tojo Hideki, who succeeded the moderate Prince Konoe Fumimaro as premier in mid-October, was determined to end indecision. The Japanese, however, still hoped war could be avoided, and extended the deadline for reaching a negotiated settlement. At the Imperial Conference on November 5, it was agreed that if diplomacy failed to reach an agreement by December 1, Japan would make the final decision for war.[53]

In the negotiations of November 1941, which largely focused on China, the Japanese and American positions remained far apart. Basically Japan sought recognition of its pre-eminent position in China, which clashed with the American assumption that any general settlement had to include Japan's withdrawl from China. In mid-November, the Japanese offered what amounted to a final offer: neither side would make any armed advances, except for Indochina which the Japanese could use as a base against China; Japan would immediately remove its troops from southern Indochina and from all of that country upon the establishment of a general East Asian peace; Japan and the United States would cooperate in acquiring the resources of the Netherlands East Indies; the prefreeze trade would be restored; and the United States would not interfere with Japan's conclusion of a settlement with China. While unwilling to agree to this abandonment of China, Roosevelt and Hull sought to enlist Japan's agreement to a modus vivendi by which both sides would pledge no military advances, and the Japanese would withdraw from Indochina in return for a partial resumption of Japanese-American trade. Obviously the differences remained significant, and with time running out, they were irreconcilable.

Roosevelt recognized the imminence of war and at last clarified the American commitment to defend Southeast Asia. As a result of its MAGIC operation, by which Japanese coded messages were intercepted and translated, the United States had become aware of Japanese plans for a military operation in early December. MAGIC did not reveal the Pearl Harbor attack plan and American leaders asssumed war would be launched against the British and/or Dutch possessions in Southeast Asia. In a Cabinet meeting in early November, Roosevelt inquired whether the public would support military action in the event of an attack on a non-American possession in Southeast Asia; all agreed that it would. On November 25, Roosevelt, in a meeting with key diplomatic and military leaders, discussed the problems of justifying a declaration of war if Japan attacked the British or Dutch colonies.[54] Roosevelt, however, was prepared to risk those difficulties, for on December 1, in a meeting with Halifax, he provided the British with their long sought commitment of U.S. assistance in the event of an attack on British or Dutch possessions, or on Thailand. For the British, the President's assurances—"we should obviously be all together"—eliminated a major concern of British diplomacy, i.e. that the remnants of European power in Southeast Asia might be obliged to fight alone against Japan. Repeatedly Netherlands government officials in London had sought a firm British underwriting of the defense of the East Indies, but Churchill had refused in the belief that the United States had to provide leadership in the Pacific. Thus, not until the eve of the Japanese attack on Pearl

Harbor did the United States finally assume the responsibilities which the British had been urging for two years.[55]

## The Atlantic Charter and the Colonial Issue

As British and American strategic interests finally merged, a series of incidents revealed Anglo-American differences over colonialism—an issue destined to cause profound disagreement and controversy. At the conclusion of their conference held at Placentia Bay in Newfoundland in August, Churchill and Roosevelt had issued the Atlantic Charter, a statement of war aims which included, as its third article, a pledge to "respect the right of all people to choose the form of government under which they live." The colonial implications of this declaration quickly became evident when the Premier of Burma and members of the legislature inquired when self-government would be applied to that part of the British Empire. The same questions were being raised about the status of India. Churchill, in a speech before the House of Commons on September 9, held that the Atlantic Charter did not apply to the British empire; rather the third article had been intended for persons living under Nazi domination. Nationalists in India and many liberal spokesmen in America criticized Churchill's stand. The American government attempted to ignore the issue, but not without the risk of becoming associated with British imperialism. On November 15, Burmese Prime Minister Maung Saw, who had failed to gain any promises of self-government in meetings with British officials in London, visited with Roosevelt. While he technically lacked diplomatic status since the British controlled Burma's foreign affairs, the Prime Minister nonetheless raised the question of the implemenation of the Atlantic Charter. In a letter to Roosevelt on November 26, he further inquired whether the President agreed with Churchill's September 9 interpretation of the Atlantic Charter. While the United States could fall back on Burma's lack of international standing to deflect these entreaties, the issue of future colonialism in Southeast Asia had nudged its way into Anglo-American relations.[56]

The emergence of the colonialism issue signified the extent to which the war in Asia would be a racial conflict. In retrospect, the appeals of the French and Dutch in 1940–1941 to perserve the dominance of the white race in Southeast Asia sound crude, but they spoke to the fundamental consideration of whether the West or Japan would control the raw materials and markets of the region. Prior to and especially after Pearl Harbor, Japan sought to exploit Asian resentment of the West. Ultimately Japanese dominance proved no more popular nor benign than that exercised by Britain, France, the Netherlands and the United States. But the era of Japanese imperialism produced far-reaching political, economic, and social changes which worked to the political benefit of the peoples of Southeast Asia and the detriment of the European colonial powers.

## Conclusions

The American search in 1940–1941 for a means to stabilize Southeast Asia without sacrificing American priorities elsewhere or undertaking serious commitments not only failed, but left lingering problems. British and American differences over Thailand resurfaced during and after the war, but, ironically, with the two nations shifting their attitudes toward the Phibun government. The subsequent position of each nation on Thailand, however, was derived directly from the pre-Pearl Harbor tensions. The ineffective French resistance to the Japanese in Indochina and the American unwillingness to bolster Indochina were an important part of a network of Franco-American antagonisms that lasted throughout and beyond the war, with important consequences for the future Indochina. While the Dutch and the British appreciated the long sought assurances of support in the event of a Japanese attack, there would remain questions of whether an earlier commitment might have discouraged the Japanese southern advance and enhanced the opposition to the militant policy within the Tokyo government.

Behind the Pearl Harbor attack were years of ineffective diplomacy characterized by miscalculations and misperceptions on all sides. A major shortcoming of British and American policies was the underestimation of Japan's capability and willingness to wage a war against the Western powers. Because of that deficiency, the British and Americans failed to contemplate the extent to which a war would change Asia. Japan's New Order was perceived as a direct challenge to Western domination, but few persons expected the Japanese to gain control over East and Southeast Asia and to effect revolutionary political changes in the process. In addition, the intense pressures on policymakers in 1940–41 and the priority given to the European war did not allow for considered analysis of the meaning and impact of a general conflict in the Pacific. Ironically, many of the changes brought by the Japanese empire in Southeast Asia worked to the political and economic benefit of the United States and facilitated the process of decolonization which became the central postwar American objective in the region.[57] As that trend became evident at war's end, the British, Dutch, and French—which a few years earlier had been anxious to involve a reluctant United States in Southeast Asian affairs—sought to limit American influence.

Once it had become the dominant power in shaping Western policy in Southeast Asia, the United States would not retreat to its pre-1940 deference to the British. Thus perhaps the most significant consequence of the crisis of 1940–1941 in Asia and the Pacific was the unmistakable assertion of American influence and the demise of the British. As Japan and the United States negotiated the issues of China and Southeast Asia and drifted to war, the British were little more than advisers to the Americans. The war in the Pacific continued the trend, for it fundamentally was an American-Japanese conflict, leaving the British and the other European nations involved only peripherally.

# 3.

# Planning for Decolonization in Southeast Asia, 1942–1943

> The western nations must now do what hitherto they lacked the will and the imagination to do: they must identify their cause with the freedom and security of the peoples of the East, putting away the "white man's burden" and purging themselves of the taint of an obsolete and obviously unworkable white man's imperialism. In this drastic reorientation of war policy, the leadership of the western nations must be taken by the United States.
>
> Walter Lippmann, February 1942

WITHIN SIX MONTHS of the attack on Pearl Harbor, Japan had established its New Order in Southeast Asia. In a series of offensive operations that shattered the foundations of the Western imperial system, Japanese forces captured Malaya, Burma, the Netherlands East Indies, and the Philippines. Thailand was pressured into collaboration and declared war on the United States and Great Britain.

To Americans, the Japanese conquest reaffirmed long-standing attitudes toward European imperialism and the sense of American destiny in Asia. Japan's conquests were attributed to the failure of the European colonial powers to build the trust of their subject peoples. Colonialism was the source of Western weakness against Japan. President Franklin D. Roosevelt held to such a view of the conflict. As reported by his son Elliott, he commented: "Don't think for a moment, Elliott, that Americans would be dying in the Pacific tonight, if it hadn't been for the shortsighted greed of the French and the British and the Dutch. Shall we allow them to do it all, all over again? . . . When we've won the war, I will work with all my might and main to see that the United States is not wheedled into the position of accepting any plan that will further France's imperialistic ambitions, or that will aid or abet the British Empire in its imperial ambitions."[1]

While Elliott Roosevelt's recounting of his father's conversations may have been exaggerated at times, this quotation is consistent with Roosevelt's attitudes and objectives. The determination of the United States to defend the Philippines and the identification of the Filipinos with the American cause seemingly affirmed the effectiveness of American colonial policy. In the article cited in the epigrah to this chapter, Lippmann captured the importance of the American-Philippine resistance: "General MacArthur leads an Army of Americans and Filipinos in a struggle which is as noble as it is glorious. For the Filipinos know that under American law, their own independence is assured to them. When they fight in the Bataan  peninsula side by side with our men, they are fighting for their independence."[2] While the promise of independence could not sustain the American and Philippine armies indefinitely, the lack of comparable heroism elsewhere in colonial Southeast Asia clearly indicated the failure of the European powers.

This resurgent anticolonialism merged with a renewed sense of an American destiny in Asia. While Americans had traditionally looked critically upon the European institutions from which they had freed themselves, the emergence of interest in Asia had been accompanied by a fascination with the exotic and a sense of mission. Throughout the nineteenth and early twentieth centuries, China and Japan had been viewed as developing markets and promising missionary fields. In fact, the American approach to Asia was based on limited contacts, over-simplified and distorted images, and insensitivity to Oriental culture. Moreover, a prevalent racism characterized American relationships with the Chinese, Japanese, and other Asian peoples.[3] Nonetheless, the sense of Asian mission endured. During the 1930s, this had centered on the peculiar American attachment to China and its resistance to Japanese imperialism.[4] The moral outrage triggered by the Pearl Harbor attack established firmly the popular image of Japan as the nation's primary enemy. The decision to concentrate American resources in a two-front war on the European theater of operations may have been appropriate militarily, but it was never popular with the majority of Americans who looked upon the Pacific theater as "our war." The disproportionate number of wartime motion pictures set in the Pacific recognized the popular identification with the campaign against Japan. The sense of Asian destiny was symbolized by the charismatic General Douglas MacArthur and was articulated by a number of writers, most prominently by Pearl Buck. "If the American way of life is to prevail in the world," she said in February 1942, "it must prevail in Asia."[4]

As the Department of State began its planning for the postwar world, it was anticipated that the establishment of a new international organization, and the realization of the principles of self-determination and the open door, would provide the basis for the preservation of peace.[5] With respect to Southeast Asia, consideration of the concept of "international trusteeship" for dependent peoples directly affected the colonies of Britain, France, and the Netherlands. While officials and committees disagreed on various aspects of the colonial question, the overall direction of planning for the European colonies, the commitment to Philippine independence, and to the restoration of Thailand's self-determination envisioned the emergence of a politically independent, economically viable, Western-oriented region.

Planning for postwar Southeast Asia was influenced by several related factors: the objective of anticolonialism; relationships with the European colonial powers; and external colonial issues, especially the 1942 crisis in India. These background considerations help to place the development of Southeast Asian planning in a proper perspective.

## Roosevelt, the State Department, and Anticolonialism

At the center of American planning for Asia was the principle of anticolonialism. In a Memorial Day address in 1942, Undersecretary of State Sumner Welles set forth the American commitment to self-determination:

> If the war is in fact a war for the liberation of peoples it must assure the sovereign equality of peoples throughout the world, as well as in the world of the Americas. Our victory must bring in its train the liberation of all peoples. Discrimination between peoples because of their race, creed or color must be abolished. The age of imperialism is ended. . . . The principles of the Atlantic Charter must be guaranteed to the world as a whole—in all oceans and in all continents.[6]

Building upon the historic American distrust of imperialism, the Wilsonian World War I appeal for self-determination and a liberal colonial settlement after that war, and the sense that imperialism had been a major cause of the two world wars, many American writers and officials believed that the concept of international accountability for colonial administration had to be made universal. The League of Nations mandates provided a limited model in the practice of international trusteeship which, it was believed, could be extended. Imperial powers would no longer be permitted to rule dependent peoples and to be responsible only to themselves; "national trusteeship" had to evolve into international trusteeship. With the American experience in the Philippines as a model, the State Department planners advanced the principle of establishing timetables of steps toward decolonization. The objectives and mechanism of an international colonial system proved to be the source of much disagreement and controversy within the American government and, later, in relations with the European powers. Should all dependent peoples be included? Did distinctions need to be made between the mandates, Axis colonies, and Western colonies reconquered from the Axis? Was independence the universal objective or, in some cases, would self-government be sufficient? How could the United States in practice insist upon acceptance of international accountability? Did international trusteeship necessitate international control or administration? While the resolution of these questions resulted in compromising of the bold statement of Welles, the United States nonetheless continued to assert throughout the war years a belief in the impermanence of colonialism.

Anticolonialism merged with pursuit of the open door in that the American assault upon the European empires meant the end of imperial preferences and promised access to commercial and investment opportunities. Anglo-American differences surfaced at the time of the writing of the Atlantic Charter when the British objected to an American draft of article 4 which specified the postwar objective of "access without discrimination and on equal terms" to markets and raw materials. At British insistence, the commitment was conditioned by reference to "due respect for existing obligations." While the British held their own in the drafting of the Atlantic Charter, the United States relentlessly sought agreement on the principle of the open door, in its pursuit of both general economic and anticolonial objectives. Not only would the United States benefit from the open door in colonial areas, American policymakers held, but so would the peoples living under European rule. With few exceptions, American officials and other spokesmen on foreign policy issues believed that European imperialism shamelessly exploited subject peoples.

The relationship between American plans for an international trusteeship system and the open door was reflected in the thinking of Benjamin Gerig, who played a central role in the formulation of the State Department's postwar objectives for colonial areas. Serving as chairman of the Committee on Dependent Areas during the war, Gerig brought to that position a background of scholarship on the League of Nations mandates and his service in the League's Secretariat. His 1930 book, *The Open Door and the Mandates System: A Study of Economic Equality before and since the Establishment of the Mandates System* argued strongly that the mandates had provided an effective means of ending national economic imperialism and securing the open door. The mandates system provided an example of the potential for a universal system of international accountability in ending economic barriers in the colonial areas.[7]

While the State Department and Franklin D. Roosevelt often operated independently from one another, the State Department's planning on colonialism coincided closely with the President's approach. Roosevelt's attitudes toward colonialism were representative of his generation. Early in his career he had thrilled to American imperialism in the Caribbean, but influenced by Wilsonian idealism and the American imperial experience, he had become, by the late 1920s, a proponent of nonintervention. As President, he supported the lessening of control over Puerto Rico, gave Latin American policy generally an anticolonial tone with his "Good Neighbor" approach, and backed the commitment to the early independence of the Philippines.[8] At a press conference in March 1941, Roosevelt set forth his anticolonial convictions: "There never has been, there isn't now and there never will be any race on earth fit to serve as master of their fellow men. . . . We believe that any nationality, no matter how small, has the inherent right to its own nationhood."[9]

During the first year after Pearl Harbor, Roosevelt gave considerable attention to imperialism. In 1942, the future of the European empires emerged as both an immediate as well as long-term problem. The British impasse with the Indian National Congress made the cause of Indian nationalism a major issue in Anglo-American relations. Roosevelt responded with a number of initiatives which sought to force modification of British policy. Beyond that problem (which will be discussed more fully later), Roosevelt also considered the postwar status of the colonies in Southeast Asia which were then occupied by Japan. In a meeting on June 1 with Russian Foreign Minister V. M. Molotov, Russian Ambassador Maxim Litvinov, and presidential advisor Harry Hopkins, Roosevelt digressed into a discourse on the impending demise of colonialism. To facilitate the transition from colonial status to self-government, administration of the colonies should be transferred to an international trusteeship arrangement. Referring to Indochina, Malaya, the East Indies (as well as Thailand) as examples of colonies where a "palpable surge" toward independence rendered prolonged western control impossible, Roosevelt foresaw that under "some form of interim international control" they might be prepared for self-government within twenty years.[10]

Roosevelt's penchant for personal diplomacy and his fascination with particular questions did result in some differences and misunderstandings—especially over Indochina—with the State Department. And on colonial questions as with other aspects of wartime diplomacy, Roosevelt distilled his idealism with realism. The results were frequently disappointing and even disillusioning to others in the American government and those in other countries who looked to the United States for a consistent, unequivocal position.[11] But whatever the limitations of his diplomacy in practice, Roosevelt's vision of a postwar world moving toward the elimination of imperialism gave impetus to State Department planning and direction to the Allied war effort especially in Asia.

## Colonialism and U.S. Relations with Britain, the Netherlands, and France

While the British, Dutch, and French shared a common interest in the reestablishment of the imperial system in Southeast Asia, their individual relations with the United States over the colonialism question and related matters followed distinctive patterns. The mutual British-American dependence established close collaboration in the fight against the Axis, but disagreements persisted over a number of military and political issues, perhaps most importantly the future of the imperial system. Alarmed at what appeared to be a simplistic American approach to the question of India's political status and at the prevalent antiimperialism in the United States, the British closely examined American postwar planning. Within the British government, considerable disagreement developed, especially between the Foreign Office and the Colonial Office, over the extent to which British interests were threatened by American objectives and the appropriate response to Washington's initiatives.[12] To uphold the colonial system in Southeast Asia, London considered the maintenance of Anglo-Dutch collaboration vital.[13]

As a result of some shrewd maneuvering, and capitalizing on Roosevelt's benign attitude toward the Dutch, the Netherlands government-in-exile managed to avoid serious strains with the United States over its Asian interests. As the Japanese were completing the takeover of the East Indies, the Netherlands minister in Washington requested that the President commit the United States to the restoration of Dutch sovereignty. At the State Department, political adviser Stanley Hornbeck and Chief of the Division of Far Eastern Affairs Maxwell Hamilton suggested to Welles that, in view of the ineffective Dutch resistance in the East Indies and the anticipated changes in the colonial world by the end of the war, the United States should avoid any commitment.[14] Yet when the Dutch government questioned the decision to concentrate resources in the battle against Germany, Roosevelt, in a letter to Queen Wilhelmina, followed an explanation of military strategy with the rather offhand commitment: "When and if that happens [Germany defeated] the combined power of the United Nations will not take long to drive the Japanese back into their own islands. The Netherlands Indies must be restored—and something within me tells me that they will be."[15]

Netherlands officials remained sensitive to the wave of anti-imperialism in the American press and maintained, in conversations with State Department officials, that it undermined the loyalty of the native peoples in the East Indies.[16] In part to appease American opinion, Queen Wilhelmina, in a widely publicized December 1942 speech, promised autonomy and partnership to the units in the Netherlands Kingdom at the end of the war. This action reduced Dutch-American problems over Southeast Asia. In particular, Roosevelt was inclined to look favorably upon Dutch policies and objectives in the East Indies. This attitude was reinforced by his admiration for Dutch resistance to the Germans and to Japan's pre-Pearl Harbor demands in the East Indies, and perhaps as well by his Dutch ancestry. But above all, his admiration for an apparently enlightened Dutch colonialism accounted for Roosevelt's support of their position in the East Indies. At a Pacific War Council meeting in July 1943, Roosevelt, after castigating the French for their record in Indochina, "concluded by mentioning twice the very splendid speech which Queen Wilhelmina had recently made which pointed toward a federation for the East Indies after the war."[17]

The American relationship with France, already strained before Pearl Harbor, further deteriorated during the following year. The maintenance of diplomatic relations with the Vichy government antagonized the Free French headed by General Charles de Gaulle. Much of American opinion was hostile to the Vichy policy and inclined toward favoring de Gaulle. Moreover, the British cultivated and supported the development of the Free French movement. Shortly after Pearl Harbor, the Free French, much to the annoyance of the United States, occupied the French North American islands of St. Pierre and Miquelon, which had been under the authority of Vichy. The Allies' North African invasion of November 1942 resulted in highly controversial American dealings with Vichy officials in France's African colonies. The Allied landings also resulted in Germany's occupation of Vichy-governed territory in southern France and to Vichy's diplomatic break with the United States. Even after

Washington's Vichy strategy had lost its usefulness, the American government remained skeptical of de Gaulle and his movement. Roosevelt and other officials questioned the extent of de Gaulle's support among the French people and were reluctant to make commitments that might prejudice postliberation French politics.[18] The personal relationship between Roosevelt and de Gaulle was strained. At their first meeting at Casablanca in January 1943, Roosevelt found de Gaulle arrogant and spoke condescendingly to him of France's weakened position.[19]

While Frenchmen divided bitterly over their response to the German occupation, collaborators and resistance elements were in agreement on the fundamental importance of the empire. The humiliation of 1940 enhanced the importance of the colonies as a symbol of France's claim to major power status.[20] The French empire, especially Indochina, became entangled in the persistent strains in wartime Franco-American relations.

The British, French, and Dutch had little concern with the Pacific war, except as it affected their interests in Southeast Asia. The European powers recognized their dependence upon the United States to defeat Japan. And while they were suspicious of American anticolonialism, differences over the future of Southeast Asia did not become a significant factor in Allied diplomacy until late 1943. In the meantime, the British cooperated with the Americans in the North Africa and Mediterranean campaigns, while the Dutch government-in-exile and the Free French looked above all to the liberation of their home countries. In the Pacific, the United States concentrated on the Pacific Island campaign against Japan. Any Allied movement against the Japanese in Southeast Asia remained a distant operation. While early American planning on the future of Southeast Asia was thus freed of the persistent bickering with Allies that characterized the later stages of the war, officials at the State Department were cognizant of the implications of anticolonialism on American relations with Britain, France, and the Netherlands.

## The India Question and Its Implications

During the year after Pearl Harbor, India's movement for independence from Great Britain raised the question of the American commitment to anticolonialism. The Roosevelt administration assumed a prominent role in efforts to resolve the British impasse with the Indian National Congress. The Indian controversy exemplified the problems of fulfilling the principle of anticolonialism. Caught between the determination for independence of the National Congress, under the leadership of Mohandas Gandhi and Jawaharlal Nehru, and the equally strong imperialist position of Winston Churchill, the Roosevelt administration deferred to its ally. The response to the British-Indian crisis of 1942 had important implications for State Department and White House thinking and planning on colonial questions.

India's cause became a symbol of the Allied commitment to self-determination. American liberals as well as a number of officials argued that failure to respond to India's aspirations would undermine the integrity of the Allied cause. Liberal spokesmen urged American diplomatic intervention to assure Indian independence. In the State Department, Assistant Secretary Adolph Berle seconded the suggestions of American officials in India to exert pressure on the British. The considerable popular interest in the Indian crisis of 1942 was intensified by the general American disenchantment with imperialism and by the desirability of gaining Indian support in the war effort. In addition, Chiang Kai-shek, widely respected in the United States at this time, strongly sympathized with the Indian nationalist movement. The Chinese leader visited India in February, 1942; his meetings with Gandhi and Nehru represented an identification of America's Asian ally with Indian aspirations for freedom.

In early 1942 as the Japanese advance through Southeast Asia threatened India, the Indian National Congress offered to support the Allied war effort in return for recognition of independence. Indian nationalists were determined to avoid repeating the mistake that they had made during the First World War when they accepted British promises of a liberal postwar policy only to feel betrayed by the subsequent limited concessions and repressive measures. In the United States, a number of journalists as well as officials at the State Department called for American action on behalf of the nationalist cause. In part to meet American pressures, the British sent a special committee headed by Sir Stafford Cripps to offer independence after the war. Their offer, however, was conditioned by provisions upholding the position of religious and racial minorities and the possible partitioning of the subcontinent. To the National Congress, the offer was unacceptable. Meanwhile Roosevelt had suggested to Churchill a scheme for the progressive realization of self-government based on the experience of the United States following its revolution against England. Churchill summarily dismissed the Roosevelt initiative, but he could not ignore the President's dispatch to India of Louis Johnson as his "personal representative." Johnson, a West Virginia lawyer who had been a controversial figure in the Roosevelt administration as Assistant Secretary of War, quickly sympathized with the position of the Indian nationalists and worked diligently to effect a compromise between the Cripps Mission and the National Congress, but without success.

To the opponents of imperialism, the failure of the Cripps Mission set back the Allied cause throughout the colonial world. A disappointed Welles wrote to Roosevelt of the potential implications of an Indian settlement: "The failure of the Cripps negotiations makes it unfortunately impossible for us to utilize the announcement of an agreement . . . providing for the freedom of India as a platform on which to base an announcement of a broader policy. If the Cripps negotiations had been successful . . . what I had in mind was to recommend the announcement of a broad policy of general liberation."[21]

Following the collapse of the Cripps Mission, the Indian National Congress, under Gandhi's leadership, moved toward accepting his demand that the British withdraw from India immediately. Gandhi and other Indian leaders sought to cultivate American support, but to most American officials and to much of the press, the "Quit India" campaign seemed reckless and ill-timed. Yet the State Department, as well as Chiang Kai-shek, urged Roosevelt to intervene as the only means of averting an anti-British civil disobedience campaign which would damage the reputation and unity of the Allies. Roosevelt made a modest effort to gain Churchill's acceptance of mediation, but by the time that the "Quit India" campaign was launched on August 8, the American government had becom reconciled to accepting British policy in India. That policy proved harsh, as the British quickly suppressed a nationwide uprising and arrested thousands of Indian leaders, most of whom remained jailed until near the end of the war.[22]

The response to the Indian crisis of 1942 had many ramifications. Basically it illustrated the difficulty of forcing the hand of an entrenched imperial power whose support on other overriding issues was considered essential. The controversy over Indian policy also indicated the problem with a universal commitment to self-determination, and it thus led to the beginning of official qualifications of the Atlantic Charter. In a nationwide radio address on July 23, Secretary of State Cordell Hull affirmed American support of movements for national freedom, but within the following context: "It has been our policy in the past—and will remain our policy in the future—to use the full measure of our influence to support attainment of freedom by all peoples who, by their acts show themselves worthy of it and ready for it."[23]

In his memoirs, Hull acknowledged that he had India in mind when he spoke on July 23 and his speech was widely interpreted as reflecting official exasperation with the National Congress for its refusal to support the war effort without a commitment to independence. The British government looked upon the Hull address as an expression of American symphy for their problems in India.[24] While committed to the ideal of anti-colonialism, Hull had not been inclined to force the Indian issue with the British. The Secretary of State sought to make certain that anticolonialism followed practical lines. The July 23 address, while consistent with the White House's deference to the British, reflected Hull's attitudes. A few months after the July 23 address, the Secretary again asserted himself by assuming direction over much of the State Department planning on anticolonialism, specifically excluding Western colonies from trusteeship plans.

Acquiescence in imperial policy, however, also led to considerable criticism, not only from Indian nationalists and the Chinese government, but from some officers in the State Department and from various journals and politicians. While Americans had looked unfavorably on the "Quit India" movement, the response of the British and the uncompromising style and rhetoric of Churchill resulted in renewed pressures on Roosevelt to reassert American interest. Most forcefully, Wendell Willkie, the Republican presidential nominee of 1940, who had just completed a worldwide tour, advocated an uncompromising stand on colonialism in a nationwide radio address on October 26:

> We are also punching holes in our reservoir of good will every day by our failure to define clearly our war aims. Besides giving our Allies in Asia and Eastern Europe something to fight with, we have to give them assurances of what we are fighting for. ... Many of them have read the Atlantic Charter. Rightly or wrongly they are not satisfied. They ask: what about a Pacific Charter? What about a World Charter? ... Many of them also asked the question which has become a symbol all through Asia: what about India? Now I did not go to India and I do not propose to discuss that tangled question tonight. But it has one aspect in the East which I should report to you. From Cairo on, it confronted me at every point. The wisest man in China said to me:
> "When the aspirations of India for freedom were put aside to some future unguaranteed date, it was not Great Britain that suffered in public esteem in the Far East. It was the United States." ... He was telling me, and through me, you, that by our silence on India we have already drawn heavily on our reservoir of good will in the East. People of the East who would like to count on us are doubtful. They cannot ascertain from our government's

wishy-washy attitude toward the problem of India what we are likely to feel at the end of the war about all the other hundreds of millions of Eastern peoples. They cannot tell from our vague and vacillating talks whether we really do stand for freedom, or what we mean by freedom.[25]

Willkie's address effectively made colonialism into a domestic political issue. In conjunction with other protests, it forced Roosevelt to reaffirm American interest in India by sending William Phillips as a special representative in early 1943. In the context of the general development of wartime thinking on the colonialism question, the frustration of American efforts in India and the adverse criticism of Roosevelt's policy must have had an effect upon the President's subsequent approach to colonial issues. The disappointment resulting from the failure of American diplomacy to resolve the Indian crisis in 1942 likely influenced Roosevelt's determination to realize anticolonialism elsewhere.

## End of Imperialism:
## State Department Planning,
## January 1942–May 1943

In the early Department of State consideration of colonial questions it was generally assumed that the war would mark the end of imperialism. Discussion centered on the preparedness of certain peoples for self-government, the process of decolonization, and whether a single anticolonial declaration could be applied equally to Axis colonies, League of Nations mandates, and the Western colonies. Officials also considered the reaction of European imperial powers and the consequent impact of anticolonialism upon long-term relations with allies.

The Advisory Committee on Postwar Foreign Policy, established three weeks after Pearl Harbor, had general responsibility for the development of postwar objectives. In view of the immensity of its task, the committee quickly decided to work through a number of subcommittees, which included members of the Advisory Committee as well as others added for their expertise. From the beginning, the planning operation included not only representatives of the State Department and other executive agencies, but private citizens and (somewhat later) members of Congress as well. The Subcommittee on Political Problems and the Subcommittee on Territorial Problems dealt in part with various aspects of the colonial questions. Among the responsibilities of the Subcommittee on Political Problems was the definition of objectives affecting an international organization, while the Subcommittee on Territorial Problems included among its duties consideration of dependent areas. The Subcommittee on Political Problems included Welles as chairman; Berle; Hornbeck; Hamilton Fish Armstrong, editor of *Foreign Affairs;* Anne O'Hare McCormick, international colunmist of the *New York Times;* Isiah Bowman, president of Johns Hopkins University; Leo Pasvolsky, special assistant to the Secretary of State; John V. A. MacMurray, former minister to China and temporarily serving as a special assistant to the Secretary of State; Myron C. Taylor, philanthropist and industrialist.

The Subcommittee on Territorial Problems, which Bowman chaired, had virtually the same membership, except that it did not include Welles and Hornbeck. This overlapping of membership helped to assure a high degree of coordination. As the committee system developed in 1942, the Subcommittee on Territorial Problems gave early attention to colonialism, especially in Southeast Asia, but the most extensive discussion and the significant recommendations emerged later from the Subcommittee on Political Problems.

A major shortcoming in formulating plans for Southeast Asia was the lack of expertise on the region. Prior to the war, the State Department had relied upon the British, French, and Dutch for information about their colonial possessions; accordingly, reporting on those territories had been generally channelled through the Division of European Affairs, not the Division of Far Eastern Affairs. The latter office was principally concerned with the independent nations of Asia and to some extent, the Philippines. During the summer of 1941, emerging

American intelligence operations brought to government service a handful of scholars with some expertise in Southeast Asia, including Kenneth Landon on Thailand, Thomas Ennis on Indochina, Amry Vanderbosch on the East Indies, and John Christian on Burma. Most of these men became involved in postwar planning, but the area clearly lacked the kind of scholarly understanding that it required. When Landon joined the Far Eastern affairs desk in late 1943, he was the first officer in that office to have lived extensively in Southeast Asia and to be familiar with the languages and cultures of the area.[26]

As the planning apparatus was taking shape, State Department officers were considering the possibility of U.S. participation in the promulgation of a "Pacific Charter" which would affirm the extension of the principle of self-determination to Asia. This plan gained considerable support from a number of political leaders and writers who were concerned about the Anglo-American differences over the universality of the Atlantic Charter, and it was endorsed by the Chinese and Australian governments. At the State Department, Berle championed the necessity of reorienting American policy in Asia, including the desirability of an Anglo-American declaration that the Allies were committed to the freedom of Asian peoples. The Division of Far Eastern Affairs and Hornbeck opposed the "Pacific Charter" on the grounds that it would tend to confirm the British interpretation of a limited Atlantic Charter. Rather, the United States should seek a worldwide anticolonial policy based on the principles of the Atlantic Charter; such a declaration became a major concern of the Territorial and Political Subcommittees.[27]

The buoyant anticolonialism of early 1942 found expression in a Territorial Subcommittee draft statement on dependent areas which was based on the assumption that the Allies "have a blank sheet of paper upon which they are writing a new chapter with colonial self-rule as the ultimate objective."[28] The rambling discussion at the committee's April 11 meeting touched upon the problems of a universal commitment to self-government. Berle, for instance, argued that it would be necessary to distinguish areas taken from the Axis, and Western

colonies reconquered from the enemy. Challenging fellow committee member Bowman's effort to deal with specific dependent
areas, Berle asserted that the committee lacked adequate information; acknowledging that he "did not know enough about the
peoples of Indo-China" Berle unwittingly revealed his ignorance
by describing them as "Chinese for the main part." Thus, they
"might well be integrally joined with China somehow."[29] Sharing Roosevelt's uncritical approach toward Dutch colonialism,
Bowman observed that Dutch administration in the East Indies
was illustrative of colonial rule that had advanced from exploitation of the native population to being responsible and beneficial.[30]

The Subcommitte on Political Problems became chiefly
responsible for developing postwar policy objectives on colonialism. It emerged as the central planning group as a consequence of its wide-ranging responsibilities and because of the
cessation in May 1942 of the meetings of the Committee on
Postwar Foreign Policy. With the Undersecretary serving as its
chairman and including a larger and more diverse membership
that the other subcommittees, the Subcommittee on Political
Problems naturally became the group to which the other subcommittees reported and looked for advice. In sum, it vitually
replaced the original overall planning committee.[31]

Although about fifteen persons regularly attended meetings of the Subcommittee on Political Problems in the summer
of 1942, the dominant figures on the colonial question were
Welles, Bowman, Hornbeck, MacMurray, and McCormick. In
August, committee consideration of a number of Asian problems
included detailed discussion on Indochina. At a meeting on the
first of August, Hornbeck introduced the Indochina issue by
criticizing the French record of exploitation and their betrayal of
the country to Japan. He concluded: "the record of the French in
Indochina in the last three years was one which did not entitle
them to consideration." While no one on the committee defended France, others did raise a number of questions: Would
China insist upon acquiring Indochina as a means of assuring its
security? Had not the United States committed itself to the res-

toration of French territory? Since the Vichy government had been responsible for France's weakness vis-á-vis Japan, would not a change in French government necessitate altering American plans for Indochina? What was the ultimate American objective in Indochina? On the first question, Hornbeck foresaw the likelihood of Chinese insistence on control of all or part of Indochina. (Although not mentioned at the meeting, on July 23 the State Department had requested that the embassy in Chungking report on China's attitude toward postwar problems. A reply received two days after this meeting, indicated that Chinese officials anticipated, among other developments, the establishment of international mandates for Indochina and the East Indies as a means of training those peoples for self-government.) On the second issue, Welles maintained that the pledge to restore French territory applied to Alsace and Lorraine and had no colonial implications. On the other questions, Welles reaffirmed the position taken in his May 30 address, i.e., the war meant the end of imperialism. He then spoke of a trusteeship arrangement as the agent for decolonization. In the course of the committee's extended discussion on these questions, Hornbeck conceded that dismissal of France's claim to Indochina was much easier than finding a workable alternative.[32]

A week later on August 8, the Political Subcommittee dealt with general U.S. postwar objectives in colonial areas, with much attention devoted to Asia. This meeting was held at a sensitive moment—the "Quit India" movement was launched that day and the first anniversary of the Atlantic Charter the following week was focusing much attention on its implications for the colonial world. The committee agreed unanimously that the United States should work for the liberation of Asian peoples. Welles then posed the fundamental problem: How should the United States respond if the colonial powers reasserted control? Hornbeck maintained that moral suasion probably represented the extent of American influence, but he conceded risks in that level of action. For if the United Nations tolerated a restoration of the prewar status quo, political instability would result. When MacMurray argued that it would be a mistake to force the hand of the sovereign colonial powers, Welles sharply disagreed. Pointing to the British intention to ignore India's demand for independence, the Under Secretary refused to become reconciled to the view that the United States was incapable of influencing nationalist-imperialist disputes. The trusteeship concept, he maintained, offered the solution, a conclusion with which other members of the committee generally agreed. Welles foresaw the establishment of a Southeast Asian trusteeship arrangement involving the powers with colonial interests in addition to the United States, Soviet Union, China, Australia, and New Zealand.

In a subsequent meeting on August 15, the committee returned briefly to Southeast Asian plans. Welles drew an important distinction between the French colony and those of Britain and the Netherlands. While international administration of Indochina was necessitated by the French record, the British and Dutch could be restored to authority in their colonies provided they agreed to the general supervision of, and to report to, the regional international trusteeship council.[33] Hence, the Southeast Asian trusteeship council, as envisioned in August 1942, would have an overall responsibility for assuring the development of self-government, but would exercise direct control only in Indochina.

American objectives for Southeast Asia were directly tied to the efforts to develop general postwar objectives. With the encouragement of Hull, two related projects were undertaken in 1942. The Division of Far Eastern affairs worked on a "World Charter" which would make clear the universal character of the Atlantic Charter principles. Meanwhile the Subcommittee on International Organization completed a draft proposal "International Trusteeship for Non-Self-Governing Peoples," which was built on the assumption that the United States should work toward the liberation of all colonial peoples. This document reflected principally the views and experience of Benjamin Gerig, who became a central figure in all planning related to colonialism. The trusteeship proposals represented an extension and elaboration of the League of Nations mandates. International supervision would be established in all dependent areas which were not prepared for self-government. While administration for practical reasons might be returned to the prewar colonial powers, it would be subject to review by regional international councils. The trusteeship system was to plan for the implementation of self-government, to enhance the well-being of the world, to provide for equal economic opportunity for all nations, and to contribute to general international security.[34]

At the same time, Hull was developing his own approach to the colonial question. Reflecting the views expressed in his July 23 address and his experience in dealing with British Ambassador Lord Halifax over the India question and colonialism generally, Hull's approval of the trusteeship plans included an important limitation. Owing to "obvious reasons of political feasibility,"[35] the Secretary insisted upon a modified plan which he titled "The Atlantic Charter and National Independence." In a November 17 memorandum to Roosevelt, Hull reviewed the trusteeship possibilities: (1) placing all dependent areas under complete international administration and control; (2) international administration and control of mandated areas and areas detached from the Axis colonies, with present colonial powers remaining as administrators of their dependent areas but under supervision of the international administration agency; (3) international responsibility for only mandated and detached areas, but with colonial powers obliged to observe certain principles with respect to administration of dependent areas and to provide essential information on colonial affairs.

The Political Subcommittee's discussions of August and the "International Trusteeship for Non-Self-Governing Peoples" had approximated the second approach. Hull's draft "Atlantic Charter and National Independence", however, considered on the third approach as "the most practical solution . . . [which] should be acceptable to all concerned and . . . offers a basis for a forward movement . . . and to our good relations with our present associates and to the peace of the world." The "Atlantic Charter and National Independence" stipulated that all governments controlling dependent areas were to help prepare them for the responsibilities of independence. In line with Hull's July 23 speech, it also specified the obligations of dependent peoples to equip themselves politically, socially, and economically for the right of independence.[36]

The Hull approach, which was approved by Roosevelt, meant that with respect to Southeast Asia and other areas of European colonies, American planning thereafter largely focused on defining the ultimate objectives of dependent areas, the obligations of colonial powers, and the relationship of the colonial powers to the international organization and regional councils. International supervision and control was now restricted to the Axis colonies and mandated areas. In fact, the Hull limitation on trusteeship arrangements was not quite that clear-cut inasmuch as Roosevelt pursued his independent course with respect to Indochina. But the position taken by Hull was important and reflected his determination to channel the colonialism plans along practical lines. Hull's November 1942 position antagonized Welles and others. Two months later Hull assumed the chairmanship of the Political Subcommittee which gave him more direct influence over much of the postwar planning apparatus.

Despite Hull's determination to accommodate the Allies, British and American plans for colonial areas, exchanged in early 1943, underscored fundamental differences. On February 4, Halifax presented Hull with a draft Joint Declaration of Colonial Policy. Aware of the American determination to have international accountability, the British prepared a document which spoke of "parent" and "trustee" states retaining responsibility for administration of their territories, and being responsible for the development of political, social, and economic opportunities that promote self-government. Regional commissions, comprising "parent" and "trustee" states with dependent peoples in the region and other states with major economic and security interests in the area, would be established for consultation and collaboration to promote the advancement of colonial peoples.[37] This effort at accommodating the American interests failed, for the British proposal left effective power in the hands of the imperial powers and made no commitment to political or economic independence.

In response to the Joint Declaration of Colonial Policy, the Department of State advanced its draft Declaration by the United Nations on National Independence. This document represented an amalgam of the work of the Far Eastern Division on a World Charter and Hull's November 1942 statement. The American proposal established the objective of independence for colonial areas. Colonial powers would be obliged to undertake specific steps leading to independence and to establish timetables for the transfer of power. The draft also anticipated the establishment of the open door principle in colonial areas. Finally, the colonial peoples themselves would have the opportunity to be represented on the regional councils. The same objectives and regional structures were proposed also for the mandated areas.[38]

The American proposal drew sharp criticism from the British government. In a May 26 aide-memoire presented by Foreign Secretary Anthony Eden to Ambassador John Gilbert Winant, the Foreign Office held that the commitment to universal independence was unacceptable in that it would result in a multiplicity of small and weak nations. Timetables were likewise unacceptable even if the objective of "self-government" replaced "independence." In addition to the impossibility of establishing such objectives for "primitive" peoples, the development of self-rule depended upon flexibility and allowance for trial and error. Hence by the spring of 1943, British and American differences over the future of the colonies had been clearly delineated.[39]

## Roosevelt, the State Department, and Indochina

As the general outlines of American objectives for dependent areas developed in early 1943, President Roosevelt simultaneously began planning for the establishment of an international trusteeship for postwar Indochina. His assumption that the French should be denied any claim to Indochina followed the thinking of a number of participants, especially Welles, in the Political Subcommittee discussions of August, 1942. It was, however, inconsistent with the "Atlantic Charter and National Independence" and the subsequent draft Declaration by the United Nations on National Independence, both of which anticipated the restoration of the colonial powers. As noted in the minutes of the Political Subcommittee's consideration of Indochina, denial of the French also was inconsistent with American commitments to restore French sovereignty in Europe as well as in their empire.

On January 20, 1942, Roosevelt, in a message to Ambassador William Leahy at Vichy, had suggested that Marshall Pétain should be reminded that the United States was France's best friend and was determined to see France reconstituted after the war. Further, the message specified that "the word 'France' in the mind of the President includes the French Colonial Empire." A year later, however, Roosevelt changed his position.[40] After the North African landings of November 1942, he was upset with his emmisary, Robert Murphy, who had served as diplomatic liaison with Vichy authorities in North Africa, for having pledged restoration of metropolitan France and the colonies. At a meeting with the Joint Chiefs of Staff on January 7, 1943, Roosevelt stated that some colonies definitely should not be returned to France; specifically, he had "grave doubts" whether French authority should be reestablished in Indochina.[41]

By the time of that meeting with the Joint Chiefs, Indochina had become a rather prominent consideration in Roosevelt's thinking about the postwar settlement in the colonial areas. Statements before the Pacific War Council beginning in the spring of 1942 indicated a persistent concern with the French empire and Indochina in particular. Roosevelt frequently used the Council as a sounding board for his ideas on Asian issues; with China, the Philippines, Australia, New Zealand, and Canada among the countries represented, he generally found support for anticolonial sentiments to the annoyance of the British and Dutch members.

In May, he commented unfavorably on the French record in Indochina; the Chinese Foreign Minister T. V. Soong added that the French had not only exploited the country, but had never made efforts to educate the people nor to prepare them for self-government. At a meeting in December, Roosevelt returned to the Indochina issue; as reported in the minutes:

> The President stated that he had received very confidential information from an excellent source that Indo-China is not anxious to see the return of the French regime. The President stated that the French had been in Indo-China since about 1832 and that little had been done towards improving conditions among the natives. The President stated that he has been informed that China has no desire to annex Indo-china, and with that as a starting point, plans could be made with reference to the post-war disposition of the territory. "It is positively refreshing that none of the big powers wants Indo-China," [Roosevelt said].[42]

When asked about Allied commitments to restore the French empire, Roosevelt replied "no firm commitment has been made." And again in early January 1943, Roosevelt told the Council that France's colonial possessions ought not be returned. Outside the Council, the President, meeting on February 22 with Hull, Welles, and a few members of the Political Subcommittee, rambled over a number of postwar questions. After alluding to uncertainty about the status of France, he stated that "France should lose Indochina, but its disposition is a question."[43]

Already Roosevelt's vague aspirations for Indochina were the source of difficulties with the British. At the January 1943 meeting of the Pacific War Council mentioned above, Roosevelt also urged the British not to make further promises to restore the French empire. This antagonized the Foreign Office as it had deliberately avoided making any such commitments and instead had confined itself to pledging the return of the "independence and greatness of France." On February 4, Halifax spoke with Hull about the contradictions between American promises made at the time of the North African landings and Roosevelt's predilections. Caught in an embarrassing situation, Hull conceded that the State Department had been excluded from North African operations and indeed was unaware of the commitments made to French authorities.[44] (Roosevelt's personal handling of the North African campaign resulted in part from his determination that the Free French not be alerted to the operations. In discussing plans with Murphy, Roosevelt reportedly stated: "Don't tell anybody in the State Department about this. That place is a sieve!")[45]

When Anthony Eden visited Washington in late March for discussions on political problems, Roosevelt stated his objective of an Indochina trusteeship. Meeting with the British Foreign Secretary on March 27, Roosevelt discussed his views on a number of questions and specified the goal of an international trusteeship for Korea and Indochina. Eden questioned whether Roosevelt was not being too harsh on France, but the President insisted that in return for needed assistance at the end of the war, France should be prepared to place parts of its territory at the disposal of the United Nations. When Welles interjected a reminder of American pledges to restore France's possessions, Roosevelt observed that this had applied only to North Africa. He dismissed Welles' rejoinder that there had been no conditions on the commitment by asserting that the situation could be clarified after the war.[46]

Welles, in whom Roosevelt placed much confidence, had modified his position on Indochina since the August 1942 meetings of the Subcommittee on Political Problems. This evidently reflected deference to the direction of Department objectives. The tendency to support and then retreat from anticolonialism had also characterized Welles's position on India. In any event, meeting with Eden on March 24, Welles said that France should regain Indochina provided France agreed to fulfill the commitments outlined in the American proposal for colonial areas.[47]

Regardless of the discrepancy with State Department planning, and the inconsistency with commitments on the restoration of the French empire, the international trusteeship had become, by the spring of 1943, Roosevelt's objective for Indochina. What accounted for Roosevelt's position? It was consistent, of course, with his anticolonialism, but the objective of an independent Indochina could have been attained by less drastic means as was envisaged in the draft Declaration by the United Nations on National Independence. Rather, the answer rests largely in Roosevelt's attitude toward France and its empire. Repeatedly Roosevelt asserted that France had exploited Indochina, leaving the country in a worse condition than prior to French domination. The President's knowledge of Indochina apparently did not go much beyond a sweeping indictment of French rule, which seemed to justify the essentially punitive measure represented by the trusteeship plan. More generally, Roosevelt looked with disdain upon France for its capitulation to Germany and Japan. Perhaps Roosevelt was thinking of both France's colonial record as well as its weakness against the Axis when he told the Pacific War Council that "we must judge countries by their actions, and in this connection we should avoid any hasty promise to return French Indo-China to the French."[48] What then of the commitments to restore French territory in Europe and overseas? They were measures dictated by the expediency of the "Vichy gamble"; that is, the United States sought until after the North African invasion to keep the Vichy government from falling under further German control. The assurances to Vichy were authorized without attention to their implications, especially in Asia. Once the Vichy tie was no longer feasible, Roosevelt was prepared to ignore the commitments.

Roosevelt's Indochina policy was a product not only of his anti-French and anticolonial attitudes but also emerged from his experiences of late 1942 and early 1943. British suppression of Indian nationalism, as discussed earlier, led to considerable domestic criticism of Roosevelt's acquiescence to Churchill's brand of imperialism. The White House was under pressure to give meaning to anticolonialism and the Atlantic Charter. In Asia, the possibilities of dislodging France from Indochina appeared more practical and justifiable than taking stern measures against the British or Dutch. In addition, Roosevelt, in early 1943, travelled to North Africa to attend the Casablanca Conference. This led to his meeting de Gaulle and the immediate Roosevelt-de Gaulle antagonisms must have enhanced Roosevelt's determination to force the French from Indochina. More importantly, the trip provided Roosevelt with firsthand observations of conditions in French colonies. As he witnessed the poverty and disease of the area, Roosevelt's anticolonialism was reaffirmed and he returned home with a determination to assure realization of the principle of international accountability in colonial areas.[49]

State Department planners devoted much time to the postwar status of Indochina, but defined American objectives differently from the President. In an October 29, 1943 memorandum, Bowman stated that there were four alternatives: (1) return Indochina to France without conditions; (2) include the country in an international system providing for review and inspection of colonial areas; (3) develop a joint international adminstration under an international organization; (4) recognize Indochina as an independent country.

By a process of elimination, the second alternative was preferred as the most practical. The first approach would be consistent with American pledges to restore French sovereignty in Europe and overseas, but it would tolerate the return of the "notoriously bad" French administration and would endanger Western interests throughout Asia. Foreseeing the possibility of widespread Asian-Western warfare, Bowman warned that the French could be restored only through Anglo-American power. With respect to the third alternative which approximated Roosevelt's trusteeship plan, Bowman argued that it had no chance of success in that it depended upon all colonial powers accepting similar international control of their possessions. Moreover, Bowman was concerned about the uncertainty of sovereignty during a period of international administration. Did it rest in the international organization? Or was it limited to the administrative powers? What would result if the international organization or administering condominium broke up? The granting of independence depended upon France's willingness to relinquish its claim to Indochina, an action which was known to be unlikely. Thus the second approach appeared to be the most practical, but it depended upon Britain and the other imperial powers accepting the same international supervision. Two specific advantages were seen in this outcome: first, it would mark an important step toward the realization of Amerian anticolonial objectives; second, it would maintain French power and influence in Asia, which was seen as a stabilizing factor.[50]

This direction of thinking also condoned the French imperial record. Reports prepared for the Territorial Subcommittee reaffirmed the established view that French administration had been corrupt and inefficient, but with all its faults, French control seemed preferable to the alternative of turning authority over to the peoples of Indochina. The lack of political training, government experience, and the historic disunity of the area were seen as preventing any effective native rule. The "government which the French had set up was the glue which held French Indo-China together," Melvin Knight and Vandenbosch argued, "and that without the French administrative system, it would not be possible to conduct any government in the area."[51]

Few officials still called for treating France differently from the other colonial powers. Joseph Ballantine, a member of the Division of Far Eastern Affairs, questioned whether France, in view of its pre-Pearl Harbor capitulation to Japan, ought to be subject to special stipulations when the colonial questions were settled. He suggested that the United States should at least obtain very precise commitments from France before agreeing to a restoration of French authority in Indochina. But the trend of Territorial Subcommittee planning followed Vandenbosch's observation that the essential task was to define the terms of a colonial settlement that would be acceptable to Britain. It seemed that regional commissions operating under a colonial charter which specified the obligations of imperial powers and established review and inspection procedures represented the most that could be expected from Britain and the other colonial nations.[52]

The conclusions of the Territorial Subcommittee were reinforced by a detailed report on Indochina written by Rupert Emerson, who like Vandenbosch was a recognized authority on Southeast Asia. Emerson's study, completed for the Council on Foreign Relations, analyzed the prewar conditions in Indochina and the various postwar options. He held that French rule should be continued but subject to international review, and the expectation that it would lead to self-government.[53] (Emerson was one of the few spokesmen on Indochina who spoke of the French regime in Indochina being "continued" rather than "restored." Inasmuch as the French still administered the country, albeit under Japanese domination, Emerson's choice of words was the more precise. This touches, however, on an important point, i.e. the fact that apparently few American officials recognized the continuation of French authority after Pearl Harbor. Not until the Japanese overthrew the French regime in March 1945 did the record of the collaborationist government receive much attention.)

Thus by the end of November 1943, the Territorial Subcommittee had reached conclusions with respect to Indochina that were consistent with the draft Declaration of the United Nations on National Independence. French Indochina was not to be singled out and treated differently from the other colonial areas.

Throughout the 1942–43 discussions on Indochina in the Territorial and Political Subcommittees, there was virtually no consideration of the Indochina political situation. Information was available from the former American diplomatic corps in the country as well as from the embassy in Chungking, but this apparently was not channeled to the planning committees or was ignored if it did reach their attention. In the fall of 1942, the Division of Far Eastern Affairs had prepared a lengthy report on

Indochina, which was based on an extensive summary of political and military conditions prepared by Charles Reed, the consul at Saigon, Kingsley Hamilton, vice-consul, and O. Edmund Clubb, consul at Hanoi. They reported that politically conscious Annamites in Indochina held strong anti-Japanese sentiments and their major objective was independence from France. Sympathy for the United States was very strong, and an American occupation was considered as the most desirable alternative to independence. Since China was an ally of the United States, the historic antagonism toward China had somewhat lessened.

In 1943, a Far Eastern Division analysis of Indochina concluded that the Vietnamese were capable of self-government; any postwar administration should be required to provide for an early transfer of political power.[54] The State Department also received reports on the activities of the Vietnamese who had fled to south China, but this information lacked completeness and accuracy. Most important, the embassy at Chungking discounted the significance of the political activity. This was understandable in view of the number of small Vietnamese organizations and the extent to which they were influenced and manipulated by the Chinese. In general, the Vietnamese nationalists were seen in 1942–1943 as instruments through which China was seeking to establish a record of sympathy for oppressed peoples.[55]

Independently of the State Department planning, Roosevelt continued his pursuit of the Indochina trusteeship, most notably at the Cairo and Teheran Conferences of November 1943. His determination on this issue made the Indochina trusteeship a matter of high level Allied diplomatic concern. And by seeking to isolate the British, Roosevelt annoyed Churchill and intensified Anglo-American differences not only over Indochina but colonialism in general.

Prior to the Teheran and Cairo conferences, Roosevelt reaffirmed and somewhat clarified his plans for Indochina. Most importantly, at a meeting of the Pacific War Council on July 21, he set forth strenuous objections to the return of the French and compared the functions of a trusteeship wilth the accomplishments of the United States in the Philippines:

> He said that he felt Indo-China should not be given back to the French Empire after the war. The French had been there for nearly one hundred years and had done absolutely nothing with the place to improve the lot of the people. He then asked Dr. Soong how many people there were in Indo-China. Dr. Soong replied about 35,000,000 and that they were somewhat like the Siamese. The President said that he felt 35,000,000 people should not be exploited; that the French had taken a great deal from them. Probably for each pound they got out of the place they had put in only one shilling. The President said that after the war we ought to help these 35,000,000 people in Indochina. Naturally they could not be given independence immediately but should be taken care of until they were able to govern themselves. He compared the situation to the Philippines. He said that in 1900 the Filipinos were not ready for independence nor could a date be fixed when they would be. Many public works had to be taken care of first. The people had to be educated in local, and, finally, national governmental affairs. By 1933, however, we were able to get together and all agree on a date when they would be ready for independence. Since this development worked in that case, there is no reason why it should not work in the case of Indo-China. In the meantime we would hold Indo-China as a trustee. The President said that even to please Generals Giraud and DeGaulle he would not change his views on Indo-China; that he felt the issue was too fundamental to be altered by French politics in the Mediterranean areas.[56]

At the British Foreign Office, Roosevelt's statement was carefully analyzed. Geoffrey Hudson, a scholar of East Asian affairs working at the Foreign Office, attributed Roosevelt's unique interest to the Willkie-led pressures. Roosevelt was forced to realize anticolonial objectives by liquidating at least one European colony in Asia. Hudson found Roosevelt's knowledge of Indochina to be shaky and vague. The trusteeship plan, moreover, was unworkable and would lead to Chinese influence and eventual domination. In preparation for the Cairo and

Teheran conferences, the Foreign Office prepared a lengthy summary of British objectives for Indochina. Following closely a position which had been advanced in August by Ashley Clarke, head of the Foreign Office's Far Eastern Department, the November 22 policy statement emphasized the importance of Indochina for postwar security in Asia. It anticipated appeasing the United States by making French readmittance dependent upon acceptance of security bases in Indochina. These might be under U.S. control or the trustees of an international organization. It was in Britain's interest to encourage the emergence of a strong France in Europe and Asia, and accordingly it wanted to avoid measures which would weaken or demoralize France. Roosevelt's plan would lead to Chinese control and eventually Japanese intrigue as well.[57] Underlying the November 22 British statement for Indochina was the objective of utilizing interest in postwar security as a common denominator for reconciling French, American, and British interests.

While that policy was being formulated, the Foreign Office also had the opportunity to discuss the President's Indochina objectives with Stanley Hornbeck, who visited London in mid-October for discussions on postwar arrangements for Asia and the Pacific. When asked about Roosevelt's July 21 statement at the Pacific War Council, Hornbeck conceded that he was unaware of it and further that the State Department generally had little knowledge of the council's meetings. Hornbeck went on to summarize both White House and State Department calculations on Indochina (without specifically acknowledging the cleavage), which only further underscored the ambiguity of the American position. In line with the President, Hornbeck admitted that he doubted whether France should be restored since "their record in Indochina was a bad one." Consistent with State Department thinking, Hornbeck maintained that conditions should be imposed on recognition of French control, but it would be difficult to impose terms on France that were not accepted by all colonial powers.[58]

In the weeks prior to the Cairo and Teheran meetings, Roosevelt kept the State Department islolated from his plans with respect to Indochina and a number of other issues. At a meeting on October 5 with Hull and a few other officers, Roosevelt casually discussed establishing international trusteeship arrangements in various situations, such as the Baltic passages, Russian access to Persia, and Hong Kong, as well as in some security points. He also observed that "Indochina might be placed under international trusteeship." Yet he went on to speak favorably of the draft Declaration of the United Nations on National Independence as an effective means for ending colonialism. It was impossible to determine the importance he attached to Indochina and whether he saw trusteeship as the preferable solution in that country or if perhaps the draft declaration (which would permit French restoration) would be sufficient. From his offhand comment about Indochina, there was certainly no indication of the attention which Roosevelt would accord it at the forthcoming conferences.[59]

At the Cairo conference of Britain, China, and the United States, Roosevelt sought Chiang Kai-shek's support of his anticolonial ideas. The two leaders met on the evening of the first day of the conference, November 23. There is no official American record of their meeting, but a Chinese official summary together with the recollections of Roosevelt himself and his son Elliott, while differing in emphasis, agree on the basic points. Beyond formulating their plans for general postwar political change in East Asia which were publicized in the Cairo Declaration, Roosevelt and Chiang also discussed the colonies of Southeast Asia, with the principal focus on Indochina. Roosevelt denied any French claim to restoration and inquired whether China wanted the country. Consistent with previous statements of Chinese leaders, Chiang demurred. On the plans for the postwar administration of Indochina, the various accounts differ in detail, although there is not necessarily any inconsistency. The Chinese record notes that Chiang proposed that the United States and China should work together to help Indochina achieve independence. The accounts of both Roosevelts stress the President's trusteeship objective. In Elliott Roosevelt's version, his father stated that the French at most could expect a trusteeship of their colonies that would be responsible to a United Nations organization which would supervise Indochina's progress toward independence. In February 1945, the President recalled suggesting a trusteeship including representatives of France, Indochina, the Soviet Union, the Philippines and the United States, to guide the colony toward self-government. Regardless of the understanding attached to trusteeship in the Roosevelt-Chiang meeting, the important consideration from Roosevelt's perspective was that he had gained Chinese endorsement of his Indochina scheme.[60]

Roosevelt's conspicuous tactic at Cairo of ignoring the British on colonial issues was repeated at Teheran where Roosevelt and Churchill met for the first time with Russian Premier Josef Stalin. In a session with Stalin on November 28, Roosevelt launched into a general discussion of his trusteeship ideas and again drew attention to Indochina. Reiterating his standard condemnation of French colonialism and building on China's support for trusteeship, Roosevelt sought and gained Stalin's assent. "The President . . . remarked that after 100 years of French rule in Indochina, the inhabitants were worse off than they had been before. . . . He added that he had discussed with Chiang Kai-shek the possibility of a system of trusteeship for Indochina which would have the task of preparing the people for independence within a definite period of time, perhaps 20 to 30 years. Marshall Stalin completely agreed with this view."[61] Later at Teheran, the French empire, particularly the future of New Caledonia and Dakar, was discussed briefly with Churchill; Roosevelt relied upon Stalin to take the initiative in denouncing the French.

## Conclusion

The Cairo and Teheran conferences thus made it clear that Roosevelt was determined to press the Indochina trusteeship issue. That objective and the manner in which Roosevelt pursued it antagonized Churchill and other British officials, thus

undermining Anglo-American relations over the future of Southeast Asia. The British never had the opportunity to use their
detailed brief against the trusteeship idea. As the Teheran Conference was ending, the Deputy Prime Minister cabled Churchill
from London that inasmuch as the British were evidently going
to be pressed further on Indochina, some guidance would be
needed.[62] Churchill responded that Britain would not prejudge
the status of Indochina any more than that of the East Indies or
British possessions. Reflecting anxiety on the question as well as
exclusion from Roosevelt's discussions with Chiang and Stalin,
Churchill added: "For your own information inter alia it is
pretty clear that the President at the moment contemplates
some change in the status of Indo-China, but he has not yet formulated any definite proposal."[63]

Churchill's annoyance foreshadowed the extent to which
differences over Southeast Asia would trouble American relations with Britain, France and even the Netherlands for the
remainder of the war and well into the postwar years. American
planning in 1942–1943 and the initial Anglo-American exchanges over colonialism constituted an important prelude to
the subsequent conflict of interests in Southeast Asia.

# 4.

# United States'-European Differences Over Postwar Southeast Asia, December 1943-October 1944

I have come to the conclusion that if this war is to be won, it's got to be won by the full strength of the virile, energetic, initiative-loving, inventive Americans, and that the British are really showing their decadence—a magnificent people, but they have lost their initiative.

Henry Stimson, April 1944

FROM LATE 1943 until the end of the war against Japan, U.S. postwar objectives in Southeast Asia clashed with the interests of Britain, France, and the Netherlands. American anticolonialism, with its emphasis on the establishment of a system of "international accountability," remained at the base of the tensions among the Western nations. Another issue—the postwar treatment of Thailand—became an important additional irritant in Anglo-American relations. During the latter stages of the war differences among the members of the Allied coalition were evident in many areas, but nowhere were the problems between the United States and the Western European allies more significant than in the struggle over Southeast Asia.

The development of American policy in Southeast Asia between the Cairo and Teheran conferences and the defeat of Japan can be considered in two phases, with the fall of 1944 as an appropriate dividing point. From December 1943 until the following October—the period considered in this chapter—the discord between the United States and the European colonial powers occurred largely within the framework of Anglo-American relations and in the context of very limited military operations in the region. At that time colonial issues seemed distant and the Southeast Asian problems were not of high priority. The British and Americans concentrated their resources and attention elsewhere. Yet the differences over the future of Southeast Asia remained clear and by the fall of 1944, as political and military developments in Europe and Asia brought Southeast Asia into prominence, a sense of desperation characterized the differences among the Allies. From October 1944 to the surrender of Japan the following August and for years thereafter, the Southeast Asian situation was a serious problem, approximating a crisis, in relations between the United States and the European colonial powers. Viewed in this context, the year after the Cairo and Teheran conferences may have provided the most opportune time for resolution of the colonialism question as it affected Southeast Asia.

## SEAC and Its Political Implications

In the struggle against Japan, American military and naval operations had, by the end of 1943, given the Allies clear superiority. The United States was in a position to launch a counteroffensive across the western Pacific. Within the next eighteen months, its forces advanced 4,000 miles from the Gilbert and Solomon Islands to Iwo Jima and Okinawa. The emphasis on striking at Japan through the Pacific reduced the strategic significance of mainland operations in China and Southeast Asia, thus reducing the resources available to the theater commanders in those areas.[1]

The relative insignificance of military operations in Southeast Asia notwithstanding, the Allied command in the region became the focal point of political tensions. In 1943, Roosevelt and Churchill agreed to establish the Southeast Asia Command (SEAC), which was to function under a British-appointed commander subject to the authority of the Combined Chiefs of Staff. Initially, the United States and Britain appeared to concur that the new theater would include Burma, Malaya, Sumatra, Thailand, and Indochina. But upon considering the likely Chinese response to having Thailand and Indochina detached from the China theater, the United States proposed that only Thailand be transferred to SEAC. Indochina, regarded as a more distant field of operations, was to remain under Chiang Kai-shek's command. This Anglo-American compromise, however, did not satisfy Chiang. In a meeting with Lord Louis Mountbatten, who had been designated Allied commander in Southeast Asia, and Lieutenant-General Brehon Somervell of the United States, Chiang insisted that both Indochina and Thailand remain in the China theater; otherwise, he would suffer a loss of prestige at home and internationally. It was then agreed by Mountbatten and Chiang to recognize that SEAC operations might eventually involve Thailand and Indochina, and at that time boundary adjustments of the two theaters might be necessary. Moreover, Chiang subsequently agreed that Mountbatten might send agents into Thailand and Indochina provided that he was informed of such activities.[2]

While the United States generally sympathized with Chiang's determination to preserve an enlarged China theater, officials at the embassy in Chungking and in the Division of Far Eastern Affairs were becoming increasingly skeptical of China's intentions in Southeast Asia. Despite China's repeated denial of territorial ambitions, there appeared to be disturbing signs of efforts to extend significantly Chinese influence and perhaps control. On several occasions beginning in late 1943, the Chinese suggested the need for inter-Allied understandings on the administration of liberated areas, especially Thailand and Burma where, it was argued, Chinese interests might clash with the British. This assertion of an interest in postliberation military administration, which was related to the controversy over the theater boundaries, was viewed with some concern in Washington. More significantly, reports of Chinese efforts to manipulate the Vietnamese nationalists in southern China led to speculation that the Chinese might claim northern Indochina or foster its own Indochinese government.[3] China's support had long been considered essential to the realization of American anticolonial objectives in Southeast Asia, but from early 1944 onward, the State Department and eventually the White House questioned China's commitment to the principles of the Atlantic Charter.

The most important source of Allied tensions centering on SEAC was the relationship of the new theater to European imperial aspirations. Concern over being associated with the efforts of Britain, France, and the Netherlands to reassert control over their colonies was a major consideration. In November 1943 John Paton Davies, political adviser to General Joseph Stilwell, recommended that the United States not assign military and political officers to SEAC headquarters.[4]

Officials at the State Department had already become suspicious of Anglo-French machinations in Southeast Asia, for in October the French Committee of National Liberation had begun pressing Assistant Secretary Adolph Berle with the argument that the use of Chinese troops in Indochina would result in massive popular resistance. These protestations, presented by the French representative in Washington, Henri Hoppenot, disturbed Berle, who wrote: "This brings us squarely up to the problem of whether, in the Far East, we are re-establishing the western colonial empires or whether we are letting the East liberate itself if it can do so. I feel the matter should be discussed on a high level with the President for his decision."[5] Reviewing the Hoppenot representations, the officers of the Division of Far Eastern Affairs concluded that they constituted a cover for the Anglo-French determination to monopolize military operations in Southeast Asia. Leaving aside the political questions at that point, Roosevelt concurred with Berle and Edward Stettinius (who had replaced Welles as Undersecretary of State) that the liberation of Indochina was to be determined by the Chiefs of Staff and commanding officers in the area.[6]

In addition to the French initiatives, the Netherlands endeavored to establish firmly its claim to a role in Allied operations in the East Indies. Through its ambassador in Washington, in August 1943 the government-in-exile reaffirmed a determination to fight against Japan and promised that immediately following the liberation of the Netherlands, the Dutch would submit a detailed plan of Pacific operations for American consideration.[7] Underlying this statement was the profound Dutch concern about American intentions in Southeast Asia. The Dutch, however, largely dealt with the British on this question rather than pressing the issue in Washington. At the Foreign Office, the Dutch ambassador expressed anxiety about American intentions in the East Indies, specifically the fear that Roosevelt's Indochina plans might be extended to that colony. The British, who considered the Dutch (in the words of the Head of the Foreign Office's Far Eastern Department) "our natural allies in Southeast Asia," offered assurance of support in making certain that Dutch administration was rapidly restored.[8] Moreover, the Foreign Office was confident of American support for the Dutch, since, unlike the French, they "were not considered immoral or decadent."[9] Anglo-Dutch cooperation within the SEAC reflected the realization of mutual interests. In November 1943 Vice-Admiral Helfrich, commander-in-chief of the Netherlands forces in the Far East, visited Mountbatten's New Delhi headquarters. After their meeting a Netherlands Staff Section was established. Initially, it was to be involved in planning for the projected 1944 landing in Sumatra but when that operation was abandoned, the Dutch concentrated on intelligence and clandestine activities in the East Indies.[10]

Reflecting the differing British and American priorities in Asia, SEAC operations were constantly the source of friction with the China theater. In early 1944, Mountbatten advanced the "Axiom plan" which called for operations against Sumatra and Malaya. Strongly opposed by Stilwell who, as commander of U.S. forces in the China-Burma-India theater and chief of staff to Chiang, feared the diversion of resources from China, the British plan was blocked by Roosevelt and the American Chiefs of Staff. Instead the American priority remained the reinforcement of China through the Burma campaign and the construction of the Ledo Road. Later in 1944 Churchill reiterated his interest in a Sumatra operation (Operation Culverin), but this encountered serious opposition from within his own government, especially the Chiefs of Staff Committee which favored building up British power in the Pacific to collaborate with the United States in the defeat of Japan. The importance of asserting British influence as a means of countering the United States was an important factor on both sides of the Culverin debate. The Chiefs of Staff's position was advanced as a means of enhancing Britain's prestige in Asia and meeting the calls of Australia and New Zealand for an enlarged British role in the Pacific. In sum, they felt that the British should not allow the United States to be given exclusive credit for the defeat of Japan. From Churchill's perspective, the Sumatra operation was seen as a means of assuring recovery of colonial territories and thus preventing the United States, in the event of an abrupt Japanese withdrawal, from establishing international control (in which the United States would presumably be the dominant factor) over the region. In the end, Churchill abandoned Culverin and supported the Chiefs of Staff's position. Nonetheless, the competing strategies persisted, with the United States looking upon Southeast Asia operations principally as a means of accomplishing its objectives in China, while the British, forever skeptical about the importance of China, regarded SEAC as essential to the recovery of Western influence.[11]

## The United States, Britain, and Roosevelt's Indochina Plan

Roosevelt's pursuit of an Indochina trusteeship at the Teheran and Cairo conferences, and upon his return to Washington, forced the issue into prominence in Anglo-American as well as White House-State Department relations. Roosevelt was buoyed by the support of Chiang Kai-shek and Stalin for his trusteeship plan. The British, in effect outvoted among the Big Four, could be ignored. By relying on personal diplomacy and denying France a role in the liberation of Indochina, Roosevelt appeared confident that his plan could be achieved. The Foreign Office responded strongly to Roosevelt's initiative and sought to force the question. Churchill, however, generally favored following the tactic he had already adopted when confronted by Roosevelt's anticolonial sentiments, i.e., to ignore such matters as much as possible and delay action until the end of the war.

At a December 16, 1943, meeting with the heads of the diplomatic missions of Egypt, the Soviet Union, China, Turkey, Iran, and Great Britain, Roosevelt coyly intimated that he had been working to prevent France's restoration in Indochina. A continuation of French administration, which had left the people uneducated and poor, could not be tolerated. Since the peoples of Indochina were not prepared for self-government, the country was to be placed under United Nations trusteeship which would develop it along the lines of the Philippines. Roosevelt admonished his audience not to repeat these plans, but certainly he recognized that the governments represented would be informed. His choice of this particular group may have been calculated as a further attempt to isolate the British in that the other governments represented had already approved his plans or could reasonably have been expected to share his antipathy for French colonialism.[12]

Roosevelt's statement stirred concern in London. Upon hearing of it, Churchill wrote to Eden: "I have frequently heard the President express these views about Indochina and Dakar and have never given any consent to them. I consider that such questions of territorial transfers must be reserved till the end of the war. . . . One can hardly suppose any intention on the part of the United States to take territory from France forcibly without agreement with France after a French government has been formed on the basis of the will of the French people. For the above reasons I am of the opinion that until we are officially apprised of these declarations we should give immediately a perfectly clear indication that we have no part in them and must reserve our opinion till the proper time comes."[13]

In anticipation of eventual difficulties, the Foreign Office, with Churchill's approval, explored the extent of White House–State Department agreement on Indochina and prepared a definitive statement of British objectives.[14] Accordingly on January 3, 1944, Halifax met with Hull, who conceded that he knew no more than the ambassador about Roosevelt's recent remarks. When Halifax reminded him of the record of American statements about the restoration of French sovereignty, Hull acknowledged that he had done his best to remind Roosevelt of those commitments. Roosevelt and Churchill could be expected to discuss the matter at a forthcoming conference. Convinced on the basis of Hull's almost apologetic stance that Roosevelt's remarks did not represent any settled policy, Halifax concluded his report to London that "this is all a bit wooly, and does not take us much further."[15]

Halifax's meetings with Roosevelt two weeks later added to British uncertainty about American policy. Finding the President in a rather whimsical mood, Halifax inquired whether his observations on Indochina represented a "considered view." The President quickly responded affirmatively and went on to develop his conventional indictment of French colonialism. He hoped that when he next approached Churchill on the matter of

Indochina, it would not be a monologue. The British had no need to fear that the trusteeship plan would be extended to their colonies or those of the Dutch, for the British and Dutch had "done a good job but . . . the French were hopeless." Roosevelt paid little attention to Halifax's arguments. He simply dismissed the pledges to restore French sovereignty. While agreeing with Halifax that France should eventually be restored as a major power, at the present, Roosevelt reiterated, they are "hopeless." In the meantime, the President wanted to remind Churchill that "I have three votes to his one as we now stand." Although sensing that Roosevelt seemed not to be taking their conversation too seriously, Halifax concluded that "I am left feeling that he has got this idea in his mind a bit more than is likely to be wholesome."[16]

Roosevelt's brief account of his meeting with Halifax conveyed a determination to press the Indochina issue regardless of British reservations. Writing to Hull that he enjoyed the "wholehearted" support of Chiang Kai-shek and Stalin, the President stated the Foreign Office could be ignored. With respect to the British, he wrote to Hull: "The only reason they seem to oppose it [trusteeship] is that they fear the effect it would have on their own possessions and those of the Dutch. They have never liked the idea of trusteeship because it is, in some instances aimed at future independence. This is true in the case of IndoChina."[17]

Roosevelt's antipathy toward the French was evident at his February 1 press conference when he issued a statement on Allied operations in Asia. Intended to offset criticism from certain groups in India that United States troops supported British imperialism, Roosevelt affirmed that the defeat of Japan was the overriding objective of Allied operations. Pointedly, he then referred to the British and Dutch as "brothers-in-arms" determined to expel the Japanese from Burma, Malaya, and the East Indies just as Americans sought to free the Philippines. Conspicuously absent was any reference to a French role in Indochina or any part in the war against Japan.[18]

Responding to Roosevelt's position, the Foreign Office prepared a lengthy policy statement on Indochina. The issue was considered urgent: the French would react violently upon learning of Roosevelt's plans; the loss of Indochina would destroy the French economy and national morale, possibly leading to its association with Russia against the United States and Great Britain; British postwar interests necessitated a friendly, prosperous France as a major power. France's restoration offered "the most tenable solution," but in tacit deference to the direction of State Department planning on the colonial question: "We should be ready, if necessary, to put pressure on France to take part in international arrangements, including, if found desirable, some system of United Nations bases in Indochina, by telling her plainly that she need not expect any support from us in maintaining her control over Indo-China or her other Pacific colonies. If she agreed, we could hardly, in decency, deprive her of her colonies."[19]

In sum, the British should seek American approval of French restoration provided it accepted international bases at strategic points and such arrangements for international consultation and security as the British would permit in their colonies. On February 24, the Cabinet approved the Foreign Office statement and directed that the support of the dominions be gained before bringing the matter to Washington's attention.[20] Churchill, however, held out against approaching the dominions immediately. Arguing that Roosevelt's personal views did not warrant an elaborate policy formulation, he fell back on his strategy of delaying the Indochina confrontation with the United States; he cautioned: "I think it is a great mistake to raise the matter before the Presidential election. I cannot conceive it is urgent. On this point the President's views are particular to himself. The war in the Far East may go on for a long time. I do not consider the chance remarks which the President made in conversation should be the basis for setting all this ponderous machinery in motion. Nothing is going to happen about this for quite a long time."[21]

Besides causing strains in Anglo-American relations, Roosevelt's Indochina policy led to difficulty in coordinating White House and State Department plans. Despite American efforts to defer the matter, the French Committee on National Liberation continued to press the State Department for a military role in Asia, especially in any Indochina operations.[22] In addition, the War Department was seeking State Department guidance in its planning for postliberation administration of areas under Japanese control. Reviewing the various alternative approaches to military administration of Indochina, State Department planners held that the most feasible approach was French military administration, since French sovereignty had remained intact and French cooperation presumably would be needed in the war against Japan. This approach to the Indochina question, however, could not be reconciled with Roosevelt's objectives. Thus, on February 17, Stettinius urged the President to approve the use of French forces, military operations, and civilian personnel in postwar administration in Indochina, which he argued, could be allowed without prejudicing the ultimate political status of the country. Roosevelt vetoed the suggestion, stating that no French troops should be used in Indochina. Following an Anglo-American military operation, a trusteeship would be established.[23]

With both Roosevelt and Churchill disinclined to force the issue, Anglo-American differences over Indochina remained at a standstill. A confident Roosevelt had made clear his determination to pursue the Indochina trusteeship and sought to deny the French any military role in the area. Despite the Foreign Office's disposition to deal with the United States on the issue, Churchill counselled the strategy of delay. For the next several months, Roosevelt himself took little interest in Indochina.

During that period Roosevelt's bargaining postion was weakened by the resurgence of French power. The Allied assault on Nazi-controlled western Europe in June 1944 and the liberation of France forced the United States to deal with a determined reassertion of French nationalism epitomized by the leadership of Charles de Gaulle. No longer could Roosevelt maintain an aloof attitude toward the French Committee on National Liberation. Roosevelt, as well as several other American officials, retained an intense dislike of de Gaulle; his visit to Washington in August did little to improve his relationship with Roosevelt. While the President reiterated that recognition of any French government depended upon evidence of popular support, the British and the State Department urged recognition of de Gaulle as a means of assuring France's reemergence as a strong power allied to the United States and Britain. Roosevelt held out until October 1944 when he, at last, acknowledged that de Gaulle's government should be granted diplomatic recognition.[24] The anomalous status of de Gaulle's movement prior to the liberation of France had facilitated the offhanded White House dismissal of the French empire, but with the reassertion of France's position in Europe and Asia, it became more difficult to insist upon the unique disposition of its colony, Indochina.

## State Department Planning
## for Southeast Asia

The need to accelerate postwar planning and the increasing importance of Southeast Asia led to two important organizational changes at the Department of State. In the planning area, the rapidly changing military situation and the increasing evidence of inter-Allied disagreements on many issues, led Cordell Hull to suspend the Advisory Committee and its subcommittees in July 1943. He replaced them with a structure that would allow for more advanced, action-oriented preparation. Two high-level committees were established, each headed by Hull with Stettinius as vice-chairman: The Policy Committee was to assist the Secretary in considering major current questions, while the Post-War Programs Committee assisted in postwar policies and in making arrangements for their implementation.

Under the revised program, the Informal Agenda Group, which had emerged during the first stage of planning to meet the need for a small coordinating committee, continued (under various names), and became the corps of advisors at the international conferences leading to the establishment of the United Nations. All of these committees relied on extensive policy summaries prepared by the research committees operating under the Committee on Special Studies; the research projects had not been affected by the suspension of the Advisory Committee and its subcommittees. To assure thorough consideration of major problems and coordination with the established department offices, a number of area and country committees were established. They combined planning personnel with desk officers from the geographical and functional units of the department. The Committee on Dependent Areas, chaired by Benjamin Gerig, had general responsibility for colonial issues, and with respect to Southeast Asia, its work was supplemented by the interdivisional Country and Area Committee on the Far East.[25]

In addition to the planning changes, the enhanced interests of the United States in a number of areas led to a reorganization of the State Department's geographical divisions. Earlier, Southeast Asian colonial areas had been handled by  appropriate officials within the Office of European Affairs. Thailand, and in some aspects the Philippines, had been the responsibility of the Division of Far Eastern Affairs. In the spring of 1944, the Division of Southwest Pacific Affairs was established; a year later, it became the Division of Southeast Asian Affairs. The new division was given general responsibility for diplomatic problems with Thailand and concurrent jurisdiction with the appropriate European Division desk officers for matters pertaining to European colonial areas. This revised structure thus allowed for influence in the shaping of Southeast Asian policy by officers with a direct interest and, in some cases, with experience and expertise in the area. Including only four officers in 1944–1945, the new division was briefly headed by Lawrence Salisbury. He was replaced by Abbott Low Moffat, who remained chief until July 1947.[26] Based on the premise that Southeast Asian policy could no longer be based on the advice of colonial "Asian hands", the new office became an advocate of anticolonial objectives in the region.

As American planning for dependent areas advanced in

1944, anticolonialism remained the guiding principle but it was tempered by political and military realities. Discussions in the planning and regional committees of the State Department paid increasing attention to the interests of the European powers in Southeast Asia, which resulted in consideration of accommodation and compromise. During the early months of 1944, the planning committees reviewed the status of each of the colonies in Southeast Asia and developed the mechanism for an orderly transition toward self-government. While native political groups and objectives received some passing attention, the expectation remained that the political progress of the region would be determined by the West.

A political summary on Burma set the tone of this advanced planning. Serious Allied differences were likely to arise because the United States, China, and Soviet Union would question an unqualified restoration of the status quo, while the imperial government of Burma, in exile in Simla, India, claimed unimpaired de jure authority. Considering the alternatives for Burma, the extreme solutions—restoration of the status quo or immediate independence—were ruled out. On the latter, the past performance of Burmese leaders provided no basis for confidence in their ability to provide political stability or to meet the problem of the Indian minority. As a result, "this solution will be unacceptable to British and is not even regarded by the Chinese as feasible without a prolonged period of tutelage." A feasible compromise anticipated British administration under a pledge of dominion status at a definite date, in association with a regional consultative council and in accordance with a general colonial charter. The British might accept that degree of international accountability.[27]

A political summary on Malaya reached similar conclusions. While the pursuit of equality of commercial and investment opportunity paralleled and augmented anticolonialism generally, the open door was an especially important consideration in the formulation of objectives for Malaya. Stability was deemed essential because of Malaya's importance as a source of rubber and tin. Moreover, all nations should enjoy access without discrimination to Malayan markets and economic opportunities. The United States should accept British restoration but in accord with the provisions of a colonial charter and as a part of a regional consultative council. Unlike Burma, however, there was no expectation of a commitment to dominion status at a definite date. Neither was there any discussion of native political groups, and immediate independence was not even considered. Those ommissions reflected acceptance of the view that political and economic stability in the racially and politically diverse Malaya necessitated an extended period of British administration. The objectives of international accountability and the open door, however, promised to modify significantly the British position.[28]

Economic interests were also prominent in American objectives in the Netherlands East Indies, but planning for that colony was complicated by the Dutch effort to gain early recognition of their claim to postwar administration. While the Dutch were relying on the British through SEAC to assure their restoration in Sumatra, the remainder of their colony was under MacArthur's Southwest Pacific Command. The initiative of the Dutch resulted in differences between the State Department and War Department, and within the former, between the offices of European and Far Eastern Affairs. This marked the beginning of a prolonged struggle over predominance in Southeast Asia policymaking between the European and Asian desks. The initial inclination of the Office of European Affairs and the Civil Affairs Division of the War Department, neither of which was informed fully on planning for Southeast Asia, was to promise a restoration of Dutch sovereignty as soon as the military situation permitted. Further, Dutch civil officers would be used fully during the period of military administration. When the Office of Far Eastern Affairs reviewed these plans, it objected to American lives being sacrificed on behalf of European imperialism and questioned the political implications of colonial restoration throughout Asia. In accord with the direction of the planning committees, it urged coordinating any promise to reestablish Dutch sovereignty with a commitment from the Netherlands to improve political and economic conditions in the East Indies.[29]

At a Policy Committee meeting in late February 1944, sharp differences developed over the European Affairs proposal. Speaking on behalf of that office, James Dunn held that the United States could not press the Dutch for concessions until it had formulated and gained Allied approval of a general plan for dependent areas. In the meantime, a military agreement had to be reached and it need not have any political implications. Moreover, the War Department sought to avoid administration in the East Indies, a responsibility which the Dutch, under the proposed military agreement, would assume. Berle questioned whether any military agreement could avoid political implications, while Joseph Ballantine, a member of the Far Eastern Affairs Office, was concerned about the ramifications of this agreement for American relations throughout Asia. Eventually, the two sides compromised. They agreed that a commitment to the restoration of Dutch sovereignty did not foreclose the American option of pressing its dependent areas proposal with the Dutch.

While the Far Eastern affairs officers resisted an unequivocal commitment to Dutch restoration, they and other postwar planners reflected the established tendency to consider the Dutch an enlightened imperial power. The political scientist Amry Vandenbosch, who was the author of a major study on politics of the Netherlands East Indies and who served on wartime planning committees, was one of the few Americans to question whether Queen Wilhemina's December 1942 statement actually promised liberalization of Dutch colonial policy. Vandenbosch noted the ambiguity of the Queen's postwar promises and the record of little political and social progress. State Department planning, however, generally assumed that the "high standards of Dutch administration" had been beneficial to the Indonesians. In sum, commentary on the Dutch empire revealed little of the bitter criticism that characterized discussion on French and, at times, British imperialism.[30]

The most extended and least decisive discussion centered on Indochina. Roosevelt's position necessitated special consideration and as his views became known, they encouraged anticolonial and anti-French sentiments. In the early 1944 deliberations the members of the Country and Area Committee on the Far East (CAC) were inclined to treat Indochina as a unique colonial question, perhaps as the place where anticolonial objectives could be achieved without compromise.

In late February, the committee reviewed the diverse elements of Indochina planning and agreed to have subcommittees prepare reports on two alternatives: a trusteeship mechanism; or conditions to be attached to French restoration. Within the committee there was a consensus that Indochina should attain independence within fifteen to twenty-five years (or at least self-government with the right of the people to choose complete independence or another arrangement like modified dominion status), but the committee was evenly divided between an international trusteeship, or French administration under international accountability as the best means of effecting the political transition of Indochina. There was a revealing vote on the basic question—should French colonies be treated the same as those of Britain? Nine members responded negatively, two others attached reservations to negative votes, and only four held that all the colonial powers should be accorded substantially the same treatment.[31]

As a follow up to that meeting, two documents—CAC 89 and CAC 114—were prepared. While dealing with two alternative approaches to postwar administration, both assumed that Indochina was to be singled out for special treatment. CAC 89 suggested that French restoration be conditioned not only on subscription to a general colonial declaration but on a number of specific commitments to economic and political liberalization as well. The French should promise tariff autonomy, the development of local industries, a more balanced economy, the abolition of compulsory labor, the establishment and development of local and central representative institutions, extension of voting privileges, and opening occupational and educational opportunities to the peoples of Indochina. The recent declaration of colonial policy at the Brazzaville Conference was noted, but its implications were unclear.[32] CAC 114 proposed that a trusteeship system could function through a committee comprised of representatives of the major nations which had responsibilities in Southeast Asia. The committee would designate a commissioner to administer the country. The progressive involvement of the peoples of Indochina in the civil service, a representative assembly, executive departments, and the judiciary would lead to independence within twenty years.[33]

The initiative of early 1944 to place Indochina in a special category encountered opposition from the representatives of the Office of European Affairs on the CAC, thus stalemating the development of Indochina policy.[34] The extent of the impasse between the Asian and European officers was evident in a third document on Indochina, CAC 239, which was prepared by a subcommittee of the principal European affairs personnel and from which representatives of the Division of Southwest Pacific Affairs were excluded. Completed shortly after the D-Day invasion of France and just before de Gaulle's visit to Washington, this paper stressed the importance to the United States of a strong, friendly France. Denial of Indochina would weaken France politically, erode national morale, and destroy Franco-American relations:

> France-American postwar cordiality is, as matters now stand, a very dubious possibility. If the United States, especially in view of its many unequivocal statements favoring restoration of the French overseas territories, is the spearhead for partial dismemberment of the French Empire, French resentment will be such as to impose a very serious strain upon our relations and thus tend to defeat basic elements underlying our policy toward France. A disgruntled, psychologically sick and sovereignty-conscious France will not auger well for post-war collaboration in Europe and in the world as a whole.[35]

Turning to the promotion of self-determination for dependent areas, it argued:

We should consider with all seriousness the question of whether that aim can be best accomplished . . . through cooperation with the French or through denial of a role to France, and operate through an international trusteeship. In reaching that decision we must determine whether it is of more interest to us and the world as a whole to have a strong, friendly co-operative France, or have a resentful France plus having on our hands a social and administrative problem of the first magnitude.[36]

Addressing the question of attaching special conditions to French restoration, the United States was in a weak position:

While French administration left much to be desired, the United States Government is in a very unfavorable position to express certain of the criticisms advanced against it. France followed an exclusive or discriminatory trade policy in Indochina, but so did the United States in the Philippines. Indeed, a far greater percent of the external trade of the Philippines was with the United States than of Indochina with France. The United States may have to continue some sort of preferential arrangement with the Philippines for some years after the war, and there are no indications that the prevailing tariff preferences for the remaining dependcies and Cuba will be discontinued after the war.[37]

It was concluded that the United States should permit restoration of the French administration provided France accepted the same conditions to which all colonial powers would be expected to subscribe. International accountability ought to be limited to the endorsement of a colonial charter, membership on a regional commission, and submitting annual reports to the commission on educational, social, economic and political progress.[38]

As they examined objectives in Burma, Malaya, the Netherlands East Indies, and Indochina, State Department planners considered the membership and responsibilities of the proposed regional commission for Southeast Asia. Initially, it was proposed that the commission include four Western powers (the United States, Great Britain, France, and the Netherlands), four neighboring states (Australia, New Zealand, China, and India), and only two Southeast Asian countries (Philippines and Thailand). When the Division of Southwest Pacific Affairs objected that this would appear to indigenous peoples as "syndicated imperialism," it was agreed that dependent areas should be represented on the commission. Accordingly, Burma, Indochina, the Netherlands East Indies, and Malaya were added to the prospective membership.[39] The question of the Soviet Union's membership was discussed at some length in the Committee on Dependent Areas (CDA); lack of a declaration of war against Japan, its relatively insignificant interests in the region, and the possibility that membership would lead to communist propaganda activities resulted in deferring any recommendation.[40] In the CAC and CDA, the relationship of the Philippines and Thailand to the dependent areas received considerable attention. Were Thailand and the Philippines to be included within the jurisdiction of the commission? Should not at least Thailand be included inasmuch as it appeared to be more "backward" than some of the colonies? At length it was decided that both countries should be members of the regional commission, but not under its jurisdiction. To do otherwise, would be insulting to the national pride of the Thais and Filipinos and would undermine the objective of utilizing their independent status as an example for the dependent peoples.[41]

These objectives for Southeast Asia were related to and were ultimately refined by State Department general planning for dependent areas. From December 1943 to July 1944, the Informal Political Agenda Group was engaged in concentrated preparation of proposals on international organization. These formed the basis for discussion among the British, Russian, Chinese, and American governments when their representatives convened at Dumbarton Oaks in Washington from August to October 1944 for extensive preliminary discussions on a new international system.[42]

Most of the modifications regarding non-self-governing areas were undertaken in an effort to accommodate the position of the British. While the British objections to American anti-colonial objectives had long been evident, the March 1944 mission to London headed by Undersecretary Stettinius, provided an opportunity for a frank exchange of views on colonialism and other issues. Before leaving Washington, the Stettinius mission met with Roosevelt and Hull, both of whom stressed the need to confront the British on the colonialism question. Roosevelt emphasized his Indochina objectives and his success in gaining Chiang Kai-shek's approval.[43] In London, Isiah Bowman, as the member of the mission who was most directly involved in planning on dependent areas, met with the officers of the Colonial Office. After some initial tensions, Bowman became sympathetic with the argument of Colonial Secretary Oliver Stanley that a general colonial declaration was impracticable and that the responsibilities of the regional commissions should be restricted. Stanley and others at the Colonial Office assumed that Bowman's conversion would result in State Department acceptance of their points of agreement. In fact, upon his return to Washington, Bowman was unable to convince his colleagues to make drastic changes in American planning.[44] He did, however, manage to channel the regional commission planning along lines consistent with the British viewpoint.

State Department preparation during this period progressed on three related matters: the declaration of principles for dependent areas; the regional commissions; and the international trusteeship system. On the first, the 1943 draft Declaration by the United Nations on National Independence was revised to eliminate the objective of "national independence." The resulting draft Declaration Regarding Administration of Dependent Territories established self-government as the objective. It also detailed the obligations of the administering powers to improve political, economic, and social conditions. Furthermore it stipulated the responsibility of dependent peoples to prepare themselves and demonstrate their capacity for maintaining stable government. The administering powers would be required to submit annual reports on conditions in dependent areas and list efforts to implement the declaration. This retreat from the earlier universal commitment to independence met with considerable opposition in the planning committee and was accepted only after extended debate.[45]

With respect to the regional commissions, the Informal

Political Agenda Group, in deference to British objections, agreed to eliminate a list of the planned commissions and to stipulate that the initiative for establishing such regional bodies would rest with the administering powers. In addition, the representation of dependent peoples on the commissions would be dependent upon its "feasibility." Finally the responsibilities of the commissions were left vague. Beyond receiving annual reports from administering powers, their duties were limited to consultative and advisory work in a number of economic and social fields.[46]

Inasmuch as it had been agreed earlier to restrict a trusteeship system to the former League of Nations mandates and areas detached from the enemy, the formulation of a trusteeship plan had implications for Southeast Asia only in the sense that it potentially related to Roosevelt's Indochina objective. With British opposition to the trusteeship idea well known, the State Department backed away from a commitment to independence in trust territories and, on the vexing question of sovereignty in such areas, it was finally determined that sovereignty would be shared jointly by the members of the international organization. The Informal Political Agenda Group approved a draft for trust territories specifying the obligations of administering powers under the general supervision of the United Nations. The preparation on trusteeship became unexpectedly complicated as a result of the determination of the American military to control, without outside interference, the Japanese islands of the western Pacific. In July 1944, Roosevelt insisted that the former mandates and the areas detached from Japan had to be placed under international trusteeship. This resulted in prolonged discussion between the State Department and Joint Chiefs of Staff over reconciling the international accountability of trust territories with the security interests of the United States. Maintaining that the United States should avoid raising any question that touched upon territorial adjustments until the war was over, the Joint Chiefs prevailed upon the State Department to eliminate consideration of the trusteeship plans from the agenda for Dumbarton Oaks.[47]

## The State Department Initiative
## on Southeast Asia, September 8, 1944

While deferring consideration of general anticolonial objectives, State Department officers concluded that Southeast Asian interests required an initiative on behalf of early postwar commitments to self-determination. During the summer of 1944, Washington had received numerous reports about the political ramifications of SEAC. Reflecting a mounting bitterness toward the British, the prevailing mood at the State Department was to have Roosevelt press Churchill on Southeast Asian issues when they met at Quebec in September.

The reports of Max Bishop, the American consul at Colombo, argued that the British were utilizing SEAC to reestablish the imperial order in the region. While the United States continued to defer action on French requests for military involvement in the war against Japan,[48] the French were gaining British support. Mountbatten approved operations, Bishop reported, to parachute deGaullist agents into Indochina. The U.S. staff officer responsible for coordinating clandestine activities had apparently been excluded from the meeting when the mission had been considered. Morevoer, American facilities in China were being utilized for these Indochina activities, but effort had been made to prevent American officers from learning of their nature. In addition to detailing this record of Anglo-French collaboration, Bishop urged Washington to reassert its interests in the region before it was lost to the European imperialist powers or to anti-Western revolutionaries.

When General Albert Wedemeyer visited SEAC headquarters, he stressed, in messages to Washington, that the British were principally interested in reasserting their prestige and only secondarily the defeat of Japan. Other American officers in the area foresaw the British establishing a federation linking Burma, Thailand, Malaya, and Indochina, which would become part of the Commonwealth.[49]

The Anglo-American differences surfaced most fully over the request of the French Committee of National Libertion that a military mission be attached to SEAC headquarters, which would permit an active French role in planning and operations against Japan. The French intentions had long been known, but did not become a matter of serious concern until August 5 when the British Chiefs of Staff, acting with the concurrence of the Foreign Office, informed the American Chiefs of Staff of their intention to approve a French mission with its functions limited to matters involving Indochina. The French, they said, were to participate in political warfare; eventually, French land and air forces might be involved in assisting the anti-Japanese resistance in Indochina. Also, the French proposed to bring into India a Corps Leger D'Intervention which would eventually operate in Indochina along Japanese lines of communication.[50]

Britain's willingness to accept the French mission directly challenged Roosevelt's ruling that the French were to be excluded from Indochina operations. The American Joint Chiefs thus restricted its approval to political warfare in the area of SEAC jurisdiction, while sending a message to the State Department suggesting that the United States should "recognize, in so far as they are consistent with our national policies, the French desires concerning Indo-China."[51] In the meantime, the British Embassy, in an aide-memoire of August 25, urged the White House and State Department to give approval to the French mission. Excluding the French from the headquarters in Kandy, Ceylon, it was argued, would result in a concentration of their activities at Chungking where they would be more difficult to control. The issue was urgent. Rene Massigli, commissioner for Foreign Affairs of the French National Committee, was then in London requesting Allied action on the French request before leaving on August 29.[52] The State Department again referred the issue of French involvement in Indochina military operations to the White House; Roosevelt ruled that the French request be deferred until the forthcoming Anglo-American conference.[53]

Differences over Southeast Asia were also straining Sino-

American relations. Concern over China's territorial ambitions again surfaced as American diplomats in Chungking and Kunming warned that the lack of clear Allied objectives in Indochina left the country vulnerable to China. Both Ambassador Clarence Gauss and Kunming consul William Langdon warned that the Chinese encouragement of self-determination for Indochina would lead to postwar efforts to cultivate a nominally independent government. Through one means or another, the Chinese appeared determined to establish hegemony over northern Indochina. The only means of discouraging the Chinese, it was maintained, was the establishment of a forthright U.S. policy.[54]

As a result of a situation in Southeast Asia which seemed to threaten American objectives on all sides, the Office of Southwest Pacific Affairs and the Division of Far Eastern Affairs urged Hull to seek the President's approval of a strong assertion of the American position. A draft memorandum was prepared by Moffat, approved by his superiors as well as by the Division of European Affairs. While not fully sympathetic with the boldness of the initiative, the latter office apparently was persuaded of its importance as a counter to Japanese propaganda.[55]

The memorandum, which Hull forwarded to Roosevelt on September 8, reflected a growing State Department view that Southeast Asia could not be treated the same as other colonial areas. It had experienced the overthrow of Western power, the establishment of Japanese rule, virulent anti-Western propaganda, and was about to become an important theater of military operations. No one in 1944 fully comprehended the extent of wartime political change in Southeast Asia, but the region was recognized as unique, not the same as the colonial areas of Africa and the Middle East. Accordingly, the September 8 policy recommendations sought to accelerate and expand in Southeast Asia the general State Department plans for dependent peoples.

After reviewing the situation in Southeast Asia and stressing the evidence of British and Chinese efforts to undermine American objectives, Hull's memorandum urged that the

United States had to take the initiative in order to gain the good will of the peoples of the area. The United States had to force a change in the European approach to Southeast Asia:

> It is suggested that early, dramatic, and concerted announcements . . . making definite commitments as to the future of the regions of Southeast Asia would save many American and Allied lives and facilitate military operations. It would be especially helpful if such concerted announcements could include (1) specific dates when independence or complete (dominion) self-rule will be accorded, (2) specified steps to be taken to develop native capacity for self-rule, (3) a pledge of economic autonomy and equality of economic treatment toward other nations. Such announcements might well be accompanied by a reaffirmation of American determination to grant Philippine independence, a joint commitment to restore the independence of Thailand, and a pledge to establish a regional commission for consultation on social and economic problems in the region, on which all countries and peoples concerned would be invited to have membership.[56]

The memorandum then touched briefly but pointedly on the issue of trusteeship:

> The value of such concerted announcements would be still further enhanced if each of the colonial powers concerned would pledge a formal declaration of trusteeship under an international organization but it might be unwise for the United States to insist upon such a declaration of trusteeship for one country if similar declarations could not be secured for others.[57]

Beyond the propagandistic and psychological benefit of such a commitment to self-determination, the State Department recommendation maintained that such development of Southeast Asia would serve the long-term interests of the United States. After noting the economic and strategic importance of Southeast Asia, it was argued:

> Their economic and political stability will be an important factor in the maintenance of peace in Asia. Emergence of these regions as self-governing countries would appear desirable as soon as they

are capable of self-rule, either as independent nations or in close voluntary association with Western powers, for example as dominions. Such association might lend them political and economic strength (the weakness of Asiatic powers had long been a cause of war) and help prevent future cleavage along regional or racial lines. Failure of the Western powers to recognize the new conditions and forces in southeast Asia and an attempt to reestablish pre-war conditions will almost surely lead to serious social and political conflict, and may lead to ultimate unifying of oriential opposition to the West.[58]

Southeast Asian questions were important not only in State Department planning for the Quebec Conference, but were also prominent in the Foreign Office preparations. Churchill's procrastination on Indochina policy, in the Foreign Office view, was largely responsible for a lack of coordination and resolution of policy. In May when the French request for a military mission at SEAC headquarters had been brought to his attention, Churchill wrote: "It is hard enough to get along in S.E.A.C. when we virtually have only the Americans to deal with. The more the French can get their finger into the pie, the more trouble they will make in order to show they are not humiliated in any way by the events through which they have passed."[59] Recalling his conversations with Roosevelt, the Prime Minister came to the reason for his reluctance to deal with the Indochina issue: "Before we can bring the French officially into the Indo-China area, we should have to settle with President Roosevelt. He has been more outspoken to me on that subject than any other Colonial matter, and I imagine it is one of his principal war aims to liberate Indo-China from France. Whenever he has raised it, I have repeatedly reminded him of his pledges about the integrity of the French Empire and have reserved our position. Do you really want to go and stir all this up at such a time as this?"[60] Despite Churchill's preferences, the Chiefs of Staff and the Foreign Office, in response to subsequent French requests, were prepared to approve the mission to SEAC headquarters. With Massigli indicating to Eden on August 24 a willingness to accept the British conditions for restoration in Indochina (as approved by the Cabinet in February), the Foreign Office argued that Churchill had to seek American approval.[61] On September 8—the same date as the State Department initiative to Roosevelt—the Foreign Office prepared a lengthy statement for Eden to share with Churchill at the Quebec meeting. Beyond recommending that the Prime Minister gain Roosevelt's endorsement of the military mission, the Foreign Office defended French colonial administration: "It cannot legitimately be said that France has misruled Indo-China . . . French rule has preserved Indo-China from tyranny and other evils and has given peace and cohesion to a territory which has no geographic unity but is, on the contrary, a mosaic of peoples, tongues, and cultures. . . . On the economic side, the French have specialized in roads, railways, dyke construction, irrigation, and the stimulation of agriculture."[62] The implications of challenging French sovereignty would be momentous: "Any attempt to interfere with French sovereignty over Indo-China . . . would be passionately resented by France and would have incalculable results not only in the Far East but in Europe. . . . It would also put in question the future of all other Far Eastern colonial possessions which have been overrun by Japan."[63]

The British and American memoranda of September 8 underscored the extent of the disagreement over Southeast Asia. While the Foreign Office was preparing to defend the imperial order, the State Department was proposing bold measures to foster its demise. Having sparred over colonialism many times, neither Churchill nor Roosevelt, however, was inclined to raise the issues of Southeast Asia at the Quebec Conference. Both leaders conjectured that time would work in their favor. Roosevelt preferred to continue his quiet battle against the French, reasserting later the American interest in Southeast Asia and planning, at the forthcoming Big Three conference, to gain a reaffirmation of Russian support. As Hull correctly suggested in his memoirs, the September memorandum was not ignored by Roosevelt; while it did not persuade him to force the issue of Southeast Asia at the Quebec conference, Roosevelt, certainly encouraged by its tone, did subsequently take important steps to assure the realization of American objectives.[64] Under pressures from the French and the Foreign Office, Churchill likewise moved cautiously but forthrightly to secure British interests. As British and American policies and strategies collided openly and directly, the struggle over Southeast Asia entered a more intense phase.

## The Anglo-American Impasse Over Thailand

Anglo-American differences over Southeast Asia extended beyond the European colonies to the region's one indepedent nation—Thailand. The postwar treatment of Thailand had been an important issue between the United States and Britain since 1942, but became more serious in 1944. The differences over Thailand were, in many ways, an extension of the clash over colonialism. British expectations that Thailand would be punished for the Pibul government's collaboration with Japan rested on the assumption of a reassertion of Western domination in Southeast Asia including Britain's prewar position in Thailand. In addition, the Thais' surplus rice offered a means of feeding the peoples of Hong Kong, Malaya, and other areas. Moreover, the possibility of increasing British influence through control of the Kra Isthmus was attractive to some officials, especially Churchill. British policy was also shaped by a sense of having been wronged by Thailand after Britain's considerable efforts to support that country against Japanese pressures in 1940–1941. Beyond the declaration of war against Britain, Thailand had assisted the Japanese invasion of Malaya and then had annexed territory at the expense of Malaya and Burma. Imperial interests thus combined with moral indignation, resulting in the determination to impose a punitive settlement. On the other hand, the United States looked upon Thailand in benign terms and sought a quick restoration of an independent, pro-Western government. Regarding the war as the beginning of the end of colonialism in Southeast Asia, the United States was not prepared to tolerate infringements on the sovereignty of the only independent nation in the region.[65] This orientation of the United States was facilitated by the effective diplomacy of Thailand's minister in Washington and was supported strongly by the Chinese government. Thus wheras prior to Pearl Harbor, the British has been tolerant of the Thai government while the Americans had been distrustful, their positions were now reversed.

While the Thailand issue became especially significant in 1944, the divergent British and American approaches dated to Pearl Harbor. As Thailand came under firm Japanese control, Prince Seni Premoj, the Thai minister in Washington, disassociated the legation from his government, repudiating the December 12 alliance between Thailand and Japan. The State Department quickly planned to recognize Seni as the representative of a "Free Thai" movement. While the British expressed no opposition to treating Seni as the leader of a Free Thai group in the United States, they were much more concerned than the Americans about the Japanese-Thai treaty. The alliance would have resulted in a British declaration of war against Thailand, the Americans were informed, except for concern about the implications for pro-Western factions in Thailand.[66]

Thailand's declaration of war against the United States and Great Britain on January 25, 1942, set the terms of the Anglo-American estrangement over Thailand. Convinced that the declaration did not represent the will of the Thai people, Seni refused to deliver it to Hull. The immediate disposition of Roosevelt, Hull, and Berle was to treat the declaration with contempt by simply ignoring it; a similar response had been followed with respect to declarations of war against the United States by German-occupied countries in eastern Europe. In the belief that the United States had nothing to gain by declaring war on Thailand, Washington adopted the position that Thailand was an enemy-occupied territory. The British goverment, however, responded to the January 25 action of Bangkok by acknowledging that a state of war existed between Thailand and the United Kingdom. Angered over Thailand being used as a base for Japanese operations against Malaya and Burma, and the violation of the 1940 nonaggression pact, Britain thus considered Thailand an enemy state.[67]

From February 1942 until early 1944, U.S. objectives for Thailand were developed in coordination with China, and with little attention paid to Britain. When Chiang Kai-shek proposed that he issue a public statement which would express sympathy for the people of Thailand and renounce any Allied territorial ambitions at Thailand's expense, the State Department encouraged the Chinese leader and indeed assisted in drafting the message which was released on February 26, 1943. Without any consultation with the British, Roosevelt quickly associated the Allies with Chiang's statement. At a press conference on March 12, he summarized the Chinese message and then asserted: "I can . . . give my solemn word that China as well as her Allies have no territorial ambitions in Thailand, and have no intentions of undermining her sovereignty and independence . . . Maybe that has been printed, but I think it is worth—worth doing, because it is a pretty simple, straight declaration of not only the policy of China but of the United Nations, in regard to Thailand."[68] Continuing their close collaboration on Southeast Asian questions, Roosevelt and Chiang, in their lengthy discussion at the first Cairo Conference in November 1943, agreed to include the restoration of Thailand's independence in their statement of postwar objectives.

In late 1943, circumstances began forcing British and American consideration of the Thailand question. The controversy between SEAC and China Command over operations in Thailand called attention to the differing British and Sino-American approaches to the country. The likelihood of early military action against the Japanese in Thailand made agreement on postwar administration essential. Also by that time, a considerable Free Thai movement had developed with representatives in China, America, England, India, and elsewhere. Its spokemen were pressing for Allied recognition as a government-in-exile. In seeking such recognition, the Free Thai pointed to a record of expanding collaboration with the Allies. Free Thai forces reentering Thailand engaged in guerilla warfare against the Japanese and also worked with the Office of Strategic Services (OSS) in establishing liaisons with the Thai underground.[69]

In Washington, the State Department's Political Planning Committee recommended basing policy on the strong pro-American sentiment, which intelligence reports indicated was emerging in Thailand. In view of the Thai confidence in American intentions, the United States should insist upon a predominant role in the postwar military administration so to assure an early restoration of independence. This determination to restore Thailand's independence rested not only on capitalizing on the changing political orientation, but as a means of enhancing American anticolonial objectives. Any restriction of Thailand's sovereignty, it was believed, would harm Western prestige in Asia. Moreover, American plans for a Southeast Commission gave priority to including an independent Thailand as one of its principal members. Thailand and the Phillipines were vital as agents within the commission for the transformation of the imperial system.[70]

Despite the extensive collaboration with the Free Thai movement, the State Department declined to formally recognize it as a government-in-exile. This position was consistent with a general wartime policy of avoiding commitments to any particular political faction from occupied countries.[71]

Meanwhile at the Foreign Office in London, there was sentiment to encourage the Free Thai movement and thus not allow the Chinese and Americans to have all the benefit of the mounting hostility toward the Japanese. It was proposed that the British should issue a declaration in support of a free, independent Thailand. In view of Churchill's interest in avoiding any commitments which might restrict claims to the Kra Isthmus, the Foreign Office agreed that the declaration should avoid reference to Thailand's territorial integrity. As the statement was being drafted, the British, through their embassy in Washington, discussed with State Department officers the coordination of policy in Thailand. Noting pointedly that the Thai had good reason to be suspicious of British intentions, Hornbeck and Ballantine urged a British statement comparable to the positions of Roosevelt and Chiang Kai-shek.[72]

The draft British declaration on Thailand greatly disappointed American officials and intensified the Anglo-American impasse. Presented by Sir George Sansom of the British embassy to Ballantine on February 26, 1944, the statement read:

> The position of Thailand is in some respects unique in the Far East though not without parallel in Europe. A country with a long tradition of friendship with us has, though admittedly under pressure from Japan, betrayed that friendship. Not content with collaborating with our enemy and despite her treaty of non-aggression with us the quisling government of Luang Pibul took the initiative in declaring war upon us. For these acts Thailand is already paying the price and will undoubtedly pay a yet heavier price as the war reaches her territories. It is still possible for the people of Thailand to do something to save themselves from the worst consequences of their betrayal, and they will be judged by the efforts that they make to redeem themselves from the position in which the action of their present regime has placed them. Like other countries in like case "They must work their way home." If they do so they can look to this country to support the emergence of a free and independent Thailand after the war is over.[73]

Elaborating on the statement, Sansom made clear that it left the British free to seek special political, economic, or strategic arrangements on behalf of collective security which might be considered appropriate after the war. Finally, the British proposed no further inducement to the Free Thai beyond that provided by the declaration.[74]

Reporting to Roosevelt, Stettinius wrote that his colleagues found the declaration "pretty rough."[75] Indeed upon receiving it, Ballantine had remarked that no statement would be preferable to the British proposal. Officers of the Division of Far Eastern Affairs regarded it as detrimental to Allied efforts throughout Asia. With Roosevelt's approval, the State Department drafted a summary of U.S. policy and objectives for London's consideration. Acting on the assumption that Thailand remained an independent, enemy-occupied country, the United States was committed to the restoration of sovereignty and the establishment of a representative government.[76] When Berle on March 20 presented Halifax with the American policy statement, he reiterated that silence would be preferable to the British draft. If the British persisted in issuing a document, at least they could add an unequivocal denial of territorial ambitions.[77]

Prior to the Berle-Halifax meeting, the British also pressed their objections to Thailand's territorial acquisitions since 1940 as a result of its collaboration with Japan. The subsequent U.S. position largely satisfied the British. Since those transfers of territory had been made under duress, they were to be considered invalid. The pre-1940 territorial status quo thus would be restored, but without prejudicing the claims of any state to territorial adjustments and subsequent territorial negotiations.[78]

After the exchange of positions in February and March 1944, the United States sought a joint statement along the lines of the American objectives. In London, the Foreign Office, in consultation with the Dominion governments, considered a modified statement. Reviewed by the Cabinet in early July, the revised draft met with strong opposition on a number of points, including the criticism of those who looked upon it as too lenient and the reservations of others who were concerned about the colonial implications. Specifically, Sir Firoz Khan Noon, representing the Government of India, questioned whether the British should be promising independence to Thailand without addressing the same question for Burma and Malaya. Following the Cabinet's conclusion that any statement would be premature, the British embassy informed the State Department on July 31 that a joint statement would serve no useful purpose.[79]

While the joint statement initiative failed, the United States had at least blunted the unilateral British policy statement. And the State Department kept pressuring for an unequivocal British renunciation of territorial ambitions. Hull instructed Ambassador John Gilbert Winant to pursue the issue with the Foreign Office.[80] The British were unyielding, as Eden, on September 8, set forth the British position: 1) recognition of Thailand's independence and sovereignty would be subject to acceptance of special security or economic stipulations that might be required by the international system; 2) the British had throughout the war avoided commitments to the restoration of territorial integrity even in the case of allied nations; 3) any pledge to Thailand's integrity would have important implications for its neighboring states; 4) any statement would require Cabinet approval and concurrence of the dominions which, judging from recent experience, would be difficult to reconcile with the interests of the United States.[81] Responding to Eden's message, the State Department sought to mollify the British by reaffirming that the United States would insist on the restoration of territory that Thailand had acquired since 1940 from Malaya, Burma, and Indochina. On the most important point of difference, the United States questioned exactly what Britain proposed with respect to special security and economic arrangements.[82] Eden, however, refused to be precise. The reservations on Thailand's sovereignty were to be determined at the time of a final Asian settlement.[83] Eden's slow-paced elaboration on British policy barely concealed his contempt for the leaders of Thailand and his lack of interest in a joint policy. In the words of one historian, the Foreign Secretary "was at his shrill worst over Siamese affairs."[84]

Thus despite several months of exchanges, the differences over Thailand remained profound. Reviewing the record of correspondance on the issue, G. F. Hudson of the Foreign Office expressed the British indignation over the issue: "The lines separating enemy, neutral, and allied nations certainly seems to have got a bit blurred. The Americans surely are being highly sophisticated in maintaining that they are not at war with Siam, although the Government of Siam has declared war on them, and in expecting us to regard Siam as an injured innocent. The doctrine that only the [Pibul] Songgram Government was to blame and that none of the consequences should fall on Siam as such is similar to the doctrine now held in the USA about Italy, and is in both cases hard to reconcile with the view that the German and Japanese peoples, and not merely their rulers, are responsible for their aggressions. . . . If they [the Thais] are to be promised their future independence and integrity without question, it surely means that is is just as good to be an enemy as an ally of Britain in war—which is not what we should proclaim to Asia."[85] Hudson's observations, upon which three of his colleagues commented favorably, underscored the extent of Anglo-American disagreement over Thailand.[86]

By the end of 1944, events in Thailand were changing rapidly and in a way that was consistent with American objectives. As the war turned against Japan, the leadership of the Free Thai movement came to power in Bangkok. In July 1944, Pridi Panamyong reemerged as the dominant figure within the cabinet and immediately made efforts to establish a secret working relationship with the Allies. The Pridi group, with the strong support of the Regent Luang Pradit, sought to make certain that the liberation of Thailand would find in power a pro-Western government prepared to repudiate the collaborationist policy of the Pibul regime. Through underground contacts with the OSS, the new government made clear its determination to cooperate openly, at the appropriate time, with the Allies. In the meantime, it collaborated with the Allies in intelligence and clandestine operations.[87]

This fluid political situation in Bangkok extended Anglo-American disagreement beyond London and Washington to the level of field operations. From late 1944 until the end of the war, the British and Americans competed for the predominant position in determining the Allied role in the liberation and occupation of Thailand.

## Conclusions

The competing interests and strategies of the United States and its European allies quickened in 1944. The points of contention centered on a number of issues: the continuation of Roosevelt's special interest in Indochina; the definition of American anti-colonial objectives and their specific application to Southeast Asia; and the postwar treatment of Thailand. In tracing these specific problems, it is possible to lose sight of the fundamental differences separating the United States from Britain, France, and the Netherlands. Above all, the American policy antici-pated and sought to encourage political and econmic change. This was evident in the American approach to all levels: the pre-paration for withdrawal from the Philippines (to be discussed fully in a subsequent chapter), the determination to establish international accountability as a working principle in colonial areas, and the conviction that Thailand's independence had to be quickly restored with political control firmly in Thai hands. While American officials differed on details, and bureaucratic competition over certain aspects of policy became evident in 1944, the overall American direction of postwar plans was still based on the belief that the days of Western control over Asia were ending. Each of the imperial powers made efforts to accom-modate the United States and internal domestic pressures by articulating an intention to modify colonial policy—Queen Wilhelmina's December 1942 proclamation, the French prom-ises at the Brazzavile Conference of January–February 1943, and later the British White Paper of May 1945. Yet none of the three measures, especially the first two, approximated the American expectations for decolonization. (As noted earlier, Queen Wil-helmina's proclamation was well received in the United States; it was not until after the war that the limitations of Dutch colonial reform would become fully evident.) Whatever their claims of liberal intentions, the British, French, and Dutch still assumed that sovereignty would be restored and would last indefinitely. The British approach to the future of Thailand rep-resented an extension of the colonial mentality. While British policy resulted partly from an understandable indignation over Thailand's behavior in 1941–1942, it also assumed that the British could reestablish their traditional predominance in the country.

For three years, Britain and the United States had tended to defer action on the problems of Southeast Asia. With military efforts concentrated elsewhere and the expectation of a prolonged struggle against Japan, it was understandable that the two allies would follow a strategy of delay in Southeast Asia. But events moved quite rapidly following the invasion of France in June 1944 and, within a few months, the French and Dutch were in a position to press their colonial interests. Moreover, the steady deterioration of China politically and militarily, and the approach of American forces to Japan, foreshadowed a series of revolutionary upheavals throughout Asia. In China the Communists and Kuomintang renewed their long struggle, and in Southeast Asia the forces of nationalism gathered strength that would surface with the collapse of the Japanese empire. No one in the fall of 1944 could have fully appreciated how closely much of Asia stood to the brink of political, military, and social upheaval, but by that time developments in Europe and Asia were already forcing the United States to reexamine and refine its objectives. By late 1944 the prospects for resolution of Anglo-American differences over the issues of colonialism and Thailand in an atmosphere free from the impending crises was ending.

# 5.

## Toward a Limited Anticolonialism: The Final Phase of Postwar Planning, November 1944–July 1945

> The President said he was concerned about the brown people in the East. He said there are 1,100,000,000 brown people. In many Eastern countries, they are ruled by a handful of whites and they resent it. Our goal must be to help them achieve independence—1,100,000,000 potential enemies are dangerous. He said he included the 450,000,000 Chinese in that. He then added, Churchill doesn't understand this.
>
> Taussig: memorandum of conversation with FDR,
> March 15, 1945

AS THE ALLIES approached victory in Europe and Asia, Americans came to realize the limitations of the Allied coalition. Long-deferred differences among the Allies became increasingly prominent. The vast power and resources of the United States, which had been vital to turn the tide against Germany and which had been responsible for the successful Pacific island offensive against Japan, could not assure the realization of postwar political objectives. In response to disagreements over eastern Europe, Germany, China, as well as Southeast Asia, American leaders confronted difficult choices which necessitated determining priorities and redefining objectives.

In Southeast Asia, the disagreements with the European powers over colonialism and (with the British in particular) over the related issue of the postwar status of Thailand reached, by late 1944, an increasingly bitter stage. Confronting a determined resurgence of European influence in Southeast Asia, and with American priorities directed toward political and military problems in East Asia, U.S. policy, in the months prior to Japan's defeat, tended to work toward adjustments with the European colonial powers. Roosevelt's personal interest in Indochina continued until his death, but afterward American officials denied any intention to challenge French restoration. Southeast Asian policy thus achieved coherence. On the problems of Southeast Asia, as with other foreign policy issues, President Harry S. Truman deferred to the Department of State. While European and Asian desk officers often disagreed on priorities, the trend in policymaking was toward resolution of differences with the European powers; American anticolonialism, based on the model of the Philippines, persisted, but in less doctrinaire and in more accomodating terms. Had it not been for the unexpectedly sudden and widespread political upheavals that accompanied Japan's surrender, the Western powers might have resolved their disagreements over the colonial questions. The nationalist revolutions, however, effectively forced the United States into choosing between supporting its anticolonial principles or permitting the reimposition of the colonial order. That situation, with all of its subtleties and ramifications, renewed tensions between the United States and its European allies.

## Political and Military Changes, 1944–1945

The transition in American policy from late 1944 to the summer of 1945 developed within the context of changing political and military conditions in East and Southeast Asia. The offensive against Japan reached a stage where operations on the Asian mainland no longer seemed essential for the attainment of military victory. While it was assumed that the defeat of Japan would require at least a year of operations following the surrender of Germany, victory in the Pacific was now virtually certain. Submarine attacks on Japanese shipping and the extensive bombing of Japan itself reduced its capacity to continue the war. In early 1945, American forces landed on Iwo Jima which, after a bitter struggle, finally fell. Meanwhile, the offensive in the Philippines, which the Joint Chiefs of Staff had never considered essential, preferring instead to concentrate on a more direct assault toward the Japanese islands, advanced steadily. Aside from the operations in the Philippines, Souteast Asia was not considered militarily important. By early 1945, the Joint Chiefs of Staff began planning for the complete American withdrawal from the Southeast Asia Command and for the extension of its boundaries.[1]

As U.S. strategic interest in Southeast Asia lessened, European influence in SEAC was strengthened. In October 1944 Winston Churchill agreed to the establishment of a French military mission. The French mission, under the leadership of General R. C. Blaizot, was to be attached to Lord Louis Mountbatten's command with the same standing as the Dutch and Chinese missions. Moreover, the French were to take a more active role in the war against Japan and to be engaged in political warfare in the Far East. This represented a larger role for the French than had been sanctioned by the American Chiefs of Staff, which had stipulated that the French mission's activities be restricted to the Southeast Asia theater. Further, the American Chiefs of Staff had reiterated that Indochina was still considered a part of the China theater. The British action also did not fully satisfy the French, who continued to seek approval of the establishment of a Corps Leger d'Intervention for Indochina operations. (From the records, it seems that Churchill, in approving the establishment of the French mission, was not aware of the conditions stipulated by the American Chiefs of

Staff. The recommendation on which Churchill acted had been drafted by the British Chiefs of Staff. They had simply re-iterated the August 25, 1944, request to Washington, mentioned in the previous chapter, on the assumption that the entire mat-ter required discussion between Churchill and Roosevelt. For whatever reason, Churchill, however, decided that he could sanction establishment of the French mission without obtaining the prior approval of the President.[2])

In addition to the military and political developments in Southeast Asia, U.S. policy was influenced by the deterioration of earlier aspirations for China. U.S. objectives for postwar Asia had anticipated the emergence of a strong China as a major stabilizing force. Roosevelt had foreseen China as one of his "four policemen" which would be principally responsible for the preservation of international order. By the end of 1944, no longer could one seriously hold to such a vision. China's military weak-ness, the inefficiency and corruption of Chiang Kai-shek's government, and the vitality of the emerging Communist move-ment produced widespread popular disenchantment with the Kuomintang. Beyond a commonly held assumption that with American encouragement the Kuomintang and Communists could be reconciled, the official response to the Chinese followed two distinctive lines. The State Department, especially career officers in Chungking and in the Division of Far Eastern Affairs, believed that the United States had to maintain flexibility, which meant avoiding any long-term commitment to Chiang, pressuring him to accept reform, and being prepared to deal with the Communists as a legitimate political group. Roosevelt, however, refused to pressure Chiang. He endorsed the views of Patrick Hurley, whom he had designated as ambassador to China in November 1944. Hurley insisted that Chiang had to be supported. Indeed the President gave in to the Generalissimo's demand that he recall General Joseph Stilwell.[3]

Roosevelt, however, recognized the seriousness of the Chinese situation. Following a conversation with Roosevelt in early 1945, Edward Stettinius, who had succeeded Hull as Sec-retary of State in November 1944, summarized the President's view: "Our policy was based on the belief that despite the temporary weakness of China and the possibility of revolutions and civil war, 450 million Chinese would someday become united and modernized and would be the most important factor in the whole Far East. China would someday assume the leadership in that area which the Japanese had attempted to seize."[4]

Acknowledging the likelihood that Chiang would not be the leader of such a China, during his last months Roosevelt treated Chiang with condescension, ignoring his requests for increased assistance and a major role in Asian affairs. At the Yalta Conference in February 1945, Roosevelt concluded a Far Eastern agreement without informing, much less consulting, the Chinese government.[5] This cavalier action contrasted markedly with the deference to Chiang and promotion of his international status which had characterized Roosevelt's diplomacy at the Cairo Conference just fifteen months earlier.

Finally, the emergence of the Soviet Union as a potential rival of the United States in Europe and Asia served to encourage a reduction of differences between Washington and the Western European allies. Repeatedly, officials in the Division of European Affairs challenged anticolonial objectives in Southeast Asia, especially Indochina, on the grounds that the United States should foster Western unity to stabilize Europe against Soviet influence. In an extensive review of postwar policy prepared by the Office of Strategic Services (OSS) in early 1945, it was argued that American interests called for maintaining the European powers in Asia; otherwise, the Soviet Union would extend its influence at Western expense.

> We should encourage liberalization of the colonial regimes in order the better to maintain them, and to check Soviet influence in the stimulation of colonial revolt. We have at present no interest in weakening or liquidating these empires or in championing schemes of international trusteeship which may provoke unrest and result in colonial disintegration, and may at the same time alienate us from the European states whose help we need to balance the Soviet power. . . . We should avoid any policy that might weaken the position of Britain, France, or the Netherlands

in Southern Asia or the Southwest Pacific. . . . None of the European powers has a strong position in the Far East. The least we can do is to avoid any action that may weaken it further; our interest in developing a balance to Russia should lead us in the opposite direction.[6]

While the OSS document offered a more explicit statement of realpolitik than was common at the State Department at the time, its essential concerns and objectives were increasingly evident in policy formulation during the last months of the war.

## Roosevelt and the Resurgence of French Influence in Southeast Asia

From the fall of 1944 until the Yalta Conference, the State Department and the White House followed different approaches to the colonial problems of Southeast Asia. The officers at the State Department reaffirmed the policy suggested in Hull's September 8 memorandum of seeking firm commitments to general decolonization based on the model of the Philippines. On October 5, before resigning as Secretary, Hull pressed again with Roosevelt the Department's position, which seemed more imperative in the context of recent developments in the East Indies. In response to Japan's promise of independence, the Indonesian nationalist leader, Sukarno, had delivered a speech which repeatedly linked the United States to the imperialism of Britain and the Netherlands. This development provided further evidence, it was believed, that Japanese policy in Indonesia and other parts of Southeast Asia would lead to postwar revolution and anti-Western sentiment. Hull wrote: "The Japanese pledge of Indonesian independence emphasizes the need for prompt formulation of American policies toward the region and the importance—as a measure of psychological warfare—of a concerted, dramatic announcement about the future of these regions."[7]

While these repeated recommendations from the State Department had some influence on Roosevelt, preventing a

French restoration in Indochina remained his overriding concern, almost to the exclusion of the remainder of Southeast Asia.
Perhaps Roosevelt regarded that objective as more attainable
than gaining British, Dutch, and French pledges to withdraw
from the region. International control of Indochina would certainly have weakened the British and  Dutch hold on their
colonies, thus hastening the transition to independence throughout Southeast Asia.

Although it is impossible to determine Roosevelt's precise
calculations, there is no doubt of his persistent effort to prevent
the French from gaining influence in Southeast Asia. The President's basic position was set forth in mid-October when he
overrode the State Department's tentative approval of an OSS
plan to provide supplies and equipment to resistance groups in
Indochina. Since the operation was to be under the American
command in Chungking in conjuction with the French mission
there, and considering that it would be directed principally
toward the defeat of Japan, the State Department was prepared
to sanction it. Roosevelt, however, vetoed the plan, insisting
that the United States should avoid involvement in any Indochina operations.[8]

But the development which gave Roosevelt as well as the
State Department officers the greatest concern was the unexpected establishment of the French military mission at SEAC headquarters in Kandy, Ceylon. American officials at Colombo,
Kandy, Chungking, and Washington questioned the process by
which this mission had been approved and, moreover, believed
that it foreshadowed an imperial intrigue to reestablish the prewar status quo in Southeast Asia. When Max Bishop, the
Colombo consul, cabled that Mountbatten was preparing to
receive a French military mission, the State Department inquired of the White House whether that development represented any agreement reached at the Quebec Conference.[9] In the
absence of any reply from Roosevelt, the officers at the State
Department were further concerned when the OSS reported in
late Octover that an officially recognized French mission was
being established; to OSS personnel at Kandy, "the strategy of

the British, Dutch, and French is to win back and control Southeast Asia, making the fullest use possible of American resources, but foreclosing the Americans from any voice in policy matters."[10] Subsequent reports indicated that diplomatic and military personnel in Ceylon assumed that an American military order had given official approval of the French mission, but with the stipulation that only military, not political, questions were to be discussed. As diplomatic personnel at Colombo noted, that distinction was meaningless.[11] In any event, as a result of Churchill's initiative and American hesitation, the French mission was established.

By the first of November, officers at the State Department had become convinced of the need to seek again Presidential clarification of Indochina policy and the French mission. In a memorandum prepared by Abbot Low Moffat of the Divsion of Southwest Pacific Affairs, the State Department informed Roosevelt of the recent developments, including the approval of the French mission, the apparent collaboration among the European nations, and the reports of British clandestine operations and propaganda in Indochina.[12] In a response written on November 3, Roosevelt reaffirmed his determination to avoid commitment or involvement in Indochina: the United States was not to give its approval to the French military mission and American officials throughout Asia were not to be involved in political decisions with the French or anyone else. Roosevelt also said that no final decision had been made on Indochina and the United States expected to be consulted on Southeast Asia—a point that he thought should be made clear to the British, French, and Dutch.[13]

Roosevelt's November 3 directive raised questions about the approval reportedly given to the French mission at Kandy. After reviewing the State Department's record on Indochina, Moffat and John Carter Vincent reported on November 10 to Stettinius that it had been consistent with Roosevelt's policy, i.e., no official statement or action of department personnel could be interpreted as approving the French mission. In a meeting that day, Roosevelt and Stettinius agreed on the necessity of issuing a general directive to all offices involved in Southeast Asian operations.[14] On November 17, the White House sent unequivocal instructions to the Secretaries of War and Navy, the Joint Chiefs of Staff, and the directors of the OSS and the Office of War Information. It concluded: "I wish to make it clear that American approval must not be given to any French military mission being accredited to the Southeast Asia Command; and that no officers of this Government, military or civilian, may make decisions on political questions with the French Military Mission or anyone else. I would like further to have it made clear that this Government has made no final decisions on the future of Indochina and that we expect to be consulted in advance to any arrangements applicable to the future of Southeast Asia."[15]

At the War and Navy departments, Roosevelt's message resulted in a review of their records and both departments uncovered that on August 30, the Joint Chiefs of Staff had informed the Combined Chiefs of Staff of their concurrence with the British request for approval of the French mission, provided that it be limited to political warfare within the boundaries of the theater. In reporting this action to Roosevelt on November 24, Secretary of War Henry Stimson maintained that withdrawal of approval would have serious repercussions, but that the War Department had issued orders, as stipulated in the President's November 17 directive, that officers were not to engage in political discussions. [16]

In the meantime, Roosevelt, having clarified within his own government his position on the French mission and political objectives in Southeast Asia, also pressed these matters with the British. This action was taken as a consequence of the mounting evidence of European collaboration within the SEAC and of French determination to participate in the liberation of Indochina. In Paris on November 4, Jean Chauvel of the French Foreign Office, informed Ambassador Jefferson Caffery of plans to recruit two divisions for use in Indochina operations.[17] From Chungking, General Albert C. Wedemeyer, who had succeeded Stilwell as commander of American forces in China and as

Chiang's chief of staff, reported that in a recent visit to Kandy, he had become convinced of intensified British, French, and Dutch plans to reestablish their predominance in Southeast Asia.[18] From Colombo, Bishop, in a thoroughly prepared statement, urged that the United States take immediate steps to convince the peoples of the region of its commitment to anticolonialism; allowing the Southeast Asia Command to restore the imperial order would lead to anti-Western revolutions from which only the Soviet Union would benefit.[19] And finally from Bishop came the report that Mountbatten was contending that the French mission had been approved in a verbal agreement between Churchill and Roosevelt.[20] Annoyed by these reports, especially the latter, Roosevelt wrote on November 24: "It should be called to the attention of our British friends that Mr. Churchill and I did not officially recognize the French Military Mission at SEAC and furthermore, I have made no agreement, definite or otherwise, with the British, French, or Dutch to retain their Far Eastern Colonial possessions.[21].

Despite Roosevelt's efforts to disassociate the United States from the Allies in Southeast Asia, "our British friends" had renewed pressures to accept the August 25 proposals on the French military role in SEAC and to resolve the Indochina question. An aide-memoire of November 22 requested approval of the French military mission, the establishment of a Corps Leger D'Intervention, and French participation in political warfare planning in the Far East. Beyond those long-standing issues, the British sought American confirmation of the understanding between Chiang Kai-shek and Mountbatten permitting both commanders to conduct operations in Thailand and Indochina with the final boundary between the China and Southeast Asia theaters to be determined later. The British would have preferred transferring Indochina to the Mountbatten command, but in view of the insistence of the U.S. Chiefs of Staff that Indochina properly belonged in the China Theater, it seemed that American approval of the Chiang–Mountbatten arrangement would eliminate confusion about the propriety of Southeast Asia Command operations in Indochina.[22] While awaiting a reply to the November 22 message, the British also urged agreement on Indochina. The emergence of a strong French government made it inconceivable to deny France a role in the liberation of its colony. In being able at last to make that argument, the British, as Churchill had long calculated, clearly had time operating on their side in the clash over Indochina.[23]

London's decision to raise the issues in the aide-memoire of November 22 was taken only after Churchill had delayed such action as long as possible. When the Foreign Office began pressing him on these matters in early October, the Prime Minister had written to Eden: "pray draft a telegram to the President *at your leisure.*"[24] But with the French urging acceptance of their role in Asian operations and with Mountbatten maintaining such support could be valuable, the initiative taken on November 22 had become imperative.[25]

The American response continued the differences over Indochina. In line with Roosevelt's pronouncements, the State Department prepared a strongly worded reply, denying all points initially raised on August 25 and criticizing the British for giving full recognition to the French mission in the absence of American approval.[26] Rather than addressing the specific aspects of the British aide-memoire, on January 1, 1945 Roosevelt directed Stettinius to follow a strategy of delay: "I still do not want to get mixed up in any Indochina decision. It is a matter for post-war. By the same token, I do not want to get mixed up in any military effort toward the liberation of Indochina from the Japanese. You can tell Halifax that I made this very clear to Mr. Churchill. From both the military and civilian point of view, action at this time is premature."[27]

Stettinius met with British Ambassador Halifax the following day, conveying the President's view and the expectation that the issue would be discussed with Churchill. Reading Halifax's report of this meeting, an exasperated Foreign Office official commented: "This throws us back where we were before the Quebec Conference. The President refused to discuss Indo-China with anyone save the Prime Minister and when he meets the Prime Minister he does not mention it."[28]

In a conversation with Roosevelt on January 4, Halifax specifically pressed Mountbatten's interest in utilizing French units for sabotage work in Indochina to break the Japanese communications network. As reported by Halifax: "The President said that if we felt it was important we had better tell Mountbatten to do it and ask no questions. He did not want in any way to be committed to anything that would seem to prejudice political decisions about Indo-China in a sense favorable to restoration of French status quo ante which he did not wish to see restored."[29] This obviously fell short of the expectations of the November 22 aide-memoire and, as Halifax noted, "off-the-record" approval of limited operations in Indochina was not a firm commitment. Since in fact Mountbatten was already conducting such activities in Indochina without American sanction, Halifax "inclined to let sleeping dogs lie."[30]

Roosevelt held to his anti-French objectives and delaying strategy in Indochina despite persistent reports of British, French, and Dutch collaboration to achieve a colonial restoration. With strident rhetoric, General Wedemeyer and Ambassador Hurley, the two most outspoken Anglophobes on the Asian scene, warned repeatedly of British-inspired intrigue against American anticolonialism.[31] In a message to Chief of Staff General George C. Marshall, which was subsequently passed on to Roosevelt, Wedemeyer wrote: "A close and coordinated relationship between British, French, and the Dutch exists with the primary purpose of retrieving pre-war favored position in this area for these countries, with the British in the dominant role. I have tangible evidence of this, General, as the result of many off-the-record discussions with Admiral Mountbatten and occasional remarks or papers which I inadvertently heard and saw."[32]

Hurley, who usually communicated directly with the President, frequently referred to the "Council of the Three Empires" at Kandy and foresaw that the "British plan to extend to the Far East the same character of imperial hegemony of the three great imperialistic nations as they have arranged for the control of Western Europe."[33] In his less passionate style, Bishop warned of the mounting evidence of European collaboration at Southeast Asia Command headquarters and the inability of the small American staff, which lacked directions on fundamental objectives in the area, to exert any restraining influence.[34]

Roosevelt's concern about Southeast Asian colonial issues led, at last, to his pressing with the British the substance of the State Department September 8, 1944 initiative. British Colonial Secretary Oliver Stanley visited Washington in mid-January for discussions on problems of dependent areas. The President's meeting with Stanley on the 16th was a vintage Roosevelt performance, combining an airy attitude with shrewd political judgment. Fully briefed by the State Department on Anglo-American differences as they had developed since the March 1943 Draft Declaration by the United Nations on National Independence, Roosevelt reaffirmed general U.S. objectives and avoided certain matters on which he preferred not to give Churchill any warning in advance of the forthcoming Big Three meeting. He mentioned Indochina and, casually but pointedly, other Southeast Asian colonies, including Burma. Warning that the status of Indochina would cause trouble at the forthcoming conference, Roosevelt reiterated his opposition to the restoration of France and his plans for administration under United Nations auspices. Continuing his discourse on Southeast Asia, the President commented that he was uncertain about the disposition of Burma and recalled Queen Wilhelmina's pledge of dominion status for Java and Sumatra. He then requested that the British commit themselves to timetables for decolonization—a move which followed substantially the State Department's recent recommendations.

Roosevelt and Stanley ranged over a number of other colonial questions and engaged in a bit of rhetorical fencing over British and American records of imperialism. Like so many of Roosevelt's conversations with British officials, this session caused concern in London not only because it seemed to reaffirm America's determination to expand in Asia at Europe's expense, but also because the President's ideas, especially regarding Indochina, still seemed, after more than three years of fighting in the Pacific, to be ill-conceived and somewhat whimsical. Nonetheless, after the Stanley meeting, Roosevelt remarked to Charles Taussig, a longtime confidante who had kept a record of the conversation, that he intended to discuss with Churchill and Stalin his plans for an Indochina trusteeship.[35]

In the weeks prior to the Yalta Conference, the anomolous status of Indochina in American planning remained a source of State Department concern and some effort was made to accommodate the department's position with that of the White House. Many officials believed that the President was undermining Franco-American relations at a time when a resurgent France was important to stability in postwar Europe. At a meeting in early January of the Secretaries of State, War, and Navy with Presidential adviser Harry Hopkins, there was a strong consensus that Roosevelt's strategy of postponing an Indochina decision was a mistake and causing unnecessary strains with France.[36] Before Stanley's visit to the White House, the department prepared for Roosevelt a lengthy report on Indochina which warned that the United States would suffer a loss of prestige if the status quo ante were reestablished; yet it also stipulated pointedly that "our policies toward Indochina should be consistent with our policies toward the other countries in Southeast Asia."[37] The department's September 8, 1944 initiative still prevailed as the guideline for Southeast Asian policy.

On the day of the Roosevelt-Stanley meeting, the Committee on Dependent Areas (CDA) approved a statement of objectives for Southeast Asia (CDA 259) which had been prepared by the Division of Southwest Pacific Affairs. While suggesting that the United States should not question the sovereignty of the European powers, CDA 259 also recommended attaching special conditions to a colonial restoration. The document reaffirmed the American interest in stability and orderly change: "Our principle objective in the areas of Southeast Asia should be the promotion of conditions which will . . . safeguard after the war our increasing interest in the maintenance of peace and the orderly political and economic development of countries in the Far East. It is important for us, therefore, that conditions of political and social stability be assured, and that we secure the good will of Asiatic peoples."[38]

Since the United States would be principally responsible for the defeat of Japan, "it cannot, in the eyes of Asiatics everywhere, escape a substantial measure of responsibility for the postwar treatment accorded those areas."[39] A return to the prewar colonial system would lead to continued unrest directed against the West. Accordingly the United States had to seek commitments to anticolonialism: "Our present policy of attempting to maintain, except in military matters, our separate identity in the Southeast Asian command theater . . . is not sufficient to protect our interests. We should also endeavor to secure from the colonial powers assurances of a more liberal colonial policy toward their dependencies in Southeast Asia, in harmony, if possible with our own policy towards the Philippines."[40]

As specified at the meeting of the CDA, this framework for decolonization in Southeast Asia was to be tied to a general United Nations declaration on dependent territories which would establish clear political objectives as well as provisions for economic development including the essentials of the open door. The revised plan for international trusteeship, also discussed by the committee, included one important change with implications for Southeast Asia. In addition to the two categories of trust territories established previously (former mandates and areas detached from the Axis), provision was also made for territories voluntarily placed under trusteeship.[41] The inclusion of the third category provided a means of accommodating the prevailing State Department assumption that France would be restored in Indochina with Roosevelt's continued pursuit of the trusteeship for that colony. Of course, the State Department planners' revised trusteeship statement depended upon France or any imperial power voluntarily relinquishing control to an international authority, which was not expected.

The relationship between this revision in the trusteeship formula and Roosevelt's Indochina project was explained later by John Hickerson of the Division of European affairs in a conversation with a British official, who reported to London: "[Hic-kerson] said that the American proposal at Yalta in connection with trusteeship had been partly phrased by the State Depart-ment in order to permit of a climb-down from the position that President Roosevelt had taken in conversations as regards Indo-China. The third category of territories . . . would enable but not compel the French voluntarily to entrust Indo-China to the Trusteeship pool. I do not imagine Mr. Hickerson expected the French to do this, but he made it clear that the State Depart-ment felt that President Roosevelt had gone too far, and the Category C was a useful face-saver."[42]

The dualism of policymaking reflected in Roosevelt's statements to Stanley and the CDA's simultaneous action set the pattern of the American approach to the Yalta Conference. Roosevelt planned to pursue his goal of the Indochina trustee-ship while the State Department readied its plans for a liberal colonial settlement in Southeast Asia. As Roosevelt continued his efforts to prevent any French military role in Indochina because of its political implications, the State Depart-ment assumed that French restoration should not be challenged. Whereas Roosevelt regarded the trusteeship concept as suf-ficiently elastic to include the imposition of a trusteeship on Indochina, the State Department, in its planning papers for Yalta, specified that territories like Indochina could be placed under trusteeship only voluntarily.

## Anglo-American Rivalry Over Thailand

On the other immediate problem in Southeast Asia—the post-war status of Thailand—U.S. policy was clear and unequivocal. In the planning for Southeast Asia, Thailand's independence was central to the realization of anticolonial objectives. Indeed added to the State Department's representations of late 1944 and early 1945 on behalf of liberal colonial policies in Southeast Asia was always the call for an Allied pledge to uphold Thai-land's sovereignty and independence. With the British strongly opposed to that commitment, officers at the State Department believed that the intractable question of Thailand could be resolved only if Roosevelt took the initiative with Churchill.

By early 1945 Anglo-American rivalry had led British and American military and intelligence to compete for control of operations in Thailand and for dominance in dealing with the growing Thai opposition to the Japanese.[43] The establishment of a strong Thai underground and its association with British and American intelligence operations led to pressures on the United States to foster a provisional Free Thai government outside of Thailand, with Washington as its most likely center. Beginning in late 1944, the OSS, operating from Kandy and Chungking and working with American-trained Thais, established an extensive intelligence network in Thailand. The British sought American assurances of a coordinated, cooperative strategy in Thailand, but OSS personnel, as well as American diplomatic representatives at Kandy and Chungking, urged their superiors that the United States be prepared to exploit fully the fluid political situation prevailing in Thailand. Otherwise, the United States might be outmaneuvered, leaving the British in control of liberation and occupation.[44] That urgency over British designs was expressed by OSS officers at a State Department meeting of January 18, 1945 with Abott Low Moffat and Kenneth Landon, both of the Division of Southwest Pacific Affairs. The OSS was planning a mission to Bangkok to establish direct contact with Pridi Panamyong, who had led the Free Thai underground and had become the Regent when the Pibul government was replaced in the summer of 1944. The new Thai government, under Premier Kuang Aphaiwong, had less military influence than the Pibul regime and reflected the reassertion of Pridi's power. Since the British were known to be making similar plans, the OSS was determined to reach Bangkok first and to offer firm assurances of American support. In particular, the Regent was known to be considering the establishment of a provisional government outside Thailand should Japan, as he feared, overthrow the government in Bangkok. Noting that the United States has generally declined recognition of such governments, Moffat suggested that the OSS reaffirm the U.S. position with respect to Thailand's declaration of war and emphasize its disinclination to treat Thailand as an enemy state.[45]

The OSS mission to Bangkok, however, failed to discourage the interest in a provisional government. When the team returned from Bangkok, they were accompanied by officials of the Thai government whom Pridi had designated to negotiate with the United States and other governments and to establish a provisional government. United Nations recognition, it was maintained, would solidify pro-Western opinion within Thailand and facilitate the establishment of a widespread resistance movement. While not acknowledged as a factor, a recognized provisional government operating outside Thailand would also lessen the chances for the imposition of harsh peace terms on Thailand. At the State Department, the impending arrival of officials smuggled out of Thailand was not exactly welcomed, for any American dealing with a provisional government risked the prospects for reconciling British and American objectives in Thailand.[46]

On the long-standing Anglo-American differences over Thailand, however, the State Department remained inflexible. In planning for the Yalta conference, officers of the Office of Far Eastern Affairs and the Division of Southwest Pacific Affairs prepared an extended analysis of the British and American positions, but the department's recommendations remained basically uncompromising. After recounting the objections to British policy, principally its infringement on Thai sovereignty and the effective continuation of prewar imperial practice, the State Department maintained that the United States could not ignore the pro-Allied orientation of the Kuang government and Pridi's reemergence as an opportunity to enlist Thailand's support in the war against Japan.[47] Toward that end, the Office of Far Eastern Affairs proposed an initiative seeking Allied agreements with Thailand, which would provide for: 1) Thailand's cooperation in the war; 2) its acceptance of pre-January, 1941 boundaries without prejudice to later adjustments by negotiation; 3) Allied respect for the sovereignty and independence of

Thailand which would be considered an enemy-occupied as opposed to an enemy state; 4) limitation of military government in the country to combat areas occupied by Allied troops, with such areas rapidly restored to the jurisdiction of the Thai government. This approach to the Thai question offered little to the British, other than the Thai commitment to renounce territory acquired since January 1941, and even that renunciation allowed for subsequent negotiation of territorial issues.[48]

Reinforcing the determination to achieve American objectives was a sense of British dependence upon the United States. Since the British evidently sought an impressive victory somewhere within the SEAC theater, some U.S. officials reasoned, control of supplies to that region gave the United States leverage in dealing with Britain over Thailand.[49]

When representatives of the Free Thai and Seni Premoj, Thailand's minister to the United States (who had maintained his diplomatic status because of the American refusal to acknowledge a state of war with Thailand), met with State Department officials in February 1945, they pressed for support of a Free Thai government which would be eligible for United Nations membership and thus would assure Thailand's postwar independence.[50] From Chungking, Chiang Kai-shek and Ambassador Hurley, (who was ever mindful of countering British intrigues), sent messages endorsing the formation of a Free Thai government-in-exile.[51] Following the Japanese overthrow of the French government in Indochina on March 12, it was expected that similar steps would be taken against the Thai government. The Thai cabinet, according to OSS sources, was prepared to resist the Japanese, but looked to the United States for support. And from Colombo, Bishop warned that failure to encourage Thai resistance would be detrimental to American interests not only in that country but throughout Southeast Asia.[52] In deference to the British, the United States discouraged the Free Thai government plan, but to help cultivate Thai-American relations, the State Department authorized increased OSS assistance to the Free Thai movement.[53]

At the same time the State Department renewed efforts

to reach an understanding with the British, but the Foreign Office, as it had in 1944, deferred consideration of Thai policy. Reaffirming the American commitment to an economically and politically independent Thailand, Washington sought recognition of a Thai government and support for its admission to the United Nations, assurances of non-discriminatory commercial agreements, and acknowledgement that any security arrangements depended upon Thai approval.[54] To the British, however, such lenient terms remained unacceptable.

## Roosevelt and Indochina, February–April 1945

At the meeting of the Big Three at Yalta, the future of dependent areas and the specific issues in Southeast Asia received little, but nonetheless significant and revealing, consideration. Differences between the United States and Great Britain over general postwar trusteeship plans were reduced, but not the troublesome questions of Indochina and Thailand. Despite his failing health and the many issues he considered at Yalta, Roosevelt demonstrated a sharp grasp of the colonial problem. He somewhat outmaneuvered Churchill, who suffered from poor Foreign Office advice on Roosevelt's strategy and priorities. Prior to the conference, Roosevelt overrode the objections of the American military which sought further postponement of discussions pertaining to trusteeship plans.[55] And Secretary Stettinius urged Eden and Molotov that there be a major powers consultation on trusteeship policy prior to the general conference to draft a charter for the United Nations organization. When the trusteeship segment of the foreign secretaries' report was presented, Churchill, who had been led by the Foreign Office to believe that Roosevelt did not attach much importance to the State Department's trusteeship plans, vehemently denounced any international infringement on the British empire. Churchill's outburst embarrassed Roosevelt and delighted Stalin. The Prime Minister's wrath subsided only when Stettinius assured him that the British Empire would not be included in the trusteeship system. Stettinius reiterated the State Department's limitation of trusteeship to three categories: existing mandates, areas detached from the Axis, and territories voluntarily placed under international supervision. Churchill then agreed to the foreign secretaries' report, which marked a significant step toward the realization of American trusteeship objectives.[56]

While the Yalta protocol ruled out discussion on specific trusteeship areas prior to and during the United Nations conference, Roosevelt again sought and gained Stalin's support of his trusteeship plans for Indochina and Korea. With respect to Korea which would fit into the "detached area" category, the President spoke of establishing an American, Soviet, and Chinese administration which would prepare the country for independence within twenty to thirty years. The two also briefly discussed Indochina:

> The President then said he also had in mind a trusteeship for Indochina. He added that the British did not approve of this idea as they wished to give it back to the French since they feared the implications of a trusteeship as it might affect Burma.
>
> Marshall Stalin remarked that the British had lost Burma once through reliance on Indochina, and it was not his opinion that Britain was a sure country to protect this area. He added that he thought Indochina was a very important area.
>
> The President . . . added that France had done nothing to improve the natives since she had the colony.[57]

Roosevelt declined to raise the Indochina issue with Churchill. He appeared to remain convinced that his objective was still attainable, provided U.S. influence was utilized effectively. In the session with Stalin, the President confided his "inability" to provide the ships which de Gaulle had requested to transport troops to Southeast Asia. In a preconference session with his advisers, Roosevelt stipulated that the United States could engage in military operations in Indochina only if they were directed against Japan and involved no alignment with France.[58] And returning from Yalta, Roosevelt, in off-the-record comments to reporters, recounted his conversations with Stalin and others and spoke of a trusteeship involving France, China, the Soviet Union, the United States, and perhaps the Philippines. But caution was dictated by British opposition: "Stalin liked the idea. China liked the idea. The British don't like it. It might bust up their empire, because if the Indo-Chinese were to work together and eventually get their independence, the Burmese might do the same thing to the King of England. . . . It would only get the British mad. . . . Better to keep quiet just now. . . . He [Churchill] is mid-Victorian on all things like that."[59]

From the Yalta Conference until Roosevelt's death two months later, the Indochina issue stirred further antagonism among the Western allies. The French, besides reiterating their determination to play a major role in operations against Japan, made clear that they would not tolerate discussion of their sovereignty in Indochina. Following the policy established at the Braazaville Conference, France and the peoples of Indochina would decide the status of Indochina within the framework of the French empire.[60] Through its embassy in Washington, France also began pressing for an agreement with the United States on the liberation and military administration of Indochina; it sought terms similar to those of the Dutch-American civil affairs agreement on the Netherlands East Indies which stipulated acceptance of Dutch sovereignty and procedures for consulting with the Dutch. Stettinius deferred this request by suggesting that unlike the East Indies, no American military operations were contemplated in Indochina. In response the French Ambassador suggested that the American reticence to discuss such matters resulted from Roosevelt's linking of Indochina to trusteeship plans, which "present difficulties."[61]

The Anglo-American exchange over Southeast Asia, like that between the United States and France, took on a sharper tone. Much to the annoyance of Mountbatten and authorities in London, Wedemeyer refused to sanction SEAC operations in Indochina which, he insisted, was part of the China theater. In the absence of instructions from Washington, Wedemeyer declined to recognize the informal agreement between Mountbatten and Chiang Kai-shek permitting both commanders to operate in Indochina.[62] The Wedemeyer-Hurley paranoia about British intentions in Asia came to be shared, although in less strident terms, by military officials in Washington. Reviewing Mountbatten's record of assisting clandestine French operations in Indochina which was considered to be of negligible military value, a Joint Chiefs of Staff report saw the British attempting to present the United States with a fait accompli: "By acquiescing in French desires rather than United States policy in Indochina, the British are successfully creating an overall situation, based on a series of seemingly minor requests by the British and French, intended to commit the U.S. to a position whereby Indochina should logically be considered in a British rather than a U.S. sphere of primary strategic interest."[63]

Roosevelt's determination to avoid association with the French was tested by the Japanese overthrow of the administration in Indochina, which abruptly transferred the French army in Indochina from part of a collaborationist regime to a potential ally. The coup of March 9 was undertaken after prolonged Japanese irritation with the French government, which, with the improvement of the Allied position in the war, had become less cooperative. With the acquiescence of the Annamese emperor, Bao Dai, and King Norodom of Cambodia, and a number of conservative nationalists, the Japanese fostered nominally independent governments in Indochina. Outnumbered and widely dispersed, the French army offered little effective resistance to the Japanese and appealed for outside assistance, especially from the United States Air Force in China.[64]

The French and British urged the United States to help the beleagured French units. Meeting with Ambassador Jefferson Caffery on March 13, de Gaulle assailed the American attitude toward France and predicted that hostility toward the French empire would cause profound popular disillusionment perhaps leading France toward communism and Russian domination. In a radio speech the following day, de Gaulle called for American arms and supplies to help the French withstand the Japanese in Indochina. From London, Churchill appealed to

Marshall that it "would look bad in history" if French resistance collapsed because the United States Air Force failed to provide desperately needed arms and munitions.[65]

The United States at length did help the French. Roosevelt, who remained reluctant to become involved in operations which might involve political commitments, was forced by circumstances to authorize assistance. Stettinius, acting in response to de Gaulle's dire predictions, proposed on March 16 that the White House issue a public statement affirming a willingness to aid the French; he maintained that this action would not prejudice postwar U.S. policy. Roosevelt vetoed this initiative, but on March 19 he did sanction operations in Indochina. A certain momentum to assist the French had developed. To deny support to the French in their resistance to the Japanese, no matter how deplorable Roosevelt might regard the French record in Indochina, was difficult to justify. Moreover, Washington received reports of enhanced French resistance capabilities being dependent upon supplies from China. The Fourteenth United States Air Force had planes loaded with supplies; only approval from the President was needed for airlift operations. Thus, Roosevelt approved assistance on the condition that it not interfere with planned operations elsewhere. Supplying the French, however, was not a high military priority. The Joint Chiefs of Staff, who were skeptical of the extent of French resistance, ignored repeated requests for a substantial increase in support and for transportation of the Corps Leger d'Intervention to support the resistance in Indochina. Accordingly, the assistance provided by the United States was limited and insufficient to salvage the resistance, which soon collapsed.[66] Altogether, the incident further strained American relations with both the French and British who were antagonized by both the delay in authorizing assistance and by its meagerness.[67]

By this time, Roosevelt, recognizing the difficulties of attaining the international trusteeship, appeared to be searching for an alternative means of assuring a commitment to Indochina's independence. A number of factors—the resurgence of British and French influence in Southeast Asia which the United States could not indefinitely restrain, the erosion of China's potential as a stabilizing force, the pressures from the Department of State to incorporate Indochina within a general colonial settlement, and the Yalta agreement on trusteeship— all undermined Roosevelt's objective of imposing an international trusteeship. His retreat from that longstanding goal was evident in an extended conversation with Charles Taussig on March 15. After speaking of the necessity of fostering independence for the Asian peoples, Roosevelt turned his attention to Indochina and New Caledonia and reaffirmed that they were to be taken from France and placed under trusteeship. Then Roosevelt abruptly modified his position; as reported by Taussig: "The President hesitated a moment and then said—well if we can get the proper pledge from France to assume for herself the obligations of a trustee, then I would agree to France retaining these colonies with the proviso that independence was the ultimate goal. I asked the President if he would settle for self-government. He said no. I asked him if he would settle for dominion status. He said no—it must be independence. He said that is to be the policy and you can quote me in the State Department."[68]

Roosevelt's refined plan thus preserved the essential objective of "trusteeship"—France could be responsible for Indochina but only with the "proper pledge" of "independence as the ultimate goal." It would seem that Roosevelt, who emphasized to Taussig that Churchill did not understand the danger of having one billion Asians turn against the West, still regarded the postwar status of Indochina as vital to the realization of anticolonial objectives in Asia. A French commitment to the independence of Indochina would, when coupled with the American withdrawal from the Philippines, have profound implications throughout Asia.

Roosevelt's conditional acceptance of French administration did not improve the prospects for Franco-American understanding. France's position that it alone could determine the postwar status of its empire, and the expectation of colonial integration within the French Union remained irreconcilable with "international accountability." Moreover, Roosevelt's toleration of a French "trusteeship" arrangement continued his practice of imposing special conditions on the French Empire.

While his postwar objectives were being refined, Roosevelt continued to resist SEAC influence in Indochina. Churchill suggested on March 17 that the antagonism resulting from Wedemeyer's refusal to sanction SEAC operations in Indochina could be resolved by the President and Prime Minister jointly endorsing the Chiang Kai-shek–Mountbatten oral understanding which permitted both commanders to operate in Thailand and Indochina.[69] In a message of March 22 ("it looks as though Wedemeyer himself drafted this!,"[70] it was observed at the Foreign Office), Roosevelt held that Wedemeyer, as chief of staff to Chiang Kai-shek, should coordinate Allied operations in Indochina until the theater boundaries were adjusted at the time of the planned Mountbatten invasion from the south.[71] Meanwhile, the Joint Chiefs of Staff, in line with Roosevelt's general directives, deferred the French request for a civil agreement on Indochina suggesting that the matter be submitted to Chiang Kai-shek, and they insisted that the French not be permitted to participate in military planning until Indochina operations had been agreed upon. They also denied a request that French officers be attached to all Allied air force units engaging in Indochina operations.[72]

While the March 15 conversation with Taussig was Roosevelt's last direct comment on Indochina, he later discussed his general trusteeship hopes within the context of a question about Indochina. This occurred in a March 24 meeting with Ambassador Hurley, who was then in Washington for conversations on the China situation. After reiterating his familiar argument against British, French, and Dutch imperial designs, the ambassador requested a written directive on Indochina. As recalled by Hurley in a letter written after Roosevelt's death, the President did not respond directly, but rather stated that at the forthcoming San Francisco conference a United Nations trusteeship would be established and would make effective the right of colonial peoples to choose their own government as soon as the United Nations considered them qualified for independence.[73] Roosevelt's last action that had any implications for Indochina was his approval of Stettinius' request that the Yalta agreements on trusteeships be made public. The April 3 announcement was subsequently used by the Truman administration to justify its claim of continuity in Indochina policy and has been interpreted to indicate Roosevelt's abandonment of an Indochina trusteeship.[74] Perhaps Roosevelt's comments to Hurley and his acquiescence in the release of the Yalta agreement indicated an acceptance of the inevitability of dealing with Indochina as part of the general colonial settlement. His expectation of a strong United Nations trusteeship, as expressed to Hurley, was difficult to reconcile with the limited number of states to be included under the Yalta agreements on trusteeship. Yet Roosevelt, like some other American officials, may have anticipated that trusteeship would become a common final phase of decolonization. It was expected that as their colonies advanced toward self-government, nations would voluntarily transfer responsibility to the international trusteeship system.

In early April, the Department of State sought to coordinate Indochina policy within the framework of Roosevelt's objectives—as best as they were understood. Officers in the Far Eastern and European divisions were aware of his approval of the release of the Yalta agreements, and of the modification of the trusteeship as expressed to Taussig. The Far Eastern division, which was responsible for drafting a lengthy analysis of Indochina policy, discounted the significance of those developments and assumed that the French might have secretly accepted a voluntary transfer of Indochina or that Roosevelt would press the issue at some future point. It was argued: "Pending further clarification . . . there would appear to be no alternative than to assume that the President's directive of January 1 . . . is still effective."[75]

The paper on Indochina, which was completed about April 5, underscored two important points: the continuation of White House–State Department differences over Indochina and the State Department's studied effort at understanding and accommodating Roosevelt's objectives. Attached to the paper was a statement, "United States Policy with Respect to the Future of Indochina," prepared by George Blakeslee of the Division of Far Eastern Affairs, which set forth the consensus of department thinking opposing the imposition of special conditions upon a French restoration. A major concern was the need for a strong France in Europe:

> If France is to be denied her former position in Indochina she will be to that extent weakened as a world power. It will probably be necessary for the United States to take the lead in any move by which France will be denied her former position in Indochina. . . . If it is to be the active policy of the United States to seek and insist upon the adoption of measures by which the peoples of dependent areas are to be lifted from their present condition and are to be given in time opportunity for full self-determination, we should consider whether that aim can best be accomplished in the case of Indochina through cooperation with the French or through denial of any role to France, and operate through an international trusteeship. In reaching that decision we must determine whether it is of more interest to us and to the world as a whole to have a strong, friendly, cooperative France, or have a resentful France plus having on our hands a social and administrative problem of the first magnitude.[76]

While the consensus of State Department thinking as reflected in the Blakeslee document opposed any special settlement for Indochina, the main body of the April 5 document endeavored to assure preservation of the President's options. Following an extensive review of Roosevelt's statements on Indochina especially his determination to avoid political or military commitments, it was concluded:

> It is assumed that the President has under consideration some proposal, to be put forward at an appropriate time, to modify French control over Indo-China, possibly by placing Indo-China under an international trusteeship. . . . It should be the endeavor of this Government to refrain from any action which would in any way weaken the effectiveness of any proposal which might here-

after be made by the United States with regard to the future disposition of Indo-China in the direction either of diminishing the
extent of French control over that territory or enlarging the political responsibilities of the native population. . . . It would be
desirable . . . that this Government refrain from making any
statement or taking any action which would operate progressively
to define the position of the United States with regard to the
future disposition of Indo-China.[77]

The ambiguous search for a policy evident in the April 5
paper provided an appropriate conclusion to Roosevelt's Indochina plans. While the President seemed to retreat from his
international trusteeship idea, the State Department continued
to anticipate that somehow he would pursue that objective.
Roosevelt's Indochina plans always lacked precision but he continued to hold to the objective of independence (following an
appropriate transitional phase); this was evident in his conversations with both Taussig and Hurley and in his expectations for
the trusteeship system. Whether Roosevelt could have achieved
a trusteeship in some form for Indochina and whether it would
have provided the basis for a rational and orderly transition to
independence can only be conjectured.[78] After his death on April
12, Indochina was no longer a topic of major interest at the
White House.

## The Accommodation with the French Over Indochina

Shortly after Truman became President, State Department
officials renewed efforts to bring coherence to Indochina policy,
but not without a resurgence of sharp differences between the
European and Far Eastern desks. Roosevelt's strong interest in
Indochina had tended to reduce internal disagreement. While
seeking to assure France's reemergence as a major power, European officers had been obliged to accommodate Roosevelt's
anticolonialism; meanwhile, the Far Eastern officers had compromised with the European desk while anticipating that Roosevelt could personally achieve objectives with which they

sympathized. With the transition in the Presidency, this artificial consensus on Indochina ended. The breakdown surfaced quickly as the European Affairs officers challenged the April 5 policy statement and backed off from the general anticolonial implications of the September 8, 1944 Hull memorandum. In a lengthy memorandum "Suggested Reexamination of American Policy with Respect to Indo-China," the Division of European Affairs maintained that Roosevelt's strategy of delaying action on Indochina had been rendered obsolete by the Yalta agreements on trusteeships, the April 3 announcement by the State Department, and the recognition that France would not relinquish control over her colony. The United States should approve France's restoration subject only to conditions that might be part of the general colonial settlement; American influence, however, should be exerted to assure a liberalization of French political and economic policies in Indochina. Reviewing these proposals, officers in the Division of Far Eastern Affairs argued for a much stronger line toward the French: the United States should insist upon the development of democratic self-government in harmony with the Western powers; otherwise, the peoples of Southeast Asia would embrace alien ideologies and become antagonistic toward the West. Accordingly, any commitment to a French restoration should be dependent upon adequate assurances of the development of democratic self-government and the establishment of commercial and economic equality. The United States should press for economic advantages, including the establishment of a free port at Haiphong and free transit facilities between Haiphong and China.[79]

The Far Eastern Affairs position, drafted by Moffat, sought to preserve the essence of the Roosevelt legacy and the State Department's September 8, 1944 recommendations. The conditions to be attached to French restoration approximated Roosevelt's insistence that a French trusteeship would be acceptable only if independence was its objective. Moreover, the economic demands—in effect, an immediate establishment of the open door in Indochina—further assured the decline of French influence and the development of Indochina's ties with the United States. In sum, the Far Eastern Affairs position, like that of Roosevelt, assumed that Indochina would be treated as a special case; American objectives were not to be limited by the terms of the general colonial settlement.

The differences over Indochina policy were resolved largely by circumstances and inadvertence. In particular, the objectives of the Far Eastern Affairs Division were undermined by military decisions which enhanced SEAC and French influence in Indochina. The transition in the Presidency facilitated the Joint Chiefs of Staff's desire to reduce American interest in Southeast Asia.[80] On April 14, Truman, who was unfamiliar with Roosevelt's concern with Indochina and was disinclined, in any event, to challenge advice from the military, accepted a Chiefs of Staff's recommendation which recognized Mountbatten's interests in Indochina. Specifically, Truman and Churchill endorsed arrangements worked out by Mountbatten and Wedemeyer which authorized SEAC operations in Indochina provided the China Command was informed and subject to its approval.[81] The British Chiefs of Staff found Truman's approval a "great improvement" over the earlier American position in that it acknowledged that Mountbatten was entitled "to have plans, intentions, and intelligence [activities]" with respect to Indochina.[82] Later in April, the American Chiefs of Staff approved transportation of the French Corps Leger d'Intervention from Algiers to Ceylon for use in Indochina as Mountbatten deemed necessary; Truman was unaware of this action, Presidential adviser William D. Leahy having ruled that the matter need not be referred to him.[83] And on April 30, the Joint Chiefs recommended that French offers of assistance in the Pacific be considered without concern for their political implications.[84]

Most importantly, the direction of American policy was shaped by assurances given to the French during the United Nations Conference in San Francisco. French Foreign Minister George Bidault, in a meeting with Stettinius, Ambassador Bonnet, and three State Department officials including James Dunn of the Division of European Affairs, complained bitterly of the dominance of the conference by the Big Three and the resulting exclusion of the French from decision making on important issues. After some angry French rejoinders to Stettinius' defense of the conference organization, Bidault expressed serious reservations over the American trusteeship proposals, especially the provision for voluntary transfer of dependencies which, he feared, would lead to pressures on the colonial powers. He emphasized that France had no intention of placing Indochina under the trusteeship system. While the United States, beginning with promises made by Welles three years earlier, had been committed to the restoration of the French empire, Bidault lamented, the American press continually implied that Indochina would be a special case. At this point, Dunn for the first time entered the discussion in a prominent way: "[Dunn] said that this was the moment for frank speaking. There was, of course, no official policy statement of this Government which has ever questioned even by implication French sovereignty over Indochina. There does exist, however, a great body of opinion in this country which condemns, rightly or wrongly, the French governmental policies and practices in Indo-China. He added that the new French colonial policy enunciated by General de Gaulle would give food for thought to public opinion."[85] Dunn's statement undercut the essential position of the Moffat memorandum of April 21, i.e., to withhold recognition pending concessions to American interests. It was, however, consistent with the preferences of the European officers at the State Department. And on an afternoon when long-deferred Franco-American differences surfaced in a frequently acrimonious exchange, assurances over Indochina must have seemed an appropriate concession. The significance of the meeting was clear; in a brief summary which Dunn prepared for Stettinius, it was observed: "Bidault seemed relieved and has no doubt cabled Paris that he received assurances of our recognition of French sovereignty over that area."[86]

Having seized the initiative in the policymaking process at San Francisco, the European Affairs Office quickly moved to coordinate American policy along lines which it had long favored. Upon his return to Washington, Dunn (whom Eleanor

Roosevelt, in discussing his views on colonial matters, once described as a "fascist") argued that no action would be preferable to the policy outlined by the Far Eastern Division. At length, Stettinius instructed the preparation of a new statement to which both units could agree. The resulting May 9 memorandum to Truman reflected the sentiments of the European office. After reviewing the need for a strong France as a means of assuring stability in Europe, and for promoting self-government in Asia, the memorandum suggested that the United States, instead of imposing preconditions on a French restoration, should seek assurances of liberal political and economic policies. Reluctant to annoy the French at all, the European officers prevailed upon Stettinius to forgo the suggested representations. In addition, the May 9 memorandum dealt with the French military role in the war against Japan—an issue that became increasingly prominent following Germany's surrender, as the French repeatedly offered military and naval forces for use in the liberation of Indochina and in the campaign against Japan.[87] In line with the recommendations of the Joint Chiefs of Staff, the French should be informed that while any large-scale operations in Indochina were unlikely, the United States was prepared to utilize French military and naval assistance against Japan.[88] In sum, American policy, in the month following Roosevelt's death, had fully accommodated resurgent French power in Asia.


## The San Francisco Conference: The Colonial Compromise

The trend toward understanding with the colonial powers was enhanced by the decisions reached at the San Francisco Conference with respect to dependent areas. While the United Nations Charter did provide for international accountability, the provisions of chapters 11 (Declaration Regarding Non-Self-Governing Territories), 12 (Trusteeship System), and 13 (Trusteeship Council) reflected a compromise between anticolonial principles and the influence of the colonial powers. Chapters 11,

12, and 13 represented a considerable retreat from the heady "end of imperialism" envisioned in the early part of the war.

In the weeks preceding the conference, an overriding concern of the American government was assuring effective military control of the Japanese mandates within the trusteeship system. After prolonged discussion among the State, War, and Navy Departments and the White House, on April 18 it was finally agreed that the conference would avoid discussion of any specific territories and that the American trusteeship formula would include provisions for assurance of strategic security. This provided the basis for the designation of the "strategic trust territories" in the Pacific. The elimination of specific territorial questions not only calmed the American military, but also reassured the British who feared that at San Francisco, the imperial powers would be pressured into "voluntarily" transferring colonies to trusteeship.[89]

Since the questions regarding dependent areas had not been discussed at Dumbarton Oaks, extensive preliminary discussions were conducted among the major powers in San Francisco. A Five Power Consultative Group, on which Commander Harold Stassen, the former Republican governor of Minnesota, served as the representative of the United States, was principally responsible for drafting articles 11, 12, and 13. Other nations with an interest in colonial matters—in particular, Australia, New Zealand, Mexico, Iraq, and Egypt—also contributed to the discussions. Frequently the United States was in the middle of disagreements between the French and Dutch, on one side, and the Soviet Union and China, on the other. Determined to achieve a general consensus among the major powers, the American delegation became an agent of compromise.[90]

On the trusteeship question, a U.S. draft proposal set forth the following political objective: "to promote . . . the political, economic, and social advancement of the trust territories and their inhabitants and their progressive development toward self-government."[91] In the meetings of the Consultative Group, the United States encountered pressures from those who sought a fuller commitment to the principle of "self-determination" and from the mandate powers for recognition of individual problems;[92] accordingly, the American delegation advanced the following addition to its earlier draft objective: "or independence as may be appropriate to the particular circumstances of each territory and its people, compatible with the freely expressed wishes of the people, and as may be provided in each trusteeship arrangement."[93] This language was adopted, with minor modifications, as article 76(b) under chapter 12. The inclusion of the word "independence" was important to many members of the American delegation and officials at the State Department, who had long believed that independence had to be the objective of a trusteeship system.

In the Declaration of Non-Self-Governing Territories, "independence," however, was not mentioned as the ultimate political objective. Stassen provided the leadership in the decision of the American delegation to accept "self-government" rather than the Russian, Chinese, and the embryonic "Third World" call for a commitment to "independence." The issue sharply divided the American delegation, with Taussig in particular challenging Stassen. In essence, he charged abandonment of the Roosevelt legacy and warned of aliention of the colonial peoples. Stassen talked of the increasing interdependence of the world, while others foresaw that an objective of independence could involve the United States and United Nations in endless disputes. Concern with preserving Anglo-American friendship in the face of Russian obstinance on a number of questions was also evident in the thinking of some officials. Isaiah Bowman, for instance, questioned whether the United States should support Russia's apparent drive to replace British and Dutch influence in Asia with its own.[94] With the United States in the pivotal position in the final decision, the Consultative Group accepted as the wording of chapter 11, article 73(b): "to develop self-government, to take due account of the political aspirations of the peoples, and to assist them in the progressive development of their free political institutions, according to the particular circumstances of each territory and its peoples and their varying stages of advancement."[95]

How did these actions affect the colonial areas of Southeast Asia? In terms of encouraging political change, the Declaration Regarding Non-Self-Governing Territories seemed to mean little, in that it left responsibilities in the hands of the imperial powers and set forth only the vague objective "to develop self-government." Yet the Declaration also assured that the metropolitan nations could be held accountable for their colonial policies and that possibly the United Nations could become involved in disputes where "the political aspirations of the peoples" were ignored or where administering powers failed "to assist them in the progressive development of their free political institutions." These provisions were, to be certain, disappointing to those who earlier in the war had foreseen the immediate end of the European empires, but they did provide for a measure of international accountability. The trusteeship formula also had potential implications for Southeast Asia, especially because some American officials expected that as colonies became more advanced under the terms of the Declaration of Non-Self-Governing Territories, the mother countries would voluntarily transfer them to the international trusteeship system. Trusteeship arrangements would thus constitute a final stage of decolonization. For that reason, many members of the American delegation regarded the trusteeship objective of "self-government or independence" as especially significant.[96]

The movement toward accommodation with the colonial powers  caused concern among many officials who argued that the concessions to France over Indochina, and the compromise at San Francisco represented a repudiation of Roosevelt's commitment to anticolonialism. At the State Department, this criticism was reinforced by Assistant Secretary of State Archibald MacLeish and others who criticized actions at San Francisco that enabled the Soviets to appear as the champions of self-determination. MacLeish believed that America's loss of prestige among colonial peoples could be reversed only by an unequivocal presidential reaffirmation of the principles of the Atlantic Charter.[97]

Despite some misgivings, political compromise was accompanied by a resolution of the related longstanding military questions. Problems between Wedemeyer and Mountbatten persisted despite the apparent agreement of mid-April. Meanwhile, the French and Dutch urgently requested that their forces be used in the liberation of their colonies, and the French again volunteered forces for the final assault against Japan.[98] By the time of the Big Three meetings at Potsdam in July, American and British military officials recognized that the confusion between the China theater and SEAC had to be resolved; moreover, the American concentration of resources in the western Pacific necessitated their withdrawal from any Southeast Asian operations. Accordingly, the SEAC was extended to include all of the East Indies, Thailand, and Indochina south of the 16th parallel. The China theater was left responsible for the northern half of Indochina. In addition, the Combined Chiefs of Staff finally agreed to accept in principle the French offer of two infantry divisions for service in the Pacific.[99]

## Conclusion

By the summer of 1945, American plans for postwar Southeast Asia had been modified considerably. As a result of changing relations with the Soviet Union and the demise of the Kuomintang in China, the United States drew closer to its European allies. In the process, anticolonial objectives became limited. By the time of the San Francisco Conference, international accountability had little substance.

Perhaps a more coherent approach to the future of the colonial empires in Southeast Asia would have brought the United States closer to the realization of its anticolonial objective. Roosevelt pursued the Indochina trusteeship as an alternative to the State Department's September 8, 1944 call for pressure on the French, British, and Dutch to make early commitments to the progressive realization of self-governing institutions leading to independence. The State Department initiative avoided the inconsistency of a colonial policy that drew a distinction between the French and the other European powers. At the very least, the State Department approach would have clearly placed the United States on the side of political change in the region. Roosevelt, who was cognizant of the necessity to recognize the movement toward self-determination in Asia, assumed that his Indochina plan would have implications for the other colonies in the region. In the end, State Department and White House differences during the war years largely dealt with strategy, not objectives. The State Department initiative, or even more vigorous pursuit of the Indochina trusteeship by Roosevelt, would have produced a postwar environment in Southeast Asia in which the United States and its European allies clearly identified with the political aspirations of the Southeast Asian peoples.

Despite the clear trend toward accommodation with the European colonial powers, disagreements on the future of colonialism persisted. Those differences became serious when the colonies unexpectedly challenged European authority following Japan's surrender. Americans soon discovered it was one thing to plan for political change for Southeast Asia when that area was under Japan's control, but quite another to respond to nationalist revolutions which looked to the United States for inspiration and support.

# 6.

# The Nationalist Revolutions in Indonesia and Indochina, 1945–1947

Such, as far as it can be reduced from scores of conversations all the way from Delhi to Seoul to Saigon to Batavia, was the hopeful picture of the American position seriously entertained by many conscious Asiatic nationalists. From it they concluded, at the very least, that while they could not trust the promises of the British, the French, or the Dutch, they could trust the Americans. But they were disappointed. They were confused. They began, in a short span of time, the passage from belief to doubt to open hostility. This process took place everywhere. It was the spectacular fact of the first postwar months, the puncturing of the American myth, the rude destruction of hopes that never had any foundations in the first place. . . .

In the broadest and most fundamental sense, the chief American failure was the failure to stand for change. The United States had a plan for a new order of things. It acted now for the old order of things.

Harold Isaacs, 1947

VJ DAY SIGNALED the beginning of the prolonged Western adjustment to the end of the imperial system in Southeast Asia.

While many observers in the West recognized that the war would stimulate nationalism, no one anticipated the extent to which the Japanese occupation had brought revolutionary changes in the former Western colonies. As the European powers sought to reestablish authority, the United States was forced to reconcile the objectives of anticolonialism and of close relations with the British, French, and Dutch. The United States continued to assume that liberal colonial policies, by fostering cooperation with dominant native elites, provided the means for orderly political change and the preservation of longterm Western political and economic influence. But in the case of Indochina, Americans confronted the problem of Communist domination of Vietnamese nationalism; that consideration led to the frustrating search for a non-Communist leadership alternative. Long after the other colonial questions had been resolved, the intractability of the Vietnamese issue remained with the result that it was not until 1975—thirty years after the end of World War II—that the United States, as essentially the successor to the French, withdrew from Indochina and accepted a Communist-dominated state.

In the aftermath of the Japanese surrender, the emerging French-Vietnamese and Dutch-Indonesian struggles were of overriding concern. In a public statement of October 20, 1945, John Carter Vincent, director of the Office of Far Eastern Affairs, set forth the State Department's basic position. The United States did not question Dutch or French sovereignty, but, at the same time, it would not "participate in forceful measures for the imposition of control." It was expected that the colonial powers would prepare the colonial peoples for the "duties and responsibilities of self-government." The United States "earnestly hoped" for agreements in Indochina and Indonesia and was prepared to lend assistance in reaching "peaceful agreements."[1] The Vincent statement put on record, within the context of the unexpectedly strong challenges to French and Dutch restoration, the general direction of American anticolonialism as it had been modified during the late stages of the war. To nationalists in Indochina and Indonesia, the acceptance of imperial sovereignty and the qualifications attached to mediation were disappointing, as they had anticipated American recognition and support of their aspirations.

In both Indonesia and Indochina, the native resistance to the reassertion of imperial authority led to efforts at negotiated settlements. Superficial agreements were reached, but neither the French nor the Dutch were prepared to compromise on their vital claim to sovereignty. In the end, the issues had to be resolved by force. The French–Viet Minh conflict began in December 1946 and seven months later, the Dutch "police action" of July 20, 1947, brought full-scale war with the Indonesians. The policy of the United States during this critical interlude between VJ Day and the launching of warfare in Indonesia and Indochina followed the basic lines of Vincent's October 20, 1945, statement—an approach which minimized American influence. While the United States later assumed a stronger role in both Indochina and Indonesia, it is unfortunate, in retrospect, that it failed to take more pronounced measures to avert conflict in the period immediately after the end of World War II.

Indeed at the time a number of officials questioned whether the United States should not adopt a more forthright position, one which would giver greater support to nationalist aspirations. By the end of 1945 the crises in Indochina and Indonesia foreshadowed warfare and an erosion of American prestige. In late November, Patrick J. Hurley, in his letter of resignation as ambassador to China, criticized the abandonment of the ideals of the Atlantic Charter and the evident underwriting of imperial restoration in Asia.[2] Responding to a State Department inquiry about American prestige in the area, Charles Yost, political adviser in Thailand, wrote that the peoples of Indonesia and Indochina were disillusioned with the American failure to support their claims for independence. They believed that the United States intended to defer to the British, French, and Dutch. Yost predicted: "American abstention ... does not seem likely to contribute to long term stability in Southeast Asia as it makes probable temporary restoration of prewar arrangements which in fact are often unsuited to present-day conditions and cannot for that reason long be maintained except by force."[3]

A State Department study, "U.S. Policy toward the Netherlands Indies and Indochina," which was completed in mid-December, observed that: "The events which are now taking place in the Indies and Indochina will play a large role in shaping the future of much of the Orient for many years to come, and it would be a major tragedy if those events should cost the United States the high esteem in which it is now held."[4] The United States could follow one of three courses: 1) "benenvolent neutrality" which would retain friendship with the European nations and serve economic interests in Southeast Asia in the short-run, but which would fail to meet the expectations of the United States as a world leader; 2) urge that the Netherlands and France place their colonies under international trusteeship, which would make clear American leadership and would be satisfactory to nationalists, but would result in some short-term loss of prestige for France and the Netherlands; 3) pressure for reform short of trusteeship, which would have the advantages of the second alternative but would be less offensive to the European powers and would enable the United States to protect its interests better than under a trusteeship arrangement. Implicitly, it was suggested that the third alternative—which essentially reinforced Vincent's October 20 statement—offered the best means for the realization of American objectives. And a few days later, Abbot Low Moffat of the Division of Southeast Asian Affairs, urged that the United States, "with a view to protecting the security, interests, and influence of Western powers in that section of Asia" should press the French and Dutch to make commitments toward full self-government within a specified time.[5]

The questioning of Yost, Moffat, and others represented a continuation of the struggle between European and Asian officers for dominance in formulating policy. The priorities given to European problems were reflected in the policymaking apparatus, where officers in the Division of Southeast Asian Affairs working with the French, British, or Dutch colonies shared responsibilities for policy recommendations with officers from the Office of European Affairs. Vincent, as director of the Office of Far Eastern Affairs to which the Division of Southeast Asian Affairs was subordinate, reported to the Secretary and Undersecretary through Assistant Secretary James Dunn, who was a strong and influential "Europe firster." Asian desk officers did manage to disassociate the United States from certain aspects of the European restoration. For political as well as military reasons, the American presence at SEAC headquarters was reduced to a liaison section. Repeatedly the deference to the colonial powers was questioned, but the imperatives of the postwar "Europe first" strategy, reflected in the politics of the State Department, gave a decided advantage to those favoring a limited role in Southeast Asia.[6]

However ineffective American policy proved to be in the initial phases of the Indonesian and Indochinese revolutions, U.S. objectives elsewhere in Southeast Asia were generally being realized. As will be discussed in the next chapter, the United States fulfilled its commitment to Philippine independence and established a relationship with the Philippine Republic which assured a predominant American political and economic influence. Also, the State Department pursued the longstanding determination to achieve lenient peace terms for Thailand. Despite continued British opposition, the United States was instrumental in the emergence of a strengthened, independent Thailand. American political influence became an increasingly important factor in Bangkok. (The development of the American–Thai relationship will be discussed in chapter 8.)

## The War and Nationalism in Southeast Asia

The conditions in Southeast Asia at the time of the Japanese surrender and the impact of nearly four years of Japanese imperialism in the area provided impetus for nationalist revolutions. When the imperial government in Tokyo sued for peace, its armies still controlled Thailand, Indochina, Malaya, and the greater part of Indonesia. Among the regions of Southeast Asia, only in Burma and the Philippines, New Guinea and some parts of Borneo had the Japanese been defeated and forced to retreat. The arrival of Allied occupation units was delayed by the decision not to enter into agreements with Japanese territorial commanders before Japan signed the general surrender document; that event occurred on September 2. Also, the British were obliged to change their military plans very quickly; the anticipated prolonged struggle to liberate the region gave way to responsibility for immediately occupying an area with a population of 128 million and disarming some 750,000 Japanese forces. The British gave first priority to liberating their own colony Malaya.[7] SEAC units did not reach Saigon until September 12 and it was another two weeks before they landed in Indonesia. The British were in a favorable position to reassert control over Burma where the Japanese had been in retreat and in Malaya, but the prolonged period between the Japanese surrender in mid-August and the arrival of SEAC forces in Saigon and Batavia facilitated the emergence of nationalist challenges to French and Dutch authority.

It would, however, be a mistake to attribute the rise of nationalism in Indonesia and Indochina to the "power vacuum" resulting from the delay in the Allied occupation. The strength of the native elites was principally a consequence of the war, especially the polices of the Japanese. After all, the British, despite their well-established position in Burma at the war's end, faced as determined and strong a nationalist movement there as the Dutch and French encountered in their colonies.[8]

The changes brought by the war almost defy generalization, since the prewar political status of the countries in the region varied considerably and the nature of Japanese dominance differed depending on local conditions and wartime exigenecies. With some important qualifications, however, Japanese imperialism stimulated political change in fundamental ways: destroying the myth of Western superiority; following policies which caused local populations to shift from initial pro-Japanese to strongly anti-Japanese sentiment; providing experience in administration, politics, and military affairs; encouraging social upheavals which led to the emergence of new elites; and accelerating, in general, the nationalistic impulse. On close examination, each of these generalizations has certain limitations. Events of the early twentieth century, especially the Russo-Japanese War and the First World War, had begun the erosion of Western superiority. As a result, imperialism had been challenged, especially in Burma, the East Indies, and the Philippines. The popular reaction to the Japanese varied, as evidenced by the prevalence of collaboration in the Philippines and the East Indies, and the importance of that issue in both countries after the war. On the other hand, in Burma, collaborators were quickly discredited. In Indochina, prior to March 1945, French collaboration with the Japanese reduced native resistance to the Japanese. The extent of political experience varied widely from the opportunities afforded by the nominal grants of independence to the Philippines and Burma in 1943, and the extensive co-option of native leadership in the administration of the Netherland East Indies, to the limited period of Indochinese independence and native political involvement following the March 1945 coup. Japanese dominance encouraged social revolution and the emergence of new political elites, but for various reasons. Whereas the principal emerging nationalist leadership in the East Indies was provided by an elite that had collaborated with the Japanese, elsewhere, notably in Burma and Indochina, postwar leadership was seized by groups that had opposed the Japanese. Thus, while Japanese imperialism strenghtened nationalism, it was in diverse ways. And in the case of the Philippines, Japanese dominance did not bring significant social changes and failed to stimulate anti-American sentiment.[9]

The political upheavals in the East Indies and Indochina were of the most far-reaching consequence for the United States. In both countries, colonial powers had suppressed nationalism before the war, but the interlude of Japanese rule provided opportunities for a resurgent nationalism. At war's end, nationalist leadership in both countries proclaimed independence and prepared to resist the reestablishment of colonial authority.

In the East Indies, the Japanese fostered in various ways the development of Indonesian nationalism. After purging the Dutch from the civil adminstration, they gave positions to Indonesians, many of whom had been imprisoned by the Dutch. As the war turned against Japan, its military administration granted additional concessions and opened more high-level positions to Indonesians. While the Japanese never fulfilled the promise of independence, their policies enabled Sukarno to consolidate his leadership of the nationalist movement and to become its symbol. The emerging nationalist elite benefitted from many of Japan's actions. The Japanese made Indonesian the national language throughout the archipelago, introduced extensive propaganda techniques, and established mass political organizations and special schools that were directed toward the nation's youth. The development of regular military and paramilitary organizations provided the Indonesians with the essential force to assert their claim to independence. By 1945, 62,000 Indonesians were in regular army units, while another 230,000 were in youth paramilitary groups. Beyond these specific policies, the Japanese notably brought a new style to Indonesian politics—centered on the dramatization of politics, rituals of state, and patriotism—which contrasted sharply with the prewar routine and remained a major characteristic of the subsequent revolution.[10]

Whatever its concessions to Indonesian nationalism, Japanese imperialism was inefficient, corrupt, ruthless, and brutal. This led to increasingly strong resentment of the Japanese. In some ways, Sukarno benefitted from the growth of anti-Japanese sentiment. For instance, the rural Indonesians' antagonism toward Japan resulting from confiscation of food and conscription into forced labor provided the opportunity for Sukarno, utilizing techniques introduced by the Japanese and their encouragement of his activities outside urban centers, to build a strong following. Yet the prevalence of anti-Japanese feeling made the policy of collaboration dangerous, especially as Tokyo delayed independence. Sukarno's claim that Indonesian aspirations would be served by Japan was challenged by the underground, led by Sutan Sjahrir and Amir Sjarifuddin.

When the war suddenly ended, Sukarno took the initiative, and on August 17, proclaimed Indonesian independence. Within three weeks, a constitution providing for a cabinet government was completed. By the time the first British units landed on September 29, the Republic had gained predominance as it had won the support of virtually all important political groups, including the underground. The popular reception to independence was almost universally enthusiastic. Prior to the British arrival, the Japanese were under instructions to preserve order, and while anxious to avoid actions which would antagonize the Allies, Japanese authorities provided moral and material assistance to the Indonesians. The outpouring of popular support for the revolution was so prevalent that it virtually defied any effort at control.[11]

The "August Revolution " in Indochina stemmed from a different background than the nationalist revolution in Indonesia. Its leadership was provided by a Communist-dominated, pro-Allied coalition which had emerged from French collaboration with Japan and the Japanese coup of March 1945. By the end of the war, the Viet Minh front not only dominated the nationalist movement but was able to establish political control over Vietnam.

The Indochina Communist Party Executive Committee headed by Ho Chi Minh organized the Viet Minh in May 1941 as a loose coalition of various political groups. Communist influence in Indochinese politics had long been significant, dating to the mid-1920s. In 1930–31, the Indochina Communist party had organized widespread strikes and rallies of peasants and workers encompassing all the provinces of Vietnam. Following its subsequent suppression by the French, the Indochina Communist party fell into inactivity until the "popular front" government in France facilitated its reemergence as a less militant group calling for democratic reform and downplaying independence and land redistribution. Then with the collapse of the popular front in late 1939, the French again suppressed the communists, imprisoning thousands and causing others to flee to southern China for sanctuary. The fall of France and Japan's persistent coercion of the French administration in Indochina provided the opportunity for the Indochina Communist party to establish a broadly based nationalist organization calling for resistance to the Japanese and independence from the French.[12]

The Viet Minh developed gradually from 1941 until early 1945. It sought to collaborate with the Kuomintang and intelligence units in China, but had little success. Several Vietnamese political groups in exile in southern China refused to join the Viet Minh. Yet it emerged as the dominant force in Vietnamese politics, facilitated by the weakness of and divisions among the noncollaborating parties. The Viet Minh also began extensive political activities in the mountainous regions of northern Vietnam near the China border, coming to exercise effective political control over much of that area. By late 1944, it had built the nucleus of an armed force.[13]

The Japanese coup of March 9, 1945, was the most decisive factor in the emergence of the Viet Minh, for it eliminated the French colonial regime and awakened a sense of patriotism among the Vietnamese. Prior to the coup, few Vietnamese in the central and southern regions of the country had been aware of the Viet Minh, but in the ensuing five months its activities and influence extended throughout the country to such an extent that it rather easily took power when the Japanese surrendered. The Viet Minh established a network of revolutionary committees, dispatched cadres throughout Vietnam, and expanded its guerrilla activities. Even the nominally independent, superficially pro-Japanese government established after the coup was susceptible to the appeal of the Viet Minh. Although Emperor Bao Dai in proclaiming Vietnam's independence promised cooperation with Japan, large numbers of the Vietnamese who filled the administrative postions vacated by the French actually detested the Japanese. They sought to exploit the situation in order to eliminate the French, and were thus easily drawn into support of the Viet Minh. The Viet Minh also drew massive support because of its response to the famine that gripped northern and central Vietnam, resulting in widespread starvation and death. Through its propaganda and actions, the Viet Minh effectively linked the devastation of the countryside with the deprivations imposed by the French and Japanese.[14]

The collapse of the Japanese provided the opportunity for the "August Revolution." When news of the Japanese surrender reached Indochina on August 13, the Viet Minh moved quickly to seize political control. It had little difficulty: Hanoi was taken without resistance on August 19, followed by Hue on the twenty-third, and Saigon three days later. With the Viet Minh's political ascendancy established, Bao Dai abdicated; in his Act of Abdication, Bao Dai stated his support of the new regime and called upon the people to support it. On Auguse 29, Ho Chi Minh established a provisional government. On September 2, Ho spoke before half a million people on behalf of the Democratic Republic of Vietnam (DRV) and proclaimed the nation's independence.[15]

## The United States and the Vietnamese Revolution

The leadership of the nationalist revolutions in Indochina and Indonesia realized their assertions of independece were ultimately dependent upon the policies of the victorious Allies, especially the Americans. Unlike the Indonesian elite which had gambled on attaining its objectives through cooperation with Japan, the Viet Minh had identified with the Allied cause throughout the war and had established a working relationship with American intelligence units. Ho Chi Minh and other leaders anticipated that this collaboration would lead to official American support of Vietnamese nationalist aspirations.

It was the Japanese coup which drew the Americans and Viet Minh into a mutually beneficial alliance. They were more clearly fighting the same enemy than had been true so long as the anomalous French regime existed. Moreover, the OSS had lost its Free French intelligence sources in Indochina, the so-called "GTB network," as a result of the coup. Captain Charles Fenn, who was placed in charge of OSS operations in Indochina headquartered at Kunming in southern China, received instructions to establish a Vietnamese network. Fenn naturally turned toward the Viet Minh. Ho was in Kunming in early 1945 where he had been seeking, without success, ties with the Americans. The Viet Minh was known to the OSS and the Fourteenth American Air Force for its assistance in rescuing an American pilot who had been forced down over northern Vietnam. The most compelling reason for working with the Viet Minh was that it was known to be the most influential of the various Vietnamese political groups in southern China. Accordingly, in meetings on March 17 and 20, 1945, Ho and Fenn worked out arrangements whereby the OSS agreed to provide radio equipment and a small amount of arms and ammunition in return for Viet Minh assistance in collecting intelligence, sabotaging Japanese installations, and rescuing American pilots. The Americans provided Ho with air transportation to the Vietnam border, and the following month OSS personnel joined the Viet Minh at Ho's headquarters fifty miles north of Hanoi.[16]

The Viet Minh–American collaboration quickly extended beyond intelligence, sabotage, and rescue operations and came to have political implications. From the time the first OSS units arrived in Vietnam as part of Operation Deer Mission, the Viet Minh cultivated American friendship. When the OSS sought to cooperate as well with Free French sources and to bring French personnel into Vietnam, the Viet Minh objected, maintaining that it would not participate in any operations  involving the French. After OSS teams had been working in Vietnam for nearly two months, Major Allison Thomas, who was in charge of Deer Mission, parachuted into Ho's headquarters on July 16. The Viet Minh enthusiastically received Thomas and his party, but insisted that a French lieutenant who accompanied Thomas be returned to the Vietnam-China border. When Thomas arrived, Ho was in a very weak condition. The OSS provided medication and treatment, which may have saved his life.[17] As he recovered, Ho had extended conversations with Thomas, who was impressed with Ho's commitment to independence. Like nearly all of the Americans who had contact with Ho and the Viet Minh in 1945, Thomas was impressed by the Vietnamese determination to achieve independence and shared their anti-colonial and anti-French prejudices. After his first meeting with Ho, Thomas recommended to his superiors: "Forget the Communist Body. Viet Minh League is *not* Communist. Stands for freedom and reforms from French harshness."[18] And a few days later in transmitting to Kunming a list of Viet Minh grievances against the French, Thomas affirmed the strength of the Viet Minh and that it was "not Communist or Communist controlled or Communist led."[19]

For the Viet Minh, the contacts with the Americans ended years of isolation. Allied promises of self-determination had been known, but they had been remote and tempered by the Viet Minh's difficult relationship with the Chinese government. Suddenly the Viet Minh had a working relationship with a group of Americans who seemed to embody anticolonialism and to promise that the French would not be permitted to return. The enthusiastic reception given to the Americans blended with the expectation of Allied support for Vietnamese aspirations. For Ho Chi Minh in particular, the American example of independence and the enlightened colonial policy in the Philippines led to a strong ideological affinity.[20]

When the war abruptly ended, the Americans in Indochina continued their cooperation with the Viet Minh as it moved to establish control and its claim to independence. This phase of the American-Viet Minh relationship has been the subject of considerable writing, reflecting two divergent viewpoints. A "French school," which includes a number of participants in the restoration of French authority, has expressed indignation over the American support of the Viet Minh. From this perspective, the United States has been held responsible for "making" Ho Chi Minh and thus contributing to postwar French frustration. On the other hand, a "lost opportunity" interpretation has been developed by Americans who reflect a liberal anticolonial tradition. The contacts of the few Americans with the Viet Minh and the strong friendship and coincidence of interests between the two groups formed the basis for official U.S. support of the DRV. In the long run, the United States could have established a strong working-relationship with an independent, albeit Communist-dominated government, that would have remained oriented toward the West in order to achieve independence from China. Accordingly, the developments of late 1945, especially the abortive Viet Minh bid for American recognition, constituted a "lost opportunity" for the United States.[21] Whether the United States exerted too much influence (as the "French school" avers) or not enough (as the "lost opportunity" holds), the American presence in Indochina in late 1945 provided a unique opportunity to comprehend the nationalist upheavals that were sweeping across postwar Asia.

For the Americans in Vietnam in August 1945 there was little choice but to associate with the Viet Minh. They paid little attention to the political implications of their activities. Diplomatic officials remained uncertain about State Department objectives in Indochina. The consul at Kunming, for instance, suggested on August 16 that, in view of the reports of anticipated Vietnamese resistance to a French restoration, the United States should be prepared for joint administration with Britain and China.[22] Whatever commitment the State Department may have made to recognize French sovereignty was unknown to the Americans in Indochina, most of whom apparently assumed that in Indochina, and elsewhere, the United States was planning an end to imperialism. The pro-Viet Minh disposition of the Americans was strongly reinforced by the mounting evidence of its popular support. In town after town in Tonkin, Americans observed the reception for the Viet Minh as its units liberated the area from the Japanese. Inevitably the Americans became identified with the "August Revolution." In some towns in Tonkin, the Americans came and were welcomed with the Viet Minh. Also, they provided Ho Chi Minh, at his request, with a draft of the Declaration of Independence which he used as a model in drafting the Vietnamese declaration.[23]

From the French perspective, the American attitude toward the reestablishment of French authority was especially aggravating. The State Department, as well as the OSS, appeared hostile to French interests. As soon as Japan's surrender became known, the French began pressing the American embassy in Chungking to permit their participation in the Chinese occupation of northern Indochina; it was maintained that the entry of unaccompanied Chinese units would cause "serious trouble" and also would "greatly prejudice" Sino-French relations.[24] The State Department attempted to dismiss the French representations on the grounds that the occupation and surrender lacked substantial political significance, but the Chinese government did agree on August 17 that some 5,000 French troops which had been evacuated from Indochina would return with the Chinese occupation forces.[25]

In the meantime, the compelling concern of the French, especially Major Jean Sainteny, the Resistance hero whom deGaulle had sent to head the French military mission at Kunming, was establishing French authority in Tonkin. When news of the Japanese surrender reached Kunming, Sainteny urged General Wedemeyer and OSS headquarters to assist in the landing of a French mission at Hanoi. For a week, the Americans delayed: Wedemeyer maintained that his role in Indochina was still restricted by Roosevelt's November 3, 1944 order. Sainteny threatened to find an alternative means of reaching Tonkin. Finally, the Americans relented and on August 22, a five man mission headed by Sainteny was flown to Hanoi, accompanied by an OSS team under the leadership of Major Archimedes Patti. By the time they reached Hanoi, the Viet Minh was in control. The Japanese, with the apparent approval of Patti, insisted that the Sainteny mission and other French citizens in Hanoi restrict their movements for their safety. (The Patti mission was sent to liberate Allied prisoners of war and thus needed the cooperation of the Japanese).[26] This humiliating return to

Vietnam—beginning with the dependence upon Americans, then being accompanied by the Patti group, and finally ending in virtual house arrest in Hanoi—embittered Sainteny. He was convinced, as were many other Frenchmen, of a "collusive Allied maneuver with the purpose of throwing the French out of Indochina."[27]

The ideological tie between the Americans and Viet Minh—or "collusion" from the French perspective—had been fully evident during the "August Revolution." The revolutionary planning of the Viet Minh included a calculated appeal for American support. At a meeting on August 15, the Viet Minh adopted a statement (which the OSS transmitted to the State Department and White House):

> The Central Committee wishes to make known to the United States Government—that the Indo-Chinese people first of all desire the independence of Indo-China, and are hoping that the United States, as a champion of democracy, will assist her in securing this independence in the following manner: (1) prohibiting, or not assisting the French to enter Indo-China; (2) keeping the Chinese under control, in order that looting and pillaging will be kept to a minimum; (3) sending technical advisors to assist the Indo-Chinese to exploit the resources of the land; and (4) developing those industries that Indo-China is capable of supporting.
>
> In conclusion, the Indo-Chinese would like to be placed on the same status as the Philippines for an undetermined period.[28]

The Declaration of Independence proclaimed at Hanoi on September 2, referred to the precedents of the American and French (but not Russian) revolutions and also held the following expectation:

> We are convinced that the Allied nations which at Teheran and San Francisco have acknowledged the principles of self-determination and equality of nations, will not refuse to acknowledge the independence of Viet Nam. A people who have courageously opposed French domination for more than eighty years, a people

who have fought side by side with the Allies against the fascists during these last years, such a people must be free and independent.[29]

Behind these appeals, however, was a strain of realism. At the revolutionary planning sessions of August 13-15, the Viet Minh considered it vital to win either Russian or American support. At that moment, the proximity of the Americans made that alternative seem more promising. Yet it was also observed that: "The contradictions between Britain, the United States, and France on the one side and the Soviet Union on the other, might lead the Americans to make concessions to the French and allow them to come back to Indochina."[30] And Ho, in a letter to Fenn, while optimistic about American sympathy for Vietnamese independence, was prepared for a struggle: "if we want to get a sufficient share [of freedom and democracy] we have still to fight."[31]

As the Viet Minh leadership recognized, independence was "quite fragile."[32] Despite the extent of its popular support, the DRV faced serious problems including a continuing food crisis, a lack of financial resources, the weakness of its army, and the arrival of British and Chinese occupation forces. By late August, the 150,000 man Chinese army had crossed into Indochina and within a week of the proclamation of independence, its units entered Hanoi. At first, the Viet Minh was hostile to the Chinese, organizing demonstrations and protests. This response developed from the Kuomintang's wartime opposition to the Viet Minh and its cultivation of the pro-Chinese rival nationalist parties: Dong Minh Hoi and Viet Nam Quoc Dan Dang. With the arrival of British units in the south on September 12, the Viet Minh's political base in the Saigon area, which had just recently been established, was undermined. Besieged in the south, the Viet Minh found it expedient to seek accommodation with the Chinese. General Lu Han, who headed the Chinese occupation army, was antagonistic toward the French and favorably disposed toward the Viet Minh. Accordingly, the Chinese army, which had the potential of crushing the DRV, provided important material and psychological support at a critical time. The Chinese turned over to the Viet Minh vast quantities of arms and war material taken from the Japanese. In addition, they humiliated the French by denying General Marcel Allesandri, whom de Gaulle had designated his representative, a role in the September 28 ceremonies marking the official Japanese surrender, while inviting the Viet Minh to participate. Much of the Chinese contempt for the French was derived from lingering resentment over the French capitulation to the Japanese in 1940–41. Allesandri, in particular, was blamed for having advised acceptance of the Japanese demands. The assistance provided by the Chinese army proved crucial in strengthening the Viet Minh's position in the north.[33]

Beyond the occupation, the Chinese, however, offered no hope for the Viet Minh. Lu Han's actions were inconsistent with the official policy of the Kuomintang, which moved toward accommodation with France. This retreat from wartime anticolonialism resulted from the Kuomintang's precarious internal situation which discouraged any adventurism in Indochina, Chiang Kai-shek's desire to avoid actions which would cause divisions among the Allies, and an interest in special economic concessions. Thus, as the war ended, the Chinese government assured the French of its recognition of French sovereignty in Indochina.[34] Clearly the Chinese were prepared to ignore the DRV in return for a favorable economic position in the country.

The British occupation in the south enabled the French to reestablish a political foothold. Mountbatten was determined to keep SEAC from involvement in any political confrontation between the French and Vietnamese. As a result, the occupation force was limited to key areas and it was not responsible for assuring French sovereignty nor for the maintenance of law and order. To hold to that limited function, SEAC relied on accompanying French units and former French authorities still in Indochina to administer the region south of the sixteenth parallel. The French, however, were able to provide only about 1,500 men when the occupation began on September 12. From the perspective of Major General Douglas Gracey, who was in charge of the occupation, the situation in Saigon quickly became intolerable. The Viet Minh claimed control but seemed unable to maintain order. Finally, on September 23, he encouraged the French to seize control of the administration with the result that a French government was reestablished in Saigon. In recognition of the general strength of the Viet Minh and its effective control of most of the southern area, Mountbatten urged that the French begin negotiations immediately.[35]

The assertion of French authority resulted in protest, demonstrations, and fighting in Saigon, events which marked the beginning of the long struggle between the French and Vietnamese. Among the first casualties of this warfare was Colonel A.P. Dewey, head of the OSS mission in southern Indochina. The death of Dewey symbolized the ironies of the American position. He had been known for his sympathy with the Viet Minh and had disapproved of the French seizure of power. Furthermore, Gracey had been antagonized by Dewey's claim to diplomatic status and the French were reportedly prepared to request his recall. Yet, according to the official investigation into his death, Dewey was almost certainly killed by Vietnamese who had set up an ambush directed randomly against any white man.[36]

With the British accommodating the return of the French in the south and the Chinese government preparing to negotiate with the French, the Viet Minh looked increasingly to the United States for support. In September, additional American personnel entered northern Vietnam. Brigadier General Phillip Gallagher headed the Combat Section of the South China Command, which accompanied Lu Han's army. Another team headed by General Stephen Nordlinger was responsible for repatriation of American prisoners of war held in Annam and Tonkin. Also, members of the Joint Army-Navy Intelligence Service landed in Hanoi. The Viet Minh cultivated the friendship of these Americans, who immediately treated the DRV as a legitimate government. The behavior of the Americans, which included discouraging the display of the French flag since it would be insulting to the Vietnamese, was humiliating to the French. The establishment, in mid-October, of a Vietnam-America Friendship Association marked the culmination of the American fascination with the Viet Minh. It was launched with an elaborate inaugural ceremony in Hanoi attended by several Americans and officials of the DRV. The affair was broadcast by Viet Minh radio. Gallagher was among the speakers, endorsing the association's plan to institute an educational exchange program. As the festivities went on, Gallagher and his aide-de-camp even rendered a song for the benefit of those assembled.[37]

The American affinity for the Viet Minh—derived initially from collaboration late in the war and the anticolonial sympathies of the Americans—came to be based principally upon respect for the Viet Minh's political organization and popular strength. The Americans were aware of the Comminist domination of the Viet Minh and, in particular, of Ho's personal Communist history, but they accepted his repeated assertion that the overriding priority was independence from the French. In sum, he emerged, from the American perspective, as, above all, a nationalist.[38] In their reports to Washington, American personnel repeatedly underscored their high regard for the Viet Minh. For instance, following an interview with Ho, an OSS officer concluded: "My personal opinion is that Mr. Ho Chi Minh is a brilliant and capable man, completely sincere in his opinions. I believe that when he speaks, he speaks for his people, for I have travelled throughout Tonkin province, and found that in that area people of all classes are imbued with the same spirit and determination as their leader."[39] With respect to the question of the Viet Minh's communist leadership and its international implications, another OSS agent wrote: "The Viet Minh is using Communistic methods in many things, such as the living of revolutionaries in the jungle, and in social situations, but does not politically embrace Russian Communism."[40]

While OSS reports following the British occupation called attention to the weakened position of the Viet Minh in the Saigon area,[41] Americans continued to emphasize the widespread support for the Viet Minh and the extent of pro-American sentiment. In an extended analysis during a two-week visit to Hanoi in October, Arthur Hale of the United States Information Service (USIS) observed:

> The enthusiasm with which liberated peoples greeted the American troops in various parts of the world is by now an old story. But nowhere did the coming of the Americans, in this case a mere handful of them, mean so much as they did to the population of northern Indo China. To Annamites, our coming was the symbol of liberation not from Japanese occupation but from decades of French colonial rule. For the Annamite government considered the United States as the principal champion of the rights of small peoples. . . . The people were made aware of our policy in the Philippines, and much of the doctrine and policy of the Vietnam Provisional Government was shaped in our own democratic formulae of government at home and in the Philippines. This was perhaps without profound analysis of the economic background of our relations with the Philippines. It was enough that it represented a political program which the Annamites considered ideal for themselves.[42]

In addition to their opinions and their extensive reporting on the political situation, Americans also transmitted a number of Viet Minh appeals for U.S. recognition and support. Repeatedly, Ho Chi Minh sought to impress upon Washington the anticolonial, pro-Allied bases of the DRV. The overriding objective remained gaining some sign of American recognition of his government's legitimacy. Upon learning of plans to establish an Allied commission on postwar problems in the Far East, Ho appealed to Truman for DRV representation, arguing that by their betrayal of Indochina to the Japanese in 1941, the French had forfeited any moral claim to govern the country. In another message, he expressed regret over the killing of Dewey and reassured Truman of the Vietnamese admiration for the American people. In still another appeal, Ho reviewed the Allied commitments to anticolonialism and called for United Nations recognition of Vietnamese independence. He further requested that the Far Eastern Commission investigate the Anglo-French policies in southern Vietnam. Shortly afterward, the DRV

requested United Nations initiative to achieve a political settlement based upon the principles of self-determination. An accompanying official pamphlet, outlining the foreign policy of the
DRV, reiterated the appeals of the declaration of independence
and the determination to achieve friendly relations with the
Western powers. In messages of early November, Ho sought a
cultural exchange program with the United States and the assistance of the United Nations Relief and Rehabilitation Administration in meeting the war-induced famine. Finally, Ho warned
that the Vietnamese were prepared to resist a French restoration; a colonial war would be the responsibility of France.[43] In
Washington, Ho's cables, received through military channels,
were duly filed at the Department of State, but went
unanswered.[44]

Ho Chi Minh's messages in the fall of 1945 and the lack of
any response from Washington symbolized the dual character of
American involvement in Indochina. For while the OSS and
other Americans tacitly recognized the DRV and gave it moral
encouragement, the direction of policy as formulated at the
State Department, did not question the resumption of French
sovereignty. Indeed the Americans in Indochina apparently were
ignorant of guidelines for U.S. personnel that Acting Secretary
of State Dean Acheson had transmitted on August 30, reiterating the acceptance of French sovereignty. Meeting with
de Gaulle at the White House a day earlier, Truman had reassured the French leader that the United States did not question the restoration of French authority in Indochina. Acheson's
statement, however, was not conveyed to the embassy in Chungking until October 5, and it was through China that American
communications and personnel reached Indochina.[45] It was not
until late October, following John Carter Vincent's outline of
America's response to the colonial struggles in Indochina and
Indonesia, that actions in the field effectively reflected official
policy.

British and French strategy and policy, as well as developments in Indochina, influenced the definition of American
objectives set forth by Vincent. The British repeatedly made

clear their intention to assume a limited role. This reflected apprehension about being caught in the middle of a colonial war. Also, the British remained uncertain of American plans in Indochina and feared being caught in Franco-American differences.[46] In early October, as British efforts to secure an effective cease-fire between the French and Vietnamese failed, they concluded a civil affairs agreement with the French, which made clear the limited responsibilities of the SEAC units.[47] The general effect of British policy, which was well-founded considering the primacy of their interests elsewhere, increased the pressures on the United States. The British determination to hand responsibilities over to the French when the French and Viet Minh were already fighting left the United States as the only possible moderating influence. Had the British interest in Indochina approximated its interests in Indonesia, Anglo-American cooperation might have been a restraint on both the French and the Viet Minh.

At the same time the French also influenced American policymaking, especially through promises of liberal economic and political objectives, from which America would benefit. For instance, Jean Chauvel of the French Foreign Office spoke to Ambassador Jefferson Caffery in Paris of concessions in Indochina and likened the economic development there to prewar Shanghai. He maintained that: "in the coming difficult period in the Far East, Indochina will be the only real foothold on the Asiatic mainland for the occidental democracies (France, Great Britain, and the United States)."[48] In his meeting with Truman on August 29, de Gaulle offered assurances of plans to take steps leading to the early independence of Indochina.[49] In addition, French officials expressed determination to send forces quickly into Indochina; they made no effort to conceal their antagonism toward the Chinese occupation units and their disapproval of the activities of the Americans in Vietnam.[50] Finally, the direction of American policy also reflected the considerable evidence of widespread opposition to the French. In this respect at least, the reports of American personnel had some effect for, together with other sources, they provided grounds for questioning the

French assertion that they could restore political control without a large-scale struggle.[51]

At the Department of State, the Indochina situation renewed the differences between the offices of European and Far Eastern Affairs. Vincent, accepting a proposal advanced by Abbot Low Moffat, of the Division of Southeast Asian Affairs (formerly the Division of Southwest Pacific Affairs) suggested that the United States and Britain establish a commission to investigate the conditions in Indochina. Pending the completion of this inquiry, no further French forces were to enter the country. The commission's report would serve as the basis for discussion among the Allied countries involved (Britain, China, France, the United States) and "Annamese elements." Acknowledging that the French would resent this intervention, Vincent argued that adverse French reaction was preferable to accepting a colonial war. The Far Eastern Affairs initiative, however, was strongly opposed by the Office of European Affairs, which believed that the French authority could be restored without a large military operation. The only effect of the proposed commission would be the ejection of the French, an eventuality which would be detrimental to the American interest in cultivating a strong France in Europe and Asia. The peoples of Indochina, furthermore, were not prepared to govern themselves. The European Affairs position prevailed within the department.[52] As a result, American interest was limited to the policy stated by Vincent on October 20: hope of peaceful agreement and willingness, if requested, to assist in negotiations.

The limited role for the United States defined in Vincent's speech was quickly symbolized, in succeeding weeks, by the withdrawal of nearly all of the American military and intelligence personnel. Their occupation-related missions having been accomplished, the various American units departed, much to the disappointment of the Viet Minh. American influence and prestige declined sharply.[53] On the reaction to Gallagher's announcement that his liason team was returning to China, Hale of the USIS commented: "Observer detected an attitude of disillusionment and disappointment on the part of government officials. And now that the French have refused to submit the Indo China question to any form of mediation on the grounds that it is an internal French problem, it would be interesting to know what affect our failure to act has had upon the Annamites' overwhelming good will toward us."[54]

While the American presence lessened, Ho refused to abandon his hope for U.S. support. On November 26, he sent still another appeal to the State Department calling for recognition in line with the ideals of Truman's Navy Day address.[55] He also befriended Frank White, who, as other Americans were leaving, arrived in Hanoi in mid-November to head a three-man OSS intelligence operation. In an extended conversation, Ho questioned whether Americans appreciated the Vietnamese determination to achieve independence. With respect to the Soviet Union, Ho conceded his admiration for the Russian Revolution but added that he was skeptical of whether the Soviets could contribute to the building of a new Vietnam. The United States, however, could provide the investment capital and technology which were especially needed.[56]

A state dinner given by Ho in mid-December dramatized the changing political situation in the country. His guests included Chinese army officers who were preparing to leave and a few French officers who had just arrived. In a breech of protocol, White was seated next to Ho. When the American pointed out that the higher ranking guests resented the arrangements, Ho replied: "Yes I can see that. But who else could I talk to?"[57]

By that time, the State Department was receiving reports from the Americans who had returned from Indochina. In separate interviews with Moffat and others on December 5, Nordlinger and Patti both emphasized the effectiveness of the Viet Minh government, their high regard for Ho's leadership, and the Viet Minh's capability of waging prolonged guerrilla warfare against the French.[58] Jane Foster, an OSS agent who had been in Saigon in October, reported on the Viet Minh's popular strength in the southern area and likewise stressed its potential for combatting the French through boycotts and guerrilla warfare. Also in a lengthy written report (referred to at points above), Hale underscored the popularity of the Viet Minh and the deep-seated antagonism against the French.[59]

Of greatest interest was Gallagher's report. Meeting on January 30, 1946 with Moffat, Charles S. Reed (who was Saigon Consul-designate), and several others, Gallagher presented the Vietnamese situation in more complicated terms. While acknowledging the popularity and effective organization of the Viet Minh, Gallagher questioned its capability of governing effectively or fighting successfully against the French. In the end, the French would crush any guerrilla campaign. Gallagher also stressed the Viet Minh's determination to resist French control. Ho Chi Minh would accept a compromise with the French only if other nations guaranteed and supervised a settlement. In reply to a question regarding the Communist nature of the Viet Minh, Gallagher maintained that, while Communist influence and tactics were obvious, the Viet Minh claimed to be principally interested in independence and "should not be labelled full-fledged doctrinaire communist."[60]

Whatever the impression in Washington of the reports of Patti, Hale, Gallahger, and others, State Department officials evidenced little concern about the character of the Viet Minh. Appraising Ho's communist and nationalist aspirations was not yet a major part of the formulation of the American response to the situation in Indochina. During the initial stages of the Vietnamese revolution, U.S. policy principally reflected an acceptance of French sovereignty and included only low-key statements on behalf of a moderate colonial restoration.

## Anglo-American Collaboration and Indonesian Revolution, 1945–1946

Upon their arrival in Indonesia, the British occupation units encountered a functioning Republic of Indonesia that enjoyed wide popular support. SEAC headquarters had not anticipated any difficulty in implementing the command's orders to occupy key towns as a means of controlling the Japanese, enforcing their surrender and disarmament, and rescuing Allied prisoners of war and interns. Recognizing the potential for Indonesian-Dutch conflict, Lieutenant General Sir Philip Christison, commander of the Allied forces, quickly pressed for a meeting between Dutch officials and Indonesian leaders and asked the Dutch to clarify their colonial plans. At Singapore, Mountbatten, with the backing of the Foreign Office, seconded the call for discussions. The Dutch, however, dismissesd the Republic as a product of Japanese imperialism comprised of collaborators and blamed its emergence on the British who had given the area low priority in their occupation plans. Acting on such assumptions, Dutch officials consistently discounted the viability of the Republic and held that a show of strength would reestablish Dutch authority. Lieutenant Governor Hubertus van Mook, who arrived on October 7 as the highest ranking Dutch official in the islands, came to regard talks with the Republican leaders as the only means of assuring British support until military units arrived from the Netherlands. The government at The Hague, however, forbade discussions with Sukarno, Hatta, or other "collaborators." When van Mook attended two British-arranged informal meetings in late October at which Sukarno was present, the Dutch government pointedly made clear that, contrary to reports in the press, no authorized negotiations had begun.

Despite their efforts at promoting negotiations, the British came under criticism from the Indonesians. In particular, the occupation of key towns in Java was seen as securing a foothold for the Dutch. In late October, ill-prepared Indonesian units resisted the British effort to occupy Surabaya in eastern Java. Only after prolonged fighting, and with support from the air and sea, did the British gain control of Surabaya. The battle underscored, however, the vulnerability of the British and the popularity of the Republic. Coinciding with the Dutch obstinance regarding discussions with Republican leaders, the Surabaya incident encouraged British reconsiderations of their objectives and strategy.[61]

From the outset, American policymakers inclined toward following British leadership in the Indonesian situation. Based on OSS reports and other intelligence sources, Washington was cognizant of the strength of the Republic. State Department officials discounted the Dutch argument, advanced by Ambassador Alexander Loudon, that the British delay in reaching Indonesia had given rise to the Republic and that the Republican leaders were all collaborators and Communists.[62] The Vincent speech of October 20, while useful in clarifying the American position, also underscored the fundamental problem confronting the United States, as well as Britain, in mediating a conflict in which sovereignty was the basic issue. After the Vincent statement, the Dutch embassy immediately inquired about the procedure for American mediation and was relieved when Vincent offered assurances that the United States would consider requests only from the recognized territorial sovereign. Unaware of that condition, Sukarno cabled an appeal to Truman for early American mediation.[63] A few days later, the Republican government, in two of its earliest political manifestos, spoke further of the desirability of close cooperation with the United States, especially to facilitate economic development, and appealed for Western recognition of the Republic.[64]

In line with established policy, efforts were made to disassociate the United States from reimposition of imperial authority, but this was not followed consistently. At State Department insistence, the "USA" designation was removed from lend-lease materials used by occupying units in Indonesia and Indochina. Several Dutch requests for the purchase of arms and ammunition, and to transfer men and material on American ships were denied. On the other hand, the United States fulfilled a commitment, dating to 1943, to train and equip a Dutch marine force of 5,000 men. The Dutch were authorized to transfer from Surinam to Indonesia more than a million rounds of ammunition; this was allowed on the grounds that it had been acquired by purchase or through lend-lease before the end of the war. Without consulting Washington, the United States Foreign Liquidation Commission in Manila sold surplus C-47 aircraft to the Dutch. Contrary to American understanding of lend-lease provisions, the British transferred aircraft, acquired through lend-lease, to a Dutch air squadron in the Indies. These inconsistent practices antagonized both sides. The Dutch questioned denials of support for their reassertion of American-recognized sovereignty. The Indonesians criticized the evidence of American equipment and supplies accompanying the British and eventually the Dutch. Republican leaders and other Asian nationalists, principally Jawaharlal Nehru in India, derided the removal of the "USA" designation from lend-lease items. And in Washington, a number of Congressmen questioned a policy whereby, through lend-lease and other means, the United States seemed to be underwriting imperialism.[65]

Within a month of the Vincent statement, it had become evident to State Department officials that it would be necessary to elaborate on American policy. After the Surabaya incident, the British appealed for American support of negotiations.[66] Changes in the Republican government seemed to improve those prospects. Leadership shifted toward younger socialist elements who had led the anti-Japanese underground; most notably this brought Sutan Sjahrir and Amir Sjarifuddin into greater prominence. Following an administrative reorganization which initiated a cabinet system, Sjahrir became Premier. His emergence lessened the stigma of collaboration which had plagued the Republic. Considering the British request as well as changes in Indonesia, the State Department, on November 20, approached the British about the advisability of an American initiative to The Hague, which would urge a "broad-minded and positive approach."[67]

The British responded that the Dutch seemed willing to meet with the Republicans, but a major problem was the Republican leadership's inability to control its extremist followers; this had resulted in repeated clashes between the British and Indonesians in eastern Java. Ambassador Halifax proposed an American press release, addressed to both sides, expressing hope for renewed conversations on a cooperative basis. At the State Department, detailed reports from American personnel recently returned from Indonesia reinforced the momentum for an American initive. Foster, who had lived in Indonesia and was familiar with the language, reported on her meetings with Republican leaders as well as people in the countryside. Lieutenant Colonel K. K. Kennedy of the Material Inspection Service had extended conversations with Sukarno and other leaders. Foster and Kennedy emphasized the Indonesian determination for independence and the unwillingness to accept a transition period under any auspices except that of the United Nations. They would resist "tutelage" under the Dutch. With the European and Far Eastern desks agreeing that the British suggestion offered an appropriate American initiative, the State Department on December 19 issued a brief statement which expressed concern about the Indonesian situation and called upon both sides for a realistic, broad-minded, and fair approach.[68]

Under Western pressure, the Dutch and Indonesians resumed their discussions and they continued intermittently throughout 1946, but within a context of changing political conditions. Most importantly, the Dutch gradually reestablished a military foothold. As they returned, SEAC forces withdrew and transferred authority—a process completed on November 30, 1946. This reassertion of Dutch authority lessened Dutch dependence on the British, but at the same time the British commitment to withdraw by November 30 enabled London to exert strong pressure on the Republic to reach a settlement before that date.[69]

The Dutch-Indonesian dispute became a matter of international concern. At the first sessions of the United Nations Security Council, the emerging Cold War quickly surfaced when the government of Iran, with American support, filed a complaint charging Soviet interference in its internal affairs and calling for a United Nations investigation. Two days later on January 19, the Soviet Union and the Ukraine charged the British with unwarranted military actions in Greece and Indonesia. In the case of Indonesia, a resolution was introduced calling for an international investigation by a special commission on which the Soviet Union would be represented. While the Security Council followed American leadership and a month later dropped the resolution on Indonesia from its agenda on the grounds that negotiations had been resumed, the brief international attention given to the Indonesian question helped force the Dutch to issue proposals in early February which formed the basis of the renewed discussions. The consideration of the issue in the United Nations was significant. It demonstrated the Soviet Union's capacity to exploit the Western, especially American, dilemma over colonial issues. Also, the United States, in opposing the Ukranian resolution, pointedly did not question that the issue was a matter of United Nations jurisdiction. American policymakers refused to consider Indonesia as an internal Dutch problem, the basis of the subsequent Dutch challenge to United Nations intervention. The United States thus demonstrated support for the principle of international accountability on colonial issues that had been incorporated in the United Nations Charter.[70]

While the Soviet Union's action in the Security Council may have been a bit of Cold War maneuvering in response to the Iranian situation, it also occurred within a context of growing interest in the Southeast Asian revolutions. In late 1945, the Russian press had devoted considerable attention to the Indonesian and Indochinese struggles, with strong criticism of Western policies. In a widely reprinted lecture, Professor A. Guber, the leading Soviet authority on colonial issues, called attention to the failure of French and Dutch policies in Indochina and Indonesia and suggested that the revolts in those colonies could be traced to the failure to establish virtual autonomy as the United States had done in the Philippines. (Such implicit praise for American colonial policy did not last long.) Along similar lines, E. M. Zhukov, writing in the leading Soviet journal on foreign affairs, praised the Indonesian and Indochinese nationalist movements and foresaw United Nations trusteeship arrangements as a feasible alternative to colonial domination. The Soviets also apparently anticipated an Anglo-American division over the colonial issue. The British were consistently criticized for their role in Indonesia, but the Soviets anticipated that the pursuit of its economic interests would lead the United States to champion anticolonialism. These considerations were instrumental in the Soviet Union's general support at this time of broadly based nationalist parties, rather than local Communist parties.

On an official level, Soviet concern with the Indonesian situation was evident at the meeting of the Council of Foreign Ministers in December 1945 when Soviet Foreign Minster Vyachelsav Molotov suggested that informal discussions among the Council might facilitate a settlement. Finally, in the United Nations, the Soviets avoided reference to the Indonesian Republic or to the independence of Indonesia, speaking only of the "popular movement." This moderation may have been intended to avoid championing a government which was not especially sympathetic to the Soviet Union, but it may also have been intended to reduce Western objections to consideration of the Indonesian issue.[71]

The Republic suffered from political instability, which culminated in an abortive July 3, 1946 coup d'etat. Moderate leadership barely prevailed. The Sjahrir government encountered strong opposition to its domestic policies and efforts at negotiation. Its commitment to establish a parliamentary democracy had little support from the older more authoritarian nationalist groups, especially the Partai Nasional Indonesia, as well as much of the civil service. The leftist nationalists who had been instrumental in Sjahrir's rise to power were bitterly disappointed by his turn toward a cautious socialism and continuation of discussions with the Dutch. Under the leadership of Tan Malaka, an opposition popular front, the Persatuan Perdjuangan or Union of Resistance (PP), was established in early 1946. The PP called for ending negotiations until the Dutch recognized the country's independence and confiscating foreign property. Eventually Sjahrir established a rival popular front, which succeeded in drawing some conservative groups away from the PP. As it appeared that the Sjahrir group was building an effective coalition, the PP struck and attempted to overthrow the government. Contrary to the calculations of the revolutionaries, the army, under the leadership of General Sudirman, remained loyal and Sukarno, vested with emergency powers, resisted their demands. The "July 3 affair" had important ramifications. It signaled the decline of Sjahrir, despite the fact he formed the cabinet which took power on October 2 after three months of presidential government. His prestige and the size of his following had clearly lessened, and he had become increasingly dependent upon the more conservative parties. The only figure to gain prestige was Sukarno, who had been instrumental in the failure of the coup. In broader terms, the "July 3 affair" assured the predominance of those groups committed to negotiations (*diplomasi*) and the demise of the parties which had championed armed resistance and social revolution.[72]

The course of the negotiations and even the settlement itself underscored fundamental Dutch-Indonesian disagreements. Following meetings between the Dutch and British prime ministers and other high level officials in London at the end of 1945, the Netherlands on February 10, 1946, put forth a plan for a federal Commonwealth of Indonesia, with a balance distribution of power between regional authorities and a central administration to be headed by a representative of the Dutch Crown. In subsequent discussions with van Mook, Republican officials backed off from the original claim of jurisdiction over all of Indonesia in return for Dutch recognition of Republican authority over Java and Sumatra. Believing that a settlement was attainable, the Republic sent a delegation to the Netherlands in April, but found The Hague government inflexible, and especially being unwilling to recognize the Republican claim over Sumatra.

Meanwhile, as more Dutch troops were landing in Indonesia, the Dutch moved to consolidate their position in Borneo, Bankia, Billiton, and other areas being handed over by the British where the Republic was not entrenched and there existed strong anti-Javanese feeling. At the Malino Conference in late July, the Dutch began implementing the federal concept by establishing ties with traditional aristocratic elites who were willing to cooperate with the Netherlands to protect them from the Javanese-dominated Republic. To resume negotiations between the Dutch and Indonesians, the British dispatched Lord Killearn (Clark Kerr) as a mediator. Under his influence, the Linggadjati Agreement was finally reached, on November 15, 1946—just before the final British withdrawal. Both sides made important concessions. The Republic claim to de facto authority over Java and Sumatra was recognized. Both sides were to cooperate in the formation, by January 1, 1949, of a United States of Indonesia as a sovereign democratic state founded on a federal basis. Also by that date, a Netherlands-Indonesian Union was to be established. This was to be headed by the Queen of the Netherlands and would have its own bodies for foreign affairs, defense, and some financial matters. Much of the Linggadjati Agreement was vague, but in general it favored the Netherlands. For the Republic, it represented a retreat from the pretentions of a year earlier. Whatever the limitations of the compromise as a workable solution, the British had forced both sides to recognize realities. The Dutch, for the moment at least, accepted the fact that the prewar status quo could not be reestablished; the Republic acknowledged that complete independence could not be immediately attained.[73]

While supporting British efforts to bring about a settlement, the United States assumed a limited role in Indonesia at this time. Much of the information reaching the Department of State suggested deferring to the Dutch. In particular, the reports of Walter Foote, the consul at Batavia who had long service in the Indies before the war, reflected a strong pro-Dutch bias. He criticized the British for fostering the Republic and enhancing their own imperial interests. The British intended, Foote was convinced, to establish control over Sumatra. The Republican government was elitist and out of touch with the majority of the population which was apolitical. Sjahrir concealed his true ideology ("halfway between Communist and left-wing Socialist") to avoid antagonizing the United States.[74] Officials in Washington, however, questioned Foote's assessments. Extensive reports from two military officers and a Department of Agriculture official, all of whom returned from Indonesia in the late spring of 1946, somewhat offset Foote's views. They stressed the decline of pro-American sentiment and argued that only immediate action in support of the Republic would keep Indonesia tied to the West. Otherwise Russian prestige, enhanced already by the Soviet Union's stand in the United Nations, would increase.[75] At the State Department, such concern about the Soviet Union's position became important, especially in the summer of 1946 when the Dutch-Indonesian talks were at a standstill. As the Russian press showed considerable interest in Indonesia and spoke of the issue being raised again in the United Nations, the State Department urged the Dutch to take a moderate and flexible approach. That was seen as essential to resuming negotiations, which would be the most effective means of keeping the question out of the United Nations. While the Dutch subsequently did bring forth proposals which led to the Linggadjati Agreement, many of their officials, including Ambassador Loudon in Washington, maintained that Western prestige was dependent upon the Dutch presence and that concessions to the Republic only enhanced the likelihood of Russian intrigue and influence.[76]

The State Department welcomed the Linggadjati Agreement and supported its early ratification. In a memorandum prepared for Acting Secretary Dean Acheson's meeting with Loudon, Vincent outlined the American position: "In the opinion of this government, a failure on either side to ratify this agreement, or a protracted delay in ratification, will lead to a deterioriation in good will so severe as to render impossible the resumption of negotiations. In this latter event, it seems likely that open warfare will break out and that in any cause the most radical elements in Indonesia will seize power. Such a situation would provide the most favorable conditions for Communist infiltration."[77]

## The Origins of the French–Viet Minh War

In Indochina, the return of the French army reasserted French authority in the south and the consolidation of the DRV in the north brought serious efforts, by early 1946, for a French–Viet Minh agreement. Fully aware of the fundamental problems dividing the two parties, the United States supported such negotiations and welcomed the limited and flawed arrangements which were worked out beginning with the Ho-Sainteny agreement of March 6, 1946.

The establishment of French predominance in the area south of the sixteenth parallel was facilitated by the lack of a strong Viet Minh foothold in Cochin China and Mountbatten's interest in a transfer of authority to the French, which was gradually completed in early 1946. Admiral Georges Thierry d'Argenlieu, whom de Gaulle appointed as High Commissioner for Indochina, arrived in Saigon in late October 1945. He refused to recognize the extent to which the "August Revolution" had stirred nationalist sentiment throughout the country and looked upon the functioning government in Hanoi as an illegal regime. In Hanoi where he represented French authority Major Sainteny had become convinced that the DRV's popular support and effective administration necessitated a new colonial policy based upon cooperation with the Viet Minh.[78]

Late in 1945 as it became evident that the French were going to be reestablished in the south, Ho Chi Minh found it expedient to solidify the Viet Minh's position. In a tactical move, the Indochina Communist Party was dissolved, although it continued to function as an underground party. The Viet Minh began negotiations with the leaders of the Dong Minh Hoi and the Viet Nam Quoc Dan Dang (VNQDD), which finally resulted in an agreement whereby both parties were guaranteed representation in the National Assembly and positions in the cabinet. Popular elections were held in Viet Minh controlled areas of Tonkin, Annam, and Cochin China. The Viet Minh claimed 97 percent of the vote, but it did give the VNQDD and Dong Minh Hoi their promised seats in the legislature. The elections enabled the Viet Minh to claim a popular mandate and to isolate further its opposition.[79]

The consolidation of the DRV's position was made all the more necessary by the impending withdrawl of the Chinese occupation units. French-Chinese negotiations, which had begun shortly after VJ day, accelerated in early 1946, as a consequence of mounting pressures internationally to liquidate occupation operations and because of the renewal of civil war in China. By the end of February, the French and Viet Minh concluded an agreement whereby the French relinquished all extraterritorial and other special rights in China and granted the Chinese economic concessions in Annam. In return, the Chinese occupation army was to be relieved by the French within the following month. For Ho Chi Minh this meant that playing on Chinese friendship and support, always recognized to be a tenuous proposition, was no longer a viable diplomatic tactic.[80]

As the French-Chinese negotiations progressed in the early weeks of 1946, Ho renewed efforts at securing U.S. support which he knew would be beneficial as he tried to negotiate with Sainteny before French units moved north of the sixteenth parallel. On January 18, Ho addressed another appeal to Truman which, after reiterating the Viet Minh position that France had abandoned any right to govern Indochina, called for U.S. intervention and reconstruction assistance. The Viet Minh's principal opportunity to secure American backing developed when the State Department dispatched Kenneth Landon, Assistant Chief of the Division of Southeast Asian Affairs, on a special fact-finding mission to Indochina. Initially Landon dealt with French officials in Saigon, but upon receiving reports of the DRV's strength in the north, he requested and received State Department permission to proceed to Hanoi. Meeting with Ho on several occasions between February 14 and 24, Landon was able to convey the claims and objectives of the Viet Minh to Washington.[81]

At his first meeting with Landon on February 15, Ho stressed the Viet Minh's popular support, peaceful goals, and determination to resist French authority. The next day Ho gave Landon messages to be transmitted to Truman and requested that he extend his stay to permit further conversations. On February 20, the Vietnam-American Friendship Association invited

Landon to an exhibition at which the organization's president, Trinh van Binh, assured him of the nationalist and noncommunist orientation of the Viet Minh leadership. The following evening, Landon met with Ho Chi Minh and Bao Dai.[82]

Landon's presence may have helped to encourage Ho and Sainteny to reach an agreement. In any case, Sainteny's report on the progress of his discussions with Ho greatly encouraged Landon. Sainteny told Landon that he had offered self-government within the French community, which apparently was satisfactory to the Viet Minh. As interpreted by Sainteny, this meant that the French would control the foreign policy of Vietnam and the Vietnamese army would be integrated with that of France.[83]

Ho's letters to Truman, which Landon relayed to Washington, indicated a lack of confidence in any arrangement with France and reflected a sense of desperation. Again requesting that the United States endorse Vietnamese independence and take steps, through the United Nations, to maintain the peace, Ho's exasperation was plainly evident:"It [French military action] implies the complicity, or at least the connivance of the Great Democracies. The United Nations ought to keep their words. They ought to interfere to stop this unjust war, and to show that they mean to carry out in peacetime the principles for which they fought in wartime."[84] Again Ho's appeal to the United States (similar messages were also sent to the Soviet Union, China, and Britain) had no effect.

Against this background of increasing isolation, Ho reached his agreement with Sainteny. Signed in Hanoi on March 6, it has been described as "simply an armistice that provided a transient illusion of agreement when actually no agreement existed."[85] France recognized Vietnam as a "free state" within the Indochina Federation and promised a referendum on Vietnam's territorial unity. The French were permitted to station troops in Tonkin and Annam. In many ways, the agreement was a defeat for the Viet Minh: the independence proclaimed six months earlier was not recognized; there was no guarantee of Vietnam's unification; French troops were to enter DRV controlled territory. Yet the accord partially recognized the legitimacy of the DRV and the French agreed to limit the number of troops in the north. Since the agreement was basically a compromise between two men who were anxious to avoid a war that would certainly become a prolonged struggle, it was criticized by many old-line imperialists in Paris and Saigon and by many followers of the Viet Minh. The VNQDD, the Dong Minh Hoi, and others denounced the treaty as an act of treason. Ho had to draw upon his immense popular esteem to convince the public that the French should not be resisted. He believed that the price of the March 6 agreement was not excessive, provided that it led to subsequent negotiations recognizing the DRV and provided the unification referendum was implemented. In addition, he likely also calculated that a left-wing victory in forthcoming French elections would facilitate a final settlement favorable to the Viet Minh. Certainly the agreement represented a retreat from the heady DRV proclamation of independence, but the resumption of French authority in the south, the presence of an invasion fleet off the coast of Haiphong, the impending withdrawal of the Chinese, and the indifference of the Americans necessitated compromise.[86] As Ho told Sainteny: "You know I wanted more than has been granted. . . . Nevertheless, I realize that one cannot achieve everything in one day."[87]

Ho seized upon the modest concession in the March 6 agreement to bid once again for international support. In messages to the United States and Britain, he requested recognition of the DRV as a "free state." Consistent with its policy of ignoring messages from the Hanoi government, the State Department did not reply, but it tacitly seconded the Foreign Office's informal denial of recognition on the grounds that Vietnam's status was still being negotiatied.[88]

The continued international isolation of the DRV weakened its bargaining position in the next phase of negotiations. The Dalat Conference, held from April 18 to May 11 and intended to serve as a preliminary to more formal negotiations scheduled for Fontainebleau, reflected d'Argenlieu's determination to reduce the DRV within an Indochina Federation. The key element in this strategy was the preservation of French supremacy in Cochin China. To the leaders of the DRV, only the unification of Cochin China with Tonkin and Annam could assure the economic and cultural foundations for a viable nation. In defining their plans for the federation, the French spoke of joining Cochin China with areas in central Vietnam, delaying any unification referendum until order could be restored in Cochin China (meaning the cessation of Viet Minh activities there), establishing an Assembly with limited powers and in which French-controlled areas of Cochin China, Cambodia, and Laos would have predominance, and giving the High Commissioner the wide-ranging executive powers traditionally held by the Governor-General. Vo Nguyen Giap, who headed the DRV delegation at Dalat, found the French position intolerable and left the conference convinced that France could never again be trusted.[89]

During the Dalat Conference, Charles Reed, the American Consul at Saigon, visited Hanoi and met with a number of high-ranking French, Chinese, and Vietnamese officials, including Ho Chi Minh. Admitting his growing skepticism of French intentions, Ho spoke to Reed of "the utmost necessity of interesting American capital and employing American technicians in Vietnam."[90] In their reports to Washington, both Reed and James O'Sullivan, who became the head of the consulate at Hanoi, emphasized the mounting tensions in Tonkin. They saw the Chinese as making desperate efforts to salvage some nationalist alternative favorable to their interests, while the French, they feared, were planning a coup as soon as the Chinese withdrew.[91]

The arrival of French units, which had begun a few days after the Ho-Sainteny agreement, produced tensions and some fighting, not only between the French and Vietnamese but between the French and Chinese. Moreover, the Chinese became disenchanted with the DRV and were concerned that the Ho-Sainteny agreement would lead to a communist government on their southern frontier. The Chinese procrastinated in fulfilling their promise to withdraw, which led to French appeals to

Washington to exert pressure on the Chinese. The French eventually occupied Haiphong, Hanoi, and other positions, but did not come to exercise effective control in Tonkin. As the Chinese gradually withdrew (a process not completed until August), Viet Minh units, following Giap's strategy, sought to gain as much territory as possible. Eliminating a number of local pro-Chinese governments fostered by the occupation forces, the Viet Minh, by early June, had reestablished control over most of Tonkin.[92]

The policies of d'Argenlieu in the summer of 1946 virtually foreclosed the prospects for French–Viet Minh understanding. On June 1 as Ho Chi Minh and the DRV delegation were leaving for the Fontainbleau Conference, d'Argenlieu announced the establishment of a Provisional Government of Cochin China. Officially justified as a popular response to Viet Minh terrorism in the south, the new government constitued a shadow for French rule. On August 1, d'Argenlieu unexpectedly called another conference at Dalat, inviting representatives from Laos, Cambodia, Cochin China, and "southern Annam." The DRV delegation at the Fontainebleau Conference (which) had begun on July 6) broke off discussions, charging the French with fostering an Indochina federation on their own terms.[93]

As reports from Reed in Saigon, O'Sullivan in Hanoi, and Ambasador Jefferson Caffery in Paris called attention to the crisis in French–Viet Minh relations,[94] Moffat wrote a memorandum August 9 that strongly criticized French policy and urged American intervention. Reviewing recent developments, Moffat argued that the establishment of Cochin China government had justifiably intensified Vietnamese hostility. French propaganda and political suppression in Cochin China rendered a representative election there impossible, and the second Dalat Conference sought to minimize the DRV's influence. The situation was serious, with warfare increasingly likely; and while the French could overrun the country, they could not pacify it except through a long and bitter military operation. The United States, Moffat maintained, should "express to the French, in view of our interest in peace and orderly development of dependent peoples, our hope that they will abide by the spirit of the March 6 convention."[95]

In Paris, Ho Chi Minh, facing the prospect of failure in his effort to reach an accord with the French, sought American action along the lines suggested by Moffat. Meeting with Caffery on September 11, Ho spoke of the necessity for a unified Vietnam and of his interest in American assistance in attaining that goal. While Caffery found Ho to be rather vague, he reported: "I gathered he would like us to get into the game and he would be very pleased if he could use us in some way or other in his future negotiations with French authorities."[96] In a conversation the next day with George M. Abbot, First Secretary of the American embassy, Ho recalled his wartime association with American units, the Vietnamese affection for Roosevelt, and admiration for American policy in the Philippines. Ho then spoke specifically of Vietnam's need for foreign capital and enterprise, which the French could not possibly provide. The DRV would resist any continuation of the French economic monopoly and would insist on the right to approach other nations. Finally he hinted that this policy might be extended to military and naval matters, mentioning specifically the possibility of a naval base at Cam Ranh Bay.[97]

Considering the strong defense of imperial interests taken by the French government in the summer of 1946 under the leadership of Premier Georges Bidault, any American action resulting from Moffat's August 9 memorandum or Ho's last-minute overtures to the American embassy would likely have had little effect. While not welcoming the result, the State Department could see little choice but to accept the indecisive outcome of the Fountainebleau Conference. While preparing to leave Paris, Ho warned that the Vietnamese would fight if necessary but, at the same time, he pleaded for some agreement by which he could forestall those leaders in Hanoi who were prepared for an immediate showdown. On September 14, an innocuous modus vivendi endorsed the March 6 agreement, but the fundamental issues of the status of Cochin China and the relationship of Vietnam to the Indochina Federation and French Union remained unresolved.[98]

Upon returning to Hanoi on October 21, Ho Chi Minh encountered mounting opposition to his conciliatory policy. During his absence, Giap, as commander of Viet Minh forces, had moved decisively against the pro-Chinese party units, had intensified guerrilla warfare in the south, and had built the army to some 60,000 regulars with another 40,000 in various paramilitary youth groups. Ho nonetheless continued to urge moderation, calling upon the public to cooperate with the French and requesting that Giap curtail the operations in the south. Shortly after Ho's return, the second session of the DRV national assembly convened in Hanoi and, on November 8, adopted a constitution. A conservative document (especially in comparison with the constitutions adopted during the same period in Indonesia and Burma), it endeavored to retain and enhance the government's support by moderate political groups. The constituiton made clear the "one and indivisible" nature of the Vietnam state, and while providing for association with the French Union, the constitution stipulated that the DRV would not be subordinate to France.[99]

Ho Chi Minh's efforts to reach an understanding with France, increasingly challenged by his own government and repeatedly undermined by the French conviction of their strength and support within Indochina, deteriorated in the last weeks of 1946. Months of tensions between the French and Viet Minh in Tonkin finally led to a major armed clash. On November 20, the French navy, which had virtually blockaded Haiphong, seized a Chinese ship loaded with contraband for the Viet Minh. After two days of fighting between French and Viet Minh forces in Haiphong, the local commanders agreed to a cease-fire. But in Paris, the French government, acting on the advice of d'Argenlieu, decided to deal forcefully with the Viet Minh. After the Viet Minh ignored an ultimatum to withdraw, a French cruiser bombarded Haiphong, killing (by conservative estimates) at least 6,000 Vietnamese. To many of the Viet Minh and their followers, the French action at Haiphong, when added to the indignities of the previous year, made war inevitable.[100]

In the aftermath of the Haiphong incident, the State Department belatedly undertook the modest level of intervention which Moffat had suggested three months earlier. With reports from the American mission at Hanoi criticizing the French for their actions at Haiphong, Caffery expressed to French officials the American concern over the consequences of an inflexible colonial policy. Also, Moffat was dispatched on a special mission to Indochina. In meetings with Phillipe Baudet, director of the Asiatic Division of the Foreign Office, and with d'Argenlieu, Caffery was assured that the French had no plans to reconquer Vietnam. Yet at the same time, French officials expressed little concern for the consequences of their recent actions and blamed the Viet Minh for precipitating the Haiphong incident.[101]

The Moffat mission to Vietnam constituted an important, but flawed, effort to encourage moderation. Reaching Saigon on December 3 and after conferring there with French officials for three days, Moffat left for Hanoi where, despite some French objections, he met with Ho Chi Minh. Acheson's instructions to Moffat, however, were not received in Saigon until after his departure, meaning that in his conversations with Ho, Moffat could only express the American interest in a peaceful settlement. Ho, who was again in poor health, assured Moffat that the Viet Minh sought independence and not the establishment of a Communist state. He told Moffat that they were determined not to surrender, and still hoped for American friendship. Moffat also met with Giap, who stressed the Vietnamese willingness to pay whatever sacrifice was necessary to attain independence.[102]

Would knowledge of Acheson's instructions have enabled Moffat to exercise an effective influence in Hanoi? The delayed instructions did give Moffat some latitude in dealing with Ho— he was authorized to affirm the American support of the March 6 agreement and the September 14 modus vivendi as the basis for a settlement, and to inform Ho that Caffery was making similar representations. He was also asked to convey Baudet's assurances that no military invasion was planned. On the issue of Cochin China, Acheson asked Moffat to determine whether Ho would consider a referendum held after prolonged disorder to be meaningful. Might he compromise on the issue, perhaps through negotiations?

In retrospect, it is difficult to believe that had Moffat spoken to Ho along these lines, the results of his mission would have been any more positive. The Viet Minh was already disillusioned by French policy and no longer trusted French promises. Few placed any hope in the agreements of March and September. Further, compromise on Cochin China was incompatible with the assumptions of Vietnamese nationhood. Only American mediation might have made a difference, and Moffat was instructed to avoid conveying any impression that the United States contemplated intervening. Finally, the Acheson instructions made clear the State Department's increasing distrust of the Viet Minh. Acheson admonished Moffat not to forget "Ho's clear record as [an] agent of international communism" and specified that the "least desirable eventuality would be [the] establishment [of a] Communist-dominated, Moscoworiented state in Indochina."[103] That overriding concern limited Washington's capacity for dealing with the French–Viet Minh impasse and, in the face of subsequent developments, left the United States a hostage to French policy.

Moffat's report, cabled to Washington on December 15, called attention to the shortcomings of French policy, but linked American interests in Southeast Asia with the preservation of French predominance. Prior to visiting Indochina, Moffat had developed strong opinions on the Viet Minh, which his stay in Hanoi served to reinforce. Moffat distrusted the Viet Minh as an agent of the Soviet Union, but he feared that French policy would enhance the appeal of communism in Vietnam. The Viet Minh leadership failed to impress Moffat. The DRV was seen as controlled by a small Communist group which possibly had direct contact with the Soviet Union and the Chinese Communists, and would eventually seek to build a Communist state in Vietnam. The DRV leaders held "almost childish" views on economic issues and the meaning of "independence" and "sovereignty" which they believed had been granted in the Ho-Sainteny agreement. While nationalist sentiment and opposition to the French ran deep, only the preservation of the French position could counter Soviet influence and possibly Chinese imperialism in Vietnam and Southeast Asia. A settlement had to be quickly reached; otherwise, the prospects for the French would steadily diminish. Neutral good offices or mediation were essential. This critique of the Viet Minh—coming from one of the more liberal officials in the State Department—was music to the ears of the Office of European Affairs. Higher officials quickly endorsed Moffat's message. The response to Moffat's report indicated that any form of American mediation would reflect a determination to extend French predominance and would expect the DRV to compromise on fundamental issues.[104]

While the direction of American policy clearly signaled the necessity to uphold the French position, the beginning of warfare forced the State Department to raise the possibility of mediation. Washington took this step hesitantly knowing that the French considered any third party involvement unacceptable. What prompted the overture to the French was the evidence that they were headed into a prolonged, unpopular war which would weaken Western interests in the region. Analyses from Reed and O'Sullivan criticized French attitudes and practices, especially the military build-up in the north leading to the ultimatum that the Viet Minh disarm its militia in Hanoi. On December 19 the Viet Minh responded by attacking French-occupied parts of the city; the French counterattacked and fighting quickly spread throughout Tonkin and Annam. While en route back to the United States, Moffat urged the State Department to offer its assistance despite the risk of French repudiation. The Chinese government suggested that through their Hanoi consulates, China, Britain, and the United States extend their good offices.[105] On December 23, Acheson, acting on the advice of Vincent, spoke with Ambassador Bonnet about France's "unhappy situation," expressing concern about the fighting and the possibility of the issue being raised in the

United Nations. Acheson offered American help in adjudicating the issues.[106]

The French did not respond to Acheson's overture until January 8, 1947. During the interval, Washington received numerous reports indicating the determination of the French to seek a military solution and suggesting the necessity for mediation. Most significantly, Moffat, in a cable from Singapore on January 7, 1947, strongly criticized French policy and called for American leadership in reaching a truce and a political settlement. His visits to Indonesia and Malaya had broadened his perspectives on the Indochina situation. Whereas his December 15 report had emphasized the need to preserve the French in order to counter Soviet and Chinese communist influences in Southeast Asia, Moffat now stressed the potential loss of Western prestige throughout the region should the United States tolerate French warfare against the Vietnamese. A permanent settlement depended upon an independent Vietnam, which would probably retain close cultural and economic ties with the French. While Moffat did not discuss the DRV directly, his expectation of an independent Vietnam with an affinity for France, provided a settlement was quickly reached, closely followed the hopes which Ho Chi Minh had repeatedly expressed. In addition to Moffat's call for American initiative, Ambassador Edwin Stanton in Bangkok, in a message also dated January 7, observed that peoples throughout the area sympathized with the Vietnamese and urged the United States to utilize its influence--either through good offices or the United Nations—to bring about a settlement.[107]

The French rejected Acheson's offer of assistance on January 8. When order was restored, they would resume negotiations with the Vietnamese. Vincent warned a French embassy official:

> There was one flaw in the French approach to the problem worth mentioning. I had in mind an apparent assumption by the French that there was an equality of responsibility as between the French and the Vietnamese. I said this did not seem to me to be the case; that the responsibility of France as a world power to achieve a

solution was far greater than that of the Vietnamese; and that the situation was not one which could be localized as a purely French-Vietnamese one but might affect adversely conditions through Southeast Asia.[108]

In response, Vincent encountered the French contention that their difficulties were not of their making:

Mr. Lacoste quickly substituted the word "authority" for "responsibility" and said that the French were now faced with the problem of reasserting their authority and that we must share the responsibility for their delay in doing so because we had not acceded to French requests in the autumn of 1945 for military assistance.[109]

The United States reluctantly accepted the French determination to pursue their own course. In the Division of Southeast Asian Affairs, Landon and Charlton Ogburn endeavored to keep attention focused on the consequences of French policy, observing that the United States could not risk alienating the Asiatic peoples.[110] Yet the Communist leadership of the Viet Minh remained the fundamental problem which precluded treating Vietnam as principally a colonial issue. The American dilemma was clearly set forth in the message of February 3 from the recently appointed Secretary of State George C. Marshall to the embassy in Paris: "We have fully recognized France's sovereign position and we do not wish to have it appear that we are in any way endeavoring to undermine that position. At [the] same time we cannot shut out eyes to [the] fact that there are two sides to this problem and that our reports indicate both a lack of French understanding [of the] other side and continued existence of [a] dangerously outmoded colonial outlook and method in [the] area. On [the] other hand we do not lose sight of the fact that Ho Chi Minh has direct Communist connections and it should be obvious that we are not interested in seeing colonial empire administrations supplanted by [the] philosophy and political organization directed from and controlled by [the] Kremlin. Frankly we have no solution of [the] problem to suggest."[111]

As indicated in the Marshall statement and earlier in Acheson's instructions to Moffat, the State Department had concluded that a Viet Minh-dominated government in Vietnam probably would be detrimental to American interests. Ho Chi Minh's repeated assertions of the Viet Minh's overriding commitment to independence, his solicitation of Western, especially American, economic assistance, his efforts at compromise with the French—all suggested an effort to orient Vietnam toward the West—were, in the end, considered too risky a basis for supporting the Viet Minh. Once the initial pro-Viet Minh enthusiasm of the wartime contacts had run its course, analyses of the DRV passed to the State Department. While officers in the Division of Southeast Asian Affairs and in Saigon and Hanoi criticized the French, they could not reconcile themselves to accept the potential consequences of a Communist-dominated Vietnam or possibly a Communist-dominated Indochina. Throughout 1946, the State Department received numerous estimates of the Viet Minh with particular attention on its relationship with Moscow and the relative importance of independence and communism within the movement. These reports, however, were limited by the lack of substantial information about the Viet Minh and especially Ho Chi Minh.[112] What became the prevailing interpretations of Ho was set forth in a late 1945 OSS biographical summary which concluded: "Ho Chi Minh has never, according to abundant evidence, adhered to the group of colonial nationalists who have put loyalty to their native land above loyalty to Moscow. On the contrary, he has remained a member in good standing of the Kremlin community through all its twists and turns, its deviations, its reversal of positions, its temporary shelving of colonial propaganda, and its pact with Nazi Germany. There is no evidence he ever demurred. There is no reason to believe he has ever done so."[113] The French repeatedly emphasized the Viet Minh's Communist character and downgraded its popular support. American officials, however, recognized the shallowness of the French position; a view expressed by Reed in August 1946 was frequently reiterated: "What the French miss, I believe is that while the Viet Minh may be disliked, the French are hated."[114] The Russian interest in Indo-china, as evidenced in the Soviet press and other sources, seemed to be limited.[115]

While mindful of the shortcomings of French colonialism and the evident negligible Soviet interest in Vietnam, American officials came to see the Communist character of the Viet Minh as the necessary dominant factor in shaping U.S. policy. The option of accepting Ho's claims to being a pro-Western na-tionalist simply seemed too risky. Moreover, as the United States moved to incorporate France within its program of con-taining Soviet expansion in Europe, it could ill-afford to alienate its ally over colonial issues.

Thus as the war began in Indochina, American policy tended to be guided largely by the desire to avoid the uncertain consequences of a Communist-controlled Vietnam. In the months that followed, the Communists moved toward victory in China, the French reestablished a strong position, and the Viet Minh took to the jungles and was isolated from the West.

## The Effort to Avoid War in Indonesia

While the United States effectively withdrew from the French-Viet Minh struggle, it took increased interest in the Indonesian situation. To secure the objective of avoiding Communist dom-ination of another Asian nationalist movement, the United States consistently sought to encourage a compromising Dutch policy that would provide for transition of authority to moderate nationalists. The early implementation of the Linggadjati Agreement seemed the most feasible means of maintaining the ascendency of the pro-Western leadership in the Indonesian Republic.

During the five months after the signing of the agreement in November 1946, however, the prospects for a peaceful settle-ment seemed remote. Dutch troops arrived almost without interruption and in late January, 1947, the Dutch imposed a blockade on Republican-held areas of Java and Sumatra. Fighting continued along the cease-fire line, much of it initiated by irregular Republican units. Occasionally the Dutch retaliated with attacks into Republican territory. Moderate groups in both the Netherlands and the Republic faced strong challenges from extremists who opposed compromise and sought a military solution. Such pressures delayed ratification of the agreement. The States General in The Hague attached a number of modifications and reservations to its ratification. Republican ratification was secured, only with assurances that the Dutch revisions of the treaty constituted an expression of views and intentions. Although no real "agreement" had been reached, the Linggadjati Agreement was formally signed on March 25, 1947. In the following weeks, the fundamental differences between the Dutch and Republican leaders undermined the implementation of the agreement. In effect, the Republic sought to retain its capacity to act independently, anticipating joint discussions and responsibility for establishing the United States of Indonesia; on the other hand, the Netherlands demanded the Republic's acceptance of its sovereignty and of a subordinate role in discussions leading to a final settlement.[116]

The international context that led the United States to virtually withdrawal from the French-Vietnamese clash encouraged an enlarged role in the Dutch-Indonesian tensions. The signing of the Linggadjati Agreement came shortly after President Truman, in his March 12 Congressional address requesting assistance to Greece and Turkey, articulated the policy of containment. In the following weeks, plans for a large scale program of economic rehabilitation assistance for Europe quickly advanced. More than any other part of Southeast Asia, Indonesia immediately became linked politically and economically to American objectives in Europe. Political stability and the open door in Indonesia were essential if the United States and its European allies were to have access to its vital resources. The United States, in the words of Acheson, "considers that immediate and unhampered trade and commerce between [the Netherlands East Indies] and [the] rest of [the] world is one of [the] most essential steps to world rehabilitation."[117]

While the Netherlands had consistently restricted non-Dutch trade, the Republic promised access to its resources and investment opportunities. During the early postwar period, the Dutch had repeatedly resisted American overtures for trade agreements that would have extended access to rubber and tin. In their meetings with American officials, Republican representatives stressed the importance of foreign capital and a commitment to nondiscriminatory trade policy. The S.S. *Martin Behrman* incident in early 1947 dramatized the American problem. Isbrandtsen Steamship Company entered into a contract with an agent of the Republic and, in February 5, the *Martin Behrman,* a U.S. government-owned ship chartered to the company, arrived at Cheribon. This was the first ship to establish direct United States–Republic trade relations. Ignoring a regulation of the Netherlands East Indies government that established a virtual embargo on exports from Republic-controlled areas, the *Martin Behrman* loaded its cargo of rubber, tin, and other commodities. The Dutch reponded quickly and effectively, putting troops on the ship and seizing its cargo. While not officially challenging the legality of the Dutch action, American officials were disturbed by the curtailing of trade with Indonesia at a time when the necessary raw materials were in short supply.[118]

With the signing of the Linggadjati Agreement, the State Department moved quickly to enhance the diplomatic and commerical status of the Republic. It seemed essential to take a more balanced approach, since the United States, in the interest of not antagonizing the Dutch during the prolonged ratification process, had raised only rather muted objections to the steady buildup of Dutch military influence and the imposition of the blockade.[119] The *Martin Behrman* incident, in particular, added to the determination to uphold the Linggadjati Agreement.

On April 3, Washington indicated its intention to recognize the de facto jurisdiction of the Republic in the areas under its control and on matters within its competence as defined in the agreement. This action met with strong objections from the Batavia consul, Walter Foote, who remained very critical of the

Republic; its leaders, he warned, would seize upon recognition to destroy the agreement. The Dutch protested that the United States was acting prematurely inasmuch as under the agreement the Netherlands remained responsible for the foreign relations of the East Indies. After considerable discussion between the Dutch embassy and State Department officials, the Americans made it clear that Dutch sovereignty was not being questioned, but that the consul at Batavia would deal directly with Republican authorities on matters within the Republic's competence as defined in the Linggadjati Agreement.[120] Despite these efforts to minimize the step being taken, this limited recognition had important political implications, for it signalled an enhanced international status for the Republic. Britain, India, China, Australia, and a few other countries also extended de facto recognition.

In addition, Washington also exerted increased pressures on the Dutch to conclude commerical agreements which would open East Indian trade on a nondiscriminatory basis; such action, it was argued, was critical to economic stability in the region and European economic recovery. Further, when the Dutch proposed an export-import bank loan for Indonesia, the State Department insisted that Republican officials be included in any discussions.[121]

These actions reflected mounting skepticism of Dutch intentions. As the Dutch-Republican disagreement over the implementation of the Linggadjati Agreement became more protracted, Washington became concerned that the Dutch would resort to military action.[122] Indeed Dutch officials repeatedly sought to enlist Western unity in Indonesia. Without strong backing from its allies, the Netherlands could not sustain Western predominance in the East Indies. The result, it was maintained, would be a communist government which would give the Soviet Union immense influence in Southeast Asia. The Dutch, seconded by the reports of Foote, argued that the Communists were rapidly gaining strength within the Republic.[123] At the State Department, however, such projections were treated skeptically; the prevailing view was set forth in a statement endorsed by officers in both the divisions of Southeast Asian and Northern European Affairs: "With respect to the danger of Communist domination of the Netherlands East Indies, we feel that Communist influence at the present is neither widespread nor effective. It is our hope that prompt measures to consolidate and strengthen the present Indonesian leadership (which we believe to be Socialist and not Communist, Nationalist and not Soviet-controlled) will eliminate those conditions which may make Communist infiltration effective.[124]

From Washington's perspective, the key was to sustain the Linggadjati process. Thus when the Dutch adopted a stronger line toward the Republic which promised some movement in the stalled negotiations, the State Department proved to be sympathetic. After the visit of a ministerial delegation from The Hague to Netherlands East Indies officials, on May 27 the Dutch demanded an interim administration under Dutch sovereignty, renunciation of claims to independent diplomatic status, and the entry of a Dutch gendermarie into Republican territory as a means of guaranteeing Dutch enterprise. Netherlands officials asked the Americans and the British to put pressure on the Republic to accept the May 27 position. The Dutch stressed their determination to keep the issue out of the United Nations and said that rejections of the May 27 plan might result in military action against the Republic. The State Department responded to the Dutch bidding. Meeting with Republican leaders, Foote urged acceptance. This support of the Dutch rested principally in the hope that such an interim arrangement would lead to implementation of the Linggadjati Agreement. That objective was shared by the British, who also had their consul in Batavia intercede with Republican officials. The only alternative, Washington and London feared, was a resort to military force—an eventuality which both Western powers were determined to avoid.[125]

When the Republic, despite the Anglo-American pressure, rejected the May 27 proposals, the United States moved quickly to discourage the Dutch from taking military action. Norman Baruch, the ambassador to the Netherlands, warned

Dutch Foreign Office officials that the use of military force would arouse adverse popular and official reaction in America. At the same time, the State Department instructed Foote to exhort Republican leaders to reconsider their position. An aide-memoire of June 26 to the Republic asked for cooperation in establishing an interim government within the framework of the Linggadjati Agreement and the May 27 proposals. Repeatedly the State Department counseled both sides to follow moderate and compromising policies. American reconstruction assistance was promised, provided the Dutch and Republic reached agreement. (Since the end of the war, about $80 million of rehabilitation assistance had reached the islands, but no money had reached Republic-controlled areas.) Officials even considered offering American administration of the gendarmerie as a means of alleviating the Republican apprehension over having Dutch-controlled units enter its territory.[126]

By this time, American policymakers attached much importance to the impact of the Indonesian struggle on Asian attitudes toward the West. A peaceful, equitable implementation of the Linggadjati Agreement followed by economic reconstruction would forestall the spread of communism not only in Indonesia, but throughout the region. Warfare would harm Western influence. American prestige, unquestionably higher than that of the British or Dutch, could be critical in assuring the ascendancy of moderate elements and the acceptance of a compromise settlement. The Indochina situation offered a sobering example: the conflict beginning there might have been avoided had the United States been insistent upon a negotiated settlement. French influence in Europe and Asia would have been enhanced by a moderate colonial policy. In Indonesia, furthermore, since American prestige was high, the risks of acquiescence in the use of military force were also very great.[127]

As reports indicated that the Dutch were preparing for military action, the State Department made strong statements, but it lacked other effective and reasonable means of restraining the Netherlands.[128] At a time when the development of Western unity was an overriding priority in the cold war battlefield in

Europe, the United States had inherent limitations on its ability to influence its allies. The reliance on compromise in the Southeast Asian colonial disputes—officially stated by Vincent on October 20, 1945—had failed in Indochina, and by the end of July 1947, had likewise run its course in Indonesia. On July 20 Dutch forces invaded Republican territory in a "police action." In reality it marked the beginning of the Indonesian war of independence. As American officials had feared, the Indonesian war became a matter of major international concern and, when the issue quickly surfaced in the United Nations, the United States was placed in a singularly embarrassing position.

## Conclusion: The Cold War and Redefined Interests

During the initial phases of the revolutions in Indonesia and Indochina, Indochina commanded far greater American attention. That resulted, in large part, from America's considerable military involvement in Indochina through the China theater, and the corresponding virtual isolation from Indonesia, as well as the priorities in wartime planning. Not only in the White House but in the Department of State, the future of Indochina was the topic of more extended analyses than any of the other colonies in Southeast Asia. Behind this, of course, was the Roosevelt fascination with Indochina, although State Department officials remained dubious whether the French would change their colonial policies and adjust to international accountability. Thus whereas American officials after 1942 had rarely questioned Dutch intentions to liberalize colonial policy, an attitude of skepticism prevailed about the French in postwar Indochina.

In the period from VJ Day until late 1946 as the opposing sides in both revolutions tried to negotiate cease-fire arrangements and political understandings, American policymakers endeavored to exert greater influence in Indochina. The British, through the activities of SEAC and diplomatic dealings with The Hague, influenced Dutch policy, while taking relatively little interest in Indochina. Again this represented a continuation of wartime calculations as the British had assumed that their "special relationship" with the Netherlands gave them leverage in dealing with the Indonesian situation. The Dutch colony was far more important to British political and economic interests in the region. In the case of Indochina, the British, while never questioning French sovereignty and assisting in the French restoration, remained conscious of the American interest and sought to avoid any unnecessary strains in Anglo-American relations. Had the State Department studied the Indonesian revolution more extensively during World War II and the early postwar period, and had it been served by representatives with a broader perspective than that of Foote's, it might have responded to the Indonesian revolution more effectively.

For by the early part of 1947, as the containment doctrine became the dominant characteristic of its foreign policy, the United States attached greater importance to the Indonesian crisis. The central objective in both Indochina and Indonesia remained the encouragement of progressive measures of self-government and the eventual transfer of authority to pro-Western nationalists. In Indonesia, the moderate leadership of the Republic had to be upheld, lest the revolution fall into the hands of unpredictable radicals. In Indochina, the Communist leadership of the Viet Minh seemingly foreclosed its capacity to integrate the DRV within the Western political and economic system. French policy, however outmoded and highhanded, offered at least the possibility of encouraging a moderate nationalist alternative to the Viet Minh. Hence, while the United States continued to counsel the Dutch and French to be moderate in their colonial policies, and was skeptical of their resort to arms in Indonesia and Indochina, by the summer of 1947 the imperatives of the cold war were already imposing limitations on approaches to the French while leaving greater latitude in dealings with the Dutch.

# 7.

# The United States' Model: Decolonization in the Philippines

> The people of the United States will never forget what
> the people of the Philippines Islands are doing this day
> and in days to come. I give the people of the Philip-
> pines my solemn pledge that their freedom will be
> redeemed and their independence established and
> protected. The entire resources, in men, and in ma-
> terial, of the United States stand behind that
> pledge.
>
> Franklin D. Roosevelt Radio Broadcast,
> December 28, 1941

THE UNITED STATES consistently upheld its record in the
Philippines as a model for the treatment of colonial peoples. The
administration of the Philippines since 1898—the progressive
development of self-governing institutions, the programs of
educational and social reforms, and the commitment to independence by a specific date—guided much of the State Department planning for dependent areas during World War II. Yet as
the United States fulfilled its promise and transferred political
authority in 1946, the term "Philippine model" took on important and ironic new meanings. The United States retained its

paramount position in the Philippines, most obviously through a trade agreement which preserved Philippine dependence on the American market. In addition, the United States gained extensive military influence. In the interlude between the the end of the war and the granting of independence, American political and military leaders also cultivated the political ascendancy of a moderate, pro-Western elite, which would preserve close relations with the United States. These measures, while important in terms of guaranteeing a substantial American presence in Southeast Asia, meant that Philippine independence was, in basic ways, compromised.

The terms of decolonization were determined, to a large extent, by the American-Philippine experience in World War II. The Japanese conquest of the islands complicated the plans for an orderly process and gave rise to a number of irritating problems: questions about the American response to the Japanese invasion, the Japanese cultivation of anti-American sentiment, the creation of a Japanese-sponsored "independent" government, the collaboration of many Filipinos with the Japanese, tensions between the Commonwealth government (whose leaders came to the United States in 1942) and the "collaborators," the postwar status of the anti-Japanese underground, Philippine demands for extensive rehabilitation assistance for its shattered cities and economy, and the disruption of established commercial relations. Perhaps the immensity of these problems meant that independence ought to have been delayed (as some observers at the time suggested), but pressures from within the United States and from the Philippines, as well as the official determination to establish the American commitment to anticolonialism, gave irresistible impetus to transfer authority on July 4, 1946.

## The Wartime Relationship

The Japanese attack upon the Philippines found the United States Army Air Force, under the command of General Douglas

MacArthur, ill-prepared, while the priorities of a global war, as determined in Washington, rendered impossible any significant assistance to the defenders of the islands. Following air attacks on Clark and Iba airfields which destroyed much of the American Far Eastern air force, the Japanese began landing forces on Luzon on December 10, 1941. MacArthur abandoned the ambitious plan to defend the entire archipelago and fell back on the essentials of War Plan Orange. He maneuvered American-Filipino forces into the Bataan Peninsula with the intention of defending it and Corregidor Island in order to deny Japan the use of Manila Bay. On December 26, MacArthur declared Manila an open city and five days later, American units evacuated the city, enabling the Japanese to capture it without opposition on January 2, 1942. The brutal fighting on Bataan took a heavy toll of lives, both from battle and disease. Although both sides suffered losses, only the Japanese could be reinforced. For the defenders of Bataan, supplies of arms, ammunition, and food dwindled. The results were inevitable. MacArthur and most of his staff were evacuated on March 12. Bataan fell on April 9 and less than a month later, General Jonathon M. Wainright surrendered Corregidor.

The conquest of the Philippines quickly brought sharp disagreements over military and diplomatic strategies, that later strongly influenced the course of Philippine-American relations. From Washington, Roosevelt called upon the Filipinos to play a "crucial role" in the defeat of Japan, praised their "greatest gallantry" and promised "their freedom will be redeemed and their independence established and protected." Behind that pledge stood "the entire resources, of men and in material, of the United States." But to the beleagured Americans and Filipinos, his words were received with growing cynicism.[1] U.S. High Commissioner Francis Sayre, OSS Director William J. Donovan, and Commonwealth President Manuel Quezon repeatedly asked Roosevelt to provide reinforcements.[2] In a message on January 28, Quezon pleaded:

> My loyalty and the loyalty of the Filipino people to America have been proved without question. . . . But, it seems to me question-

able whether any government has the right to demand loyalty from its citizens beyond its willingness or ability to render actual protection.

This war is not of our making. Those that had dictated the policies of the United States could not have failed to see that this is the weakest point in American territory. From the beginning they should have tried to build up our defenses. As soon as prospects looked bad to me, I telegraphed President Roosevelt requesting him to include the Philippines in the American defense program. I was given no satisfactory answer.[3]

As the situation on Bataan became more desperate, Quezon urged the United States to grant immediate independence, after which he would propose the neutralization of the Philippines. If accepted by Japan and the United States, all occupying forces would be withdrawn. In a cable of February 8 to Roosevelt, Quezon argued:

> While enjoying security itself, the United States has in effect condemned the sixteen millions of Filipinos to practical destruction in order to effect a certain delay. You have promised redemption, but what we need is immediate assistance and protection. . . . Shall we further sacrifice our country and our people in a hopeless fight? I voice the unanimous opinion of my War Cabinet and I am sure the unanimous opinion of all Filipinos that under the circumstances we should take steps to preserve the Philippines and Filipinos from further destruction.[4]

Quezon's proposal was endorsed by Sayre on the condition that its premise of no additional American reinforcements was correct, and by MacArthur, who considered it a useful propaganda ploy to counter Japan's promise of independence.[5]

In Washington, Chief of Staff General George C. Marshall and Secretary of War Henry Stimson counseled Roosevelt to reject the independence-neutralization plan. Instead the Americans and Filipinos should continue the resistance in Bataan. Roosevelt's terse response to Quezon reminded the Commonwealth leader of America's record in the Philippines—"unique in the history of the family of nations"—and of the futility of trusting the Japanese.[6]

The neutralization of the Philippines following independence was not a new idea in 1942. It had been advanced in the Congressional debates over the Hare-Hawes-Cutting Act of 1933 as well as in the Tydings-McDuffie Act of 1934. Yet in 1942 it was unacceptable to both the United States and Japan, as the Philippines experienced the ultimate futility of being "between two empires." Even if the neutralization plan had been accepted earlier by the Japanese, their drive to eliminate American influence in Asia after Pearl Harbor virtually dictated moving against the Philippines. So the Filipinos and Americans fought on Bataan, which did at least serve to sustain morale and enhance a unity of purpose in the Philippines and in the United States.[7]

Following the collapse of resistance to the Japanese, the United States moved to preserve the integrity and prestige of the Commonwealth government. Quezon, Vice-President Sergio Osmena, and other officials were evacuated first to Australia, and were later brought to Washington. They functioned, in effect if not in name, as a government-in-exile.[8] The Commonwealth government became a part of the Allied war effort, most importantly by adhering to the United Nations Declaration. Assistant Secretary of State Adolph Berle first raised the possibility of inviting Philippine adherence and was strongly supported by Undersecretary of State Sumner Welles and a number of other State Department officers, all of whom considered it an important means of improving Philippine morale and affirming American anticolonial principles in the Pacific. Roosevelt was reluctant, being apprehensive that such a step might imply an early recognition of independence. When it was noted that the government of India had been an original signer without any such ramifications, the White House accepted the proposal. As a result, on June 13, 1942, the Philippine Commonwealth formally adhered to the declaration. At the same time, Roosevelt added Quezon to the membership of the Pacific War Council.[9]

For Quezon, exile in the United States provided an opportunity to remind Americans of his country's present acute situation and anticipated postwar needs. He challenged the "Europe

first" strategy, which he considered principally a means of preserving the British empire. Calling attention to the failure to
provide for the defense of the Philippines, he sought acceptance
of American responsibility for postwar reconstruction and rehabilitation. As the Japanese moved toward granting independence to the Philippines, Quezon advocated acceleration of
American plans for independence. The Philippine leader, who
had a flair for self-dramatization (one argument advanced for
bringing him to Washington was that he and MacArthur could
not share theatrics in Australia), enjoyed close relations with a
number of key members of Congress. Secretary of Interior
Harold Ickes, however, regarded Quezon as a subordinate
(which technically he was), rather than as a head of an Allied
government. Accordingly, Quezon preferred to deal with Roosevelt, who rather liked him and always treated him and his ideas
with respect.[10]

While Quezon had no success in reversing Allied military
strategy and received only tentative commitments to postwar
assistance, his major and most controversial efforts were directed toward preserving his own political power and advancing
the date of independence. In the summer of 1943, Quezon was
nearing his constitutional limit of eight years as president. On
November 15, he was scheduled to turn the presidency over to
Osmena. Quezon initiated a movement to extend his term of
office. Roosevelt and Stimson, both convinced that his leadership was necessary for military reasons, gave their encouragement. Initially the State Department and Interior Department
criticized such a step, regarding any deviation from the constitutional process as compromising the American record in the
Philippines and as ultimately beneficial to Japanese propaganda. Yet with the White House sympathetic to Quezon's
remaining in office, neither of the departments pressed its reservations. In the end, the White House and Quezon worked with
congressional leaders, principally Senator Millard Tydings, to
pass legislation that provided for Quezon's continuation in office
until conditions permitted an election. Senate Joint Resolution
95, however, touched off an extended debate in the House of

Representatives. Critics argued that the United States ought not interfere in the constitutional process, questioned what harm would result from Osmena becoming president, and ridiculed the notion that Quezon was somehow indispensible. In the end, the measure carried the House by a margin of 181 to 107. The Senate gave little attention to the matter and passed SJ Resolution 95 by a voice vote.[11]

A great deal of the administration's attention was directed toward controlling the movement in Congress to advance the date of Philippine independence. Roosevelt supported the movement, but his choice of a plan was never clear. Sometimes he advocated acknowledging independence immediately and other times he seemed to prefer delaying it until the islands were liberated. On August 12, 1943, the forty-fifth anniversary of the American occupation of the Philippines, Roosevelt pledged that "the republic of the Philippines will be established the moment the power of our Japanese enemies is destroyed."[12] The following month, in a meeting with Tydings and Quezon, Roosevelt endorsed the idea of immediate independence. Assuming White House support, Tydings then planned to seek such legislation. When a number of officials pointed out that action would appear to give legitimacy to the "independent," puppet government about to be established under Japanese tutelage, an alternative approach—advancing independence to whenever the islands were liberated—drew increased support.

The State and Interior departments, however, raised a number of compelling arguments against that measure: 1) rehabilitation and trade legislation—both time-consuming matters—needed to be resolved prior to independence; 2) Philippine collaborators could easily control any government established at the time of Japan's defeat; 3) American naval facilities, provided for in the Tydings-McDuffie Act, could best be negotiated for after the war; 4) Congressional action would enable Japan to claim that its policies had driven the United States to advance independence as a wartime expediency; 5) a change in the status of the Philippines might have unsettling effects upon the British and Dutch in relations with their dependencies in Asia. Accord-

*
ingly, the administration, with Roosevelt taking little interest in
the matter, worked with Tydings to modify his resolution. In
November, Tydings introduced Senate Joint Resolution 93
which authorized the President to proclaim Philippine independence following the liberation of the islands, and the restoration
of constitutional processes and the Commonwealth government.
In addition, the resolution authorized the President, following
negotiations with the President of the Commonwealth, to withhold or acquire bases beyond those specified in the Tydings-
McDuffie Act. The insistence on providing for additional bases
represented pressures from the Interior Department and the
Chiefs of Staff, which assumed that the long-term security of the
Pacific necessitated a substantial postwar naval and air presence. SJ Resolution 93 was approved by both houses of Congress
the following spring.[13]

After the extension of Quezon's term and the passage of
the resolution on Philippine independence, the Commonwealth
leadership could do little more than await the American invasion of the Philippines, which did not begin until October 1944.
Quezon's dream of returning to the Philippines as president was
not fulfilled. He died on August 1, 1944, a victim of tuberculosis
which had caused a progressive deterioration of his physical condition for several years. Osmena, succeeding Quezon to the presidency, was reluctant to return to the Philippines with Mac-
Arthur's invasion force, arguing that he was needed in Washington to secure rehabilitation assistance. Under pressure from
Roosevelt and MacArthur, he yielded and led the group of
Philippine officials which went to Australia in early October in
preparation for accompanying MacArthur on a triumphal
return.[14]

By that time, the issue of Philippine collaboration with
the Japanese—an outgrowth especially of the Japanese-sponsored Republic—had become a major problem in Philippine-
American relations. The Japanese decision to foster an independent government was intended to improve the morale of the
Japanese and the conquered peoples at a time when the United
States had gained the military initiative in the Pacific. From

Tokyo's perspective, Philippine independence countered the Atlantic Charter and established Japan's commitment to liberating subject peoples. On October 14, 1943, the Philippine Republic was inaugurated with widespread publicity and much fanfare. In the United States, the Republic was immediately denounced; in a radio broadcast directed to the Philippines, Roosevelt stressed that the Commonwealth was the only legitimate government and reaffirmed America's commitment to drive out the Japanese and establish a truly independent government.

Prior to the establishment of the Republic, the Japanese prevailed upon the prewar oligarchy—the group experienced in government and in control of the country's political, social, and economic institutions—to retain their offices. Indeed, this association with the Japanese was encouraged by the Commonwealth leadership. Upon leaving the islands in 1942, Quezon ordered his secretary Jorge Vargas to remain behind to deal with the Japanese and protect Philippine interests. The Japanese made Vargas chairman of an Executive Commission which was comprised of prominent leaders and served as the administrative agent of the Japanese military. Few Filipinos were attracted to the Japanese and their institutions, and the overwhelming majority retained their loyalty to the Commonwealth and the United States. The harsh and intimidating rule of the Japanese reinforced those sentiments. The deep-seated hatred of the Japanese limited the usefulness of the collaborators and in turn undermined the defense of their actions. Since the Vargas administration lacked popular support, it could not bargain with the Japanese. Instead the collaborators consistently sought to prove their usefulness to their conquerors, which left them increasingly dependent upon the Japanese. In sum, Philippine leaders relied on the Japanese more than the Japanese relied on them. As a result, it was questionable whether collaboration restrained the Japanese in any way. Accordingly unlike other parts of Southeast Asia, the Japanese could not exploit nationalist sentiments against the Allies. For that reason, a gesture as dramatic as the granting of independence was seen as the only means, clearly a desperate one, to break the Filipino-American bond.

As the Japanese planned to fulfill General Tojo's promise of independence for the Philippines, the major problem was finding a cooperative leader who could approximate Quezon's appeal and prestige. They worked, but without success, to recruit Manuel Roxas, who was widely considered Quezon's political heir. Eventually they settled upon the Japanese-educated Jose Laurel, who had served on the Executive Commission and had pro-Japanese sympathies. Laurel and other leaders of the Japanese puppet government, which became commonly known as the Laurel Republic, tried to resist Japan's demand that the Republic declare war on the United States. After some delays, and fearful of reprisals, on September 22, 1944 Laurel issued a proclamation of war against the United States and Great Britain. While the Republic's leaders did not intend to wage war against the Americans, the Japanese took advantage of the state of war to form volunteer militia from opportunists and Japanophiles.[15]

Judgment on collaboration is always difficult. The number of actively pro-Japanese Filipinos remained very limited, although collaborators were fully exploited for political, military, and propagandistic purposes by the Japanese. The vast majority who worked with the Japanese retained their loyalty to the Commonwealth and the United States, but believed cooperation provided the only means of lessening the severity of Japanese rule. Indeed the war years enhanced the emotional tie of Filipinos to Americans. In his final letter to Roosevelt, Quezon cautioned understanding in dealing with the collaboration question:

> Anyone who has betrayed the interests of the Filipino people by actively and wholeheartedly cooperating with the Japanese should not only be removed from any position of influence and punished, but even more, completely and thoroughly discredited in the eyes of the Filipino people. I therefore feel sentence must be passed upon the collaborationists by the Government of the Com-

monwealth of the Philippines itself and decided in conformity
with Philippine standards and jurisprudence. . . . In considering
the case of the apparent collaborationists, it seems to me we must
take into account the element of brutal coercion; and even more
important, the possibility—more than that, the probability—
that many of these seeming collaborationists are cooperating with
the Japanese only on the surface, and are actually using their
positions and power to assist and sustain the guerrillas, and in
other ways hamper the Japanese.[16]

The existence of a widespread resistance movement complicated the issue of collaboration. While many of those associated with the traditional oligarchy argued (as did Quezon)
that the resistance benefited from the extent of cooperation with
the Japanese, the underground held no sympathy for collaborators. Throughout the countryside, those Filipinos who cooperated with the Japanese were summarily tried by guerrilla units.
Laurel was critically wounded by a would-be assassin in early
1943, and shortly afterward the publisher of Manila's largest
newspaper was killed because of his alleged pro-Japanese
activities.

Guerrilla forces operated throughout the islands, and
some 300,000 Filipinos were active in the movement. While the
guerrilla forces were generally isolated and lacked coordination
with each other, all remained loyal to the Commonwealth and
most followed instructions from MacArthur's headquarters and
provided it with important intelligence. The extent of the anti-
Japanese campaign was much stronger in the Philippines than
in other parts of Southeast Asia—an outgrowth of the prevailing
pro-American sentiment and of the dislike of the Japanese.
Those feelings intensified as the Japanese military became
generally more harsh in its rule, and in its reprisals against captured guerrillas. Thus as the war progressed, the fighting between the Japanese and the guerrillas became increasingly
brutal.

Among the many guerrilla bands, the Hukbalahap, which
operated in central Luzon, was the most effective. Led by left-

wing intellectuals who represented the strong social revolutionary movements that had developed in Luzon during the 1930s, the Huks called for a struggle against the Japanese on behalf of economic and social justice. Taking advantage of dislocations resulting from the Japanese invasion, especially the flight of much of the landlord class and traditional officials to Manila, the Huks came to exercise extensive political control in central Luzon. The Japanese lacked adequate forces to suppress the Huks and with strong support from peasants, laborers, and tenants, they laid the foundations of a far-reaching agrarian revolution aimed at breaking the prewar political and social structure. In addition, the Huk-controlled territory became the safest refuge for American airmen who had been forced down and for Filipinos escaping the Japanese.

After the war the traditional Philippine elite seized upon Communist influence within the Hukbalahap to discredit the movement. It was, however, impossible to measure the extent of that influence. Luis Taruc and Casto Alejandro, the most prominent leaders, had been closely associated with the socialist movement. Certainly the Philippine Communist party infiltrated the Huks and may well have been decisive in determining its ideology, activities, and organization. Having functioned as an illegal party during the Commonwealth period, the Communists had gained experience in underground activities which proved important to the success of the Huks.

Whatever the extent of Communist influence, the Huks clearly established themselves as the most prominent of the underground forces and as a valuable ally of the Americans prior to the invasion of October 1944, as well as in the subsequent campaign against the Japanese. Their promise of revolutionary change and their uncompromising position toward collaborators drew wide support from middle- and lower-class groups in Luzon, but caused profound apprehension among the Philippine elite. For American and Philippine leaders, the Huks complicated consideration of the issues of collaboration as well as the nature of postwar Philippine politics and society.[17]

## The "Return" to the Philippines

The liberation of the Philippines marked the beginning of the final phase of decolonization, but under conditions unique in Philippine history. However enlightened American colonial policy had been since 1898, it could not have prepared Americans or Filipinos for the immense problems caused by the war. Food was scarce—crop production in 1944–45 was only 60 percent of the normal output and much of it was consumed by the armies. Industrial production and the transportation system were at a standstill. Manila, which MacArthur had tried to save from destruction by declaring it an open city in 1941, was by 1945 one of the war's most devastated cities; about 85 percent of the capital had been destroyed. The islands had become a land of homeless, starving people. Disease was widespread, and medical and sanitation facilities virtually nonexistent. Law and order had collapsed; only the black market seemed to flourish. The widespread death and destruction left the people stunned, seemingly comatose. It was certainly not the situation in which constitutional processes could be easily revived or complex issues like collaboration judiciously resolved. A scholar of Philippine collaboration has observed: "it was not the optimum time for Philippine society to have to confront the human imperfections of an imperfect world."[18]

These conditions strained Philippine politics, relations between the Philippine elite and American authorities, and decisionmaking within the American government. Tensions developed between the returning commonwealth officials and those who had endured Japanese rule, leading to a situation in which the collaboration issue came to dominate Philippine politics. Philippine leaders differed with the United States over the timing of independence, policy toward the collaborators, postindependence commercial relations, and rehabilitation assistance. Within the American government, differences over Philippine policy emerged. MacArthur intervened in Philippine politics in ways seemingly inconsistent with official objectives,

while in Washington, the State Department, White House,
Interior Department, and Congress competed for predominance
in determining the principal directions of Philippine-American relations.

Following the landings at Leyte on October 20, 1944,
MacArthur's forces, with strong air and naval support, overcame
determined Japanese resistance. By January 1945, the Americans began invading Luzon and on February 3, the first units
reached Manila. The city was bitterly defended by the Japanese,
and only after a month of house-to-house combat was resistance
effectively ended. While military operations in the Philippines
continued until V-J Day, military priority by the spring of 1945
shifted to building up the islands as a massive staging area for
the projected invasion of Japan. Accordingly, MacArthur was
anxious to install a civil administration as soon as feasible. In a
ceremony on February 27, he restored full civil government. In
practice, the devastation of the Philippines, the divisions within
the Philippine leadership, and the continued military campaign
against the Japanese meant that effective political power still
rested with MacArthur.

The establishment of civil government virtually obligated
President Osmena to convene the Philippine Congress. The last
Congress, elected in 1941, had never met and most of its members had cooperated with the Japanese, holding positions in the
Vargas administration and the Laurel Republic. Osmena suggested reviewing the wartime records of all members of Congress, only to be accused of being a dictator. Under much
pressure from MacArthur and Philippine leaders, Osmena sum-
moned Congress; it finally convened on June 9. Of the 110 members who met in joint session that day, 77 had, in one way or
another, served the Japanese.

Leading the opposition to Osmena was Manuel Roxas
who, although having declined to lead a puppet regime, had
nonetheless served in the Laurel government. MacArthur was
instrumental in Roxas' reemergence as a major political figure.
After the American landings, the Japanese had taken members
of the Laurel cabinet to Baguio in December 1944; from there

Laurel and a few others were flown to Formosa and eventually to Japan, while others were released. In April 1945, Roxas was freed and "rescued" by the American army; other Laurel government officials were "captured." The distinction in Roxas' case was on orders from MacArthur, who held that Roxas' participation in the wartime government was justified by his participation in a Manila-based intelligence group which had maintained contact with MacArthur's headquarters. Clearly MacArthur preferred Roxas, a friend and former aide, to Osmena. In ensuing weeks, other American military officers came to share MacArthur's assessment of Roxas; and as Osmena appeared less effective (largely a consequence of American actions), military personnel in the Philippines looked to Roxas as the only leader who could restore stability and direction. Roxas quickly became Osmena's principal rival and the leading defender of the collaborators. When Congress convened, he was overwhelmingly elected President of the Senate.[19]

In Washington, the liberation of the Philippines revived discussion on the timing of independence. In early 1945, the State Department recommended granting independence "as soon as possible" and MacArthur, from Manila, urged advancing the date to August. He encouraged Osmena to return to the United States in order to gain a firm American commitment to an early transfer of authority. Ickes opposed the seemingly unreasonable haste to withdraw before commercial relations and other important matters were resolved. Roosevelt, however, sided with the State Department, MacArthur, and Osmena, who visited the President at Warm Springs, Georgia, on April 5. At a press conference later that day, Roosevelt expressed hope that he would be able to proclaim Philippine independence "long before" July 4, 1946.[20] The movement toward early independence abruptly lost momentum, partly as a consequence of Ickes' influence on Truman following his succession to the presidency, and also because of the increased awareness in Washington of the serious political and economic problems in the Philippines. When Truman and Osmena met, on April 19 and again on May 4, the Philippine President recalled his conversation with Roosevelt and sought Truman's endorsement of his predecessor's intentions. Truman, however, cautiously committed himself to Roosevelt's general policy and, in a press release following his second meeting with Osmena, he pledged only the fulfillment of SJ Resolution 93.[21] While the military, economic, and commercial problems justified avoiding any commitment to independence before July 4, 1946, Truman's decision made Osmena's mission appear a failure.

## The Collaboration Issue, 1945–1946

Most detrimental to Osmena was the burden of implementing U.S. policy on collaboration. That policy had been stated by Roosevelt on June 30, 1944: "those who have collaborated with the enemy must be removed from authority and influence in the political and economic life of the country."[22] Roosevelt's statement reflected basically an emotional response to a sense of betrayal; American authorities had not considered the immense problems of defining collaboration and implementing an extensive review and judicial process. Had the Truman adminstration carried out Roosevelt's intention to transfer power in the fall of 1945, the treatment of collaborators would have been handled by Philippine authorities on the basis of their definition of disloyalty. Instead Osmena was obliged to implement a policy which was established in Washington prior to liberation and was directed against the oligarchy of which he was a part. While endeavoring to fulfill American policy, Osmena's leadership steadily eroded. Roxas and his followers blocked Osmena's appointment of two guerrilla leaders to positions in the cabinet. When Osmena proposed the establishment of courts to try those charged with disloyalty, with a stipulation that the judges could not have collaborated, he met strong opposition from the Roxas camp and modified his plans. As the war against Japan ended and MacArthur handed over to Philippine authorities the names of large numbers of persons charged with aiding the enemy, the debate became intense. While leaders of the elite defended their record on the grounds that it lessened the severity of Japanese rule, their opponents charged that suffering had not been alleviated, and that the elite had followed a spineless course; resistance or martyrdom would have been preferable.[23]

When it appeared the Osmena was vacillating on the collaboration issue, Washington exerted strong pressure to uphold American policy. By early September, Osmena was preparing to grant the release on bail of hundreds of political prisoners on whom the American army had collected evidence of collaboration; moreover, he was allowing officials who had served in the puppet regime to hold offices in the Commonwealth government. While it was widely recognized that Osmena's personal political position as well as American objectives on collaboration had been seriously undermined by MacArthur's actions, both the State Department and Interior Department took initiatives to remind Osmena of his obligation to fulfill Roosevelt's policy. Most important, Ickes, in a cable of September 11, suggested that failure to remove the collaborators from political life would jeopardize Congressional allocation of funds for Philippine relief and rehabilitation.[24] Osmena immediately defended his actions: those persons released would still face charges and trials would be conducted by a special People's Court under judges who were not associated with the Japanese adminstration. Officials, however, who had continued in positions held under the puppet government but had been found, by American military personnel, to have taken no actions against the American or Commonwealth government had been reinstated. Moreover, Osmena reminded Washington that the United States was largely to blame for the confusion on collaboration: the release of Roxas and his subsequent activities had created domestic divisions. Beyond the general outlines of Roosevelt's statement, the American government had failed to define its policy in the context of the actual situation in the Philippines.[25]

Ickes' statement, which was released to the press, was resented by Philippine leaders. Filipinos saw Ickes' act as a blatant effort at coercion. Some compared it to the contemptuous treatment they had suffered under the Japanese. While Ickes

anticipated that the threat to reconsider assistance would enhance Osmena's position, in fact it weakened his credibility. In
the Philippine press and Congress, calls were heard for a leader
who would stand up to Washington. Altogether the incident
enhanced the standing of Roxas and the people who supported
the collaborators.[26]

Beyond the representations made to Osmena, the Truman administration endeavored in other ways to influence the
outcome of the collaboration issue. In a September 29 memorandum to Truman, Paul McNutt, about to return to the Philippines as High Commissioner, and Abe Fortas, Undersecretary of
the Interior, baldly stated the fundamental concern: "we do not
want to be placed in the position of granting independence to a
Philippine government composed of enemy collaborators."[27]
Two days later, Osmena, on one of his frequent trips to Washington, met with Truman, who warned strongly against any soft line
toward the collaborators. As Fortras reported the conversation:
"He [Truman] said that the Philippine collaborationists ought
to be hanged first—even before the war criminals in Germany—
because the Philippine collaborationists had been guilty of
treason to the U.S. He said that he was interested in putting the
Philippines back on their feet, but that he was not interested in
doing that for the sake of 'Jap collaborationists' "[28]

However firm the American position, the removal of
collaborators from political life, assuming (as Truman may not
have) that was to be accomplished through the Philippine judicial process, would take months, even years. The first trial of a
relatively prominent political figure to be charged with treason
began in early October. In the meantime, the Roxas forces were
calling for early elections of Congress and the President, which
would almost certainly result in enhancing the position of those
who had worked with the Japanese and in the election of Roxas
to the presidency. In Washington, the State Department and
Interior Department were reluctant to interfere in the election
process, inasmuch as it had been four years since the last elections. After considerable debate, Osmena succeeded in gaining
support for holding the elections in the spring of 1946. At the urg-

ing of the Interior Department, Truman took steps to bring the review of alleged Philippine collaborators under American jurisdiction. The Justice Department was instructed to send a mission to the Philippines to investigate cases of disloyalty against the United States and the Commonwealth. Using intelligence provided by the army and navy, the mission was to recommend appropriate action that might be taken by the United States. In early November, Attorney General Tom C. Clark appointed Walter Hutchinson to head the mission; this initiative placed direct pressure on the Philippine government to pursue its prosecution of collaborators.[29]

The decision to send McNutt back to the Philippines as High Commissioner also reflected a renewed determination to exercise influence on Philippine politics, especially the collaboration issue. The office had been unfilled since Sayre, disillusioned over MacArthur's lack of preparedness to defend the islands and unable to work with Ickes, had resigned in June 1942. Earlier in 1945, the prevailing consensus among the White House, State Department, and MacArthur's command had been to send a special representative who would be concerned with working out the details of commercial relations and other matters preceding independence, rather than dispatching a High Commissioner—the office which symbolized American rule. Osmena had strongly advised against the appointment as an unpopular act, but the Interior Department had consistently advocated designating a High Commissioner. With Ickes pushing the matter and with conditions worsening in the Philippines, Truman decided to reappoint McNutt. After his term as high commissioner from 1937 to 1939, McNutt had headed the Federal Security Agency, a position which he held until the end of the war.[30]

The appointment of a High Commissioner would in any case have caused adverse reaction in the Philippines, but McNutt in particular generated widespread criticism. During his earlier tour of duty, he had been widely known as an advocate of "reexamination" of the American pledge to independence by 1946. Apparently his views had not changed during the intervening six years. In March 1945, he suggested that independence be postponed until the islands had been rehabilitated. And in a Toyko press conference in late December 1945, McNutt was quoted to the effect that the United States would be responsive to a Philippine movement to continue its rule beyond July 1946. His statement brought a wave of protest in the Philippines. In Washington, officials at the State Department were appalled by McNutt's insensitivity to Philippine and Asian sentiment generally. As Abbot Low Moffat noted, Philippine independence was the one tangible application of American's lofty ideal of anticolonialism; nationalists elsewhere looked to the Philippines as a model. Hesitation in fulfilling the promise of independence, Moffat warned, would be detrimental to American prestige and influence and would stimulate a resurgent pan-Asiatic movement from which only the Soviet Union would benefit.[31]

The Hutchinson report was submitted to Clark and McNutt on January 28, 1946. It recommended strong American action to assure full prosecution of the collaborators. Blaming the American military for handing the issue over to the Philippine authorities before they were adequately prepared, Hutchinson found the Osmena administration's procedures lacking adequate investigators, prosecutors, and justices. Moreover, the political leadership of the country and much of the press had minimized the seriousness of collaboration with the result that the public had become indifferent. If Roxas became president, a general amnesty was expected to follow. To remedy the situation, Hutchinson urged that in addition to providing financial and other support for the Philippine special prosecutor, the United States participate directly and fully in all cases involving treason. This could be accomplished through one of the following procedures: a war crimes tribunal which would continue beyond independence; an extraterritorial court which would remain in effect after independence; or the prosecution of officials of the Vargas administration and Laurel Republic in the United States.[32]

By the time the Hutchinson report reached Truman in early March, its recommendations had been subjected to strong criticism. McNutt favored limiting American involvement to support of the Philippine special prosecutor and making certain that cases were disposed of speedily. Clark, on the other hand, urged action along the lines of the final alternative in the Hutchinson report, i.e. the assumption of responsibility for prosecuting officials of the Vargas administration and the Laurel Republic. A war crimes commission under the Allied command in the Far East would assure that those guilty of treason were prosecuted. Clark, however, opposed U.S. involvement in other cases, suggesting that it make known that the Philippine government would have full responsibility. At the War Department, Secretary Robert Patterson criticized Clark's recommendations, maintaining that because established policy dating to the Roosevelt administration delegated responsibility for collaboration issues to civilian authorities, the Filipinos would resent American intervention.[33] MacArthur strongly influenced Patterson's position; in a cable of March 3, he opposed any initiative on the grounds that it would be counter to policy followed elsewhere and would undermine Philippine sovereignty and American interests:

> While there is no question that the crimes committed were against both the United States and the Commonwealth, the unalterable fact remains that these men were Filipinos, [and] the incident involved occurred on Philippine soil. . . . The priority action of the United States cannot fail to be deeply and accumulatively resented by a majority of the Philippine people. In all other liberated countries collaborationists have been released to their respective governments for action. . . . The only possible valid reason to intervene would be the doubt of adequate Philippine punishment. Even if this doubt proved legitimate, I still believe that paramount interest in this matter lies with the Filipinos. It was their loyalty, their devotion and their gallantry which contributed markedly to our success and in my opinion, it would be a churlish act indeed to reciprocate this magnificant performance by an exhibition of superior national sovereignty on incidents connected therewith, and with full independence only four months away. In my belief, the United States in its future relationships with the Far East would have everything to lose and

nothing to gain by not trusting the Filipinos to take action in the premises.[34]

The Patterson-MacArthur position ultimately prevailed in the White House, resulting in the virtual end of Philippine prosecution of collaborators. In a public statement on March 16, Truman indicated that he saw no need to change the policy of leaving disposition of collaborators to civil authorities in the Philippines. This disavowal of the Hutchinson recommendations and retreat from the earlier signs of pressing the collaboration issue came shortly after Philippine authorities had gained the conviction and sentence to life imprisonment of the first (and as events proved only) trial of a relatively prominent political official. Without American backing, the Philippine government shied away from vigorous prosecution. In the end, of 5,603 cases filed before the People's Court, only 156 or 2.7 percent were convicted. The oligarchy which had cooperated with the Japanese went unpunished. Among the 165 most influential political figures listed by the United States Army in its dossiers of collaborators, 122 were never indicted, the cases of 28 were dismissed, 13 others were listed as bonded but without further action, and only 1 was ever tried and convicted.[35]

The American retreat on collaboration policy strongly influenced Philippine politics, for it meant an abandonment of Osmena. He lost interest not only in the collaboration issue but in his campaign for election to the presidency, and in the April 1946 elections, suffered a predictable loss to Roxas. In the campaign, Osmena had become increasingly dependent for support upon leftist groups and the wartime guerrillas, especially the Huks. Much of the middle class, apprehensive over the nature of Osmena's backing, gave strong support to Roxas, as did the oligarchy which was attached to him by his stand on collaboration. Osmena also suffered from his inability to gain satisfactory rehabilitation and commercial agreements with the United States. Considering his many liabilities, the only surprising aspect of Osmena's defeat was that it was not more decisive: he received 1,130,000 votes to 1,333,000 cast for Roxas.[36]

Although the United States officially took no sides in the

election, American officials welcomed Roxas' victory. While MacArthur had facilitated his rapid reemergence, others in Washington and Manila came to share the assumption that Roxas could provide decisive direction to the Philippines as it attained independence. Before the election, McNutt and his staff had already become identified in Philippine eyes with Roxas; clearly the High Commissioner preferred Roxas to Osmena. The American attachment to Roxas resulted principally from concern about the necessity to provide stable leadership. Behind the reversal on the collaboration issue was the recognitition of the stubborn American tie with the oligarchy. At a time when the United States was vitally concerned about Communist expansion in Eastern Europe, China, and mainland Southeast Asia, Washington was not prepared to accept the possibility of Communist influence in a Philippine government. To trust the development of the Philippines to a group which might be Comminist-dominated constituted a risk Washington was not prepared to take. While intelligence sources reported that the Huks enjoyed broad support, had responded to genuine social and economic unrest, and could not be simply labeled as "Communist,"[37] the context of the emerging cold war meant that, in practice, "Washington, considering the Hukbalahap to be the international conspiracy of communism, ignored the noncommunist, indigenous, albeit radical, quality of peasant unrest."[38]

## Economic and Military Relations, 1945–1946

The policy on post-independence economic relations constituted, like the resolution of the collaboration issue, a reestablishment of the American association with the Philippine elite. It signified as well a determination to resume the prewar patterns of trade, which meant continued Philippine dependence upon the United States. A trade agreement, moreover, became tied to the American program on rehabilitation assistance, which from the Philippine perspective was deficient and, in any event, clearly retarded Philippine reconstruction and economic development. The American action on trade policy and rehabilitation assistance reflected largely the opinions of McNutt, who took initiative on these matters at a time when the White House seemed to lose interest and when congressional leaders, the State Department, and the Interior Department were frequently in disagreement. To many observers in the Philippines, the economic policies undermined political independence and constituted a disregard of Philippine interests and of earlier American promises and commitments.

During the war, Roosevelt had encouraged the Philippines to expect a substantial program of rehabilitation assistance, but neither the President nor Congress had moved decisively to establish a program for its implementation. In August 1943, Roosevelt stated that the Philippines would be compensated in "full repair" for war damages. At his urging, Congress established a rehabilitation commission, composed of American and Philippine representatives, but it proved ineffective, largely because of inadequate information about conditions in the islands and waning American interest as the end of the war approached. Shortly after becoming President, Truman promised Osmena substantial rehabilitation assistance, but then provided no leadership on the matter. The Commonwealth government, during its exile in Washington, had established the Philippine Technical Committee, which in March 1945 estimated war damages at $1.1 billion. The War Damage Corporation, which had been charged by Congress to receive Philippine claims and had conducted its own investigation, set the damages substantially lower: $800 million. In Congress, the sentiment in late 1945 was to limit Philippine war damage claims to $500 million.[39]

Philippine-American differences, as well as disagreements within the U.S. government, likewise characterized consideration of commercial relations. The Tydings-McDuffie Act provided for Philippine trade preferentials to end at the time of independence, but during the war Filipino representatives in Washington pressed for their continuation as a means of facilitating rehabilitation. While a number of American officials came to favor extension of free trade or a limited period of preferentials, others opposed any special policy for the Philippines. To these officials, the overriding concern was the inconsistency between continuing a preferential relationship with the Philippines at a time when the cornerstone of postwar trade policy was the elimination of imperial preferences and other forms of trade discrimination. By March 1945, Roosevelt endorsed a compromise formulated at the State Department which called for a period of declining preferential trade, but in the summer of 1945, Congress challenged the adminstration's position, thus beginning a prolonged controversy over postindependence trade relations to which rehabilitation assistance became subservient.[40]

Congressional action on Philippine trade policy represented a series of compromises among various competing special interests: traders and investors who sought to sustain thier position in the Philippine economy; agricultural producers who feared competition from Philippine products; proponents of extended free trade as a boon to American interests; those favoring an early, if not immediate, end to special priviledges as part of the pursuit of the global open door. When Congressman C. Jasper Bell as chairman of the House Insular Affairs Committee introduced a Philippine trade bill in September 1945, it called for a twenty-year period of free trade, quotas on major Philippine exports in the American market (most importantly sugar, cordage, and coconut oil), and American parity rights in various phases of Philippine economic development. The White House, under prodding from the State Department, and Senator Tydings spoke out against the prolonged period of free trade, but whereas the Roosevelt administration had supported a twenty-year period of declining preferences, circumstances now virtually necessitated accepting a brief period of free trade preceding declining preferences. Tydings proposed a five-year interlude of free trade followed by the twenty-year period of declining preferences. Opponents of the Bell measure argued that it would not only prolong Philippine dependence and encourage export industries, but would also undermine State Department efforts to negotiate with the British government for an end to its system of imperial preferences.

Acceptance of at least a few years of free trade, however, had become politically advisable because Philippine leaders lobbied for the Bell proposal. Osmena maintained that it would facilitate economic reconstruction and would assure a market for Philippine exports at a time when dislocations resulting from the war precluded the establishment of viable trade relations anywhere in Asia. In November, with McNutt and the Interior department strongly supporting continuation of free trade, a White House conference of congressional leaders and various administration officials agreed to a modification of the Bell trade bill providing for eight years of free trade and twenty-five years of declining preferences.[41]

As Congress acted upon the revised Bell proposal, supporters justified the measure principally as a means of rehabilitating the Philippine economy. In testimony before congressional committees, McNutt emphasized the devastation of the Philippines and argued that free trade would help revive agricultural production and the economy generally. While not stated in such bald terms, McNutt and others implied that the Bell trade proposal provided an alternative to the large scale program of rehabilitation assistance promised by Roosevelt. It also offered incentives to American investors and benefits to the largely American-owned sugar and coconut interests. Domestic agricultural interests did press, with some success, for modification of the period of free trade and quota provisions. In March 1946, the Bell proposal was revised again, reflecting generally the objectives of McNutt and his considerable influence. The preferential period was reduced to a total of twenty-eight years (free trade for eight years and twenty years of declining preferences) and American parity rights were specifically designated to the development and exploitation of Philippine natural resources and public utilities. Further, the value of the Philippine peso in relation to the American dollar could be changed only with the approval of the American president. The Bell Trade

Bill, incorporating these provisions, was passed by Congress in April 1946.[42]

By that time, Congress was also acting upon a rehabilitation bill. By the terms of a measure introduced by Tydings, the United States would provide $620 million in compensation for war damages—about one half of the Philippine estimate of the actual cost of wartime losses. As stated bluntly by Tydings: "the purpose . . . is to rehabilitate the Philippines in the least costly way we can."[43] After the measure passed the Senate, Bell, who steered it through the House, responded to critics who suggested the amount was inadequate: "if we give that much help, private industry will be able to carry the balance of the load and we want to do it as cheaply as we can."[44] In addition, the bill contained a proviso which was especially obnoxious to many Filipinos. At the urging of McNutt, rehabilitation was tied to the trade act, specifically by stipulating that no damage claim in excess of $100 would be paid until the Philippine and American governments had reached an executive agreement implementing the Bell Trade Act. While many Americans recognized that the rehabilitation measure constituted an affront to Philippine national pride, most members of Congress accepted McNutt's position that the rehabilitation and trade acts were the "heart of the program for Philippine recovery."[45]

When the trade and rehabilitation bills went to the White House, Truman, at the urging of James Brynes, whom he had appointed as Secretary of State, and Henry Wallace, who was Secretary of Commerce, accompanied approval with a statement acknowledging the inequitable features and calling for remedial measures at a later time.[46]

Despite Truman's efforts to reassure them, political leaders and others in the Philippines resented the economic policy being imposed by the United States. The Philippine press strongly criticized the Bell Trade Act and Tydings Rehabilitation Act. In some cases, they were compared with the degradation imposed by the Japanese. Commenting on these developments in a forty-page report, "The Deterioration of Philippine-American Relations," D. L. Worcester of the High Commissioner's Office warned that by its economic policies and intervention in Philippine politics, the United States had lost its credibility among the Filipinos.[47]

Despite the affront to Philippine sovereignty, Osmena and Roxas, as the office of the presidency changed hands, urged acceptance of the measures. Before the Philippine Congress, Roxas defended the trade act. The provision for parity would attract American capital; the quotas guaranteed export markets for Philippine agricultural products; finally, implementation of the Bell act enhanced prospects for approval of a $250 million rehabilitation loan which Roxas had requested. On July 2—just two days before the transfer of power—the Philippine Congress approved the provisions of the Bell Trade except for the granting of parity rights to American nationals. Since the Constitution reserved the exploitation of natural resources to Filipinos or Filipino-owned corporations, a constitutional amendment was required for that provision to go into effect. This meant that as power was formally transferred on July 4, a trade agreement had not yet been completed and, as a result, the Tydings Rehabilitation Act could not be fully implemented.[48]

While economic and political objectives fundamentally reestablished prewar relationships, military planning anticipated a considerable expansion of American influence. The Tydings-McDuffie Act had provided only for naval bases and fueling stations, but during the war, the Philippines came to figure prominently in plans for an enlarged security system in the Pacific. The Japanese conquest gave a strong moral imperative to guaranteeing Philippine security. During the war, Roosevelt had pledged that independence would be established and protected by the full resources of the United State, and SJ Resolution 93 provided for additional military bases. By the spring of 1945, the War and Navy departments had developed plans for some thirty sites to be used as infantry, air force, coastal defense, radar and communication bases. In the meantime, MacArthur's command established bases as part of the campaign against Japan in the islands and in support of operations in the north. In June 1946, the United States retained some seventy-one bases in the Philippines.[49]

In the meantime, Philippine and American officials were negotiating a comprehensive military agreement. As a first step toward postindependence cooperation, on June 26, 1946 Truman signed the Philippine Military Assistance Act, which provided for the training of Philippine military and naval personnel as well as transfer of equipment and supplies to the Philippines; $100 million in arms and equipment was immediately earmarked for the Philippine army. While Philippine leaders strongly supported American military plans, Roxas and others insisted that the Amerian military presence be removed from the Manila area and questioned the insistence of the War and Navy departments that military authorities exercise jurisdiction over military personnel even when they were outside the bases. On the latter point, the State Department supported the Philippine position; John Carter Vincent, Director of the Office of Far Eastern Affairs, argued: "A provision such as that desired by the War and Navy Departments would be regarded not merely by the Filipino people but by other friendly Far Eastern peoples as a revival of extraterritoriality; . . . it would create popular opposisiton to the bases agreement in the Philippines . . . and this country's good will among Far Eastern peoples would suffer without commensurate advantage to this country."[50] Despite efforts to work out a compromise, no military agreement had been reached by July 4, 1946.

## The Promise Fulfilled: Independence

Independence thus came to the Philippines with important questions unresolved and American hegemony preserved. Yet the significance of the transfer of political authority could not be denied. The United States had fulfilled its promise. Sukarno and Ho Chi Minh, who were just beginning the struggles which would lead to independence from the Dutch and French respectively, extended congratulations, as did many other nationalist spokesmen. For those in the United States who had been disappointed by the wartime compromises with the colonial powers, the withdrawl from the Philippines reestablished America's anticolonial credentials. The continued American influence could not be ignored and led to a certain cynicism about Philippine independence. The strongest criticism came from nationalist leaders in India, who tended to regard their movement for independence from Britain as a more appropriate model for colonial peoples.[51] Jawaharlal Nehru, then President of the Indian National Congress and destined to be Prime Minister after independence was attained in 1947, sent a message of congratulations to the Philippines which set the tone of India's reservations: "We hope that this really signifies independence for this word has become rather hackneyed and outworn and has been made to mean many things. Some countries that are called independent are far from free and are under the economic or military domination of some great power. Some so-called independent countries carry on with what might be termed 'puppet regimes' and are in a way client countries of some great power. We hope that is not so with the Philippines."[52]

The compromised independence and the attendant unsettled questions troubled Philippine-American relations beyond July 4, 1946. Philippine dependence upon the United States, especially for rehabilitation assistance, forced the newly independent government in Manila to support the obnoxious provision in the Bell Act providing for parity rights in the exploitation of Philippine resources. At length, on September 18, the Philippine Congress approved a resolution proposing a parity rights amendment. The resolution was adopted by a narrow margin and constitutionally questionable process; Roxas and his Liberal party followers arbitrarily ruled that seven members of the House of Representatives and three Senators, all representing other parties, could not take their seats on the grounds that their elections failed to represent the will of the electorate. With a sufficient number of opponents thus purged, the resolution was barely approved by the required three-fourths margin.

Finally in March 1947, a plebiscite ratified the amendment by an eight-to-one margin; only 40 percent of registered voters, however, participated in the referendum and many observers interpreted that small turnout as a silent rebuke of the special rights being given to Americans.[53]

In addition to their resentment over the provisions for rehabilitation assistance and trade relations, many Filipinos also objected to the American indifference to the Republic's serious financial problems. The independent government immediately faced a shortage of revenue for which it was not responsible. Roxas appealed to Washington for loans of $400 million to meet budgetary needs over the next five years and $250,000 from the Export-Import Bank. With the Truman adminstration showing only modest concern over the plight of the Philippine government, the National Advisory Council of the Export-Import Bank disapproved the application and Congress authorized a loan of only $75 million through the Reconstruction Finance Corporation.[54]

Philippine sensitivity on these economic issues led some officials in Washington, especially at the State Department, to urge moderation on military plans. As a result, the War Department abandoned its earlier demand for exclusive jurisdiction over American military personnel and was prepared to limit off-base jurisdiction to cases where both parties were Americans. In the fall of 1946, Filipinos increasingly criticized the plans for military bases. McNutt urged Truman to take the initiative by declaring that the United States and Philippines were about to enter a "solemn compact for the national defense of the Philippines." Officials at the State Department, joined by those at War and Navy, prevailed upon the White House to veto McNutt's suggestion which would have offended Filipinos and antagonized the Roxas government to which American interests had become closely tied.[55]

The War Department also came to favor, for different reasons, a reduction of military forces in the Philippines. At a time of rapid demobilization which had not been anticipated a few months earlier, the Chiefs of Staff reassessment of military priorities downgraded the importance of the Philippines. More-over, acceptance of the Philippine insistence that forces be removed from the Manila area necessitated construction of facilities elsewhere, which, owing to budgetary constraints, would have to be limited. Accordingly, the State-War-Navy Coordinating Committee, by December 1946, endorsed the policy of withdrawing all American forces (except for units con-cerned with immediate postwar problems) and suspending military construction. Roxas and McNutt, however, strongly objected to these plans, maintaining that they represented an abandonment of wartime pledges to the Philippines. It was recalled that the Philippine Congress, in one of its first acts after being reconvened in 1945, had passed a resolution which called for tying Philippine security to a continued American military presence. Eventually Truman, while agreeing that American forces should be withdrawn from the Manila area, stipulated that limited forces be retained elsewhere pending the comple-tion of a formal agreement on military bases.

The military base agreement, which was initialled by Roxas and McNutt in March 1947, designated sixteen sites for American retention (seven being operational bases, and nine miscellaneous facilities) and listed seven additional sites subject to subsequent negotiations. The agreement was to be effective for ninety-nine years. As worked out earlier, the Philippine government held jurisdiction in criminal cases involving Amer-ican personnel outside the bases (except when both parties were American). With Roxas strongly supporting the agreement, the Philippine Senate gave its approval virtually without debate. The unanimous Senate endorsement (eighteen votes in favor) was, however, deceptive as a measure of Philippine opinion. Three prominent senators, who opposed the treaty, declined to vote, and at least one of the affirmative votes was cast under pro-test. While specific reasons for the opposition varied, an under-lying concern in all cases was resentment over the compromise of Philippine sovereignty.[56]

The Philippine-American relationship which developed between the liberation of the islands and first months of independence troubled many observers in both countries. Joseph Abaya, a journalist who had served in the Philippine underground during the war, and David Bernstein, who had been an adviser to Quezon and Osmena, set forth, in separate books, strong indictments of American policy. Abaya's *Betrayal of the Philippines* and Bernstein's *The Philippine Story,* published in 1946 and 1947 respectively, criticized MacArthur's role in manipulating Roxas into power as the decisive act in determining the direction of Philippine-American relations. Abaya, who strongly defended the Huks as representatives of genuine nationalist sentiment, warned that Philippine democracy would be plagued by civil strife and dependence upon one-man rule, which was already personified by Roxas. To Bernstein, the United States had failed to fulfill its obligation to rehabilitation and to real economic and political independence. As suggested in the writings of Abaya and Bernstein as well as later scholars of Philippine-American relations, the United States in 1945–46 had a unique opportunity to accompany rehabilitation with thorough social and economic reform. The kind of commitment to reform evidenced in the occupation of Japan could have brought far-reaching and fundamental changes to the Philippines. Instead the limited vision of Washington led only to months of haggling over funding, terms of assistance, and military arrangements.[57]

As has been noted, some officials were troubled by the insensitivity of American policy, the inadequacy of rehabilitation assistance, and the perpetuation of the power of the traditional elite. When the Philippine government moved in late 1946 to suppress the Huks and other dissidents (an action justified in part by the allegation that Chinese Communists in the islands were behind the insurgency), officers at the American embassy in Manila warned Washington that the reliance on military measures ignored deeply rooted political and economic grievances.[58]

In the end, American objectives and tactics in the Philippines seemed contradictory. Maintaining a close economic and political relationship became dependent upon trade and rehabilitation policies that undermined the confidence of the elite, to which American interests were closely tied. The Huks and others who had resisted the Japanese felt completely betrayed and could only continue a desperate and isolated struggle for political influence. While they were antagonized by American actions, the Philippine elite under Roxas and later leaders, facing serious internal problems, lacked maneuverability and had no choice but to remain dependent upon the United States—the former colonial power which was at once admired, needed, and despised.

# 8.

# The Emergence of United States' Influence in Thailand, Burma, and Malaya, 1945–1948

> For the discernible future, we must recognize that on no important question can we [British] hope to achieve results here [Thailand] unless we can move forward in unison with the Americans.
>
> C. M. Anderson, Foreign Office, November 19, 1946

AMERICA'S SOUTHEAST ASIAN policy after World War II focused on Indonesia, Indochina, and the Philippines, but at the same time, the United States faced important problems in Thailand, Burma, and Malaya. The interests of other Western powers in Thailand and Burma challenged American objectives. In Thailand, the wartime Anglo-American differences continued, producing serious tensions before the substantial realization of goals set by Washington. Whereas Burma had been of negligible concern to the United States earlier, and its postwar status had not caused difficulties between London and Washington, that situation changed quickly as a result of the emergence of a strong nationalist movement by the end of the war. To the

United States, both Thailand and Burma provided opportunities to demonstrate that the West could fulfill promises of
self-determination. In Thailand, this meant assuring that independence was not jeopardized by a punitive peace settlement,
while in Burma it called for pressing for early independence. At
the same time, and especially as Communist armies moved
toward victory in China, American policy sought to assure the
political ascendancy of Thai and Burmese leaders who would
follow pro-Western policies.

In Malaya, however, British and American political and
economic interests tended to converge. This reflected the common perceptions of Malayan nationalism as relatively weak and
ineffective, and of the threat posed by the emergence of a strong
Communist movement. By the time that the British were imposing virtual martial law to counter Communist-inspired unrest,
the United States was reestablishing its prewar trade with
Malaya, especially imports of rubber and tin.

## The Reemergence of Thailand

While the British persisted in approaching Thailand as a defeated enemy, the United States sought the early establishment
of diplomatic relations with a Thai government provided it
repudiated the Pibul government's association with Japan.
Moreover, the United States was prepared to assist in Thailand's relief and rehabilitation and encourage credits for the
Thai government and industry; open door economic rights and
privileges remained central to American objectives. Britain
planned to include in agreements ending its state of war, provisions for a prolonged period of military control and stringent
economic penalties. These measures threatened Thailand's
sovereignty and foreshadowed a British protectorate. In particular, the Department of State objected to the stipulation of a
levy of 1.5 million tons of rice. The British regarded the levy as
an appropriate punishment for Thailand' s declaration of war
and as essential to meeting war-induced food shortages in

Burma, Malaya, Singapore, and India. According to American estimates, Thailand's rice reserves approximated 500,000 to 800,000 tons, meaning that the proposed levy would seriously strain the Thai economy. Not only did this undermine the American objective for an economically and politically viable Thailand, it also ran counter to the general American approach to postwar reparations which rested on the principle of balancing a country's capability with Allied demands on its resources. Disregarding the American position, SEAC put forth the British terms to representatives of the Regent of Thailand in the name of the "Allied military authorities" thus implicitly associating the United States with British objectives.[1]

In the fall of 1945, Washington repeatedly pressured London over the Thailand issue. When it became known on September 6 that Mountbatten had given the Thai delegation at Kandy 48 hours to sign an agreement embodying British demands, Assistant Secretary of State Dean Acheson instructed Ambassador John Gilbert Winant to protest and request delaying the procedure. The Joint Chiefs of Staff had approved the first part of the agreement dealing with occupation policy, but Acheson and Winant strenuously objected to the long-term economic and military arrangements, and said that their inclusion would necessitate disavowal of the agreement. While the British altered Mountbatten's instructions telling him to insist upon signing only the first part of the agreement, they remained adamant on the economic issues. In an aide-memoire of September 8, the British argued that contrary to American projections, Thailand did not face serious economic problems; the country had suffered relatively little war damage, foreign exchange holdings had been conserved during the war, and alone among the countries of the region, it had accumulated a large surplus of rice. To allow Thailand to unload that surplus at scarcity-induced high rates would permit the country to increase substantially (perhaps by three times) its foreign exchange holdings at the expense of suffering by other peoples.

The American response, embodied in a strongly worded aide-memoire of September 19, stipulated that the rice levy should not be included in any agreement put forth in the name of the Allies. As an alternative, the State Department suggested a voluntary Thai gift of perhaps 500,000 tons of rice—an allocation deemed reasonable based on American estimates of the rice surplus and the 1945 crop. In addition, Washington challenged the provision that Thailand accept a SEAC military mission to advise on organizing, equipping and training the army; the Americans held that Thailand should be free to negotiate its own military assistance programs. Further, the State Department reiterated its intention to restore diplomatic relations with a Thai government dependent upon abrogation of the agreements with Japan.[2]

In a move which further underscored the American determination to disassociate itself from British policy, on September 21 Washington dispatched Charles Yost to Kandy. (Yost had recently been designated chargé d'affaires at Bangkok pending the establishment of diplomatic relations.) This move gave the United States direct high-level contact with SEAC officials and Thai representatives. Yost's presence at Kandy suggested the potential of a Thai-American agreement undermining British plans. When Thai officials in early October indicated that the Japanese treaties had been formally renounced, the State Department informed the Foreign Office that diplomatic recognition could be delayed only for a "reasonable period" to allow for coordinating it with the signing of a British-Thai agreement. As the British remained adamant on the rice levy issue, on October 31 Acheson authorized sending Yost and his staff to Bangkok. In deference to the British, the Yost mission went without official status; the State Department, however, intimated that his presence could lead to formal diplomatic relations by December 1, 1945. Although the United States did not reestablish diplomatic relations with Thailand until January 1, 1946, Yost's presence in Bangkok during the interim signified an assertion of American influence that put substantial pressure on the British.[3]

The Anglo-American exchange became increasingly acromonious, leading to Washington's decision to break openly with the British by intervening in Thai-British negotiations. Developments in Thailand and elsewhere in Asia reinforced the State Department's conviction that American interests necessitated full and immediate recognition of Thailand's sovereignty. From Bangkok, Yost urged recognition as the only means of countering a defeatist attitude prevalent among Thai leaders who had become convinced of American complicity in British policy. Further, as he and other officers at diplomatic posts in Asia warned, the British ascendancy in Thailand and the American deference to colonial powers in Indochina and Indonesia were eroding the American image among the peoples of Southeast Asia.[4] When the British dismissed the State Department's suggestion that the United States be represented on a claims commission to determine Thailand's capacity to absorb a rice levy, Washington took sharp issue in an aide-memorie of November 29. Acheson's comments upon presentation of the note to Halifax further accentuated the American position.[5] The British did modify their attitude toward the commission, but at the same time they renewed pressure on Thai officials by presenting them with an ultimatum to sign the military and economic agreements by December 15. Concerned with American interests in Thailand and the region generally, Washington intervened in the negotiations and encouraged the Thais to resist the British demands.[6] With the United States now lending support to Thailand, the British had no alternative but to accept the essential American positions on the rice issue, which meant recognition of the Thai's capacity to meet the levy, and their freedom to work out their own security arrangements.[7]

The British-Thai agreement, signed at Singapore on January 1, 1946, represented an important acheivement for American diplomacy in Southeast Asia. Thailand was prohibited from exporting rice until September 1, 1947, except in accord with the policy set by a British-appointed board; any exports were to be limited to the surplus available and could not exceed 1.5 million tons. (In fact, the rices clauses were not implemented. The Thais smuggled surplus rice into Hong Kong and Malaya at substantial profit. In May, 1946, the agreement was modified to provide that the British would have to pay for the rice delivered through the board's directives, but at prices below the world market. As smuggling continued, it was finally agreed, in December 1946, that the world market prices would be paid.) In the other provisions, Thailand renounced territory seized from Burma and Malaya during the war and granted the British veto power over the construction of a canal across the Kra Isthmus. British commercial and banking institutions were permitted to reopen in Thailand, and Britain agreed to support Thailand for membership in the United Nations.[8]

After the signing of the Singapore Treaty, difficulties between France and Thailand became prominent, and again the United States worked toward a solution which enhanced Thailand internationally and strengthened its government internally. The controversy stemmed from the 1941 agreement in which Indochinese territory had been transferred to Thailand. France refused to recognize the treaty since it had been concluded by the Vichy government; Thailand held that the agreement had been signed with a government with which it had not been at war, and thus ought not be compared with the wartime annexations of territory from Burma and Malaya. To resolve the dispute, Thailand proposed that plebiscites be conducted in the ceded territories. Maintaining, as it had in 1941, that the cessions had been made under duress, the United States supported the French position on restoration, but with the proviso that it should not prejudice subsequent peaceful and orderly adjustment of conflicting border claims. Accordingly, the State Department repeatedly sought assurances from France that retrocession would be followed by examination of the Thailand-Indochina border questions, but France declined on the grounds that such a concession would enhance Thailand's claims and foster instability along the frontier.[9]

In early 1946 the French-Thai dispute was intensified by the crisis in Indochina. As the French reasserted control over their colony, Cambodian and Laotian nationalists took refuge in Thailand. Thai officials allowed them to operate in Thailand without restraint. In May, several incidents along the border resulted in skirmishes between French and Thai forces; Thailand charged France with seizing their territories while the French accused the Thai of protecting Laotian and Cambodian revolutionaries and diverting attention from Thailand's obligation to return the disputed territory. While the United States officially urged restraint on both sides, its officials in Bangkok and Washington tended to side with Thailand, resulting in stronger statements to France and a reiteration of requests for full review of the boundary issues. In addition, the United States modestly encouraged Thailand's plan to take its case to the United Nations; it was assumed that France, facing the prospect of prolonged Security Council consideration of the Thai complaint, which was filed on May 31, would modify its position. Washington, likewise, did not enthusiastically seek United Nations consideration, for an open dispute with France risked delaying Thailand's admission to the international organization. Accordingly the United States quietly advocated direct negotiations and welcomed France's proposal that the dispute be submitted to the International Court and that an interim neutral administrator ( or "conservator") be placed in charge of the provinces ceded in 1941. On August 1, the United States endorsed the French plan and volunteered to serve as "conservator." This overture, however, proved abortive for after fighting resumed on August 10 in the Seam Reap area, instigated in part by Cambodian nationalist activities in Thailand, France withdrew its offer to accept arbitration through the International Court and threatened as well to block any United Nations consideration of Thailand's case.[10]

Despite the failure of the International Court-conservator approaches, the essential U.S. objective represented in that overture—a negotiated settlement—was realized. This required, however, insisting that Thailand accommodate France's demands. This shift in the American position reflected various considerations. First, it was obvious that France enjoyed international support. International opinion was influenced by evidence of Thailand's toleration, perhaps encouragement, of Laotian and Cambodian nationalist activities within its borders. Second, Washington gave high priority to Thailand's membership in the United Nations. Membership was considered essential to enhancing Thailand's international position, but was threatened by the Franco-Thai dispute. Third, the United States was encouraging the French to seek a settlement with the Viet Minh, which suggested the desirability of not antagonizing them over the Thailand issue.

In a meeting on August 28 with Prince Wan Withayakam, chief of the Thailand delegation to the United Nations, Acheson ruled out further American representations to the French and noted the unlikelihood of any United Nations action favorable to Thailand. Instead, Acheson urged direct negotiations, which in effect obligated Thailand to accept France's position.[11] Six weeks later, the State Department unequivocally advised Thailand to accept French terms which annulled the 1941 treaty, restored the ceded territory, resumed diplomatic relations, and reiterated a provision in the 1937 French-Thai treaty for an international conciliation commission to review border claims. In return, France promised to support Thailand's request for United Nations membership. The French proposal came close to the American objective on the border dispute, but it disappointed leaders in Thailand. In the Thai parliamentary debate on annulment of the 1941 treaty, the advice of the United States was frequently cited by those members who argued that the country had no choice but to accept France's terms. Edwin Stanton, who had become the U.S. minister in Bangkok, warned Washington that American prestige would be damaged if the French mistreated Thais living in the retroceded territories and if the international commission ignored legitimate Thai border claims. On November 17, 1946, the agreement between France and Thailand was signed in Washington.

As Thailand came to terms in 1945–46 with its colonial neighbors, the United States had played an important role. American support had enabled Thailand to escape the more punitive aspects of British peace terms, while pressure from Washington had induced Bangkok to accept the border settlement with France. From the perspective of the State Department, the Anglo-Thai agreement gave Thailand the opportunity to advance toward political and economic stability, while the French-Thai treaty at least assured French support for Thailand's membership in the United Nations, which was approved on December 12, 1946. Further enhancing Thailand's international position, the American and British legations in Bangkok were elevated in early 1947 to embassy status; Stanton served as the first United States Ambassador—a position he held until 1953.[12]

Political developments in Thailand which were partially influenced by American policies, ran counter, however, to Washington's objective of cultivating a stable, democratic government. In early 1946, general elections and the promulgation of a new constitution brought Pridi Panyamyong into the position of Prime Minister; Pridi had emerged as the dominant leader following the overthrow of the collaborationist Pibul regime. Pridi had long been a prominent spokesman for parliamentary government, opposed to the militarists still surrounding Pibul, and the royalists led by Seni Premoj. From the American viewpoint, Pridi and his followers were, in Yost's words, "more progressive than their opponents, more realistic politically, and offered a somewhat better prospect of establishing a firm, stable government."[13] These hopes for democratic progress under Pridi were shattered when his leadership was discredited following the mysterious death of the young King Ananda Mahidon on June 9, 1946. Unable to explain the death and in the midst of charges of regicide, Pridi resigned and was succeeded by one of his followers, Luang Thamrong Nawasawat. His leadership, however, was quickly undermined by the terms of the agreement with France. The international commission of conciliation, provided for in the agreement, met in Washington in the spring of 1947 with the representative from the United States as chairman (Peru and Britain were the other neutral members), and submitted a report on June 27 which supported none of the Thai claims to territory and called for only a few changes in border relations.[14]

As the prestige of the parliamentary forces eroded, the military gradually regained influence. On several occasions in early 1947, Stanton expressed concern to Thai officials over the possibility of Pibul's return to power; his avowed fascist principles and leadership of the wartime government made him an anathema to the United States and Britain. Yet at the same time, the State Department became increasingly concerned with communism in Thailand. The Soviet Union resumed diplomatic relations with Thailand on January 12, 1947 and charged in *Izvestia* and other sources that the British and Americans were exploiting the country. While reports from Bangkok indicated little communist activity, Washington feared that chronic instability could stimulate its emergence or, more likely, subversion originating in neighboring China, where the communist ascendancy was now established, would spread to Thailand.[15] Hence, in formulating its objectives for Thailand, the United States began to experience tensions between its interests in a constitutional, democratic system and the need for political stability.

In November 1947 the American dilemma sharpened when the military overthrew the Pridi forces and reestablished itself in power. Partly out of concern over the Western reaction, Pibul remained in the background and Khunag Aphaiwang became prime minister in a cabinet comprised principally of moderate leaders. The United States, together with Britain and France, fearing the resurgence of the ultranationalist, anti-foreign policies of the earlier Pibul regime, withheld diplomatic recognition until March 1948. Although uneasy about the drift toward militarism, the United States ignored overtures from Pridi's followers and some monarchists to intervene either by forcing a coalition government or supporting a countercoup.[16]

Recognition of the government, however, was quickly tested when in early April, Pibul's political dominance came into the open as he regained the position of prime minister. This marked the sixth change in government in Bangkok since V-J Day. Stanton urged nonrecognition of this change in government as a means of demonstrating moral disapproval of his means of gaining power and support for a constitutional system. But in Washington, the State Department overruled Stanton and recognized the Pibul regime. In defending this decision to a much annoyed Stanton, the Division of Southeast Asia Affairs observed that Pibul exercised de facto control and that recognition did not connote approval or support. Yet the United States had delayed recognition of the preliminary phase of the military takeover for four months. What made a difference by April 1948? In large part, recognition of Pibul was dictated by concern with communism in the region. The Soviet Union had just established it legation in Bangkok. The communist conference at Calcutta in February had issued its call for armed revolt in the region, and communist forces were making advances in neighboring Burma and Indochina. It seemed that hostility from the West might drive Pibul toward the Soviet Union. Moreover, Pibul, however regrettable his wartime record and political philosophy, seemed to offer the only available prospect for stabilizing Thailand. Following recognition by the United States, Britain, and France, Pibul took action against Chinese and Annamese communist elements in northeast Thailand and moved as well against the communist-dominated Free Thai movement. Thus, by late 1948, the American interest in Thailand had become increasingly dependent upon a government headed by Pibul Songgram, who just three years earlier had been an enemy of the United States.[17]

In the process the United States was emerging as the dominant external power in Thailand. Both Americans and Thais were intent on expanding economic and commercial interests, as well as strengthening the political relationship. While the British continued to exercise a larger economic role than the United States, clearly the American position politically and economically was in the ascendancy.[18]

## Burma: Expectations and Disillusionment

Thailand's western neighbor, Burma—unlike Thailand, Indochina, Indonesia, or the Philippines—had been of negligible concern to the United States during World War II as it planned for the future development of Southeast Asia. But at the war's end, rapid political changes in Burma increased American interest and influence, for Burmese nationalists looked to the United States for support as they broke from British control.

The decolonization of Burma, as elsewhere in Southeast Asia, reflected the changes brought by Japanese domination. For nationalists in Burma, the war presented an opportunity to regain the country's independence. The Thakin Party, which had dominated prewar nationalist activity, allied itself with Japan in the founding on December 26, 1941 of the Burma Independence Army (BIA). Participating in the Japanese conquest, the BIA was widely welcomed and supported by virtually all segments of Burmese society. After the Japanese disbanded the BIA in July 1942 and replaced it with a smaller Burma Defense Army, the Thakins participated fully in the Japanese-sponsored provisional government, which was headed by Ba Maw. On August 1, 1943, the Japanese granted nominal independence. Within the limits allowed by Toyko, and with Japanese authorities in Burma, Ba Maw became a virtual dictator. While they initially admired his efforts to win independence, other Burmese leaders came to resent Ba Maw's arbitrary policies and close relationship with Toyko. As it became evident that the Japanese did not intend to foster genuine independence, the Anti-Fascist People's Freedom League (AFPFL) emerged. Its leadership came from within Ba Maw's cabinet: Aung San, who was Defense Minister and headed the Burma National Army (BNA), and Than Tun, who served as minister of agriculture, both joined. The AFPFL was an effort by Thakin leaders to build a united nationalist front to eliminate the Japanese and to carry on the struggle for independence whenever the British returned. It was broadly based and included Socialist as well as Communist Thakin leaders, the BNA, and mass peasant and worker organizations affiliated with the Socialist and Communist parties. By the time the British began their attack against the Japanese in Burma, the AFPFL dominated native politics.[19]

Beyond being a part of general postwar plans for colonial

areas, Burma was of marginal interest to the State Department until late in the war. As the Japanese conquered the country, American officials did consider inviting Burma to adhere to the United Nations Declaration as a means of countering Japan's strong appeal. Colonial Governor Sir Reginald Dorman-Smith, whose government fled to India, rejected that possibility on the grounds that the Burmese were not yet capable of self-rule. Officials in Washington shared that view, regarding Burma as more backward than the other colonies of the region.[20] To Isaiah Bowman, the Burmese were "a mess of people." Even Roosevelt held the Burmese in contempt; he wrote to Churchill in 1942: "I have never liked the Burmese and you people must have had a terrible time with them for the last fifty years. Thank the Lord you have He-Saw, We-Saw, You-Saw under lock and key. I wish you could put the whole bunch of them into a frying pan with a wall around it and let them stew in their own juice."[21]

As the British formulated plans for restoration of their authority, however, the United States became increasingly concerned with Burma. Dorman-Smith and other officials of the government-in-exile at Simla, recognized the growing strength of Burmese nationalism and sought a liberal policy pronouncement as a means of facilitating the return of British forces and the reestablishment of British rule. In 1943 Dorman-Smith went to London and gained Colonial Office support for a statement promising self-government "as soon as possible" and establishing a maximum period (the Governor favored seven years) for postwar British administration. Churchill, however, bitterly opposed such a policy and prevailed upon the War Cabinet to delay any meaningful commitment.[22] After returning to Simla, Dorman-Smith lamented to American officials about the shortsightedness of London's position. In the hope that the United States might exert some influence, he requested that an American diplomatic officer be attached to his government. But in Washington, the State Department demurred; any identification with the British empire, even if for a liberal purpose, would only harm American standing among Asiatic peoples.

Despite the renewed efforts by Dorman-Smith to mod-

erate colonial policy, the War Cabinet eventually adopted a conservative approach—the Burma White Paper of May, 1945.
Based on the assumption that the British would be welcomed by
the Burmese people, the White Paper stipulated that Burma's
progress toward self-government had been set back by the war
and that economic and social recovery had to precede the revival
of prewar political institutions. Accordingly, only after a three
year period of direct rule by the governor would the prewar form
of government be reestablished. While the White Paper included
a provision for preparing for full self-government, no date was
set for transfer of authority; moreover, treaties were to be signed
"safeguarding the continuing obligations of His Majesty's Government in Burma." Virtually all members of the Burmese
nationalist movement, including the Burmese who served in
Dorman-Smith's government, were offended by the White Paper's outdated colonialism. Throughout the country, press comment was highly critical, even in some semiofficial newspapers.
To nationalists in Asia as well as disappointed American officials, it seemed a presumptuous policy considering the
strength of Burmese national sentiment, Britain's failure to protect the country three years earlier, and the pledge of the Atlantic Charter.[23]

In the meantime, Mountbatten's strategy and objectives
somewhat modified the British approach. Mountbatten considered cooperation with the AFPFL as essential militarily. Sensitive to American opinion on colonial issues and anticipating
that Burma would become a base for later operations in other
parts of Southeast Asia, he believed that the British  had to
establish in Burma a record of liberal treatment of dependent
peoples. When the AFPFL on March 27, 1945, revolted against
the Japanese, Mountbatten issued orders to his officers to
welcome BNA assistance (while warning, as he realized London
would insist, that past association with the Japanese would not
be forgotten). Faced with a fait accompli, the War Cabinet reluctantly approved Mountbatten's policy. The BNA played an
important  supportive role in the continuing campaign against
the Japanese which led, by early May, to the liberation of

Rangoon. The resulting enhaced status of the AFPFL—symbolized by the BNA participation in the Allied victory parade through Rangoon on June 15—rendered the White Paper all the more out of touch with reality.[24]

In ensuing months, tensions developed between Dorman-Smith, who returned to Burma in October 1945, and the AFPFL. The British continued to insist that economic recovery had to be given priority, while the Burmese pressed for a commitment to self-government. Adding to the problem was the status of Aung San, who was accused of having murdered a village headman in 1942, a deed which he did not deny. The British, concerned about preserving the integrity of their rule, but also mindful of Aung San's continual standing as a national hero, handled the situation badly. They procrastinated, then ordered Dorman-Smith to arrest Aung San, only to later remand the instruction. Having lost what little credibility he still had among the Burmese, Dorman-Smith was dismissed.[25]

State Department officials followed developments in Burma during Dorman-Smith's seven month second governorship with a mixture of apprehension and guarded optimism. While British policy in 1945 and early 1946 seemed to be shortsighted, it was believed that the Labour government would ultimately adopt a more liberal approach. Also, it appeared that the future of Burma would be directly affected by developments in India; and by the end of the war, it was evident that the British could retain control of India only at a high political cost, domestically and internationally. These considerations made the Burma situation seem manageable, especially when compared with the crises in Indochina and Indonesia. By April 1946, Washington was giving serious consideration to long-term political and economic relations with Burma. In planning for negotiations regarding the disposal of lend-lease and other supplies, it was agreed that the United States should seek an air transportation agreement and a cultural and educational exchange program.[26] Glenn Abbey, who headed the consulate in Rangoon, warned that it would be difficult keeping Burma associated with the West. Beyond the "distinct Russian leanings . . . of influential Burmese politicians," all politically conscious Burmese were sensitive to anything resembling imperialism. "If and when the United States moves to help Burma develop its economy," Abbey wrote, "it will be an extremely delicate undertaking to find a middle ground between outright philanthropy and that degree of good business which will not arouse suspicions of imperialism."[27]

Concern over Burma's long-term stability increased during the summer and fall of 1946, as American officials, particularly those at the consulate in Rangoon, and John Cady, a leading historian of modern Burma who was working at the Division of Southeast Asian Affairs, became critical of British delay in implementing measures leading to self-government. A general strike, which confronted Dorman-Smith's successor, Sir Hubert Rance, upon his arrival in September 1946, symbolized the widespread discontent. From the American perspective, it raised again the specter of communist influence.[28] In response to the strike, Rance brought AFPFL leaders into a reconstituted governor's council. After ending the strike and purging the recalcitrant communists from its ranks, the AFPFL demanded on November 10 that the British agree to the election of a constituent assembly in April 1947 and proclaim by January 31, 1947 that Burma would be granted independence within a year of that date.

At this point, the State Department exerted pressure on the British. Further delay, it was feared, would discourage the AFPFL, enhance the appeal of the Communists, and reduce Western commercial and economic influence. On three occasions between November 8 and December 17, 1946, Acting Secretary of State, Dean Acheson, instructed the embassy in London to urge the British to move quickly in order to assure a peaceful transfer of authority. Following a heated exchange with an embittered Churchill in Parliament, on December 21 Prime Minister Attlee invited the leadership of the AFPFL to come to London for discussions on the implementation of Britain's constitutional pledges to Burma.[29]

The delicate negotiations in London, which occurred against a background of considerable Burmese distrust of British intentions evident in renewed strikes and protests (in part, Communist inspired), prepared the way for independence. Among the many points raised in the meetings, the AFPFL sought the early establishment of direct diplomatic relations with the United States, as well as with Thailand and China. With British approval, the Department of State began plans for such a diplomatic exchange. A comprehensive agreement was reached on January 27, 1947 which realized the substance of the AFPFL demands. In the ensuing weeks after the delegation returned to Burma, the leadership of Aung San was critical in winning support for the London agreement and in bringing the various frontier minorities into a united government. As a result, the April elections of a Constituent Assembly gave an overwhelming popular endorsement to the AFPFL and the London agreement.[30]

As the Burmese moved toward independence, the United States exerted pressure on the AFPFL to maintain a strong anti-Communist position. The Communist movement, while divided and eclipsed by the AFPFL, remained nonetheless the second most numerous political group with considerable potential for stirring opposition, especially among the minority peoples. Officials in Washington perceived parallels between Burma and China and sought to prevent the Burmese Communists from gaining the influence that their counterparts enjoyed in China. A statement of American objectives approved by Secretary of State George C. Marshall maintained: "Our policy . . . of preventing them from gaining influence by obtaining a foothold in the government is similar to that in China in that it is one of preventing, if possible, civil war. . . . Only by excluding the communists will the nationalist democratic elements . . . be able to unite among themselves to an extent which will make possible the setting up of enlightened self-government in that country."[31] Accordingly, William Packer, who had succeeded Abbey as Consul-General in Rangoon, pressed upon Aung San and other leaders that allowing Communists any influence would lead to disruption of the democratic process and prove disastrous to Burma.[32]

That the United States would have to assume a major role in encouraging the preservation of Burma's association with the West became more evident when the AFPFL and Constituent Assembly decided in early June 1947 to sever all ties with Britain, thus repudiating its dominion status within the Commonwealth. The United States, meanwhile, enjoyed considerable prestige, with Aung San speaking of the necessity for close relations and assuring Americans that nationalization, contrary to British fears, was a long-term objective which would be implemented cautiously. On the basis of the progress being made by the Constituent Assembly, President Truman approved a diplomatic exchange at the ambassadorial level. In Rangoon, Packer offered help in establishing a professional foreign service and encouraged Burmese expectations of economic assistance.[33]

Burma's development suffered a tragic setback on July 19, 1947 when Aung San and six other cabinet members were assasinated. Aung San, at age thirty-two, held the confidence and respect of the Burmese public to an extent unmatched by any leader before or since. In leading the country toward independence, he had followed pragmatic political and economic policies which had been instrumental in reducing Communist influence, winning over the minorities, and reassuring the British and Americans. Leadership of the AFPFL fell to the competent but untested U Nu, who steered the Constituent Assembly through the completion of a liberal-socialist constitution. With that fundamental task finished by late September, decolonization proceeded rapidly. Over the objections of Churchill, who still maintained that economic rehabilitation should be given priority, Parliament in November 1947 approved a bill granting independence on January 4, 1948.[34]

While welcoming the final steps leading to independence, the United States feared that under U Nu, Burma would move toward the left politically. Official denuniciations of capitalism and renewed talk of rapid nationalization were discouraging, as was Burma's favorable comment about the Soviet Union for its support of nationalist revolutions in Indonesia and Indochina. Repeatedly Packer sought to impress upon U Nu the danger of inviting Communists to join the government, drawing upon examples of obstructive tactics followed by Communist parties in Europe. To American officials, the Burmese evidenced a naive attitude toward communism; to Packer's considerable annoyance, U Nu, for instance, talked of having only "personal" disagreements with Communist leaders. As independence approached, Communist-inspired unrest, however, was limited and ineffective politically, but the likelihood of Communist and minority rebellions persisted. To help stabilize the country and region, Packer urged that Washington be prepared to act favorably on requests for technical or economic assistance. As he had also encouraged, American and Burmese officials completed an agreement for an educational exchange program under the terms of the Fulbright Act.[35]

Despite misgivings about Burmese leadership and the stability of the country, the United States could only welcome the transfer of authority on January 4, 1948. Coming eighteen months after independence had been granted to the Philippines and within five months of the British withdrawal from India, it demonstrated again that decolonization could be accomplished through essentially peaceful means and power transferred to moderate nationalists. American pressure had helped assure that outcome in Burma. At the same time, the influence of the United States had been considerably enhanced.

The government in Rangoon quickly confronted difficulty maintaining the fragile political and ethnic unity fostered by the common interest in gaining independence. After the Communists broke from the government and began warfare in March, U Nu announced a "leftist unity program" which was intended to resolve differences among the various factions in the AFPFL by clarifying domestic and foreign policies. Defending the decision to receive a British military mission which had been strongly criticized by the Communists, U Nu insisted that the government would never accept assistance which infringed on the county's sovereignty. He also affirmed his interest in friendly relations with the Soviet Union and the "new democracies of eastern Europe."[36]

To American officials in Rangoon and Washington, U Nu's leadership seemed ineffective and naive. J. Klahr Huddle, who became ambassador following independence, described the Burmese as "bewildered" and "timid" in dealing with domestic problems and as following a foreign policy which suffered from "ignorance, mistaken concepts, chauvinism, and inexperience."[37] To Huddle, the "leftist unity program" constituted a "frankly Communist line" amounting to an unwitting invitation to Russian imperialism.[38] The Prime Minister's private assurances to Huddle that his program was intended for domestic purposes only, reconfirmed the embassy's assessment of an inept leader. The failure of the Burmese government to take strong and effective measures against the Communists and to counter the signs of disaffection, especially among the ethnic Karens, led officials in the Division of Southeast Asian Affairs to strongly suggest Marshall meet with Burmese Foreign Minister, Kyaw Nyein, in October when both were in Paris attending the meeting of the United Nations General Assembly. In their conversation, Marshall encouraged expectations of American assistance provided Washington was convinced that the Burmese were sufficiently cognizant of the Communist menace, while Nyein took the occasion to affirm his government's opposition to communism and determination to acheive democratic institutions and friendship with the United States and Britain.[39]

From the American perspective, Burma by late 1948, despite protestations of anti-Communist resolve by Burmese officials, remained a poor risk. The Karens broke from the AFPFL and began fighting against government forces. The country appeared headed for chronic instability which would presumably benefit the Communist movement above all others. The incipient Communist victory in China added further to the bleak prospects for Western interests in Burma.[40]

## Malaya: Anglo-American Collaboration

While the United States questioned efforts to reassert the colonial order elsewhere, it did not challenge the reestablishment of British rule in Malaya. Even during the war years, American officials had placed Malaya in a separate category among the colonial areas of Southeast Asia. Malayan nationalism had developed slowly and was hindered by the sharp racial distinctions in the pluralistic Malayan society—which the British rule had exploited through divide-and-rule practices. That tendency to regard Malaya as less prepared for self-rule continued into the postwar period. When Kenneth Landon visited Southeast Asian countries in early 1946, he found strong nationalist sentiments elsewhere, but in Malaya only "some talk of independence" and that "in general discussion [did] not exceed the primary step of self-government with an eventual goal of dominion status."[41] When Malaya was quickly plagued by labor and racial unrest, food shortages, and political turmoil after the war, State Department officials deferred to the British, readily accepting the argument that colonial rule was essential to the preservation of stability.

To the United States, a stable Malaya was important for the reestablishment of trade. A major postwar objective was the reopening of Malayan raw materials for the American market. The International Resources Division of the State Department sought to secure adequate supplies of Malayan tin and rubber. Under American leadership, the Combined Tin Council, representing the United States, United Kingdom, France, Belgium, and the Netherlands, was established for the purpose of assuring equitable international allocation of tin, principally through the early rehabilitation of Malayan mines. By 1946, the United States was buying nearly half of Malayan rubber exports and, with the reopening of the mines, it was purchasing 60 percent of its tin exports in 1948 and fully 90 percent the following year. At the same time, the United States, in contrast with the prewar trading pattern, managed to find a growing Malayan market for its exports, so that by 1949, it had become the third largest supplier of Malayan imports accounting for about 12 percent of the total value of imports.[42]

The emergence of a strong Communist movement seemingly challenged this expanding American economic influence. The Malayan Communist party, which had never been very strong in the prewar period and drew most of its support from the Chinese community, played a prominent role in the resistance to the Japanese. At the end of the war, it sought increased influence, and organized strikes and other forms of political and economic protest. While initially it seemed that the British might accommodate the Communist movement, serious tensions soon developed. In the aftermath of the Calcutta Conference and a series of British-communist confrontations in early 1948, the Malayan Communist party shifted its tactics to support armed revolt and began a campaign of terrorism and sabotage. The British quickly responded, imposing the Emergency Regulations which gave the authorities in the Malay Federation and Singapore virtually unlimited power to suppress the Communist revolt.

To American officials in Southeast Asia and in Washington, U.S. interests clearly necessitated support of the British. The Soviet Union was generally held to be responsible for the uprising; the Kremlin, in Malaya as elsewhere in the region, appeared ready to exploit indigenous grievances. But in Malaya, in contrast to Indochina, communism was not closely linked with nationalism. The British policy during the Emergency seemed essential to upholding the American political and economic position. Hence, American and British interests converged more clearly in Malay than elsewhere in Southeast Asia. Only somewhat later would the colonial relationship be seen as a hindrance to the British anti-Communist effort.[43]

## Conclusion

American diplomacy in Thailand, Burma, and Malaya was generally realizing its basic objectives. The United States had helped to assure the realization of self-determination in Thailand and Burma—not insignificant achievements. Washington had worked as well for representative government, but in Thailand the constitutional experiment failed, while in Burma a democratic system was floundering. Stability seemed to require strong leadership; from the perspective of policymakers in Washington, this necessitated accepting the return of Pibul to power in Thailand. In Burma, no one could truly replace Aung San; with his death, political unity quickly eroded. Malayan self-rule was deferred, for there the priority was resisting Communist insurgency—which the British undertook with unquestioning American approval. The evident Communist success in China contributed to the recognition of the once-discredited Pibul, the apprehension about the future of Burma under U Nu, and the support of the Emergency in Malay, and forced still greater attention to these countries when America's Asian policy was redefined in 1949–1950.

# 9.

# The Indonesian Revolution, 1947–1949: The Fulfillment of Anticolonialism

Sucessive United States Representatives on the Committee of Good Offices together with other neutral observers whose opinions this Government has reason to respect have come to identical conclusions. . . . (1) The welfare of Indonesia is vitally dependent upon the continued availability . . . of the experience and judgment and of the technical and adminstrative proficiency of the Dutch. (2) In the long run, the influence of the Netherlands . . . will be proportional to the confidence and good will accorded the Dutch by the Indonesian people. (3) The preponderant desire of the Indonesian people to govern themselves finds its chief expression in the Republic of Indonesia, which must be considered not as a geographical concept but as a political force.

State Department Aide-Memoire
to Netherlands Embassy,
December 8, 1948

BEGINNING IN THE summer of 1947 when the Netherlands resorted to military force against the Republic of Indonesia, the

Indonesian Revolution became a major international issue. More starkly than any other postwar colonial question, the warfare in Indonesia ultimately forced the United States to decide between supporting a European ally or insisting upon decolonization. Once the Dutch began their "police action" on July 21, the possibilities of compromise virtually ended. The American response satisfied neither side fully, but after some uncertain initial steps, the United States gradually moved toward identification with the Indonesian cause and, in the end, assumed a decisive role in the attainment of Indonesian independence. But the change in American policy came very slowly and, at times, indecisively. This hesitant transition began with steps which the United States took reluctantly in late 1947, but by then the American-Indonesian relationship had deteriorated. It reached its nadir in the three months following the Dutch resort to arms.

The police action was a military success, but a political and diplomatic failure. Moving relentlessly against the ill-equipped and outnumbered Indonesian units, the "limited" objectives—occupation of the major towns of East and West Java, the agricultural areas of the East Coast Residency, and the major oil and coal areas—were realized. The offensive, however, failed to intimidate the Republic. The more moderate leaders who had earlier sought compromise with the Dutch were discredited, the control of the Republican government over extremist groups was reduced, resistance to the Dutch continued, and Indonesians in occupied areas avoided openly siding with the Dutch. Many Dutch officials wanted to crush the Republic entirely by occupying Jogjakarta, but the Netherlands government resisted going that far, realizing that it would produce even more serious international repercussions.

## The Good Offices Committee

The extent of the international reponse surpassed Dutch calculations and placed the United States in an especially difficult position. The Indonesian cause drew sympathy from peoples in the Middle East and other parts of Asia. For two years, the Republic had developed contacts through the activities of unofficial representatives in the Middle East, India, the United States, England, and Australia. As a result, despite the persistent Dutch strategy of isolating the Republic militarily, it managed to maintain a substantial international reputation. Nationalist newspapers and leaders in colonial areas denounced the Dutch and frequently criticized the United States as well for it was commonly assumed that the Dutch would not have taken such drastic action without American approval. A sense of Islamic solidarity dominated much of the commentary from the Middle East and the Muslim leadership in India. Pro-Indonesian sentiment was strong not only in the colonial areas, but also in Australia, New Zealand, and the newly independent Philippines. The normally progovernment press in Manila criticized the Philippine leadership for failing to give unequivocal support to the Indonesians and for not disassociating the Philippines from the United States on this issue. The Soviet press and Communist spokesmen and propaganda throughout Asia fully exploited the Indonesian situation, depicting the police action as a desperate Anglo-American-Dutch conspiracy to retain Western imperialism. For months prior to the military offensive, *Pravda* maintained a steady criticism of Dutch policies in Indonesia, predicting that the United States would provide economic and military assistance in return for the opening of the islands to American trade and investment.[1]

India, then on the threshold of independence, took the initiative in forcing United Nations consideration. Jawaharlal Nehru immediately denounced the police action and called upon the United States and England to insist that the Dutch cease hostilities. When they failed to act promptly, Nehru assailed this evident continued deference to the Dutch and, in conjunction with Australia, insisted that the Indonesian question be taken before the United Nations.[2]

For ten days following the beginning of the police action, the United States and Britain sought to keep the issue out of the

United Nations. Actually, the British attitude was not too different from that of India in that both nations assumed that Dutch dependency gave the United States considerable leverage; for instance, the head of the Southeast Asian Department at the British Foreign Office suggested to an American embassy official that the threat of withdrawing financial assistance would force the Dutch to settle the Indonesian question. From London's perspective, the Dutch move was singularly ill-timed and would lead, it was feared, to prolonged warfare in Indonesia and to disturbances in India, Malaya, and the Middle East. Accordingly, on July 24, three days after the start of the police action, the British suggested that the United States join in an offer of mediation under the Linggadjati Agreement; if mediation failed, the Dutch and Republic would commit themselves in advance to accept an Anglo-American arbitration settlement.

In Washington, Dutch officials repeatedly assured State Department officials that their military operations were progressing successfully and were limited in scope; the Indonesian issue, the Dutch insisted, was an internal matter, not subject to United Nations jurisdiction. In deference to the Dutch position, Truman on July 26 rejected the British overture. At the State Department, a number of officials, however, argued that the United States needed to take some initiative.[3] Charles Wolf, who had just returned to Washington following a seventeen-month tour of duty as vice-consul at Batavia, maintained that prolonged warfare would lead to serious economic dislocations and enhance the appeal of communism. John Carter Vincent and Henry Villard, speaking for the Offices of Far Eastern Affairs and African Affairs respectively, stressed the adverse international repercussions of deferring to the Dutch. As it had in earlier stages of the Dutch-Indonesian crisis, the State Department leadership compromised between its European and Asian interests. With the objective of avoiding United Nations debate on resolutions which might bitterly divide the non-Communist bloc, Truman on July 30 approved a plan whereby the United States would extend its "good offices"—either unilaterally or jointly with the British—to achieve a mediated settlement.[4] This overture, which was considerably weaker than the British mediation-arbitration plan, guided American strategy in the United Nations.

The day that Truman approved the good offices initiative, Australia and New Zealand brought the Indonesian crisis before the Security Council. With the Republic's supporters calling for an immediate cease-fire and submission of the dispute to arbitration, and the Netherlands denying United Nations jurisdiction in the matter, the United States sponsored a compromise resolution that avoided the jurisdiction issue and left open solutions through means other than arbitration. The American resolution, approved on August 1, called for a cease-fire and for a settlement by arbitration or other peaceful means; in addition, the Security Council was to be kept informed of the progress made toward a settlement.

This resolution provided the basis for continued Security Council cognizance of the Dutch-Indonesian dispute and was widely praised at the time as an appropriate assertion of United Nations authority. From the perspective of the Republic and its supporters in the United Nations, however, the Dutch military position threatened the Republic's very existence; stronger international action seemed essential for an equitable settlement. Having attained their basic military objectives, the Dutch informed the United States on August 2 that they would accept American good offices and announced the following day that a cease-fire would go into effect at midnight August 5. The State Department then instructed Walter Foote, consul at Batavia, to seek Republican acceptance of the good offices overture, an assignment which Foote, who remained strongly pro-Dutch, and was reporting that the Indonesians overwhelmingly supported the police action, carried out with considerable reluctance.[5] In Jogjakarta, Foote met over several days with Sukarno and other Indonesian leaders, but found them unwilling to accept the American offer unconditionally, preferring instead to have an arbitrated settlement. After considerable delay, and despite much pressure from Washington, the Republic on August 19 tacitly rejected the American offer.[6]

The Republic's decision was reinforced by the continued support for its position in the United Nations, which reopened the Indonesian debate as it became evident that the cease-fire had failed and hostilities were continuing. The Republic's insistence on arbitration drew considerable international backing while the American good offices plan was frequently criticized. Soviet delegate Andrei Gromyko charged that it showed contempt for the Republic and for the Security Council. The Indonesian cause was greatly enhanced by an impassioned speech before the United Nations by Soetan Sjahrir, whom Sukarno had designated ambassador-at-large. Invited to speak over the objections of the Dutch, Sjahrir's presence at the United Nations further improved the Republic's international standing.

As the American good offices plan floundered, the Dutch, on August 15, suggested the establishment of a three-nation good offices commission. The Netherlands and Republic would each designate one nation whose representative would serve their interests and would mutually agree on an impartial third nation. From the beginning the Dutch anticipated that the United States would be the third member. While considering the Dutch plan, State Department officials received a visit from a Republican delegation headed by Sjahrir who asked for American support of a United Nations commission to supervise implementation of the cease-fire resolution. Still refusing to take steps being advocated by the Republic and its supporters in the United Nations, and in the face of continuing criticism in the Asian nationalist press for its deference to the Dutch, the United States proposed the establishment of the good offices committee, which the Security Council approved on August 25. At the same time, the Soviet Union, following substantially the proposal of the Republic, suggested the establishment of a commission, comprised of representatives from the member nations of the Security Council, to supervise the cease-fire. In a maneuver intended to exclude the Soviets from any commission, the United States countered with a plan restricting the commission to Security Council members which had career consular offices in Indonesia. Moreover, under this new American plan, the Consular Commission's function would be limited to reporting on the implementatin of the cease-fire. Following France's veto of the Russian resolution, the Security Council approved the American alternative. Again on August 26, the Council issued a cease-fire request, calling upon both parties to adhere to the August 1 resolution. On August 29, the Dutch military command announced a new demarcation line which included their most advanced military positions and enclosed far more territory than had been occupied during the official action. "Mopping up" operations proceeded against the Republican units left behind the new line.[7]

Deference to the Dutch during the crisis resulting from the July 21 police action cost the United States its good relations with the Republic and the peoples of Asia and the Middle East. Meanwhile, the Soviet Union's consistent support for the Republic enhanced its prestige in the nonwestern world. Press comment repeatedly praised Gromyko's uncompromising stand while criticizing Anglo-American vacillation. The leadership of the Republic, which earlier had been strongly pro-American, became suspicious of Washington's intent, as was evidenced in the rejection of the unilateral good offices proposal. The major objective of the Republic—international arbitration—was defeated largely because of the United States. In early August, it seemed evident that at least four members of the Security Council (Australia, Poland, Syria, and the Soviet Union) favored arbitration. Had the United States lent its support, Brazil, Colombia, and China would likely have followed its leadership. Behind the American opposition to arbitration was concern for the position of the Netherlands which recognized that arbitration would work to the advantage of the Republic. The good offices approach, which provided only for mediation and would require several weeks before being implemented, was the extent of international involvement acceptable to the Dutch. The American three-nation good offices plan and the consular commission plan both followed Dutch suggestions. The means of selecting the third member of the good offices committee was

important in that the United States was the only nation acceptable to both sides. An alternative approach, advanced in an Australian arbitration proposal, was to have the Security Council
select the third member, thus assuring recognition of the Council's pro-Republican sentiment.

American actions, at points, did differ from Dutch preferences. Washington refused to accept the Dutch claim that the
issue lay beyond United Nations jurisdiction. Likewise the State
Department viewed permitting Sjahrir to speak before the
Council as preferable to the adverse reaction which would have
resulted from denying him that opportunity.[8]

In general the actions taken by the Security Council in
August 1947—which were certainly favorable to the Dutch, but
not wholly subservient to their position—helped to establish the
effectiveness of the United Nations. Having passed its series of
resolutions, the Security Council could not henceforth ignore the
Indonesian situation. In the process, the United States had
become the mediating force between the Dutch and the
Republic.

The effectiveness of the United Nations was immediately
tested by developments in Indonesia. The Consular Commission, which began investigating conditions in early September,
found that the Netherlands and Republican interpreted the
resolution quite differently. The Dutch assumed that their continued military operations were appropriate, while the Republic
considered them to be a violation of the cease-fire. In its reports
of September 22 and October 11, the commission warned that
full-scale fighting might well resume. In the Security Council,
the Soviet Union and Australia proposed resolutions specifically
calling for the withdrawal of Dutch forces to their prepolice
action position. As it had throughout the Security Council
debates in August, the United States, again in deference to the
Dutch, opposed any suggestion of troop withdrawals; accordingly, the Security Council on October 31 defeated two such
resolutions. The following day, the Council approved an American compromise resolution calling upon the Good Offices Committee (GOC) to help implement a cease-fire.[9]

The GOC had, at that time, just arrived in Indonesia. In September, the Netherlands and the Republic had designated Belgium and Australia as their respective representatives and, as expected, the United States became the third member. Frank Graham, the president of the University of North Carolina, headed the American delegation. The committee faced a difficult situation. The Dutch, in command of two-thirds of Java and the major areas of Sumatra, were determined to prevent the committee from exercising any effective mediating influence. Indeed Dutch officials continued to maintain that even this limited United Nations involvement constituted an unjustified intervention in an internal matter. By keeping the Republic isolated militarily and economically, the Dutch assumed that they could impose a United States of Indonesia on their own terms. The GOC suffered from a lack of substantial authority—it could offer suggestions, but only when both sides requested it.

## The Graham, duBois, and Cochran Initiatives

At about the time that the GOC began what many assumed would be an impossible task, the American approach to the Indonesian Revolution began a prolonged transition toward greater identification with the interests of the Republic. To a large extent this change reflected the impressions and objectives of the men who comprised a considerably enlarged official presence in the war-torn country. They recommended that the State Department abandon its deference to the Dutch, but European priorities made Washington hesitant to challenge Dutch policy. There were also changes in personnel that resulted from the recognition that reporting on the Indonesian situation had been superficial and one-sided. In September the pro-Dutch Foote was replaced by William Livengood as the American Consul-General in Batavia.

When the Consular Committee began functioning that month, an army-navy advisory group was sent to assist. In its report, the advisory group said that the Dutch were badly overextended militarily, the Republic remained cohesive and determined, and only third party mediation could achieve a settlement. Frank Graham, who was a widely respected labor arbitrator, was frustrated by the limitations of the GOC. To resolve the delicate question of where the committee would meet with representatives of both sides, Graham prevailed upon the State Department to use an American ship, anchored in Indonesian waters. Consequently, meetings were held on the U.S.S. *Renville*, beginning on December 8. Charlton Ogburn of the State Department's Division of Southeast Asian Affairs, who was assigned to Graham's staff, reported thoroughly on developments, stressing the extent of native hostility toward the Dutch, the vitality of the Republic, and its expectation of support from the West.[10] Graham, Livengood, Ogburn, as well as other diplomatic and military personnel, thus began in late 1947 to press for a change in American policy.

While fully cognizant of the GOC's very limited authority, Graham worked diligently to bring the two parties to an understanding. The Dutch, more openly contemptuous of the Republic than ever, regarded the committee as a meddlesome nuisance. Graham immediately supported the Republic's grievance concerning Dutch economic pressures resulting from the naval blockade and the severance of the Republic from major food-producing areas. In addition, the committee, owing to the American position, decided to send an inquiry team to investigate charges of Dutch violation of the cease-fire. On both of these issues, Lieutenant Governor-General Hubertus van Mook and other Dutch officials strongly criticized the committee. After several days of frustrating efforts at mediation, Graham, in a message to Washington, addressed the dilemma of the American position: if the Republic was eliminated or survived as a minor state, the United States would be blamed by the Republicans and nationalists throughout Asia; if the Republic was not substantially impaired, then the United States, as the pivotal member of the Good Offices Committee, faced the seemingly impossible task of trying to reconcile two parties which differed on the most fundamental issues. In a lengthy report on December 20, Graham advised that the only feasible long-term solution was the recognition of the Republic's position either as the sovereign government or as the dominant element within a sovereign United States of Indonesia. While this would lead to some factional disputes and economic dislocations, the competent, resourceful, Western-oriented, Republican leadership would be capable of meeting those problems. To achieve that end, it would be necessary to exert pressure on the Netherlands to modify its demands and to offer concrete suggestions on a resolution of the dispute. A few days later Livengood warned Washington that unless the United States took a stronger position, the GOC would fail, and, in that event, the Republic would blame the United States and move toward the Soviet Union for support.[11]

Already the concerns of Graham and others had reached the attention of high level officials, with the result that the State Department made clear to Graham that the GOC should take a "firm stand" so that "substantial discussion can proceed."[12] With that encouragement and the support of both the Australian and Belgian members of the committee (even the pro-Dutch Belgian representative did not want to see the committee fail), Graham drafted and gained committee endorsement of a special statement, the "Christmas message" which offered the basis for a compromise settlement. In many respects, the Graham proposals favored the Dutch position—at least in their immediate impact—but that was simply the military reality. Graham believed it essential to gain Dutch acceptance of some bargaining proposals which recognized the continued legitimacy of the precarious Republic. The "Christmas message" provided for troop withdrawals within three months to the prepolice action lines, the reestablishment of Republican civil administration in occupied areas, free elections within six to twelve months to determine the relationship of the Republic to the United States of Indonesia, and the establishment of a United Nations agency to observe the implementation of the United States of Indonesia. While the "Christmas message" was acceptable to the Republic, the Dutch responded with their own twelve principles which basically ignored the existence of the Republic and the troops withdrawal issue. In addition, van Mook, on December 29, proclaimed the establishment of the "state" of East Sumatra, the richest of the areas taken militarily from the Republic. In sum, the Dutch, without reference to the Republic or the committee, set out to unilaterally construct their own federated Indonesia.[13]

In anticipation of the difficulty gaining Dutch acceptance of the Graham initiative, the State Department cabled a detailed statement to Graham on the last day of 1947. The statement, sent by Robert Lovett, as Acting Secretary, reflected the fullest effort since the beginning of the Indonesian Revolution to relate American interests there to major objectives in Europe. The stability of the Netherlands government, which strongly supported American policy in Europe, would be undermined if it lost its very considerable stake in the East Indies; thus, Washington looked unfavorably upon any solution which required an immediate and complete withdrawal from Indonesia. Yet in line with established policy favoring self-determination for "qualified" peoples, Washington also supported establishing a date for Indonesian independence. Immediate stability in Indonesia, however, was critical. Indonesian trade had to be reestablished and accelerated; it was potentially indispensable as a supplier of food and other commodities necessary to meet the demands of the Marshall plan. Lovett concluded by authorizing Graham to take steps to prevent the failure of negotiations.[14]

Reinforced by this encouragement from Washington and realizing that the Republic could not accept the Dutch principles, Graham advanced "six additional principles" which provided for: Dutch sovereignty until after a "stated interval" when it would be transferred to a United States of Indonesia; the Republic's inclusion among the states within the United States of Indonesia; fair representation of all states; a continued United Nations presence during the interim period; and plebiscites in certain areas to determine preference for the Republic or another state. Graham's action was strongly supported by the State

Department in conversations with Netherlands embassy officials. Republic leaders were hesitant to approve, detesting the Dutch principles and considering the Graham principles vague. The GOC, in four days of meetings with Prime Minister Amir Sjariffudin, President Sukarno, Vice-President Muhammad Hatta, and other nationalist leaders at Jogjakarta, argued that nonacceptance would effectively end the committee which stood as the most effective Republican link to the international community. Moreover, the inclusion in the Graham proposals of plebiscites, presumably under United Nations auspices, would certainly result in overwhelming Republican victories, thus enhancing the Republic's prospects for dominating any federated government. After three months of contacts with Graham and his staff, the Republican leadership had acquired much confidence that the Americans would insist upon a fair process of plebiscites and transition of sovereignty. Nonetheless, bitter memories of negotiations with the Dutch persisted, and only after long discussions and much agonizing did the Republican leadership approve the two sets of principles.[15]

On January 17, 1948, representatives of the Netherlands and the Republic signed the Renville Agreement embodying the twelve Dutch principles and the six additional principles of Graham—an agreement described a decade later as "one of the wonders of postwar diplomacy."[16] The attainment of any agreement was a singular achievement for the GOC, but at the time it seemed to offer no basis for a negotiated settlement; rather the agreement appeared to sanction the Dutch reconquest of the East Indies. It accepted the results of the police action and diminished the status of the Republic from that attained in the Linggadjati Agreement. The Indonesian opposition to this humiliating agreement forced Sjarifuddin's resignation as prime minister. Yet the agreement, in an important sense, rescued the Republic and gave its leadership confidence that the United States, through the United Nations, would insist upon implementation of the Graham principles. Considering its military and economic situation, the Republic had no choice but to gamble on the GOC; hence, despite Sjarifuddin's resignation, his successors continued to pursue the strategy of negotiation and reliance upon the United Nations. While many difficult times lay ahead for the Republic, the Renville Agreement helped to reaffirm the Republic's legitimacy and to renew the United Nations interest in a peaceful settlement.

The effectiveness of the agreement depended upon the United States, and as the Dutch arbitrarily took steps which ignored the agreement, American initiative was again required. In response to the GOC's suggestions for discussions with the Republic, the Dutch procrastinated for two months and in that period unilaterally began establishing new states in areas seized from the Republic during the police action. On March 9, von Mook announced the formation of an interim federal government; the Republic was invited to participate but on condition of negotiation of a final political settlement. These actions contradicted the Renville Agreement stipulations for plebiscites and joint Dutch-Republican planning of an interim government. In effect the interim government annouced by the Dutch amounted to a continuation of the Netherlands East Indies regime with the addition of a few anti-Republican Indonesian leaders.[17]

Graham's efforts had little effect upon his superiors, for State Department officials remained reluctant to press the Dutch. As the Dutch proceeded as though the Renville Agreement had never been signed, American officials in Washington and Batavia advocated restraint and renewal of discussions, but avoided any strong declarations. Because of Department displeasure over his pro-Indonesian sympathies, Graham resigned to return to the University of North Carolina. His successor, it was assumed, would be more favorably disposed toward the Dutch. Coert duBois, who had recently retired from the Foreign Service following a long career which included duty as Consul General in the East Indies before World War II, replaced Graham; he was widely considered to be pro-Dutch. Indeed upon arriving in Indonesia in late February, duBois, in his initial meetings with Republican leaders counseled trusting the Dutch and urged participation in the interim government.[18] DuBois and other American officials were frequently annoyed by Republican tactics, especially the threat to seek renewed Security Council consideration of their grievance.[19]

Yet like the other Americans who went to Indonesia during the nationalist revolution, duBois eventually became very critical of Dutch policy and sympathetic with the Republic. Of considerable importance were duBois' contacts with Sukarno and Hatta and his tours of areas formerly under Republican control. He became convinced of the quality of Republican leadership and the widespread popular support for independence under the Republic. In a cable of May 10, duBois concluded that the situation demanded Dutch compromise. But the Dutch continued their unilateral formation of an interim government, annoucing plans for a conference of thirteen "states" to be held at Bandung beginning on May 27. DuBois warned the State Department that unless the GOC insisted upon implementation of the Graham principles, the Dutch would soon present the world with a United States of Indonesia as a fait accompli. By the end of May, duBois pressed the Dutch to conduct plebiscites and to deal directly with the Republic. In a subsequent message to Washington, he argued that the continued western orientation of Indonesia depended upon American support of a settlement favorable to the Republic. An independent Indonesia, duBois confidently predicted, would welcome American investment, trade, and economic and technical assistance.[20]

Convinced that the initiative of the GOC was again needed, duBois worked with Australian delegate, Thomas K. Critchley, to advance a set of proposals which were intended to counter the Dutch strategy. Building upon the Renville principles upholding fair representation of all states and plebiscites to determine the areas of Republican representation, the duBois-Critchley proposal called for the GOC to conduct elections throughout Indonesia for delegates to a constitutional assembly which would also function as a provisional parliament. As a parliament, it would elect a cabinet which would administer internal and external affairs, but ultimate authority and sovereignty would remain invested in the Netherlands. In drafting a constitution for a United States of Indonesia, it would safeguard legitimate Dutch interests. Following Dutch and Indonesian ratification of the new constitution, sovereignty would be transferred to the United States of Indonesia.[21]

When duBois and Critchley informally presented their proposal to Indonesian and Dutch officials on June 10, duBois realized that he was acting without clear authorization from his government. After the session at which von Mook icily received and read without comment the Australian-American document, duBois remarked that he had followed his conscience and would have taken this step even without Australian support. The State Department, which did not receive the text of the duBois June 5 message outlining the proposal until June 22, had, nonetheless, given duBois considerable latitude and reasonable expectation of support for his initiative. Secretary Marshall, responding on June 8 to duBois' messages of May 21 and June 1 in which he set forth the general points later made more explicit in the duBois-Critchley proposal, stated that he should consider himself a "free agent making such choices on the spot as . . . [he] believes will lead to agreement . . . and in accordance with larger interests of the United States."[22] Yet at the same time, duBois' impatience with the mediating process annoyed the State Department. On the same day that Marshall authorized the American delegate to be a "free agent," a message from the Office of Far Eastern affairs suggested that he return to Washington for consultations, and that during his absence, negotiations need not be pressed. That message certainly indicated the department did not anticipate, nor wish to encourage, any immediate initiative from duBois. And as soon as the Dutch began complaining about the proposal which duBois put forth on June 10, Washington restrained duBois; an urgent cable the next day implored him to avoid placing the Dutch in a "squeeze play."[23] Dutch protestation became more strident when they learned a few days later that correspondent Daniel Schorr had obtained a copy of the proposal and was planning to publish it in *Time*. The Dutch immediately charged duBois with leaking the documents, but duBois, as well as other Western officials and correspondents, believed that the Dutch themselves were responsible, since it provided a pretext for refusing further discussions.[24]

As the Dutch criticism mounted, duBois sought repeatedly but futilely to force Washington's consideration of the proposal itself. Acknowledging that the initiative was not impartial, he reiterated that support of the Republic offered the only means of keeping Indonesia tied politically and economically toward the West. The Indonesians, he maintained, were clearly capable of governing themselves; he had done all he could—the rest was up to the State Department. Such pleas failed to convince his superiors who reminded duBois that the GOC lacked powers of arbitration, and made clear that the department opposed any reference to the proposal in GOC reporting to the Security Council.

When the GOC met with Dutch and Republican officials on June 22, the Dutch refused to receive the proposal which the Republic had requested be included on the agenda. However, the GOC report referred to the duBois-Critchley proposal as an agenda item; duBois cast the deciding vote for including that reference. He well realized that the State Department would criticize that action and thus the next day, duBois, who was in poor health and disillusioned by the failure of his mission, resigned. In deciding to break with the department's instructions, duBois played his one last card, i.e., that the Security Council would take action on the report. Yet when the Security Council received the report, and on July 1 China moved that the Council study the duBois-Critchley proposal, the U.S. delegate voted against the motion, thus ending the duBois initiative.[25]

DuBois' failure deeply disappointed Indonesian leaders. It seemed that the United States had failed to act in good faith. The Republic had signed the Renville agreement with the understanding that the United States would assure its implementation. Yet when duBois had attempted to force serious consideration of the Renville principles, he had not been supported by Washington. His departure was widely interpreted as a recall and repudiation. In the ensuing weeks the Dutch increased economic pressure on Republican territories by shutting off trade and access to agricultural surplus areas, thus causing serious shortages of food, clothing, and other commodities. At the same time, the United States began substantial Marshall Plan assistance to the Netherlands. To the disillusioned Republican leadership, Dutch colonial policy seemed to be underwritten by the United States.

The failure of Washington to support duBois did result principally from the priority given to European economic recovery. The launching of the Marshall Plan strengthened Dutch-American relations. It was assumed, furthermore, that the rebuilding of the Dutch economy depended upon the revitalization of the Dutch economic position in the East Indies. While officials in the State Department recognized that Dutch colonial policy was shortsighted, they saw the importance of the Netherlands in the program of containment. This policy necessitated toleration of an outdated colonialism in the expectation that eventually the Dutch would become more moderate in dealing with the Indonesians. From the global perspective of the State Department in the summer of the Marshall Plan, the duBois-Critchley proposal was singularly ill-timed.[26]

Beneath the decision to support the Dutch, there remained strong undercurrents pushing American policy in the opposite direction, with the result that between July and October 1948, a consensus developed among high officials at the Department of State which accepted the essential premise and formula of the duBois plan. Viewed in the context of the overall development of American policy, the duBois initiative, while failing to achieve its objective immediately, was thus one of a series of factors forcing continued reassessment of the American response to the Dutch-Indonesian conflict. In the month between duBois' departure and the arrival of his successor, H. Merle Cochran, officials in Washington endeavored to modify the duBois-Critchley proposal so that it would be acceptable to the Dutch as a basis of negotiation. In an unusually blunt conversation between Dutch Ambassador van Kleffens and Undersecretary of State Robert Lovett, Lovett reprimanded the Dutch for their inflexible position and urged moderation.

This effort to revive negotiations reflected growing awareness that American interests were being undermined by Dutch
colonialism. Reports from Indonesia stressed the Republican
disenchantment with American policy. In addition, Australia
pressed for further cooperation on behalf of the Renville principles. The Indonesian cause continued to elicit strong sympathy among Asian peoples, especially in the newly independent
nations of India and Burma. Ogburn, the ranking member of the
American delegation on the GOC, and Livengood constantly
pressed Washington to recognize that American interests necessitated association with the Republic's aspirations for independence. At a time when communist uprisings were occurring
against independent governments in Burma and the Philippines
and were disrupting British rule in Malaya, and when the Viet
Minh was challenging French restoration in Indochina, American officials in Indonesia argued that support of the Republic
would assure its stability and prevent the movement of Indonesian nationalism to the left.[27] (On the other side, the Dutch told
Americans that the Indonesian "inclination to be governed in a
totalitarian way" would simplify a communist takeover in the
event of the withdrawal of the Netherlands' military power.)[28]

The arrival of Cochran on August 9, 1948, seemed, however, to offer little hope for the Republic. While the Dutch
appeased Washington by making some gestures in the direction
of negotiations, they continued to exert strong economic and
military pressures designed to isolate the Republic. It was difficult to conceive how the GOC could effect any change, unless it
acted with strong American backing. Cochran, a career Foreign
Service Officer who, like his predecessor was considered pro-
Dutch, had extended conversations in The Hague while en route
to Indonesia. While there he also met with Eugene Black, Director of the International Bank, who urged Cochran's uncompromising support of the Dutch in order to protect the islands
from political chaos and a Communist takeover. Altogether,
Cochran's conversations in The Hague instilled "great confidence" among Dutch officials.[29] Shortly after Cochran's arrival
in Indonesia, Livengood, gloomily wrote that "the present

outlook for further or successful ... negotiations appears slim."[30]

Yet the concerns of officials like Livengood strongly influenced thinking in Washington. Charles Reed of the Division of Southeast Asian Affairs, reflected on reports from Indonesia and saw American options becoming more limited and more difficult. In a lengthy assessment, he concluded: "It is tragic that we may be called upon to choose between (1) denying independence to the deserving dependent peoples of the areas so as to assure the flow of strategic materials—such denial even being supported by the force of arms; (2) insisting that those dependent peoples be given independence notwithstanding the possibility that the left-wing or Communist element will take over—take over to our disadvantage. . . . Unless a pessimistic picture in Indonesia as set forth in recent reports is reversed by action in the not too distant future, such speculation will become a bitter alternative."[31] Soon afterwards, facing the prospect that Dutch actions were forcing the moderates from power within the Republic, and responding to reports of renewed Communist activities in Indonesia, Secretary Marshall instructed Cochran on September 1 to work quickly within the committee on behalf of a revised version of the duBois–Critchley proposal.[32]

The Dutch reaction to what became known as the Cochran plan disappointed American officials, who, for two months, had been encouraged by indications of a willingness to negotiate within the spirit of the Renville Agreement. In the first week of September, the State Department's sense of urgency about the situation was reinforced by a lengthy report from James W. Barco of the Division of United Nations Affairs who had just returned from Indonesia. His detailed observations gave strong support to those who maintained that the only hope of a settlement was through the GOC and American pressure on the Dutch to negotiate in good faith.

The Cochran plan, presented to both sides on September 10 in the form of an "oral note," followed the duBois–Critchley proposal but with several modifications intended to appease Dutch interests on a number of points, including strengthening the federal character of the United States of Indonesia and enhancing Dutch authority during the interim period. In contrast with the presentation of the duBois–Critchley proposal, the State Department mounted an immediate diplomatic offensive on behalf of the Cochran plan; representations were made to Dutch officials in Batavia, Washington, and The Hague and strong calls for support were made to Britain, Australia, and Belgium. While the Republican leadership indicated immediately a favorable reaction to the plan (formally accepting it on September 17), the Dutch criticized it. Foreign Minister Dirk Stikker undertook a special mission to Washington to set forth the objections. Dutch intransigence, exemplified in the Stikker mission, annoyed Secretary Marshall and Lovett.[33] Increasingly officials in Washington were inclined to look favorably upon the advice of Graham, who still followed Indonesian developments closely; on September 16 he wrote to the State Department that the time had come to tell the Dutch: "This is *it* and *now!*"[34]

## The Communist Uprising
## and American Pressure on the Dutch

As the Stikker mission was leaving Washington, the long-feared Communist uprising in Indonesia was launched—an event which strongly influenced American thinking toward the Republic. The Indonesian left-wing, which since early in 1948 had centered around former Prime Minister Sjarifuddin, had steadily criticized the moderate leadership of the Republic for its reliance on negotiations and resultant dependence upon the GOC. Many second level leaders had attended the Communist-sponsored Southeast Asian Youth Conference held in Calcutta in February 1948 where they had been influenced by the Soviet line of a divided world and the call to abandon narrow nationalism in favor of supporting the long-term struggle against capitalism. In August, Musso, the leader of the Indonesian Communist party twenty years earlier, returned from his long exile in the Soviet Union and organized a rather loose left-wing coalition. On September 18 a Communist meeting in East Java proclaimed a revolt against the Republic and two days later Communists seized control of Madiun, a city in eastern Java. The Communist rebellion, however, lacked coordination and its leadership badly misjudged the extent of popular support for the Republic.

For the Republican government, the revolt provided not only a challenge but an opportunity. Indeed Cochran on September 20 pointedly reminded Hatta of the immense international advantages of suppressing the Communists; Cochran made clear American sympathy for those who resisted communism. Within two weeks, Republican military units crushed the rebellion, thus enhancing its reputation in the West. The action assured that the Indonesian Revolution—contrary to Dutch predictions—would not follow communist leadership. At a time when communism seemed to be advancing steadily in Asia, the ascendancy of the pro-Western, anti-Communist leadership in the Indonesian Republic emerged as a valued asset in America's Asian interests.[35]

While the Republic moved against the Communist insurgents, the United States exerted more pressure on the Dutch to accept the Cochran plan. Repeatedly—on at least eleven occasions between September 24 and October 13, 1948—officials in Washington, The Hague, and Batavia made strong representations to the Netherlands government. By this time, the State Department was threatening disassociation from the Dutch in the event that the Security Council considered the Cochran plan. For a month, Dutch replies dealt only in part with the plan; instead they focused on repeated criticisms of the Republic for truce violations. On occasion, they threatened an immediate withdrawal, leaving the islands to political and economic chaos.[36] The Dutch finally responded formally to the Cochran plan on October 14 with a conditional acceptance. They failed, however, to mention the Republic, and referred instead to the eleven constituent states set up in Java and Sumatra under their unilaterally established federal program. The numerous Dutch amendments to the Cochran plan amounted to virtually a new basis for negotiations. To offset Republican criticism as well as

American disappointment, The Hague announced that the un-popular van Mook would be replaced as Lieutenant Governor General by Louis Bell, and that Stikker would head a special negotiating mission to the islands. While Stikker conveyed a favorable impression and personally appeared to seek accommodation with the Republic, fundamentally the Dutch position remained one of opposition to negotiation under the Renville formula. Their strategy still was clearly directed toward imposing a federated Indonesia in which the Dutch position would remain paramount. An increasingly disillusioned Cochran warned Washington that the lack of good faith on the part of the Dutch continued to undermine the prospects for a settlement.[37]

Facing this determined Dutch colonial policy, in early November the leadership of the Department of State tentatively decided that the time had come to follow Graham's "this is *it* and *now!*" advice. A draft aide-memoire of November 5 set forth a virtual ultimatum. Premised on the assumptions that the Republican government had to be supported and that only national elections could establish a representative interim government, the aide-memoire held that the United States, in the event of Dutch failure to negotiate under the Cochran plan, had to be prepared to disassociate itself from the Dutch. Dutch policy was leading to conflict which would be disastrous to the country and to American economic and political interests in Europe and Asia. Clearly the circumstances demanded Dutch flexibility and accommodation. If the Dutch refused to change their approach, the United States would act independently in the United Nations. In view of popular and congressional sympathy for the Republic, Congress might well suspend Marshall Plan allocations for Indonesia and possibly even the Netherlands itself.[38] The aide-memoire was kept in the State Department for another month as conversations continued and Cochran and the State Department worked desperately to salvage negotiations. In the end, the Stikker mission failed amidst expectation that the Dutch would again resort to arms against the Republic. During the last efforts of the Stikker mission, it was agreed in Washington that the November 5 aide-memoire should be presented but without reference to the Marshall Plan. This significant modification was agreed upon in the interests of preventing any disruption of the European recovery effort and avoiding any threat which it might not be possible to implement.[39]

The State Department presented its aide-memoire to the Dutch on December 7. The aide-memoire claimed that since the Republic represented the aspirations of the vast majority of Indonesians and served Western interests, military action would result in adverse international reaction and would lead to prolonged guerrilla warfare. The resources of the Netherlands would be drained, thus nullifying the impact of the Marshall Plan. The blunt warning had no effect: the Dutch responded in an angry and defiant fashion, defending their colonial policy, castigating the leadership of the Republic, and threatening the use of force. Australia and India urged American action to avert open warfare. The United States tried desperately to prevent that eventuality by supporting a conciliatory initiative from Hatta and warning the Dutch that economic aid earmarked for Indonesia might be cancelled, but ultimately to no avail. On the morning of December 18, Lloyd V. Steere, the American in chargé d'affairs in The Hague, acting under urgent instructions from Washington, sought to see Stikker to make strong statements against the reportedly imminent use of force. Strikker declined to meet the American official, delaying until the afternoon by which time the Dutch Cabinet had made the decision to launch a second police action. Stikker told Steere the march on the Republican capital Jogjakarta was about to begin: "it simply had to be done."[40] Meanwhile, just before midnight in Batavia, Cochran was informed by Dutch officials that the Renville Agreement was being repudiated, and shortly thereafter the army moved against the Republic.

## The Second Police Action

The Dutch military campaign, intended to eliminate the Republic quickly, was based on serious miscalculations. To be certain, the Dutch accomplished their basic military objectives with little difficulty—Jogjakarta and Republican areas of Java and Sumatra were overrun and the leadership of the Republic including Sukarno, Hatta, and Sjahrir were captured—but at the price of outrage from the international community. The Dutch planning assumed that by presenting the United Nations with a fait accompli, they could withstand international criticism and proceed with their plans for a United States of Indonesia. From throughout Asia, much of the Middle East, Europe, and the Americas came expressions of indignation; especially strong were the criticisms for India, Australia, Pakistan, Burma, the Philippines, and the Arab League. The United States and Australia called a special session of the Security Council on December 20 at which almost all members denounced the Dutch action. Besides miscalculating the extent of international opposition, the Netherlands planning also failed to appreciate the extent of popular support for the Republic; it was assumed that the Indonesian people would respond favorably to the assertion of authority. Instead, the Dutch encountered popular resistance, noncooperation in captured areas, and a growing guerrilla movement. In sum, to control the territory gained by the end of 1948, the Dutch had to be prepared to pay an excessive price: strong opposition from the Indonesian people and diplomatic isolation internationally.

To many critics of the police action, the United States was ultimately responsible for Dutch colonial policy. Without American economic assistance, the Netherlands, it was widely assumed, would not have the capacity to wage war against the Indonesians. By the end of 1948, the United States under the Marshall Plan had provided the Netherlands with $298 million and another $61 million to the Dutch in Indonesia; besides, Holland had received since 1945 over $300 million in credits from the Export-Import Bank. The significance of this assistance was underlined by the fact that Dutch military expenditures in Indonesia in 1948 totalled about $437 million. The strident criticisms of American policy could be heard from a variety of prominent figures including CIO President Philip Murray,

NAACP Secretary Walter White, and Senators Margaret Chase Smith of Maine and George Malone of Nebraska. They called increasingly for an end to Marshall Plan aid to the Netherlands.[41]

Despite such pressures, the initial response of the United States was cautious. When the question was discussed at the White House on December 20, Truman advised Lovett to avoid any position which could not be maintained owing either to the defection of allies or the inadequacy of American power. The President's views paralleled the considered opinion of high officials at the State Department as they planned strategy for Security Council consideration of the Indonesian issue. In a message to Ambassador Phillip Jessup, Deputy Undersecretary of State Dean Rusk set forth the basic position: While the United States was committed to support of independence and could not condone Dutch action, at the same time it would not break with the Dutch over Indonesia. Instead, the United States should seek to work through the United Nations to build pressure on the Netherlands (particularly from France and Britain) to alter its policy. This approach rejected the possibility of curtailing Marshall Plan aid to the Netherlands and other stringent measures, such as United Nations economic sanctions, then being advocated by Australia, India, and Republican representatives in Washington. To exert some economic pressure, the State Department prevailed upon the Economic Cooperation Administration to halt authorization of Marshall Plan funds earmarked for Indonesia; this amounted to $30 million of the $74 million allocated for the Netherlands in the first quarter of 1949.[42]

In the Security Council, the strongest support for the Indonesian position came from the Soviet Union which introduced a resolution condemning Dutch aggression, calling for troop withdrawals and establishment of a United Nations commission (comprised of all Security Council members) to assist in reaching a settlement. With the United States and other Western nations opposed, the Russian resolution failed. Instead the Council on December 24 passed a resolution, cosponsored by the

Untied States, calling for a cease-fire. In deference to the Dutch, the Security Council eliminated a provision calling for troop withdrawals and an Australian amendment requesting GOC assessment of responsibility for the hostilities. As the Dutch simply ignored the December 24 resolution while continuing their offensive against the Republic, the Council four days later passed two resolutions, both supported by the United States, which called for the release of all Republican leaders and for a consular commission to report on the situation and on the compliance with the cease-fire request. These moderate resolutions, all passed under American auspices, bitterly disappointed Republican leaders; the Security Council failed to determine responsibility for what was obviously an act of Dutch aggression and did not even call for troop withdrawls. It seemed that the resolutions constituted a tacit confirmation of Dutch conquest. That, however, was not the American intention, as the State Department hoped that such limited measures would bring sufficient pressure to force modification in Dutch policy.[43]

Yet as it became evident that the Dutch had no intention of complying with the Security Council resolutions, high officials at the Department of State considered more fully the consequences of failing to take a stronger stand. Reports from diplomatic personnel emphasized the extent to which the police action had weakened Western interests in Asia and the Middle East. In a lengthy assessment of the American position sent to various diplomatic personnel on the last day of 1948, Lovett acknowledged that the Dutch were undermining much of America's postwar Asian policy and that the time was approaching when it might be necessary to "take steps unpleasant to The Netherlands."[44]

On January 3, 1949, Cochran informed Washington that he would remain in Indonesia only if his government publicly disassociated itself from the policies of the Netherlands, suspended economic assistance until a settlement was reached, and insisted that the Dutch cease military operations and free all Republican leaders. Four days later, the Office of Far Eastern Affairs, acting in part on Cochran's ultimatum, recommended that the United States threaten curtailment of Marshall Plan aid and sponsor a resolution in the Security Council stipulating the steps leading to a transfer of sovereignty by a specific date. When the Indonesian issue again came before the Security Council on January 11, Ambassador Jessup placed the United States on record as finding no justification for the Dutch military action and criticized the Dutch for failing to pursue peaceful means. In a meeting with Dutch Ambassador van Kleffens that same day, Lovett warned that adverse public and congressional reaction to the military offensive might jeopardize congressional approval of economic assistance.[45] The tougher American position, evidenced in Jessup's public statement and Lovett's conversation, clearly indicated that the United States by mid-January was at last prepared to "take steps unpleasant to The Netherlands."

By January 12, this momentum brought officials to consider seriously a draft Security Council resolution which signalled the unequivocal disassociation from the colonial policies of the Netherlands. Adding considerably to the urgency was a call issued by Indian Prime Minister Nehru for an international conference, to be held at New Delhi beginning on January 20, to consider the Indonesian situation. Clearly the competence of the United Nations to deal with the issue was being challenged; the New Delhi conference, it was feared, would attract representatives of Asian and Middle Eastern countries and would be embarrassing to the United States while offering propaganda opportunities for the Soviets. Based on the January 7 suggestions of the Office of Far Eastern Affairs, the draft American resolution, after criticizing the police action and the failure to comply with the cease-fire, called for an immediate cessation of hostilities and the return of Republican officials to Jogjakarta to resume governmental functions. Moreover, it stipulated the establishment of an interim federal government, the election of a representative constituent assembly, and the transfer of sovereignty by July 1, 1950. The GOC, to be renamed the United Nations Commission for Indonesia (UNCI), would have strong authority to implement the resolution.[46]

As the draft resolution circulated in advance of formal Security Council consideration, Dutch officials protested strongly. They reiterated familiar arguments in defense of their policies and warned that the resolution would lead to chaos, but the United States made no significant concessions. Through extensive preliminary discussions with Security Council members and backed by GOC reports criticizing the Dutch for failing to abide by the December resolutions, wide support for the American position was achieved. With China and Norway joining as cosponsors, the Security Council on January 28 approved the American resolution.[47]

While the resolution marked an important assertion of United Nations authority and of the power of the United States, it disappointed the leadership of the Republic; the Dutch were not called upon to withdraw from other than the Jogjakarta area and, in view of the impotence of the GOC, there was understandable skepticism whether the reconstituted United Nations agency could enforce the resolution. The views of many Indonesians were expressed by the Soviet delegate in the Security Council who abstained on the grounds that the resolution gave an aggressor the opportunity to consolidate its position. To most Republicans, the economic relationship of the United States with the Netherlands still determined Dutch colonial policy, but beyond Lovett's warning to van Kleffens on January 11 (which, of course, was not known in Indonesia), the United States declined to consider severing that vital link in its European recovery program.[48]

Whatever the limitations of the January 28 resolution, it represented an important step in the development of the American response to the Indonesian Revolution and in the aftermath of the Security Council action, the United States exerted pressure on the Netherlands to implement its provisions. Of particular importance was the decision to appoint Cochran to the UNCI, ignoring the informally expressed Dutch reservations because of his support of Republican aspirations. Before returning to Indonesia from Washington where he had been called for consultations, Cochran was sent to The Hague in early February for meetings with Queen Wilhelmina, Stikker, and other leaders. In marked contrast with his earlier solicitous visit with Dutch officials, Cochran talked bluntly about the necessity to implement the Security Council resolution, warning that otherwise the situation confronting the Dutch internationally and in Indonesia would worsen dramatically. The determination to press the Dutch at this time was reinforced by pressures to impose harsh economic measures unless a settlement was reached. The Australian government, impatient with the lack of immediate progress, talked of sanctions, while in Congress, Senator Owen Brewster presented a resolution, endorsed by nine other Republican senators, calling for the cessation of all Marshall Plan and other assistance to the Netherlands.[49]

In response to international pressure, Dutch strategy shifted toward apparent compromise in a plan advanced by High Commissioner L.J.M. Beel. Reflecting the ascendancy of more moderate elements within The Hague, the Beel Plan, which was officially announced on February 26, called for a Round Table Conference to which all Indonesian groups, including the Republic, would be invited. To be held at The Hague beginning on March 12, the conference was to discuss the possible transfer of sovereignty; the plan anticipated that an interim government would be established by May 1, 1949 and the full transfer of sovereignty was to be accomplished by July 1, 1949. While the Dutch defended the Beel Plan as an acceleration of the timetable established in the January 28 resolution, the proposal continued the long-established contempt for the Republic. Republican authority in Jogjakarta, the Dutch argued, could not be restored before the conference, which would be held regardless of Republican participation. Because of this failure to comply with the intent of the Security Council resolution that the Republic had to be accorded equal status in subsequent negotiations, the Beel Plan was criticized by American officials. Republican leaders rejected the Round Table invitation. In addition, the leaders of the Dutch-fostered federal states—the backbone of the Dutch strategy for the United States of Indonesia—likewise repudiated the Beel Plan. Their reasons varied from an instinctive sense that the Republican leadership was representative of nationalist sentiment to a crass calculation that events were overtaking their Dutch patrons. Whatever their reasons, this defection proved devastating to the Netherlands strategy.[50]

Faced with the prospect of a continuing impasse between the Dutch and Indonesians, the leadership of the State Department concluded by late March that threatening the curtailment of economic assistance would be necessary to achieve implementation of the January 28 resolution. This decision resulted from several related factors. First, reports from Indonesia suggested that time to achieve a negotiated settlement was running out. The strong opposition to the Beel Plan led Cochran to strongly recommend that the State Department press the Dutch, and in particular Stikker, who was visiting Washington at the end of March, for immediate moderation of Dutch policy.[51] Second, the Truman administration's deference to the Dutch came under strong criticism in Congress during the debates on the extension of the Marshall Plan. In the Senate, Owen Brewster, joined by George Aiken of Vermont and Wayne Morse of Oregon, led the call for ending the indirect support of Dutch military operations through economic and military assistance to the Netherlands. The mounting congressional opposition to the semblance of Dutch-American cooperation in Indonesia underscored the possibility that continuation of Dutch rule would undermine the entire structure of economic and military planning for Western Europe. The Brewster amendment threatened to end assistance to the Netherlands unless the Dutch accepted the mandate of the January 28 resolution.[52] Third, international pressures intensified. Repeatedly the United States was in the unenviable position of being essentially held accountable for Dutch actions. India, in an aide-memoire of February 24 and in other statements, called upon the United States to take a stronger stand on behalf of the Indonesian cause; Indian officials warned that prolonged isolation of the Republican leaders from the people of Indonesia would provide a context for the reemergence of a strong Communist movement. Finally the Dutch were simply failing to achieve their military objectives. The strong guerrilla opposition to the police action placed the Dutch on the defensive and widespread civilian noncooperation set back any pacification plans. For the first time since the beginning of the revolution three and a half years earlier, the Dutch conceded that a military solution might not be feasible. The surprising developments in Indonesia forced officials in The Hague to reconsider their policy, touching off a cabinet crisis in early 1949 which led to indications of a more conciliatory approach. The Beel Plan had reflected those pressures, and the Indonesian reception to it only increased the difficulties of the Dutch government. In sum, the essential Dutch justification for the police actions—that they would restore order and stability—now lacked substance.[53]

As a part of an effort to encourage Dutch compromise, the United States on March 23 joined with seven other Security Council members to endorse a Canadian resolution, which called upon the UNCI to assist in reaching an agreement on the implementation of the January 28 resolution, in particular the provisions calling for a cessation of hostilities and the restoration of Jogjakarta.[54]

The direction of State Department thinking on the Indonesian situation found clear expression in the Policy Planning Staff's detailed, thirty-nine page statement on American interests in Southeast Asia. This report was endorsed on March 29, following extensive review by all relevant department offices, and was forwarded to the National Security Council. Eventually designated NSC-51, it basically sought to make certain that Southeast Asia would not follow China's path to communism. The significance of Indonesia in maintaining a noncommunist Southeast Asia was stressed, and the Dutch-Republican struggle necessitated prompt action. It was argued: "Timing is of prime importance in the Indonesian situation. The longer the delay in accomplishing a transfer of authority from the Dutch to representative Indonesians, the weaker becomes the position of both the non-communist native leaders and the Dutch and the stronger becomes the influence of all extremist elements including the communists. The earliest feasible cessation of hostilities and transfer of authority from the Dutch to the Indonesians is therefore imperative, and will probably require additional pressure on the Dutch."[55]

Convinced that American interests in Europe and Asia dictated a firm position with the Dutch, Dean Acheson, who had succeeded Marshall as Secretary of State, decided to confront Stikker. Meeting with the Dutch foreign minister on the last day of March to discuss the Atlantic Pact, Acheson spelled out the American dissatisfaction with Dutch policy in Indonesia. The public and Congress generally held the Dutch guilty of aggression and the depth of that sentiment jeopardized continuation of the Marshall Plan assistance to the Netherlands. Even if the Brewster Amendment should fail, the Indonesian issue would threaten legislation for further military assistance. Acheson's warning was precise: "I made it plain that in my opinion, in the absence of a settlement in Indonesia, there was no chance whatever of the Congress authorizing funds for military supplies to The Netherlands."[56] Stikker requested elaboration: Did Acheson mean that in the absence of a settlement, the Netherlands would not participate in the military assistance program? Acheson's reply made clear the extent of his concern: continued Dutch military involvement in Indonesia would possibly threaten the entire military assistance program in Congress. He closed the conversation by emphasizing the need for prompt action leading to a settlement under the auspices of the United Nations.[57]

Through Acheson's warning, the United States had at last followed the advice offered six months earlier by Graham, for Acheson unmistakably warned the Dutch that unless they moved quickly to achieve a settlement with the Republic, the United States would be forced to consider ending economic assistance to the Netherlands. This bald use of power assumed that the Dutch government, faced with the choice between continuing American assistance and endeavoring to maintain its increasingly vulnerable position in Indonesia, would calculate that its interests dictated maintenance of its economic relations with the United States. The Acheson warning had its intended effect. Combined with the continued strong guerrilla resistance and the defection of the federal leaders in Indonesia, the threatened loss of American support left the government in The Hague no real choice but to adopt a conciliatory approach toward the Republic. Under the auspices of UNCI, the Dutch entered into discussions with Republican leaders which led to the signing, on May 7, of the Roem-vanRoyen Agreement—the terms of which represented a major Dutch concession. The Netherlands agreed to restore the Republican government in Jogjakarta following which the Round Table Conference at The Hague would immediately be convened. In return, the Republic promised to end guerrilla warfare and to participate in the Round Table Conference. After the withdrawal of the last Dutch forces from Jogjakarta on June 30, Sukarno and the other leaders of the Republic returned to their capital. With Republican authority reestablished, the armistice went into effect on August 1 and the Round Table Conference—which would work out the details leading to independence before the end of the year—convened later that month.

While the Dutch concessions following the Acheson-Stikker conversation gave momentum to the end of Dutch rule, at each of the steps preceding the Round Table Conference, the UNCI played a conciliatory role. In particular, Cochran repeatedly reassured the Republican leaders who remained skeptical of the Dutch and (until the time of the Round Table Conference) American intentions.[58] And at the Round Table Conference (which will be discussed in chapter 11), the United States was instrumental, helping to resolve the remaining differences.

# Conclusion

By the summer of 1949, the American response to the Indonesian Revolution had thus undergone a far-reaching change. The two years of fighting which began with the first police action of July 1947 had forced the Department of State to reexamine the relationship of American interests in Europe with those in Asia.

Slowly a profound transition in American policy developed from deference to the Dutch position to support of Republican aspirations. This change resulted from several related factors: international denunciation of the Dutch decisions to resort to arms not only in July 1947 but again in December 1948; the resultant establishment of a United Nations presence in Indonesia which, however weak in terms of its initial authority, helped to assure that the Indonesian issue would remain a matter of international concern; the persistant pressures upon Washington from American officials (Graham, duBois, Ogburn, Cochran, and Livengood) who believed that American interests were tied to Indonesian independence under the Republic; and the growing domestic pressures, ultimately represented in the Brewster Amendment, to disassociate the United States politically, economically, and militarily from the Dutch effort to preserve its colony. In the two years of warfare, American actions satisfied neither of the protagonists. The Dutch, even when the United States largely deferred to them, resented the intrusion of the United Nations and American contacts with the Republic. The Republic, bitter over the weakness of American involvement prior to the second police action, and convinced that Dutch militarism was underwritten by American economic assistance, remained suspicious of Washington's intent until the very eve of independence.[59]

The deliberate character of the change in American policy ought not, however, obscure the significance of the position ultimately adopted by the United States. The American commitment to anticolonialism, admittedly tarnished, was finally upheld, much more dramatically in the Indonesian revolution than in the other colonial areas of Southeast Asia, thus helping to assure the preservation of Western interests in Indonesia. That it required substantial international and domestic pressure and the force of events in Indonesia to induce unequivocal support for the Indonesian cause underscored the dilemmas of balancing European and Asian interests.

# 10.

# The Vietnamese Revolution: The Evolution of the Commitment to France, 1947–1950

> The choice confronting the United States is to support the French in Indochina or face the extension of Communism over the remainder of the continental area of Southeast Asia and possibly farther westward. We would then be obliged to make staggering investments in those areas and in that part of Southeast Asia remaining outside Communist domination or withdraw to a much-contracted Pacific line. It would seem a case of "Penny wise, Pound foolish" to deny support to the French in Indochina.
>
> Indochina Problem Paper, February 1, 1950

THROUGHOUT THE PERIOD when the United States gradually adjusted its policy in Indonesia to support nationalist aspirations centered in the leadership of the Republic, it also responded to the other major nationalist revolution in Southeast Asia: the struggle between the French and Viet Minh in Indochina. American interests in that conflict, however, came to be defined quite differently from those in Indonesia. The United

States moved toward close identification with French political and military actions intended to isolate and defeat the Viet Minh. This orientation of American policy culminated in the acceptance of the "Bao Dai solution"—the French fostered nationalist alternative to the Viet Minh.

## International Implications

The different policies adopted by the United States resulted, in part, from the sharply varying international contexts of the two revolutions. The struggle in Indochina never attracted the wide international attention that focused on the Indonesian revolution. The Viet Minh lacked the extensive diplomatic representation abroad which enabled the Indonesians, even at their darkest moments, to enlist wide support. Also, the nature of the fighting in Indochina worked against attracting international attention. It was generally a persistent, guerrilla campaign; and unlike Indonesia, the Indochina war was not interrupted by truces followed by the massive resort to arms such as characterized the Dutch police actions. For various reasons, the Viet Minh failed to gain strong supporters within the international community. Even the Soviet Union, which took every opportunity to champion the Indonesian Republic's cause, took relatively little interest in the anticolonial campaign of its fellow Communists in Indochina. To some extent, Moscow doubtless calculated that a show of sympathy for the Viet Minh would harm the French Communist party. Not only the Russians but the colonial and newly independent peoples of Asia and the Middle East gave only modest support to the Viet Minh, especially when contrasted with that accorded the Indonesians. A sense of Islamic solidarity facilitated the appeal of the Indonesians in South Asia and the Middle East. Most striking, India, the self-proclaimed champion of anticolonialism, barely identified with the Viet Minh; this resulted from concern with the Viet Minh's Communist orientation, as well as from a reluctance to antagonize France.

That consideration touches on another fundamental difference between the two revolutions—the relative international status of France and the Netherlands. Despite its humiliations in World War II, France had been restored to major power status. Its presence as one of the five permanent members of the Security Council, at a time when the Indian-Pakistani dispute over Kashmir was a major international issue, made the Indians pause before they denounced French colonialism in Indochina. In addition, India sought cordial relations with France in the interest of resolving French colonial claims in India. Not only India, but the United States acknowledged the relative difference between the two colonial powers. American objectives in Europe depended much more substantially on France than on the Netherlands. This enabled the French, unlike the Dutch, to withstand American pressure; indeed the French came to exert leverage over the United States with respect to Indochina.[1]

A part of the reason for the differing international responses to the two revolutions, and the major factor in the differing American responses, was the relationship of communism to nationalism in the two countries. The pro-Western, anti-Communist character of the Indonesian Republic, so forcefully demonstrated in the suppression of the Communist rebellion of September 1948, ultimately drew the State Department to conclude that American interests necessitated identification with the Republic. The Communist-led Viet Minh, on the other hand, always appeared to be an unacceptable replacement for French colonialism. Whatever the protestations from Ho Chi Minh of his nationalism and interests in Western economic assistance, and however uncertain the relationship between the Viet Minh and the Soviet Union, the perceived risks inherent in a Viet Minh-dominated Indochina led Washington to support of France.

## The Bao Dai Solution

From 1947 to 1950, the French sought to convert the struggle into a civil, as opposed to a colonial war. While many Asian leaders saw this as a deceptive tactic, it helped to reduce the international criticism of French policy. By the end of 1947, the French army had control, in addition to its initial foothold in Cochin China, of a number of towns in Annam including Hanoi, a string of frontier fortresses, and the industrial areas of the Red River delta. But the French had failed to destroy the Viet Minh, which retained the loyalty of the overwhelming majority of the population and remained capable of waging guerrilla warfare throughout the country.

To support its precarious position, the French government moved decisively away from negotiating with the Viet Minh and sought instead collaboration with anti-Viet Minh leaders. By late 1947, this search for a non-Communist nationalist alternative centered on former Emperor Bao Dai—the "Bao Dai solution." While he and other Vietnamese leaders were initially reluctant to cooperate unless they were granted genuine self-government, the French capitalized on their strong anti-Viet Minh sentiments to force acceptance of a superficial, diluted independence. In the so-called Elysée Agreement of March 1949, France committed itself to granting Vietnam's independence but retained responsibility for foreign affairs and defense as well as various special privileges. Further, Vietnam and the other "associated states" (Laos and Cambodia) were obliged to become members of the French Union in which real power rested with France.

A dissatisfied Bao Dai returned to Vietnam in July 1949 to become "head of state." On December 30, the terms of the Elysée Agreement were formally instituted by the Conventions of Saigon. On February 7, 1950—five days after the French Assembly ratified those agreements—the United States recognized the Bao Dai regime as an "independent state within the French Union." For France, the establishment of this government and its international recognition were important steps toward the preservation of its position in Indochina.[2]

As French policy emerged between 1947 and 1950, American calculations of the French—Viet Minh struggle reflected a few clear assumptions which led to support of the Bao Dai solution. At the base of American policymaking was the calculation that the United States could not accept the risks of a Viet Minh-dominated state. Repeatedly, official analyses of the Vietnamese situation expressed uncertainty about the nature and orientation of the Viet Minh. Despite the uncertainty, however, the United States concluded that it had no choice but to calculate its policy on the most unfavorable consequences of a Viet Minh-dominated state—Vietnam becoming a satellite of the Soviet Union. Ho Chi Minh's professed commitment to nationalism, his expressed admiration for the United States, his apparent neutrality in the early Cold War, the inclusion of noncommunists within the Viet Minh, and the apparent lack of contact between the Viet Minh and Moscow led to the possibility that "this government, if confined in power, would follow a nationalist rather that a Soviet line."[3] But the communist background of the Viet Minh leadership caused apprehension: "On the other side, there remains the fact that the Vietnamese leaders include seasoned Communists, men who for years collaborated with the Third International—including Ho Chi Minh in particular—and that no change of heart has been publicly confessed by them."[4]

In an effort to gain a more comprehensive overview of the contingencies in Vietnam, the State Department in July 1947 instructed its consuls at Saigon and Hanoi to report fully on the implications of a Viet Minh controlled government: its orientation toward the Soviet Union, the importance of its sensitivity to American opinion, and the likelihood that it would provide stability with relatively free political expression. This request came at a time when the French repeatedly stressed Ho Chi Minh's communism, maintaining, for instance, that recently decoded secret Viet Minh messages gave clear evidence of a pro-Soviet orientation. The reports of James O'Sullivan at Hanoi and Charles Reed at Saigon both advanced, with much qualification, the viewpoint that the United States could attain influence in and a reasonable relationship with a Viet Minh-dominated state. O'Sullivan argued that Vietnam's isolation from the Soviet Union and the proximity of American influence in the Phillippines would prevent full association with the Communist bloc. The United States, O'Sullivan implied, ought not allow concern with communism dictate policy. Ever skeptical of the French, he cautioned that they never talked of a "communist menace" in Indochina until late 1946 when French-Viet Minh efforts at negotiation gave way to war. While agreeing that the Viet Minh would not immediately become affiliated with the Soviet Union, Reed maintained that an existing remote Soviet control of the Viet Minh could lead to an open association once the Viet Minh government was firmly established. Both consuls, however, agreed that the Vietnamese admired the United States and that American influence could be established, principally in the form of economic assistance. Neither consul, however, doubted that the Viet Minh would be successful in establishing a one-party state.[5] Those reports thus suggested, at best, an uncertain American position in a Viet Minh-dominated state.

At the State Department, Kenneth Landon, of the Division of Phillippine and Southeast Asian Affairs, advanced the possibility of factionalism undermining the predominance of the Viet Minh. In November 1947, Landon, who following a meeting with  Ho Chi Minh in early 1946 had advocated American mediation at that time, suggested: "It is not a foregone conclusion that if the Annamese win their objective they will establish a communist state. If and when they have a victory, the ardent leadership of the small Communist group will become less vital and the various Annamese factions will turn from facing the French to facing one another. Then will come the time for the natural development of political parties as Annamese regroup themselves for the purpose of self-government."[6]

A comment in the margin of Landon's report by Woodruff Wallmer of the Division of Western European Affairs expressed the essential department reservation on risking the consequences of a Viet Minh victory: "It may not be certain, as Ken Landon says, that Ho and Co. will succeed in setting up a Communist State if they get rid of the French, but let me suggest that from the standpoint of the security of the United States, it is one hell of a big chance to take."[7]

Repeatedly, appraisals of the Vietnamese political situation concluded that the United States could not risk a Viet Minh-dominated state. This consensus among American officials was reinforced by an analysis of the Indochina situation prepared by the British Foreign Office in late 1947 and shared with Washington. Basically, the British maintained that endeavoring to distinguish nationalist from communist motivation was unproductive and futile; as one British official observed: "Clearly Communists always disguise themselves as Nationalists when they can, but this does not make it any easier to decide whether a Nationalist is also a Communist at heart—nor, in the last resort, does it really matter."[8]

What of the evident lack of contact between the Viet Minh and the Soviet Union? Rather than raising questions about Ho Chi Minh's objectives, this came to be considered as further substantiation of his allegiance to Moscow. As a Russian-trained communist leader, Ho, according to American analyses, did not need direction. Clearly, the Viet Minh, whatever its nationalist aspirations, was serving Russian interests by draining French resources and thus dissipating Marshall Plan assistance. Hence, when Ho requested in early 1948 that an American observer visit Vietnam to reestablish contacts between his movement and the United States, the State Department dismissed the initiative on the grounds that whatever the results of such a mission, it could not conclusively challenge "the basic assumption of this government vis-à-vis Ho, . . . [i.e.] that we cannot afford to assume that Ho is anything but Moscow-directed."[9]

As doubts about the Viet Minh emerged, the Department of State considered the implications of acquiescing in French military and political strategy. In September 1947 Reed recommended that the United States discourage the evident French plan to restore, by force of arms, the pre-World War II status quo.[10] Skeptical of France's military prospects, Reed and O'Sullivan expressed concern that a French victory could be achieved only at the expense of the interests of the United States. In terms similar to those of his Saigon colleague, O'Sullivan argued: "Such action [a French restoration of its prewar status] would, of course, be catastrophic to United States prestige, would turn Vietnamese who distrust and hate the French into a violent anti-white bloc, and would insure the irretrievable orientation of intellectuals and the people toward communism and Moscow and against the West."[11] With additional intelligence reports reaching the Division of Philippine and Southeast Asian Affairs projecting the failure of the French military campaign launched that fall, Landon argued that the United States should register with the French its opposition to the use of arms.[12] That initiative, however, received no support at higher levels.

In early 1948, as the French began advancing the Bao Dai solution and the futility of the military campaign against the Viet Minh became evident, a few officials in Washington believed it necessary to enlarge the American role in Indochina. American policy in the Dutch-Indonesian war seemed to offer a model; specifically, the mediating influence of the United States through the Good Offices Committee might be paralleled in Indochina. In the end, however, such an initiative was deemed inappropriate in Indochina, not only because of French aversion to third party interference, but, more importantly, because any negotiated settlement would give enhanced status to the Viet Minh. A French-Viet Minh agreement, American officials had come to believe, would result in the eventual communist domination of Vietnam.[13]

## The Recognition of Bao Dai

As policymakers concluded that American interests could not countenance a complete victory by either side or support a negotiated settlement, a process of elimination led toward acceptance of the Bao Dai solution. That orientation of American policy, however, resulted in sharp bureaucratic disagreement over the terms of making a commitment with such important implications. While French colonial policy unfolded in 1948 and 1949, the critical question within the Department of State was not whether to back Bao Dai, but rather whether the United

States should insist on French concessions to Vietnamese nationalism as a condition of American support. Two competing strategies—one " Asian-oriented" and the other "European-oriented"—emerged. The process by which the United States came to recognize the Bao Dai government reflected a struggle between two bureaucratic groups within the Department of State and, in a broader sense, the priorities which each represented.

The Asian-oriented strategy was advanced by the consuls at Saigon and Hanoi and received the endorsement of the officers in the Division of Phillippine and Southeast Asian Affairs and the Office of Far Eastern Affairs. In a cable of June 30, 1948, George M. Abbott, who had replaced Reed as the consul at Saigon, set forth the basic Asian-oriented approach which called for withholding and support pending significant changes in French policy. In a conclusion that was later underlined by his superiors in Washington, Abbott argued: "If the Bao Dai solution fails, the United States will be on record as advocating a liberal solution crucial to the political problem but in no wise committed to monarchist, as distinct from non-communist, solutions."[14]

At the base of this approach was the recognition of the lack of popular support for Bao Dai and the inability of the French to attract non-communist nationalists to his side. To counter the influence of Ho Chi Minh among the peoples of Vietnam presented a formidable challenge. Reed once observed: "Unfortunately, the majority of natives stoutly maintain that Ho Chi Minh is the man, and the only one, who represents them and they will oppose the putting forward of any other candidate as the creating of but another puppet and the erecting of a smoke screen of France's real intentions."[15]

As the French plans to foster Bao Dai's return gradually developed, no American official in Indochina or Washington anticipated success; the prevailing analysis held that the former emperor not only lacked popular support, but was politically naive and incapable of leadership. In the absence of French concessions enhancing the status of any government headed by Bao

Dai, his return under French auspices would drive the Vietnamese more fully toward the side of the Viet Minh.[16]

Just prior to Abbott's June 1948 recommendations, the installation in Hanoi of the French-sponsored government headed by Nguyen Van Xuan—the first phase of the Bao Dai solution—provided vivid evidence of the distance between French colonial policy and its puppets, and the mass of the Vietnamese people. Reporting on the ceremonies, Edwin C. Rendall, the vice consul in Hanoi wrote to Washington:

> The pervading atmosphere at all these gatherings celebrating the birth of the "first provisional government of Vietnam" was more that of a funeral than a christening. . . . The expressions on the faces of both the participants and the spectators gave one the impression that the whole thing was a rather poorly managed stage show, with the actors merely going through the motions. The appearance of Xuan, his stocky figure clothed in mandarinal robes which he quite obviously did not know how to handle, almost succeeded in introducing a note of low comedy. Gilbert and Sullivan came to mind. . . . An obvious attempt was made to identify Bao Dai with the proceedings. . . . A gigantic likeness of the ex-emperor imposed on a map of Indochina dominated the entrance way to the presidential palace, and paintings and photographs were in evidence at other points. . . . At the installation ceremony the small number of Vietnamese civilians allowed to watch the affair was in particularly striking contrast to the amazing number of armed men who literally hid behind every bush. . . . No attempt was made at any time to show popular support for the new government. . . . It is difficult to see how even a puppet can serve any useful purpose if the gulf betweeen those who govern and those governed is admittedly so wide that even the briefest visual contacts cannot be permitted.[17]

With this and similar reports predicting failure for French colonial policy, in the summer of 1948 the State Department recommended that the French make significant concessions to Bao Dai so that upon his return to Vietnam, his government would attract substantial support. It was essential, American officials argued in conversations with French colleages in Washington, Paris, and Saigon, that Bao Dai not be perceived as a

French puppet.[18] Two considerations, however, always limited America's ability to influence French policy. First, France held a high card. France could always suggest the possibility of withdrawing from Indochina, leaving the United States with the choice between intervening itself or accepting a Communist victory. Recognizing that Washington would tolerate a continued French presence rather than face the consequences of withdrawal, Paris indeed was in a position to extend less generous terms than the United States advocated. The threat of withdrawal had been expresssed before. In the spring of 1948, the State Department and French embassy officials met to discuss the implications of criticism in Congress that the French were draining their resources and Marshall Plan assistance for the Indochina war. In response, an embassy official warned that any congressional reduction in economic assistance might necessitate leaving Indochina and its insoluble problems to the United States.[19] The lingering effect of this threat, which subsequently became a more prominent feature of the Franco-American exchange over Indochina, reduced the feasibility of the Asian-oriented strategy.

The United States was also restrained by its cold war strategy which held that France was needed to assure the security of Western Europe. The preservation of a close association with a stable French government was a high priority. To many American officials, acquiescence in France's colonial policy was dictated by imperatives of the cold war. A policy statement, drafted by the Division of Philippine and Southeast Asian Affairs in late July 1948, and subsequently endorsed by Secretary of State, George C. Marshall, stressed the continued impotence of the United States in Indochina:

> The objective of United States policy can only be attained by such French action as will satisfy the aspirations of the peoples of Indochina. . . . Our greatest difficulty in talking with the French and in suggesting what should and should not be done has been our inability to suggest any practicable solution. . . . We are naturally hesitant to press the French too strongly or to become deeply involved as we are not in a position to suggest a solution or

until we are prepared to accept the onus of intervention. The above considerations are further complicated by the fact that we have an immediate interest in maintaining in power a friendly French government, to assist in the furtherance of our aims in Europe. This immediate and vital interest has in consequence taken precedence over active steps toward the realization of our objectives in Indochina.[20]

Despite its inherent limitations, the Asian-oriented strategy set the tone of American policy until the discussions leading to the Elysée Agreement. By that time, the European-oriented strategy was becoming predominant in the policymaking process. Advanced by the American embassy in Paris, and supported by the Office of Western European Affairs at the State Department, this approach called for virtually unconditional acceptance of French colonial policy, principally on the grounds that the fragile political situation within France prevented significant concessions to Vietnamese nationalism. The only feasible remedy for the acknowledged shortcomings of the Bao Dai solution was American recognition and support, not a liberal French colonial policy.

The struggle over Indochina policy crystallized in late February 1949. In a message to the Paris embassy on February 25, Secretary of State Dean Acheson, indicated that the French should be informed that support of the Bao Dai government depended upon concessions vital to its success.[21] Ambassador Jefferson Caffery blunted this approach to the French, arguing that the United States should not prejudge the agreement. After his review of the March 8 letter from President Vincent Auriol to Bao Dai that constituted the Elysée Agreement, Caffery immediately advocated American support as vital to strengthening Bao Dai's position. While mindful of Bao Dai's weakness, the ambassador argued that since he was the only alternative to Ho Chi Minh, the United States had to take risks on his behalf.[22] This approach, supported by the Office of Western European Affairs, drew strong criticism from the Division of Philippine and Southeast Asian Affairs, whose new chief, the former Saigon consul, Charles Reed, maintained:

Because we have the power to render impotent the Bao Dai solution, we should not delude ourselves into thinking that we therefore have the power to make such an experiment succeed. Merely because he offers at present the only possible non-Commuist solution in Indochina is no reason, in view of his very dubious chances of succeeding, in committing the United States at this time to his support, as in event he turns out to be a puppet, we then must follow blindly down a dead-end alley, expending our limited resources—in money and most particularly in prestige—in a fight which would be hopeless.[23]

The issues set forth in the February confrontation over Indochina policy were reaffirmed as policymakers anticipated the American response to Bao Dai's return to Vietnam. From Saigon, Abbott suggested that as conditions of its recognition, the United States should insist that Cochin China be linked to Vietnam in response to the nationalist demand for national unity, and that Bao Dai form a cabinet of leaders of sufficient stature to provide a chance of success. In the meantime, he urged pressure on France to implement the Elysée Agreement liberally and rapidly. Underlying Abbott's position was the assumption that "our support will not assure Bao Dai's success but the lack of it will problably make certain his failure."[24] In opposition, the Office of Western European Affairs and the Paris embassy continued to argue that France, given its internal political divisions over colonial policy, could not be expected to grant additional concessions and, more importantly, that the Bao Dai government needed American support, which had to begin with an official statement welcoming the establishment of the Vietnamese state.[25]

In June 1949, the scenario of the preceding February was replayed as the Paris embassy again prevented a straightforward statement of the Asian-oriented strategy from being presented to the French government. On June 6, the State Department, acting with the knowledge of Acheson, who had left Washington to attend a Foreign Ministers meeting in Paris, instructed David Bruce, the new ambassador to France, to present a memorandum to the French government which maintained that the

Elysée Agreement provided insufficient concessions to attract nationalists away from Ho Chi Minh and to Bao Dai. To save Indochina from Communist control and to perserve some French influence there, the French were obliged to give assurances of genuine Vietnamese independence and to provide an early transfer of authority to the Bao Dai government.

Taking advantage of Acheson's presence in Paris, embassy officials gained his support of their opposition to this memorandum, persuading the secretary that political conditions in France prevented reconsideration of colonial policy, and that it was inappropriate to prejudge the Elysée Agreement. In addition to blunting this initiative, the European officers also gained unexpected support from Abbott. The Saigon consul was impressed by the arguments of the Paris embassy; he was also being pressured by Vietnamese associates of Bao Dai. He seconded the embassy's call for immediate American support of the Vietnamese state. This would build up Bao Dai as the cohesive figure in uniting noncommunist nationalists.[26] Accordingly, by mid-June, the State Department was preparing a public statement expressing its hope that the Elysée Agreement would bring together the "truly progressive elements within Vietnam" and would lead to a full realization of Vietnamese aspirations. Despite the opposition of a number of other important governments (principally Great Britain, India, the Indonesian Republic, and Thailand) to endorsement of French colonial policy, the United States, on June 21, issued its statement in support of the Elysée Agreement.[27]

By the end of June, the Asian-centered strategy had been effectively abandoned. In a memorandum of June 28 to his superiors in the Division of Philippine and Southeast Asian Affairs, Charlton Ogburn, who had been instrumental in drafting the abortive June 6 memorandum, expressed profound disappointment:

> What has happened is that Southeast Asia's policy has been junked, nothing effective is being done to promote a non-Communist solution in Indochina. . . . This is the culmination of three years of consistent effort on the part of Western Europe to set

aside all considerations of our position in Asia and to keep a free hand for the French. This has been done on the grounds that a stern attitude on the part of the United States would cause the French government to fall. We have been gagged by this consideration beyond all reason, in so many contexts that the thing has become a joke.[28]

Then comparing the American reponses to colonial policies of European allies in Indochina and Indonesia, Ogburn concluded:

So long as we were hogtied by this fear in our dealings with the Dutch, developments in Indonesia went from bad to worse. If the situation in Indonesia is now improving, I believe it is solely because the Dutch were threatened with the loss of ECA [European Cooperation Administration]. . . . We have spoken far more drastically to the Dutch than we have dreamed of speaking to the French. And there has been no sign of the Dutch Government's falling. I think we are heading into a very bad mess in the policy we are now following toward Indochina.[29]

During the next few months, developments in Indochina confirmed Ogburn's prediction of a "very bad mess" for American policymakers. Concerned about the lack of international support for the Elysée Agreement, the United States urged officials of the Bao Dai government to take measures that would enhance its appeal. At the same time, officials in Washington and Manila pressed the Philippine government to recognize the Communist danger in Indochina and the necessity for the success of the Bao Dai solution. But by September, the Bao Dai regime remained lacking in popular and international support.[30]

As the United States confronted a worsening situation, its policymakers were cognizant of, but quickly discounted, renewed public affirmations from Ho Chi Minh of his overriding commitment to Vietnamese nationalism. Ending two years of isolation from the West, Ho, in the summer of 1949, issued several statements directed toward France and the United States. Through radio contact, letters, and the Viet Minh propaganda outlet at Bangkok, Ho reiterated to French and American correspondents many of the themes that had characterized his earlier appeal to the West between the end of World War II and the beginning of the French-Viet Minh War. In particular, he defended the Viet Minh as representative of many political groups, affirmed his commitment to national independence and neutrality in the cold war, and promised investment opportunities for foreign capital.[31] In America, his views received some attention, especially in *The Nation.* In that journal, Andrew Roth argued that Ho constituted an "Asian Tito" worthy of American support and cultivation. In an article of September 10, Roth maintained: "Although there has been much talk in Washington about the possibility of Chinese Titoism, the situation in Vietnam suggests that the State Department is incapable of recognizing Titoism when it sees it."[32] In view of the established assumption that the United States could not risk a Communist-dominated Vietnam, the State Department declined any consideration of Ho Chi Minh as an "Asian Tito."

While the United States dismissed the "Ho Chi Minh alternative," its tendency toward unconditional acceptance of the Bao Dai solution continued to present serious problems, principally the possibility of becoming the lone partner of France in a losing colonial enterprise. The meeting of the Big Three Western foreign ministers and their staffs in Washington in early September underscored differences among France, Great Britain, and the United States. The American disposition to proceed with the recognition of Bao Dai—there being no acceptable alternative—ran counter to British reservations, which were based not only on the doubt that the government met established criteria for recognition, but also on whether international recognition by itself would strengthen the Bao Dai regime internally. Accordingly, the British advocated pressuring France to interpret the Elysée Agreement liberally as soon as it was ratified.[33] Yet when Acheson met with French Foreign Minister, Robert Schuman, the latter took the initiative and asked for an enlarged American military and economic commitment. Maintaining that the French army was preventing the Communist domination of Southeast Asia, Schuman pressed for United States military assistance to the associated states. Tacitly promising a liberal policy, the foreign minister also stressed the lack of preparation for independence, while claiming the necessity for early Asian recognition as the key to strengthening the Bao Dai government.

In sum, the three foreign secretaries could agree on little more than the necessity for some appropriate French gestures toward Vietnamese nationalism (principally transferring the adminstration of Indochina from the Overseas France Ministry to the Foreign Office) which would be followed by Anglo-American pressures on governments in South and Southeast Asia to recognize Bao Dai. They could also agree that Western recognition alone would be the "kiss of death" for the Bao Dai solution.[34]

Following the Washington meeting, conversations between American officials and representatives of Asian governments, principally India, further revealed the deep-seated antagonism toward French policy in Indochina and the need for significant changes to gain the vital support of Asia governments.[35] Moreover, as foreshadowed in the discussions at Washington, the British appeared to be moving toward dissociation from French policy in Indochina.[36] It seemed that the United States might be placed in a very isolated position, committed to a government that lacked popular and international respectability. The situation in Indochina potentially paralleled the American association with the discredited Chiang Kai-shek government in the Chinese Civil War.

Concern about American credibility led Asian desk officers in the Department of State to make another effort to increase the pressure on France as a means of salvaging Western influence in Indochina. The Division of Philippine and Southeast Asian Affairs advocated that France be called upon to follow ratification of the Elysée Agreement with the announcement of a timetable detailing the transfer of authority in Indochina and the establishment of an international commission to supervise the transition.[37] Against a background of the Communist victory in China and the Viet Minh's military successes against the French, this plan was viewed favorably by higher officials, with the result that on December 1, Acheson informed the embassy in Paris of the Department's anticipated representations to the French government.[38] Again, however, the embassy blunted a plan that called for taking a strong stand with the French. Bruce argued that no French government could survive internally if it undertook such commitments. Instead, he called for more moderate expectations from France—transferring responsibility for Indochina from the Overseas France Ministry to the Foreign Office, and a statement affirming that the Elysée Agreement constituted an evolutionary step in the changing French-Indochina relationship. In return, the United States, Bruce urged, should recognize the Bao Dai government and provide economic and military assistance.[39] As it had in similar circumstances in February and June of 1949, the leadership of the State Department deferred to the European-centered approach which, by this time, meant minimal modification of French policy in return for a substantial American commitment to France's position in Indochina.

## The "Grievous Political Defeat": The Final Imperative

That direction of American policy was reinforced by reports from Indochina and by the diplomatic-military implications of the Chinese Civil War. In December 1949, Washington received some encouraging estimates of the prospects for Bao Dai's success. Malcolm MacDonald, the British commission general in Southeast Asia, visited Indochina and quickly became a strong advocate of Bao Dai's position. He recommended early support as a means of evidencing Western good will.[40] Samuel Welles, a *Time-Life* correspondent who toured Indochina in the fall of 1949, provided State Department officers with a very optimistic appraisal of Vietnamese developments.[41] From the field, the consuls at Saigon and Hanoi, while remaining skeptical about the Bao Dai solution, reported that the situation had become more stable. Robert S. Folsom, who joined the Saigon consular staff in November, following tours of duty in China and Hungary, suggested, with the strong backing of the Consul General, Abbott, that recognition need not depend on Bao Dai's attaining popular support. Instead, the United States should extend recognition as a means of helping his government gain credibility and popular backing.[42]

By late 1949, the victory of the Communists in the Chinese Civil War provided irresistible momentum to the movement toward early, unconditional recognition of the Bao Dai government. The outcome of the Chinese Civil War profoundly affected the thinking of American policymakers with respect to Indochina. Most evidently, if focused attention on Southeast Asia as the next likely battleground in the struggle with international communism. As a result, American concern with Southeast Asia intensified, and plans were made to utilize economic and military assistance extensively in the region as a means of assuring the survival of Western-oriented governments in Indonesia, Thailand, Burma, the Philippines, and Indochina.[43] Moreover, the devastating defeat of America's longtime ally, Chiang Kai-shek, threatened to demoralize non-Communist nations throughout the world. American credibility seemed to be threatened by the Communist victory in China which made a strong stand against communism in Southeast Asia all the more necessary. The National Security Council (NSC) in its policy statement 48-1, set forth clearly the significance of Indochina: "The extension of communist authority in China represents a grievous political defeat for us. . . . If Southeast Asia is also swept by communism, we shall have suffered a major political rout, the repurcussions of which will be felt throughout the rest of the world. . . . The colonial-nationalist conflict provides a fertile field for subversive movements, and it is now clear that Southeast Asia is the target for a coordinated offensive directed by the Kremlin."[44]

With the implications of the Chinese Civil War increasingly prominent in the policymaking process, American officials called vigorously for the development of a consensus among the non-Communist governments of the region. By the end of 1949,

Washington was urging Asian governments to extend diplomatic recognition of Bao Dai as soon as the French Assembly ratified the Elysée Agreement. Inasmuch as the Bao Dai regime appeared to be gaining strength, the United States argued, recognition could be vital in attracting nationalists away from Ho Chi Minh and in pressuring the French to meet the legitimate demands of the Vietnamese.[45] But the American appeal to the governments of India, the Philippines, Burma, Indonesia, and Thailand failed. Those nations were unwilling to recognize a government whose independence was compromised and which lacked substantial popular support.[46] To Secretary Acheson, this position of Asian leaders reflected an inadequate appreciation of the overriding danger of communism: "This general indifference or lack of understanding may prove to be disastrous for those nations as Communism relentlessly advances. It is impossible for the United States to help them resist Communism if they are not prepared to help themselves."[47]

In an effort to make the Bao Dai solution more acceptable to Asian nations, the United States asked the French for a commitment to further concessions, but that initiative also failed. In response to American suggestions that ratification of the Elysée Agreement be coupled with a statement on the evolutionary progress of Indochina toward independence, French officials repeatedly maintained that internal constraints prevented any elaboration on Indochina policy.[48] Moreover, the French realized that American and British plans for recognition were already well advanced and would be forthcoming without additional concessions.

Finally, the American momentum toward recognition was enhanced by the Soviet Union's decision, announced in late January 1950, to recognize the government of Ho Chi Minh. That action seemed to provide evidence of a Soviet–Viet Minh link. It also confirmed the assumption of NSC 48-1 that Southeast Asia, and especially Indochina, should be given economic and military assistance. In a public statement on February 1, Acheson asserted that the Soviet recognition ought to remove any illusions about the alleged nationalist character of the Viet

Minh and clearly reveal Ho Chi Minh as the enemy of Vietnamese aspirations for independence.[49] In sum, by the first week of February 1950, the United States had become fully committed to the Bao Dai solution and was prepared to recognize that government unconditionally.[50]

In the weeks after the recognition of the Bao Dai government, the United States became more fully involved in Indochina. Commitment quickly followed recognition. From the perspective of Washington, Indochina became a military question, thus reducing concern with French colonial policy. Contemplating America's options a few days after recognition, Acheson was wary that "our bargaining position disappears the moment we agree to give them aid."[51] Despite the Secretary's misgivings, military and economic assistance had already become the unquestioned next step in stabilizing Vietnam. No one doubted the necessity of preventing a Viet Minh victory in Indochina as the key to preventing Communist expansion into Southeast Asia. Failure to aid the French would only result in larger expenditures of American resources at a later date. The French were seen as determined to maintain a strong military effort against communism in Indochina, but they needed American assistance. Otherwise, they would become demoralized and might withdraw, leaving the defense of Indochina and the remainder of Southeast Asia to the United States.[52]

## Conclusion

Reflecting on the decision to recognize the Bao Dai government and the attendant commitment to French colonial and military policy, it is evident that the United States accepted a solution that was given only a marginal chance of success. To some extent, the prognosis for Indochina improved in late 1949 and early 1950. The encouraging estimates of Bao Dai's prospects provided by Welles, Folsom, and MacDonald were reinforced by the favorable analyses of Ambassador-at-Large Phillip Jessup and the new counsel at Saigon, Edmund Gullion. In this environment, even the most modest suggestion to seek modification of French policy failed. For instance, in late March, the Asian desk officers proposed that the French be asked to prepare an "evolutionary statement" explaining the means by which full independence would eventually be accomplished within the framework of the Elysée Agreement. Gullion strongly opposed such an overture on the grounds that the Bao Dai government, which was already experiencing serious internal problems, would become increasingly irresponsible if the French position were weakened. Accordingly the plans for military assistance progressed without any evolutionary statement being requested.[53]

Before and after recognition of the Bao Dai government, the United States basically lacked leverage in dealing with France over Indochina—a consequence of the pressures of the cold war and the Communist victory in China. The French presence in Indochina, whatever its imperfections, was considered vital to the preservation of Western interests in Southeast Asia.[54] The extent to which the United States had become a captive of the French program was evident in the State Department's retreats of February, June, and December 1949, from projected representations on behalf of a liberal colonial policy. Whether attaching conditions to American recognition and support of the Bao Dai government would have made any difference in the long run is uncertain, but at least requests for significant French concessions would have dissociated the United States from a colonial policy that was an anathema to the majority of Vietnamese as well as to the independent nations of Asia. At the time, however, Americans perceived only very limited options in Indochina and the priority, it appeared, had to be given to anticommunism and the slender hope that the French, through the Bao Dai solution would somehow establish a viable nationalist alternative to the Viet Minh.

# 11.

# The Redefinition of United States' Policy, 1949–1950

If we are to ally Southeast Asia to ourselves, the decision to do so must be taken now. The issue of China has been settled. The future and meaning of Korea are still unsettled and uneasy. The role and attitude of India are a growing shadow across the face of Asia, influenced by events in China and, in turn, influencing Southeast Asia. Under these pressures the time of decision on the future of Southeast Asia has long since arisen above the horizon and is reaching the zenith. Everything we have seen and heard convinces us that the area can be held if we will it. But it must be done now. In the eyes of Asia, failure will for the predictable future compromise, if not destroy, American influence and prestige. America without Asia will have been reduced to the Western Hemisphere and a precarious foothold on the western fringe of the Eurasian continent. Success will vindicate and give added meaning to America and the American way of life.

Final Report of Joint MDAP Survey Mission
December 5, 1950

THE MOVEMENT OF the Chinese Communist army toward victory in their long struggle against the Kuomintang brought Southeast Asia into greater prominence in U.S. strategic planning. Throughout 1949, as the Communist forces in China solidified their position and approached the frontiers of Southeast Asia, American policymakers urgently searched for means to prevent the further extension of Communist influence. The United States accordingly allocated economic and military assistance in an effort to assure political stability.

The Communist victory in China provided the immediate impetus for the redefinition of American interests in Southeast Asia, but broader interests were also giving higher priorities to the region in American global strategy. With the establishment of the Marshall Plan and the North Atlantic Treaty Organization, the links between European economic recovery and remilitarization, and the Southeast Asian interests and commitments of European allies, made it ever more essential that U.S. actions in Southeast Asia not undermine its European priorities. That consideration was strongly reinforced by the persistent weakness of the European economies which was aggravated by the imbalance in world trade and the enormous "dollar gap." This led to the prevalent American fear that its carefully structured multilateral economic system might collapse. Revitalizing the economies of Southeast Asia served to benefit European recovery. And as the United States moved toward reestablishing Japanese industrial and commercial power, Southeast Asia took on even greater significance as a source of raw materials and as a principal outlet for manufactured goods.

The unexpected outbreak of war in Korea on June 25, 1950, and the immediate decision of the Truman administration to support South Korean resistance to the attack from the north, increased the determination of Washington to preserve the American position throughout Asia. This meant an acceleration of commitments to the countries of Southeast Asia. The Communist aggression in Korea, together with the forthright American response, enhanced the position of the United States in most of Asia, and brought closer relations with the Philippines,

Thailand, and Burma while solidifying further the Franco-American ties in Indochina.[1]

## The Policy Review

At the direction of Secretary of State Dean Acheson, the Policy Planning Staff (PPS) reappraised Southeast Asian interests which resulted in PPS 51, a comprehensive thirty-nine page policy review endorsed by the staff on March 29, 1949. Reflecting the then common assumption in Washington of rivalry between the Chinese Communist party (CCP) and the Soviet Union, PPS 51 maintained that until the previous year, the Russians had been content to allow the CCP, through the influence of the Chinese community in Southeast Asia, to carry communism into the region. But within the last year, Russian interests had evidently increased. The Soviets had established an embassy in Bangkok, convened and guided the Southeast Asian Youth Conference at Calcutta, and dispatched Musso to lead the communist rebellion in Indonesia. The PPS saw Soviet motivation in Southeast Asia as principally directed against the United States and its allies, rather than as driven by any immediate strategic or economic needs:

> Southeast Asia is important to the free world as a source of raw materials, including rubber, tin, and petroleum and as a crossroads in east-west and north-south global communications. . . . In seeking to gain control of Southeast Asia, the Kremlin is, of course, motivated in part by a desire to acquire Southeast Asia's resources and communications lines, but its immediate and perhaps even greater desire is to deny them to us. While Southeast Asian resources could help satisfy Soviet and satellite economic needs, it must be remembered that the USSR has never relied on Southeast Asian raw materials and markets. And although control over the Southeast Asian airways and seaways would, assuming that China is overrun by the communists, afford the dramatic spectacle of the world divided in half by communism on a north-south axis, such an achievement would be

largely negative in value, a denial to us rather than a positive gain.[2]

For the United States, the prospects of a Russian-dominated Southeast Asia threatened security interests throughout Asia and the Middle East:

> The outstanding positive gains to be attained by the Kremlin . . . are political in nature. The extension of communist authority in China represents a grievous political defeat for us; if Southeast Asia also is swept by communism we shall have a major political rout the repercussion of which will be felt throughout the rest of the world, especially in the Middle East and in a then critically exposed Australia. . . . Without China being overwhelmed by communism, Southeast Asia represents a vital segment on the line of containment, stretching from Japan southward to the Indian peninsula. The security of the three major non-communist base areas in this quarter of the world—Japan, India and Australia—depends in a large measure on the denial of Southeast Asia to the Kremlin. If Southeast Asia, particularly the Philippines and Indonesia, is lost, then these three base areas will tend to be isolated from one another. If Southeast Asia is held, the links will exist for the development of an interdependent and integrated counterforce to Stalinism in this quarter of the world.[3]

To assure the preservation of a non-Communist Southeast Asia, PPS 51 recommended that the United States pressure the Dutch and French to liberalize their colonial policies, and pursue regional collaboration among non-Communist states in Southeast Asia and with India, Australia, and Japan. To assure the preservation of Western interests in Southeast Asia, PPS 51 made specific recommendations for each country, and strongly suggested that the United States support non-Communist regimes through greater political involvement, dissociate itself from Europen colonialism, and foster regional cooperation among the Southeast Asian states.[4]

PPS 51 clearly set the tone for American policymaking in

Southeast Asia. As the Asian situation became more critical, PPS 51's assumptions that Southeast Asia was a target of Soviet expansion, and that the area had to be held for economic and strategic purposes, were accepted without question. The National Security Council (NSC) undertook the definitive reexamination of Asian policy, which culminated in NSC 48-2 approved by the Council and then by President Truman in December. The central assumptions and objectives, and indeed much of the very language of PPS 51, determined the NSC's policy formulation.[5]

The relationship of the external threat to regional vulnerability was explicitly drawn by Secretary Acheson in his often-cited public address, "Crisis in Asia: An Examination of United States Policy" delivered at the National Press Club on January 12, 1950. While Acheson's purpose was to defend the record of American diplomacy in the aftermath of the China debacle, the part of the speech which attracted the greatest attention had to do with his definition of the American "defensive perimeter" in the Pacific which stretched from the Aleutians, to Japan, the Ryukus, and the Philippines. The Secretary carefully added that response to military attack in areas outside the perimeter would rely initially on the resistance of the victims of aggression and subsequently on the fulfillment of commitments made by members of the United Nations under its charter. Stressing throughout his address the complexities facing the United States on the Asian continent, Acheson closed by summarizing the major problems in Japan, Korea, Southeast Asia, and South Asia. In the Philippines, he noted that the $1 billion in American assistance since the end of World War II "had not been used . . . wisely" and that the country likely faced "serious economic difficulties." In the rest of Southeast Asia, the situation was "difficult." In Burma it was "highly confused"; in Indochina, the French "although moving slowly, are moving"; Indonesia was "full of encouragement although [also] full of difficulty." The most favorable assessment was given to Malaya

where the British and native people were making "progress."
With respect to the American position in Southeast Asia,
Acheson noted that "our responsibilities, except in the Philippines . . . are very small." He also reiterated a willingness to provide large-scale technical assistance.[6] That willingness had been
underscored a year earlier by President Truman in his presidential inaugural address with its call for the Point Four program of
technical support for underdeveloped areas. Acheson's speech—
which included more references to Southeast Asian problems
than any earlier public statement by a Secretary of State—
signalled the increased importance of the region. Appropriately,
State Department planning by January 1950 clearly foreshadowed a substantial increase in American involvement.

In the comprehensive overview of American policy—
NSC-68— Southeast Asia was seen as an important part of the
worldwide confrontation with the Soviet Union. Completed in
April 1950, NSC-68 originated in Truman's directive that nu-
clear weapons strategy be reexamined in light of the Soviet
Union's successful testing of an atomic bomb in August 1949.
The resulting document exceeded that objective and issued a
detailed justification for a vastly accelerated rearmament program. At the base of NSC-68 was the assumption that the
Soviets sought "complete subversion or forcible destruction" of
governments outside the Communist sphere with their immediate efforts directed toward "domination of the Eurasian land
mass."[7] In reviewing critical political-economic trends, Asia,
along with central and western Europe, seemed especially
vulnerable to Soviet influence. With respect to Asia, it was
argued:

> The communist success in China, taken with the politico-eco-
> nomic situation in the rest of South and South-East Asia, pro-
> vides a springboard for a further incursion in this troubled area.
> Although Communist China faces serious economic problems
> which may impose some strains on the Soviet economy, it is prob-
> able that the social and economic problems faced by the free

nations in this area present more than offsetting opportunities for Communist expansion.[8]

To maintain the Western position in Asia presented a serious challenge:

> Throughout Asia the stability of the present moderate govern-
> ments, which are more in sympathy with our purposes than any
> probable successor regimes would be, is doubtful. The problem is
> only in part an economic one. Assistance in economic develop-
> ment is important as a means of holding out to the peoples of Asia
> some prospect of improvement in standards of living under their
> present governments. But probably more important are a
> strengthening of central institutions, an improvement in admin-
> istration, and generally a development of an economic and social
> structure within which the peoples of Asia can make more effec-
> tive use of their great human and material resources.[9]

American strategic planning of 1949–1950, as reported in PPS 51, NSC 48, and NSC 68, clearly saw Southeast Asia as a region in which the United States needed to enhance its politi-cal, economic, and military position. While those documents addressed in general terms the challenge facing the United States in the region, they did not elaborate on the immediate problems in each individual country. Close examination of the political situation in the Philippines, Indochina, Burma, Thai-land, and Indonesia added to the sense of crisis which prevailed in Washington's reexamination of Asian policy. The situation in those countries made the consequences of the Communist vic-tory in China all the more ominous. By 1949, the governments in the Philippines, Thailand, and Burma appeared increasingly unstable and incapable of dealing effectively with Communist pressures. The situation in Indochina was the most critical as a result of the Communist domination of the nationalist move-ment and the failures of French colonial and military policies. The attainment of independence in Indonesia, while bringing peace to that war-torn nation, also presented serious challenges if ties with the West were to be preserved.

## The Revitalization of the Southeast Asian Economy

As the principal National Security Council and State Department documents stated, holding the line against Communist expansion required, as an integral objective, the revitalization of the economic structure of Southeast Asia. Basically the United States sought to establish a neo-colonial system that approximated the prewar commercial relationship—a relationship which would especially benefit Western Europe and Japan. In the process, the United States would enhance its global political and economic interests.

By 1949, the United States was encountering a serious international economic situation. The objective of a multilateral system, free of restrictions on trade and investment, was undermined by the imbalance of postwar trade. The demand for American goods, the effects of the war, and the decline of colonialism led to an annual $10 million surplus of exports over imports. The resultant "dollar gap" was balanced only by U.S. foreign economic assistance. The Marshall Plan for Europe's economic recovery was justified principally as a means of containing Soviet expansion, but it also served the basic economic objective of financing American surplus exports, thus assuring dominance over international markets and reducing the prospects of tarriffs and controls. The fear persisted among American officials and business leaders that the world economy would become stagnant and then deteriorate, undermining American productivity and enhancing the prospects for leftist movements everywhere.

As the Marshall Plan moved forward, American global strategy anticipated a world with three major industrialized centers: the United States, Western Europe, and Japan. With the emergence of the Communist state in China, close economic and political cooperation with Japan became a cornerstone of America's Asian policy. Japan, linked to the West politically, economically, and ideologically, would serve as the principal deterrent to further Communist expansion. Japan's economic recovery—a key aspect of this program—required trade outlets and raw materials, which Southeast Asia could provide. If denied access to Southeast Asian materials and markets, Japan would have no alternative but to seek accommodation with the Chinese People's Republic. Hence, American interests pointed toward the stabilization of Southeast Asia as a means of facilitating Japan's reemergence as a major industrial power. Just as German reconstruction was seen as the key to Western European recovery, so too was the defeated enemy in Asia seen to be the basis of Asian economic revitalization. The Japanese were to be encouraged to reestablish prewar trading patterns with Southeast Asia; in return for raw materials, it would provide exports and technological leadership, thus contributing to the region's pro-Western orientation. Southeast Asia was not to be developed, rather it was to retain its historic colonial economic role. Large-scale American economic assistance would not be necessary, because Japan, stimulated in part by American assistance, would fuel its economic revival.[10]

The Southeast Asian economic connection was vital not only for American interests in Asia, but in Europe as well. American policymakers assumed that the stability of the British economy and the sterling area was vital to American interests. Yet despite the large postwar loan from the United States and the beginnings of Marshall Plan assistance, the British economy was sluggish and recovery was disappointingly slow. Its precarious situation was worsened by the dollar gap which could be reduced only by increasing exports to the United States. In that situation, Malaya took on special significance for its rubber and tin exports had long been an important source of dollar earnings. By 1949, Malayan rubber and tin production, while recovered from wartime devastation, surpassed world demand. Declining American demand was the principal cause of the surplus. The United States alone could reverse the situation by reducing the surplus, thus increasing prices and reestablishing the prewar "triangular trade" relationship with Malaya and Britain. In the process, the dollar gap would be reduced. While American officials in 1949–50 disagreed on the means, none questioned the necessity to alleviate the Malayan surpluses.[11]

## Another China?—The Crisis in the Philippines

The shortcomings of Philippine democracy especially aggravated the United States and led many analysts by 1949–50 to
conjecture the loss of American influence in China was about to
be repeated in the Philippines. American and Philippine leaders
tended to blame one another for the problems confronting the
Philippines—problems which threatened the stability of the
Philippine economic and political systems. The resurgence of
the Huks—an outgrowth of ineffective Philippine leadership,
widespread corruption at all levels of government, and the
inadequacy of agrarian reform—placed the Philippines, and the
American hopes embodied in the half-century "special relationship," in a singularly precarious position.

   To the Philippine leaders, the United States failed in the
immediate post-independence period to recognize the importance of the islands and gave only nominal military and eco-
omic assistance to its loyal Asian ally while pouring billions into
European recovery and the futile effort to save Chiang Kai-shek.
Indeed in 1947–48, the Truman administration decided to
reduce substantially the number of American forces in the
Philippines, disbanded the 29,000 Philippine Scouts contingent,
and rejected the repeated requests of the Philippine government
for additional military and financial assistance.[12] To the United
States, this limiting of American influence reflected not only the
relatively low strategic priority of the Philippines, but a sense
that commitments were being fulfilled and that the independent
nation was making progress. Through disbursements under the
War Damage Act, the Philippine Rehabilitation Act, and other
means, the United States contributed about $1.4 billion in
overall assistance between 1945 and 1949. In addition, the
government's financial condition stabilized and the economy
improved as production reached prewar levels and inflation was
brought under control. The government under the leadership of
Roxas and, following his death, Elpidio Quirino seemed to be
dealing effectively with the communist insurgents. In a dra-

matic move shortly after assuming the presidency, Quirino announced an amnesty for the Huks provided that they presented themselves and their arms to official authorities by August 30, 1948. Despite initial signs that the amnesty might end the Huk movement, Quirino's initiative failed. As a result, the Philippine army in September 1948 moved quickly against the Huks in an effort to eliminate that threat to internal stability.[13]

In 1949 the American perception of the Philippines changed dramatically. This resulted from the increased attention to Southeast Asian developments generally, the considerable publicity given to some glaring and long ignored problems within the Philippines, and the "lessons" of the Chinese War. As early as April 1949, Truman, speaking to Acheson of the "recent catastrophe" in China, ordered a reexamination of Philippine policy since the islands were "more important than ever" and "must be kept close to the United States."[14] Indeed the situation in the Philippines seemed strikingly similar to the conditions in China which had led to the Communist victory. To officials in Washington, the Philippine government was seen as increasingly corrupt, its leadership losing credibility at home and abroad, its anti-Communist efforts failing politically and militarily, and its domestic programs alienating large segments of the population. Another American ally was following the same road to destruction as the Kuomintang in China.

In the 1949 Philippine presidential election, the Liberal party resorted to widespread fraud, intimidation, and terrorism to assure Quirino's victory over the Nacionalista party candidate, Jose Laurel. The election was symptomatic of corruption at all levels of the government. Disposition of $200 million worth of war surplus property transferred by the United States as a part of the rehabilitation act was especially scandalous; theft, fraudulent auctions, and mislabeled materials had promoted a flourishing black market.

In the rural areas, longstanding agrarian problems were ignored. The erosion of the democratic process renewed the vitality of the Huks who steadily gathered support; by February 1950, they emerged as the People's Liberation Army calling for the overthrow of the Republic.[15] In Washington this demise of Philippine democracy was seen as partly the result of American policy: "The spread of communism in the country can be prevented, if the problem is handled properly. But the people have seen with consternation the speedy deterioration of the situation in China. They see that our Armed Forces are not strong in the Islands. . . . These events, coupled with action of the part of this Government is strengthening its ties and commitments in other areas, create the danger that the Filipinos will come to the erroneous conclusion that the US is losing interest in the Far East and that their resistance to anti-American and anti-Western agitation may consequently be weakened."[16]

To help correct the situation, a State Department study recommended increasing military assistance, providing economic and technical aid through the Point Four program, and allocating an additional $150 million in war damage funds. In addition, the United States, it was maintained, should enhance the position of the Philippines internationally, especially by supporting Carlos Romulo, the Philippine representative at the United Nations, in his efforts to provide leadership in the international organization.[17] Perhaps the most important phase of the reexamination of Philippine policy was the agreement, reached by Truman and Quirino in a meeting on February 4, 1950, to have an American mission undertake an extensive survey of the country's economic and financial problems. That agreement came after the United States had deferred repeated Philippine requests for large-scale economic and military assistance. In effect, the survey mission became a prerequisite to any substantial commitment of American resources. Indeed just three weeks before the Truman-Quirino agreement, Acheson, in his January 12 address on Asian policy, had specifically criticized the Philippine government "for not us[ing] . . . wisely" the $2 billion of assistance provided since the end of the war.[18]

While the United States in 1949–50 was prepared to increase its economic and military involvement in the Philippines, policymakers recognized that the principal impetus for change had to come from the Philippine government, and, in that respect, they were not sanguine about the prospects for leadership by Quirino. To officials in Washington and at the embassy in Manila, Quirino had become a liability to American interests in the Philippines. He seemed to act impetuously and to suffer from an exaggerated sense of self-importance. Instead of confronting his nation's serious internal problems, Quirino engaged in international and domestic posturing. For instance in 1949, he made numerous public statements suggesting an alliance in Asia modeled on the North Atlantic Treaty Organization. To America's chagrin, this led to Chiang Kai-shek's unexpected visit with Quirino on July 5, 1949 which resulted in a joint call for a regional anticommunist alliance. As expected in Washington, only South Korea showed interest, while the more prominent Asian countries, especially India, criticized the suggestion.

After Quirino's agreement with Truman on the survey mission, he asserted, upon returning to Manila, that the mission would be comprised of both Americans and Filipinos; he and Truman, however, had spoken explicitly of exclusive American membership. Quirino's refusal to accept that condition, despite repeated representations from Ambassador Myron Cowen, delayed establishment of the mission.[19] Annoyed by these and other actions, a draft State Department memorandum prepared for Secretary Acheson in April 1950 concluded that Quirino was the "principal obstacle" to political and economic reform; lacking capacity to provide leadership, Quirino was driven by "overwhelming vanity and arrogance, pettiness, and vindictiveness." Such inept leadership reminded department officers of the China example: "If there is one lesson to be learned from the China debacle it is that if we are confronted with an inadequate vehicle it should be discarded or immobilized in favor of a more propitious one."[20] Quirino, who later attempted to gain a guarantee of a development grant in return for accepting an exclusively American mission, finally was forced by Washington to accept its terms. His tactics not only delayed establishment of the mission until July 1950, but also further eroded his standing among American officials and with his own countrymen.[21]

## The Crises in Burma,
## Thailand, Indonesia, and Indochina

As the United States moved to reinforce its position in the Philippines, it was also being drawn into an enlarged role in Burma. By 1949, Washington could no longer afford to consider Burma as largely a British responsibility. The unstable situation—which had been a source of concern to American officials since the assassination of Aung San in July 1947—seemed to leave that country vulnerable to Communist subversion or Chinese aggression.

In the first year after independence, the leadership of U Nu encountered rebellions from the Communists, the People's Volunteer Organization, and, most significantly, from the Karens. By early 1949, the central government had made considerable progress in asserting its authority, particularly in dealing with the first two rebellious groups. This resulted from the lack of coordination among the dissidents (and the divisions within the Communist ranks), the government's ability to prevent the rebelling groups from receiving external assistance (which was especially important to the Karens), and the unexpectedly effective leadership provided by U Nu. Yet even with the gains made by the central government, its forces controlled less than half of Burmese territory. The Karen rebellion, which sought the establishment of an independent state, presented the major threat to national sovereignty. The continuing struggle between the Burmese and Karen forces caused considerable concern in India, Britain, and the United States. Accordingly, the State Department quietly supported Jawaharlal Nehru's initiative of February 1949 inviting representatives from Britain, Australia,

Pakistan, and Ceylon to a conference at New Delhi which led to an offer of mediation. The behind-the-scenes American role resulted from Washington's recognition of the Burmese sensitivity to any action which might hint of Western manipulation. That position proved to be well-founded in that U Nu rebuffed the New Delhi action as an unwarranted interference in Burmese affairs. His government, he averred, would soon bring the Karen rebellion under control.[22]

As the Communists approached victory in China, the Burmese government worked to strengthen its position externally as well as internally. In a meeting with U.S. Ambassador J. Klahr Huddle in April 1949, Prime Minister Nu stated that he now considered communism to be a major threat and that Burma was prepared to cooperate with others in an anti-Communist bloc. Burmese concern about the implications of the Chinese Civil War increased in the summer as the Chinese Communists denounced the Burmese for their alignment with the "imperialist-capitalist camp." Foreign Minister U. E. Maung and Deputy Prime Minister General Ne Win visited London and Washington where they reiterated an interest in a Pacific alliance and a need for military assistance. At this time the United States declined to pursue a closer relationship with Burma. Washington remained skeptical about the viability of the Burmese government and encouraged British influence as a stabilizing force. In the summer and fall of 1949, Anglo-Burmese relations were strengthened as a result of Burmese relaxation of regulations restricting private investment and the Commonwealth's extension of a $70 million loan. Burma's Western orientation was limited, however, by its proximity to China and internal politics (strong leftist criticisms of Maung's policies forcing his resignation), and on December 16, Burma extended diplomatic recognition to the Chinese People's Republic—the first non-Communist nation to take that step.[23]

At the time, however, neither Washington nor Rangoon considered recognition to be detrimental to a pursuit of closer relations. The Burmese continued to seek economic and military assistance and to speak of the possibilities of an alliance with the

West. And the United States, while still wary of Burmese leadership and the prospects for long-term stability, concluded in early 1950 that U.S. security dictated an investment of resources and prestige in Burma. The reasoning behind that commitment found expression in a State Department policy statement on Burma, drafted on June 16, 1950, which maintained that Burma and Indochina stood as the keys to the future of mainland Southeast Asia. If these countries were held against communism, the region would be secure; if either were lost, Thailand would quickly follow.[24]

In Thailand, the United States sought a means of forestalling the Thais' historic tendency to find security through identification with prevailing political trends in the region. From the perspective of Bangkok, developments in China and Indochina foreshadowed the emergence of a strong Vietnam allied with China. As observed in a Department of State memorandum: "It would be strange if during a period of communist ascendancy in the Far East Thailand would not assume the popular political coloration in order to be inconspicuous among its neighbors. Many Siamese who do not believe in Communism per se will support a government which will assume the Communist political pattern out of expediency."[25]

The government headed by Pibul Songgram seemed especially vulnerable. While generally supported by the armed forces, various elements in the military sought Pibul's overthrow. An abortive coup of February 1949 was followed by a purge of numerous officials. The reestablishment of a bicameral legislature in which representatives to the lower house were elected by universal adult male franchise, brought into prominence leaders of the anti-Pibul Democratic party and generally threatened the position of the military.[26]

Ambassador Edwin Stanton and officials in the Division of Philippine and Southeast Asian Affairs at the State Department suggested that the United States reassure Pibul of U.S. interest in the preservation of a strong, anti-Communist Thailand. In 1949 Stanton repeatedly warned that without such expressions of interest, the leadership in Bangkok would fatalistically assume that opposing communism was futile. Accordingly, he recommended immediate action on requests for military and economic assistance which, Stanton maintained, would benefit the Thais psychologically by convincing them that the United States considered the country to be of importance in its anti-Communist policy. The United States, by early 1950, was moving toward a clear association with Thailand, but uncertainty about whether the country could achieve stability and could resist the temptation of identifying with communism made any commitments a risk.[27]

Among the countries of Southeast Asia, Indonesia appeared the most stable. The ending of the Dutch-Indonesian war and the attainment of independence on December 27, 1949 constituted an important achievement for American diplomacy. When Ambassador-designate H. Merle Cochran delivered President Truman's message of congratulations to President Sukarno signifying formal American recognition of the Republic of the United States of Indonesia, the Indonesian leader remarked that he might not have been in the presidential palace that day had it not been for Cochran's support of the nationalist revolution.[28] America's principal rival had little influence in Indonesia; the Soviet Union, while quickly extending diplomatic recognition to the new nation, criticized Indonesian independence, maintaining that the Indonesians were trading Dutch for American dominance.[29]

Although Cochran and other American diplomats in Indonesia during the revolution deserved Sukarno's praise for their efforts on behalf of the Republic during its most difficult period, the United States emerged from the final stages of the Dutch-Indonesian negotiations with a tarnished image. During the Round Table meetings which included the United States, Australia, and Belgium as members of the United Nations Commission for Indonesia (UNCI), and which began at The Hague on August 23, 1949, a number of issues threatened to delay independence and, at times, to disrupt the conference. Most importantly, the Dutch insisted that all public debts at the time of the transfer of authority—totaling 6.1 billion guilders (about

$1.5 billion)—be taken over by the Republic. Indonesian leaders —from both the Republic and federal areas—objected to the assumption of debts incurred after the surrender of the islands to the Japanese in 1942. They objected most strenuously to absorbing any debts incurred as a result of the Dutch military campaign against the Republic. At length, the debt controversy was resolved through negotiations in which Cochran played a pivotal role. The UNCI pressured the Indonesians to accept a settlement which obliged the Republic to assume debts totaling approximately two-thirds of the Dutch demand—an amount which far exceeded what the Indonesians considered to be a reasonable compromise. The American position reflected the conviction that the Netherlands could not assume a greater share of the debt without it leading to serious domestic ramifications; the country had suffered a humiliating loss and national morale could not sustain a heavy debt from the Indonesian enterprise.[30]

The Indonesian leadership also resented the American role in the resolution of differences with the Dutch over the status of Western New Guinea (Irian). As the disposition of that area emerged at The Hague conference, the State Department favored Dutch retention on the grounds that it was "not politically articulate" and its peoples were not related ethnologically to Indonesia.[31] Cochran urged a compromise whereby New Guinea remained under Dutch control with the stipulation that by the end of the first year of the transfer of authority to the Indonesian Republic, its final status would be determined by further negotiation between the Netherlands and Indonesia. The Republican delegation criticized the Cochran plan for failing to assure Indonesian control of New Guinea. With the Dutch, backed by Cochran, maintaining that they could not make further concessions, and threatening to end the conference over the issue, the Indonesians finally conceded and accepted the compromise on the New Guinea question.[32]

While the American position in The Hague negotiations annoyed Indonesian leaders, the United States and Indonesia were drawn into a close relationship by the time of independence. The Republic looked to the United States for economic assistance as it was endeavoring to establish effective democratic processes and to build a unitary state, while the United States looked to Indonesia, with its vast resources and strategic location, as a vital part of the efforts to preserve a non-Communist Southeast Asia. Beginning in early November 1949, American officials indicated their receptivity to requests for technical and economic assistance and suggested an International Monetary Fund mission to help in implementing needed currency reform. Within two weeks of the attainment of independence, President Truman approved a joint State Department–Defense Department proposal to provide $5 million in military assistance to maintain internal security against Communist encroachment. Shortly thereafter American and Indonesian representatives entered into discussions on the extension of credit through the Export-Import Bank, and by mid-February 1950 an initial line in the amount of $100 million was provided.[33]

In Indochina, the American effort to stabilize the situation through recognition of the Bao Dai government failed to bring any immediate improvement. The French pressed for military and economic assistance. Edmund Gullion, who was designated Charge d'Affairs to the Associated States, strongly backed such an undertaking as the means of increasing the self-confidence and popularity of the Bao Dai regime. While Gullion's assessment drew some criticism at the State Department, particularly from Charlton Ogburn who argued that French concessions provided the only effective means of building a strong anti-Communist alternative to Ho Chi Minh's leadership, pressures to rely on military means proved increasingly irresistible. The French continually protested that they had made significant concessions which were not properly understood in the rest of Asia and in the United States and threatened (at least implicitly) to withdraw, thus leaving the intractable Indochina problems to the United States alone.

As that threat underscored, the United States found itself increasingly without leverage in dealing with the French over

Indochina. The situation in Indochina became linked with NATO and the tentative American plan to remilitarize Germany. France was seen as vital—"the keystone of the arch"—in the Western system of European defense. Accordingly, the French received the largest allocation of U.S. aid under NATO, but the effect of that assistance, and the French contribution to NATO, was drained by the war in Indochina. In 1950, over half of the French army was spending about 35 percent of France's total military budget in Indochina. So long as the war was taking such a large share of French military expenditures, the government and public would never countenance German remilitarization. Only if France were strong militarily on the European continent would it support the arming of its historic enemy. For the United States, the only solution seemed to be the underwriting of the French military operation in Indochina. Hence, the deepening American commitment in Indochina became ever more determined by European considerations. In early May 1950, Truman approved an urgent military assistance allocation of $10 million, and shortly thereafter commitments were made to provide extensive economic assistance. Throughout the three-month period following recognition of the Bao Dai government, Gullion and other officials requested immediate U.S. assistance on the grounds that the United States was in a race against time; without such support, the French-Bao Dai foothold would be lost. Yet as the military assistance began in the spring of 1950, the American quandary in Indochina clearly was more profound than ever. On the one hand, Bao Dai repeatedly criticized the French for failing to provide the reforms which he had been promised; on the other hand, the French reminded their Vietnamese and American allies of their sacrifices on behalf of the anti-Communist cause. Progress in this situation remained unlikely.[34]

## The Special Missions:
## Jessup, Griffin, Melby-Erskine, Bell

To implement the objectives outlined in PPS 51 of March 1949, and later in NSC 48 and NSC 69, the Department of State sent a series of missions to Southeast Asia. On December 15, 1949, Ambassador-at-Large Phillip Jessup departed Washington on an extensive tour of Asian capitals which was to lead to specific policy recommendations. On February 27, 1950, a special economic survey mission, headed by R. Allen Griffin, editor-publisher of the Monterey *Peninsula Herald,* left San Francisco for a six week visit to countries of Southeast Asia (except the Philippines) with the purpose of recommending implementation of economic and technical assistance programs. On June 29—four days after the outbreak of the Korean War—President Truman announced that a long-discussed economic mission to the Philippines would undertake a detailed survey of the Philippine economy and the government's fiscal and revenue policies; Daniel Bell, president of the American Security and Trust Company, headed this mission. Also in the aftermath of the war in Korea, the State and Defense departments dispatched a Joint Mutual Defense Assistance Program survey mission headed by John Melby and Major General Graves B. Erskine to Southeast Asia with instructions to report on means by which military assistance could be used to prevent Communist advances into the area. Like the Bell Mission, the Melby-Erskine Mission—while being launched in the crisis surrounding the outbreak of the war in Korea—had been anticipated for some time; the war was thus more the immediate impetus, than the reason, for these missions. As a consequence of these missions, American influence in Southeast Asia significantly increased and policy achieved greater coherence and direction.

The Jessup Mission centered on a conference of U.S. chiefs of mission from countries ranging from Pakistan on the west, to Korea on the east, which was held in Bangkok from February 13 to 15, 1950. Reflecting a strong consensus on most issues, the participants spoke against any plans to build up either Japan or India as a dominant power (as some State Department analysts were then suggesting), urged consultation with the British and the Commonwealth countries in formulating policy, and called for a clear expression of American interest in providing Point Four assistance to each of the non-Communist Asian countries. Another important point of agreement, which Jessup quickly endorsed, was that contrary to PPS 51/ NSC 48 formulations, the Indian subcontinent, with its own political and economic problems, needed to be considered separately from Southeast Asia. Also the American diplomatic corps stressed that Asian leaders had little interest in regional anti-Communist cooperation. The sentiments expressed at Bangkok impressed Jessup; when he reported to Acheson and other high-ranking officials at the Department of State on March 23, he reiterated much that had been expressed at the Bangkok Conference.[35] Speaking of the "weakness of our friends," Jessup said that the non-Communist countries generally lacked democratic institutions and traditions, were militarily weak, and were distrustful of the West. Yet there were also "strengths of our friends"—signs of political and economic progress in some areas, antipathy toward communism, and a general pro-American sentiment. On balance, Jessup saw the situation "bad but not desperate" and advocated, above all, movement toward implementation of economic assistance.[36]

Jessup's cautious optimism for the region was particularly influenced by his visit to Indonesia in early February where he met with Sukarno, Cochran, and others, and came away convinced that the United States could not overlook the young nation's importance. With proper external assistance, Indonesia, Jessup was convinced, would become stable and could resist Communist pressure. Accordingly, he urged early action on the request to the Export-Import Bank; this facilitated the extension of the $100 million loan shortly after Jessup departed Indonesia.[37]

Jessup's conclusions gave impetus to the Griffin Mission which, by the time that Jessup was reporting in Washington, had completed half of its tour of five Southeast Asian countries. The appointment of Griffin to head the mission served a useful political purpose. Griffin was a prominent California Republican associated with Senator William Knowland, one of the leading critics of Truman's Asian policy. Griffin had been the deputy chief of the China mission of the Economic Cooperation

Administration. Samuel Hayes, the deputy chief of the Griffin mission, was an economist with extensive government service, notably in the administration of the Lend-Lease program and, more recently while in the Department of State, he had been instrumental in the development of the Point Four planning. Assisting the small mission were representatives of various government agencies in each of the countries visited. As it began, the mission anticipated that from $50 million to $100 million would be available from various sources, including the Export-Import Bank, the Mutual Defense Assistance Act, and, pending congressional action, Point Four funds. The mission faced a difficult choice between emphasizing programs which would bring immediate political benefits and making efforts at long-term economic development which would likely have more enduring appeal among Southeast Asian peoples.

The mission visited Vietnam, Malaya, Burma, Thailand, and Indonesia, spending about seven to ten days in each country and eventually recommending a total of about $66 million in economic and technical assistance through the end of the 1951 fiscal year. In general, the mission, reacting to the immediate crisis emanating from the Communist victory in China, urged measures which would bring production back to prewar levels, develop skilled manpower, and encourage private and public capital investment; there was also considerable emphasis on educational and public health measures which would bring quick and visible results. In its recommendations for each country, the mission concentrated on utilizing economic assistance to meet the pressing political challenges facing the United States: in Vietnam, $23.5 million in well-publicized technical and economic assistance would help Bao Dai's government achieve a genuine independence and enhance its popular appeal; in Burma, $12.2 million, largely directed toward stimulating agricultural production, would foster political stability; in Thailand, $11.4 million channeled principally into agriculture and transportation-communication facilities would reassure the government of Western friendship; in Indonesia, $14.5 million would help to bring agricultural production to prewar levels and would buttress the government against Communist-inspired political unrest; in Malaya, $4.5 million would reinforce British political objectives.[38] Overall, the mission found reason to believe that such relatively limited allocations could bring significant results; its members were optimistic that "a small group of good men and the expenditures of small amounts of money could accomplish wonders in the area."[39] The recommendations, except for that pertaining to Malaya which was vetoed on the grounds that it should remain an area of British responsibility, were endorsed by the Truman administration. On June 5, Congress enacted the Foreign Economic Assistance Act, which included the substance of the Griffin Mission recommendations. This step marked the beginning of substantial American economic and technical assistance to Southeast Asia.[40]

The implementation of the Griffin Mission recommendations coincided with reconsideration of the extent of military assistance which would be necessary to preserve Western interests in the region. The dispatch of the Melby-Erskine mission was based on the assumption that beyond programs of economic and technical assistance, long-term political and economic stability depended in large part on establishment of adequate military forces within each country to resist Communist pressure and subversion. Prior to the mission, the United States had provided limited military assistance from a $75 million allocation for the "China area" in the Mutual Defense Assistance Act. In early 1950, Truman approved $15 million in military assistance for Indochina, $10 million for Thailand, and $5 million for Indonesia, but by the spring of 1950, officials at the State Department and Defense Department believed that a comprehensive review of military assistance had become necessary. The utilization of the allocations for Indochina, Thailand, and Indonesia depended upon clearly defined programs in the recipient countries, which were slow in developing. Also, it was assumed that only through additional military assistance could Thailand, Indochina, Burma, and the Philippines be stabilized.[41]

Against that background and the urgency resulting from the Korean War, the Melby-Erskine Mission visited Indochina,

Malaya, Thailand, the Philippines and Indonesia, but political unrest forced cancellation of the planned stop in Burma. This extensive four-month survey of military resources and the potential impact of American assistance, concluded with a generally pessimistic prognosis. The situation in Indochina was seen as weakening the American position throughout the region because of Asian identity with the Viet Minh and the popular association of the United States with French military and colonial policy. While deeply concerned about developments in China, Indochina, and Burma, the mission believed that American influence in Indonesia, Thailand, and the Philippines could be preserved through cooperation with and military support of those governments. The mission thus reaffirmed the assumptions of the necessity to hold Southeast Asia and called unequivocally for increasing military assistance.[42]

The final mission—that headed by Daniel Bell to the Philippines—reflected Washington's profound disappointment with conditions in that country and provided the basis for pressuring the Philippine government to undertake sweeping reform. Besides Bell, the mission included Major General Richard J. Marshall, Superintendent of Virginia Military Institute, who served as Deputy Chief; Edward Bernstein, director of Research of the International Monetary Fund, who was in charge of the economic survey; August Strand, president of Oregon State University, who headed the agricultural investigation; and Francis McQuillan of the Western Pennsylvania Power Company, who was responsible for an industrial and power survey. Assisted by eighteen specialists, the mission completed within three months a 107-page report with numerous additional technical memoranda. The situation was so serious that problems could be resolved only by fundamental changes in the policies of the Philippine government. Its far-reaching recommendations included: 1) reorganizing government finances to eliminate chronic shortness of funds and to control inflation; 2) developing a diversified economy and improving agricultural production; 3) imposing a 25 percent import tax on all goods except basic foodstuffs in order to reduce demand for imports and avoid further deterioration of the country's international payments position; 4) undertaking a systematic program of public health and extending educational opportunities; 5) improving public administration with particular attention to assuring efficiency and honesty. To assist in this program, the United States should provide $250 million over a five-year period, but only if the Philippine government committed itself to undertaking the reforms outlined by the mission, and permitted the United States to have full responsibility for administering economic aid missions.

Quirino, objecting to the criticisms of his government and blaming the United States for the country's problems, resisted the Bell Mission recommendations, but could do so only briefly. Not only did Ambassador Cowen and ultimately Truman put considerable pressure upon him, but in the Philippines itself, many leaders and much of the press considered the Bell Report to provide a fair assessment (indeed many expected criticism of the government to be much harsher) and a reasonable set of recommendations. After some delaying tactics, Quirino, on November 14, 1950, signed an agreement which embodied the recommendations of the Bell Mission; the Philippine government was to confront directly the problems outlined in the report, and Quirino was to present appropriate reforms to the Philippine Congress. In return, the United States would provide social, economic, and technical assistance over the next several years.[43]

As a consequence of the policy review occasioned by the Chinese Civil War and reinforced by the Korean War and the recommendations of the special missions, the American military and political position had become, by late 1950, much more substantial. Southeast Asia had become a major theater in the struggle against communism, and American resources were directed increasingly toward the preservation of friendly governments in the region.

## The Stabilization of Southeast Asia

American officials recognized that Southeast Asia could not be easily stabilized, but in general an optimistic assessment prevailed by the end of 1950. Just five days before the signing of the Philippine-American agreement based on the Bell Mission, the National Security Council, in its continuing review of the Philippine situation, reiterated the importance of the Philippines to American security which required that the islands "become and remain stable, anti-communist, pro-American and an example for the rest of the world of the intention of the United States to encourage the establishment of progressive and responsive governments."[44] The struggle against the Huks remained an overriding concern to officials in Manila and Washington. An NSC report of November 1950 made clear that US intervention would be justified if that seemed to be the only means of preventing Communist domination. That alternative seemed remote, however, for encouraging reports predicted that the Philippine army would be sufficient to crush the rebellion. The Philippine government and public, moreover, had rallied behind Truman's response to the North Korean attack, and Philippine units were sent to fight with the United Nations in that conflict. In sum, the Asian crises of 1949–50 drove the United States and the Philippines into a closer relationship and greater interdependence.[45]

Likewise, the United States and Thailand forgot lingering differences and moved toward a closer relationship. From the perspective of Bangkok, the signs of American commitment to prevent further communist expansion ended questions about the appropriate course for Thai diplomacy. Jessup's meeting with Thai leaders in early February 1950 proved to be especially important in removing mutual doubts—both the Thai uncertainty about American resolve and American skepticism about the character of the Pibul government lessened. Thailand's support for the American position in Asia was quickly forthcoming when on February 28, it extended recognition to the Associated States in Indochina, thus supporting the American hopes for the Bao Dai solution. The outbreak of the Korean War shocked Thailand and served virtually to end questions about seeking security through reliance on the United States. On July 21, 1950, Thailand became the first Asian country to offer a military unit for service with the United Nations. Reflecting on the status of relations with Thailand, a State Department report of October

1950 found the situation to be very encouraging—the Pibul government had brought badly needed stability, the economy benefited from a favorable trade balance (and the resumption of trade with Japan), and United States economic and military assistance as well as cultural exchanges were welcomed. The American position thus seemed secure with considerable potential for enhancing Thailand's orientation to the West.[46]

The troubled situation in Burma had improved significantly by the fall of 1950, and, while to lesser extent than in Thailand, its movement toward the Western democracies was clearly evident. U Nu's government withstood the multiple rebellions which had threatened national unity since the attainment of independence, and began the formidable assignments of developing an effective government throughout the country, building a stronger army, and undertaking economic and social reform. The North Korean invasion chillingly reminded the Burmese of their own vulnerability to communist aggression. This led to unhesitating support of the United Nations resolution condemning the attack. The earlier decisions of Burma to recognize the Chinese People's Republic and to withhold recognition of the Associated States in Indochina had annoyed the United States, but the Korean War brought Burmese diplomacy toward the West. The United States supported Burma's concern over the implications of the movement in 1949–1950 of the remnants of the Kuomintang army into eastern sections of Burma which, it was feared in Rangoon was well as Washington, invited Chinese Communist incursions into Burmese territory. The State Department interceded with the Nationalist government, requesting that its forces in Burma voluntarily disarm. While the American suggestion was resisted, this initiative on Burma's behalf helped Burmese-American relations. Altogether Washington was reassured by Burma's diplomacy and internal developments of late 1950. As the embassy in Rangoon projected, Burma, by moving away from its earlier emphasis on leftist programs domestically, and by appreciating its stake in the Asian crises, could now be counted on in the event of a showdown with the Communist powers; Burma would certainly be in the Western camp.[47]

In Malaya, American interests were being served on two levels. Politically, the British campaign against communist insurgency was at least holding firm, although progress was not as great as the British military superiority might have suggested. The success of that effort was tied to Malayan economic development, and the export trade showed considerable vitality. The Truman administration took various steps to enhance rubber and tin imports, with the result that Malayan sales to the United States significantly increased. In 1949–1950 Malaya built a considerable trade surplus with the United States, thus contributing to the sterling area's dollar pool. There were limits to the American demand and the United States would not become as dependent on Malayan markets as it had prior to World War II. The development of domestic synthetic rubber production and the emergence of Indonesia as a major source of natural rubber reduced the American-Malayan connection. Yet the Korean War generally stimulated the Malayan economy, as world demand for rubber soared and prices significantly increased. Thus, the prospects for economic stability and political development under British tutelage had considerably improved.[48]

Relations with Indonesia were troubled in some ways, but there was no reason to doubt the newly independent nation's aversion to communism and its fundamental orientation toward the West economically and politically. During the first year after independence, the Indonesian government encountered serious internal problems which centered on the nature of the federal system inherited from the Dutch and ultimately led to the abrupt decision of July 1950 to establish a unitary state. Domestic political rivalries reinforced the disposition of the Indonesian leadership to avoid any actions internationally which implied deference to a Western power. To the annoyance of officials in Washington, the Indonesians adopted a policy of neutrality in response to the Korean War; Prime Minister Hatta also declined to receive a proposed ten-man military assistance advisory group and to enter into any military agreement which would require parliamentary approval. Ambassador Cochran steadfastly defended Hatta's position to the State Department, maintaining that toleration of such policies was essential to the perservation of Hatta's position politically. Nonetheless, Hatta was replaced in August by Mohammad Natsir, who also declined to participate in the Military Defense Assistance Program and even repudiated a Hatta-negotiated agreement providing for transfer of police equipment. In addition, the Indonesians took exception to American failure to pressure the Netherlands to withdraw from West Irian; Washington's position on that issue was dictated by the desire to improve relations with the Dutch which still suffered from the antagonism resulting from American support of the Indonesian Republic in 1948–49. Despite these problems in the Indonesian-American relationship, the Natsir government, like that of Hatta, was basically pro-Western and entered into an economic and technical assistance agreement with the United States which was signed on October 16, 1950. A month earlier, the United States strongly supported Indonesia's admission to the United Nations; in the process, it exerted considerable pressure on the Chinese Nationalist government to abandon a threatened veto of Indonesian membership.[49]

## Indochina: The Military Solution

While the American position in Southeast Asia generally had improved by the end of 1950, in Indochina the fundamental problems underlying American objectives not only continued, but in fact were made more serious as a result of the outbreak of the Korean War. The commitment of American resources to the defense of South Korea reduced Franco-American differences over Indochina, as the United States reinforced anti-Communist positions throughout Asia. Truman quickly announced an acceleration of military assistance to Indochina. The conflicts in

Korea and Indochina came to be seen as two phases of the same struggle against communism. In an article in *Foreign Affairs,* Jacques Soustelle wrote:

> The glow from the Korean battlefields lights up the whole Asiatic front from Manchuria to Malaya. On certain sections of this front calm reigns—in appearance at least. On others, for example in the Philippines and in Burma guerilla warfare is endemic between the native governments and rebel forces. Finally, along two portions of this immense arc, the cold or tepid war has given place to, simply, war. There two Western powers have engaged their armies. The United States has been in Korea since June 26, 1950 and France has been in Indo-China since December 19, 1946.
>
> The two conflicts differ from each other in many ways. However, each clearly has a place in the same strategic and political complex. They share a basic common factor. Each results from the expansion of Soviet power toward the area, pushing its satellites ahead, and exploiting against the West the nationalism, even xenophobia, of the Asiatic masses.[50]

Yet the sense of common purpose could not remove the American questions about the nature of French policy and strategy. Reflecting on reports from Indochina, including the assessment of the Erksine-Melby mission, the PPS, in a lengthy analysis completed on August 16, 1950, observed that the objective of a credible and viable anti communist government still depended upon a French commitment to complete independence. The outlook remained bleak: "If Paris does not feel it can adopt a bolder political approach . . . we must recognize that the French and we will be heading into a debacle which neither of us can afford. For our part, it will be necessary promptly to reexamine our policy toward Indochina."[51] As a consequence, the United States endeavored again to encourage liberalization of colonial policy, including the establishment of a Vietnamese national army. In addition, the State Department pressured Emperor Bao Dai to take his role more seriously, pointedly calling attention to his prolonged summer holiday on the French Riviera.[52]

Such efforts had little effect and circumstances forced the acceptance of French reliance on a military solution. During the

evacuation in October of the frontier fortress at Cao Bang, the
French suffered their worst military setback in the nearly four
years of fighting. This touched off renewed debate in the French
National Assembly between the advocates of a military conquest
and those favoring a negotiated settlement, which led the
French government, under the leadership of Overseas France
Minister Jean Letourneau, to seek additional American military
assistance as the means of destroying the Viet Minh and building up the government headed by Bao Dai. For the United
States, the preservation of the French position had become
increasingly critical, which meant that it could not insist upon
political concessions in return for military assistance. A National Security Council report of December 21 reiterated the
objectives set forth in earlier documents: the overriding concern
of the United States was the denial of Indochina to the Communists; the attainment of that objective depended principally
upon the French army. While that report like others stressed the
importance of French concessions to the attainment of a strong
anti-Communist alternative to the Viet Minh, the Mutual
Defense Agreement signed on December 23 by the United
States, France, and the Associated States made military commitments which reduced any American leverage on the French.
Thus by that time, the United States was in the position of
underwriting the French military effort, but without significant
ability to influence colonial policy. The PPS's proviso a few
months earlier for a prompt reexamination of policy if the
French failed to make concessions thus now lacked any
feasibility.[53]

The commitment in Indochina, with all its complexities,
remained the most troublesome aspect of America's Southeast
Asian policy. The determination to hold the line against communism, which took shape definitively in 1949–1950, brought
substantial economic and military resources into the region. The
enlarged American involvement caused some apprehension and
suspicion, but generally Southeast Asian leaders, responding to
the need for American assistance and disturbed by the conflicts
in China and especially Korea, welcomed the initiatives from

Washington. Clearly by 1950, the United States and the non-Communist governments of Southeast Asia had been driven toward greater interdependence.

# 12.

# Conclusion

AT THE END of the 1940s, as at the beginning of that decade, Southeast Asia was a critical area in American diplomacy. In 1940, Japan's New Order threatened Western predominance, while by 1950, Soviet-based Communism seemed determined to extend its influence southward following the Communist victory in the Chinese Civil War. During the intervening years, immense political changes had occurred, principally as a consequence of World War II, meaning that while the Japanese had challenged a region that, with the exception of Thailand, was part of Western imperialism, the Communist threat was to a region whose countries were at varying stages of decolonization. The United States had anticipated the end of imperialism and had consistently sought to channel political change along peaceful and gradual lines.

In the pursuit of that objective, the United States encountered, during and after World War II, serious difficulties with its European allies—Britain, France, and the Netherlands—who were reluctant to recognize the extent of changes brought by the war. While European powers had sought American involvement in the region in 1940–41 in order to counter Japanese expansion, they wanted, by the end of the war in 1945, to limit American influence. American political interests, however, necessitated concern with Southeast Asian developments. As the United States ultimately compromised its anticolonial principles, it became the target of criticism from nationalist leaders. In the face of mounting Communist insurgency—which the Soviets and Chinese seemingly abetted—the American ability to force moderation in the colonial policies of its cold war allies was considerably reduced. To help stabilize the region, the United States by 1949–1950 was encouraging the renewal of Japanese economic influence. The defeated, demilitarized Japan, unlike the militaristic and aggressive Japan of the New Order, was integrated within the American global political and economic strategy. In sum, the problems confronting American policymakers in Southeast Asia during the 1940s defied simple solutions.

As it became a power in Southeast Asia, the United States consistently sought to promote political stability through the cultivation and support of pro-Western elites. The region's economic importance, which was clearly established during the early decades of the twentieth century, made it essential that its raw materials and markets remain open to the United States, Western Europe, and (as noted above) eventually Japan. All of the wartime planning for colonial areas, the commitments to the Philippines, and the objective of a lenient peace for Thailand signaled the American determination to foster the end of Western political dominance as part of the broader vision of liberalizing international political and economic systems. To achieve that objective, on September 8, 1944, Secretary of State Cordell Hull—in one of the most important initiatives on Southeast Asian policy—urged President Roosevelt to press for "early, dramatic, and concerted announcements" by Britain, France, and the Netherlands promising independence or self-rule, and establishing timetables toward those ends. Behind this recommendation was the recognition by key State Department officers that the experience of Southeast Asia under Japanese rule, and the forthcoming Allied liberation under the British-led Southeast Asia Command, risked an immediate alienation of the peoples of the region. Roosevelt, while fully cognizant of the issues being raised and apprehensive himself, as he said a few months later, of losing the friendship of over 1 billion Asians, never acted on Hull's recommendation. He had become very cautious in dealing with his colleague Winston Churchill on colonial issues.

One can thus only speculate whether vigorous representations to the European powers might have forced moderation in their policies or, at least, might have left the United States in a less vulnerable position among Southeast Asian peoples. Clearly nationalist leaders in Indochina, Indonesia, and Burma believed the idealistic promises of the Atlantic Charter. While the British, French, and Dutch acted predictably, the American deference to the European colonial powers eroded the immense Asian good will toward the United States.

Throughout the 1940s and long afterward, Indochina presented the most intractable problems. Elsewhere the United States had its difficulties, but by 1950 its interests were being substantially realized in the Philippines, Indonesia, Thailand, Burma, and Malaya. The United States may have compromised Philippine independence and offended Philippine pride in countless ways, but Philippine-American relations were still manageable and by 1950, the Truman adminstration had made at least some steps toward remedying the Philippines' chronic economic problems. However the United States may have procrastinated before confronting the Dutch over the Indonesian revolution, the eventual support of the Republic marked a significant turning point and a merging of American-Indonesian nationalist political and economic interests. However inconsistent the American embrace of wartime collaborator Pibul Songgram's return to power in Thailand, the United States had played a critical role in the favorable 1946 peace terms which enabled Thailand to emerge as an independent force in regional affairs. However precarious Burma appeared under the leadership of U Nu, and however uncertain the course of British policy during the Emergency in Malaya, both countries remained clearly oriented toward the West.

Indochina was always the exception, and a critical exception, for changes in Indochina held, at every step, implications for the rest of the region. Japan's expansion at France's expense had to be discouraged for it posed a threat to the Dutch Empire in the East Indies. During the war, Roosevelt's plan for an international trusteeship was motivated partly by his determination to demonstrate that anticolonialism was a viable objective. The gradual American movement to support of the French colonial and military policy against the Viet Minh was driven, in part, by apprehension that the success of Communist-led nationalists in Indochina would encourage Communist insurgency elsewhere. That the United States failed to halt the Japanese in 1940–41, that Roosevelt's trusteeship policy—already undermined by various forces—finally died with him, and that the support of the French ultimately could not sustain their empire—all speak to the persistent shortcomings of Indochina policy. If the American frustrations in Indochina over the next quarter century can best be understood as a process of incremental involvement, then the first critical steps were taken during the 1940s.

While Southeast Asia was an area of growing concern and involvement, it was not equal in importance to Europe and East Asia. As a consequence, Southeast Aisan policy was always largely shaped by conditions in those other areas. The collapse of European influence, a result of the war in Europe, forced the United States to defend Western interests against Japan. The postwar compromise of colonial issues resulted principally from the importance of the emerging cold war strategy in Europe. As global policy was redefined in 1949–50, the region took on greater significance not only because of the increased signs of regional instability but because of economic and political needs in Europe and Japan. The nationalist movements were not approached on their own terms, but principally as developments to be accomodated within bilateral relationships with European allies. This did not mean that Americans were ignorant of the strength of the Viet Minh or the Indonesian Republic; indeed analyses from the field as well as in Washington consistently pointed to the dim prospects for colonial restoration. And American officials were aware of the implications of becoming associated with outdated colonialism.

By 1950, the United States had accomplished the substance of its decade-long search for orderly political change and the transition of power to political leaders who would keep the area oriented toward the West politically and economically. Democratic institutions were functioning in Indonesia, Burma, and the Philippines. Malaya and Thailand were stable, and in Malaya, the British would gradually transfer political power. American concern over Communist expansion was widely shared by the non-Communist countries, especially in the aftermath of the outbreak of war in Korea. Indochina remained the exception to the prevailing conviction that American economic, political, and military influence could assure a politically stable, economically viable, and non-Communist Southeast Asia.

# Abbreviations

IN AN EFFORT to keep endnote references brief, I have utilized the following means of abbreviating major documentary holdings and published collections. Locations of the documetary collections and full citations are included in the Bibliography. References to various committees and agencies have also been abbreviated.

| | |
|---|---|
| AMSSO: | American Staff Services |
| CAB: | British Cabinet Conclusions and Memoranda |
| CAC: | Country and Area Committee(DOS) |
| CAC-FE: | Country and Area Committee-Far East (DOS) |
| CCS: | Combined Chiefs of Staff |
| CDA: | Committee on Dependent Areas (DOS) |
| CIB: | Committe on India and Burma (DOS) |
| COS: | Chiefs of Staff |
| CTP: | Committee on Colonial and Trusteeship Problems (DOS) |
| DOS: | Department of State Records |
| DOS: (followed by numbers) | (refers to decimal file) |
| DOS: IAC | Interdivisional Area Committee on the Far East |
| DOS: Inter-Intra Comm. | Inter-Intradepartmental Committee Files |
| DOS: Notter | Harley Notter Files |

| | |
|---|---|
| DOS: Pasvolsky | Leo Pasvolsky Files |
| DOS: NSC | National Security Council Files |
| DOS: PSEA | Division of Philippine and Southeast Asia Affairs |
| DOS:SWNCC | State-War-Navy Coordinating Committee Files |
| DOS: SC | Secretary of State Staff Committee Files |
| FDR Papers: | Franklin Delano Roosevelt Papers |
| FO: | British Foreign Office Files |
| *FRUS:* | *Foreign Relations of the United States* |
| HST Papers: | Harry S. Truman Papers |
| JCS files: | Joint Chiefs of Staff Files |
| JSM: | Joint Staff Mission (British, in Washington) |
| OSS: | Office of Strategic Services |
| PREM: | British Prime Minsters' Files |
| SACSEA Files: | Supreme Allied Commander, Southeast Asia |
| SC: | Secretary of State Staff Committee |
| SEAC: | Southeast Asia Command |
| SWNCC: | State-War-Navy Coordinating Committee |
| WM: | War Cabinet Minutes (British) |

# Notes

## 1. The United States and the Colonial System in Southeast Asia

1. Peter W. Stanley, *A Nation in the Making*, pp. 51-278.

2. Thomas R. McHale, "The Philippines in Transition," pp. 331-42.

3. Grayson L. Kirk, *Philippine Independence*, pp. 136-226.

4 Russell H. Fifield, *Americans in Southeast Asia*, p. 3-5; Benito Legardo, Jr. and Robert Y. Garcia, "Economic Collaboration," pp. 130–31; Theodore Friend, *Between Two Empires*, pp. 156-60.

5. Friend, *Between Two Empires*, pp. 169-71.

6. Quotation by General Stanley D. Embrick, commander of Corregidor garrison in 1933, cited in: Ronald H. Spector, *Eagle Against the Sun*, p. 57.

7. *Ibid.*, pp. 54-59.

8. D. Clayton James, *The Years of MacArthur*, 1: 506.

9. *Ibid.*, pp. 510-42.

10. Friend, *Between Two Empires*, pp. 151-95, 226-68.

11. Fifield, *Americans in Southeast Asia*, pp. 12-15; Kenneth T. Young, "The Special Role of American Advisers in Thailand, 1902-1949," 1-31; James V. Martin, "A History of the Diplomatic Relations Between Siam and the United States of America, 1833-1929"; Donald G. Lord, "Missionaries, Thai, and Diplomats," pp. 413-31; Benjamin A. Batson, "American Diplomats in Southeast Asia in the 19th Century: The Case of Siam," 64: 39-111.

12. Russell H. Fifield, *The Diplomacy of Southeast Asia, 1945-1958*, pp. 230-34; James V. Martin, Jr. "Thai-American Relations in World War II," pp. 451-54; Edward T. Flood, "Japan's Relations with Thailand, 1928-1941," pp. 1-280; Vivat Sathachuay, "United States-Thailand Diplomatic Relations during World War II" pp. 1-19, 67-84.

13. Pamela Sodhy, "Passage of Empire: United States-Malayan Relations to 1966", pp. 1-61; Department of Commerce, *Foreign Commerce Yearbook 1935*, pp. 283-311; Department of Commerce, *Foreign Commerce Yearbook 1939*, pp. 234-317.

14. Mira Wilkins, *The Maturing of Multinational Enterprise*, pp. 8-9, 58-59, 101-2.

15. *Ibid.*, pp. 120-22, 238-41.

16. Irvine H. Anderson, Jr., *The Standard-Vacuum Oil Company*, pp. 126-231.

17. Christopher Thorne, *Allies of a Kind*, pp. 17-20, 35-38, 71-76; William Roger Louis, *British Strategy in the Far East*, pp. 241-67; Peter Lowe, *Great Britain and the Origins of the Pacific War*, pp. 14-135; David Reynolds, *The Creation of the Anglo-American Alliance, 1937-1941*, pp. 30-31, 58-62; Bradford Lee, *Britain and the Sino-Japanese War, 1937-1939;*, pp. 15-22, 45-49.

18. Lee, *Britain and the Sino-Japanese War*, p. 19.

19. Abbot Low Moffat, Diplomatic Journals, Dec. 16, 1937, cited in: James R. Leutze, *Bargaining for Supremacy*, p. 18.

20. *Ibid.*, pp. 19-57.

21. Waldo H. Heinrichs, "The Role of the United States Navy," pp. 197-218; Leutze, *Bargaining for Supremacy,* pp. 3-55.

## 2. The Rivalry of Japan and the United States Over Southeast Asia, 1940–1941

1. Akira Iriye, *Across the Pacific,* pp. 200-20; Akira Iriye, *Power and Culture,* pp. 1-15; Nobutaka Ike, ed. and tr., *Japan's Decision for War,* pp. 3-13.

2. Waldo H. Heinrichs, "The Role of the United States Navy," in Dorothy Borg and Shumpei Okamoto, eds. *Pearl Harbor as History,* pp. 218-23; Leutze, *Bargaining for Supremacy,* pp. 178-96.

3. Reynolds, *Creation of the Anglo-American Alliance,* pp. 143-44, 226-27; Robert Dallek, *Franklin D Roosevelt and American Foreign Policy, 1932-1945,* pp. 269-71; James C. Thomson, Jr., "The Role of the Department of State," pp. 81-106.

4. Hull to Mattews, Sept. 9, 1940, *FRUS 1940* 4:104-5.

5. Memorandum of Conversation (Hull), Sept. 16, 1940, *FRUS 1940* 4:120-21.

6. Herbert Feis, *The Road to Pearl Harbor,* pp. 52-54; Arnold A. Offner, *The Origins of the Second World War,* pp. 185-89; Dickover to Sec. State, April 16, 1940, *FRUS 1940* 4:8-9; *Department of State Bulletin,* April 20, 1940.

7. Robert K. Wolthuis, "United States Foreign Policy," pp. 13-18, 37-41, 80, 97-100, 150-73; Kramol Tongdhummachart, "American Policy in Southeast Asia," pp. 20-28; Charles Wolf, Jr., *The Indonesian Story,* pp. 1-5.

8. Peter Lowe, *Great Britain and the Origins of the Pacific War,* pp. 139-51; Sir Llewelyn Woodward, *British Foreign Policy,* pp. 92-101; Flood to Hull, June 25, 1940, *FRUS 1940* 4:37-38; Memorandum of Conversation (Hull), July 12, 1940, *FRUS 1940* 4:46-47; Arnold A. Offner, *Origins of the Second World War,* p. 189.

9. Embassy of China to Dept. of State, June 22, 1940, *FRUS 1940* 4:32-33; Chinese Minister for Foreign Affairs to Dept. of State, July 10, 1940, *ibid.,* pp. 45-46; Johnson to Hull, July 12, 1940; *ibid.,* p. 46.

10. Memorandum of Conversation (Ballantine), July 31, 1940, *FRUS 1940* 4:58-59.

11. Embassy of France to Dept. of State, Aug. 6, 1940, *FRUS 1940* 4:63-64; Memorandum by Dunn, Aug. 6, 1940, *ibid.,* pp. 64-65; Grew to Hull, Aug. 7, 1940, *ibid.,* pp. 68-69.

12. Murphy to Hull, Aug. 17, 1940, *FRUS 1940* 4:80-81; Matthews to Hull, Sept. 11, 1940, *ibid.,* pp. 109-11.

13. E. Thadeus Flood, "The 1940 Franco-Thai Border Dispute," pp. 304-25.

14. Grant to Hull, Aug. 17, 1940, *FRUS 1940* 4:79-80.

15. Acting Sec. State to Grant, Aug. 21, 1940, *FRUS 1940* 4:84.

16. Grant to Hull, Sept. 5 and 13, 1940, *FRUS 1940* 4:98-99, 113-15.

17. Hull to Grant, Oct. 10, 1940, *FRUS 1940* 4: 176-77; Grant to Hull, Oct. 11, 12, and 19, 1940, *ibid.,* pp. 177-79, 181-82, 187-88.

18. Embassy of Great Britain to Dept. of State, Jan. 6, 1941, *FRUS 1941* 5:2-5.

19. Embassy of Great Britain to Dept. of State, Jan 6, 1941, *FRUS 1941* 5:9-10; Butler to Eden, Jan. 8, 1941, FO 436/11; Butler to Eden, Jan. 8, 1941, FO 436/11.

20. Memorandum of Conversation (Hull), Jan. 13, 1941, *FRUS 1941* 5:16-17; Hull to Leahy, Jan 13, 1941, *FRUS 1941* 5:20.

21. Embassy of Great Britain to Dept. of State, Jan. 22, 1941, *FRUS 1941* 5:28-32; Butler to Eden, Jan. 22, 1941, FO 436/11; Halifax to Eden, Feb. 1, 1941, FO 436/9/.

22. Reed to Hull, Feb. 1, 1941 *FRUS 1941* 5:53; Memorandum of Conversation

(Welles), Feb. 4, 1941, *ibid.*, pp. 55-56.

23. Fifield, *Diplomacy in Southeast Asia*, pp. 234-35.

24. Grew to Hull, Feb. 7, 1941, *FRUS 1941* 5:62-64.

25. Halifax to Hull, Feb. 11, 1941, *FRUS 1941* 5:74-77; Australian Legation to Dept. of State, March 6, 1941, *FRUS 1941* 5:103-5; Consul General Batavia to Eden, Feb. 9, 1941, FO 436/11; Eden to Halifax, Feb. 20, 1941, FO 436/11; Churchill to Halifax, March 1, 1941, FO 436/9; Memorandum of Conversation (Hull), Feb. 15, 1941, DOS: 711.94/2040.

26. Grew to Hull, March 13, 1941, *FRUS 1941* 5:109-11; Hosoya Chihiro, "The Role of Japan's Foreign Ministry and Its Embassy in Washington," in Dorothy Borg and Shumpei Okamoto, eds., *Pearl Harbor as History*, pp. 149-52; Dallek, *Roosevelt and American Foreign Policy*, pp. 272-73.

27. Offner, *Origins of the Second World War*, pp. 220-22.

28. Memorandum of Conversation (Hull), April 8, 1941, *FRUS 1941* 5:120-24; Halifax to Eden, April 10, 1941, FO 436/11.

29. Eden to Halifax, April 18, 1941, FO 436/11.

30. Winant to Hull, April 21, 1941, *FRUS 1941* 5:133-34; Aide-Memoire, British Embassy to Dept. of State, April 21, 1941, *FRUS 1941* 5:134-36; Memorandum of Conversation (Hull), April 22, 1941 *FRUS 1941* 5:136-37; Halifax to Eden, April 23, 1941, FO 436/11.

31. Memorandum of Conversation (Hornbeck), May 9, 1941, *FRUS 1941* 5: 148-49.

32. Grant to Hull, May 8, 1941, *FRUS 1941* 5: 146-47.

33. Grant to Hull, May 22, 1941, *FRUS 1941* 5:155.

34. Acheson to Hall, June 17, 1941, *FRUS 1941* 5:178.

35. Netherlands Embassy to Hull, April 28, 1941, *FRUS 1941* 5: 140-41; Halifax to Hull, May 6, 1941, *FRUS 1941* 5:142-43; Memorandum by Hornbeck, May 27, 1941, *FRUS 1941* 5:160-61; Embassy of Great Britain to Dept. of State, June 2, 1941, *FRUS 1941* 5:163-65; Memorandum of Conversation (Hull), June 3, 1941 *FRUS 1941* 5:165-66; Memorandum of Conversation (Hull), June 3, 1941, *FRUS 1941* 5:166-67; British Embassy to Hull, June 4, 1941, *FRUS 1941* 5:169-72; Memorandum of Conversation (Welles), June 3, 1941, *FRUS 1941*, 4:248-51.

36. Ike, *Japan's Decision for War*, pp. 77-90; Iriye, *Power and Culture*, pp. 26-27.

37. Acting Secretary of State to Leahy, July 16, 1941, *FRUS 1941* 5:212; Leahy to Hull, July 19, 1941, *ibid.*, p. 218.

38. Memoranda of Conversations (Hamilton), July 18, 1941, *FRUS 1941* 5:329-330, 330-31.

39. Harold L. Ickes, *The Secret Diary of Harold L. Ickes*, p. 567.

40. *Ibid.*, p. 567.

41. Dallek, *Roosevelt and American Foreign Policy*, pp. 274-75.

42. Memorandum of Conversation (Welles), July 24, 1941, *FRUS: Japan 1931-1941*, 2:527-30.

43. Feis, *Road to Pearl Harbor*, pp. 236-41; Irvine H. Anderson, Jr., "The 1941 De Facto Embargo on Oil to Japan," pp. 201-23; Jonathon G. Utley, "Upstairs, Downstairs at Foggy Bottom," pp. 17-28; Dallek, *Roosevelt and American Foreign Policy*, pp. 275-76; Reynolds, *Creation of the Anglo-American Alliance*, pp. 234-36.

44. Spector, *Eagle Against the Sun*, pp. 74-76, 324-26; Russell F. Weigley, "The Role of the War Department and the Army," pp. 180-85.

45. War Plans Division Report, cited in Spector, *Eagle Against the Sun*, p. 75.

46. Leahy to Hull, Aug. 1, 1941, *FRUS 1941* 4:246-27; Memorandum of Conversation (Berle), Sept. 12, 1941, *FRUS 1941* 5:287-89; Memorandum of Conversation (Hull), Sept. 16, 1941, *FRUS 1941* 4:452-54.

47. Grant to Hull, July 4, 1941, *FRUS 1941* 5:195-6; Memorandum by Peck, July 11, 1941, *FRUS 1941* 5:204-5; Acting Sec. State to Grant, July 12, 1941, *FRUS 1941* 5:205-6; Hall to Acheson, July, 14, 1941 *FRUS 1941* 5:207-8; Grant to Hull, July 17, 1941, *FRUS 1941* 5:216-18; Memorandum by Feis, July 16, 1941, *FRUS 1941* 5:211-12; Grant to Hull, July 20, 1941, *FRUS 1941* 5:219-20; Grant to Hull, July 27, 1941, *FRUS 1941* 5:235-36; Memorandum by Welles, July 31, 1941, *FRUS: Japan 1931-1941* 2:539-40.

48. Memorandum by Peck, July 30, 1941 *FRUS 1941* 5:240; Memorandum by Gray, July 31, 1941, *FRUS 1941* 5:242; Acting Sec. of State to Grew, Aug. 1, 1941, *FRUS 1941* 5:245; Halifax to Acting Sec. of State, Aug. 2, 1941, *FRUS 1941* 5:248-50; Memorandum of Conversation (Welles), Aug. 4, 1941, *FRUS 1941* 5:254-56; Memorandum of Conversation (Hull), Aug. 9, 1941, *FRUS 1941* 5:268-69; Memorandum of Conversation (Peck), Aug. 14, 1941, *FRUS 1941* 5:271-73; Eden to Halifax, Aug. 1, 1941, FO 436/11.

49. Peck to Hull, Oct. 4, 1941 *FRUS 1941* 5:306-9; Peck to Hull, Oct. 15, 1941, *ibid.*, pp. 320-22; British Embassy to Dept. of State, Oct. 25, 1941, *ibid.*, pp. 325-26; British Embassy to Dept. of State, Oct. 25, 1941, *ibid.*, pp. 326-27.

50. Memorandum by Hornbeck, Oct. 28, 1941, *FRUS 1941 5:* 327-29.

51. Peck to Hull, Oct. 29, 1941, *FRUS 1941 5:* 330-31; Peck to Hull, Nov. 6, 1941, *ibid.*, pp. 335-37; Memorandum by Hornbeck, Nov. 7, 1941, *ibid.*, pp. 337-38; Peck to Hull, Nov. 15, 1941, *ibid.*, pp. 342-43; Hull to Peck, Nov. 22, 1941, *ibid, pp. 345-46.*

52. Peck to Hull, Nov. 26, 1941, *FRUS 1941* 5:355; Peck to Hull, Dec. 3, 1941, *ibid.*, p. 367; Peck to Hull, Dec. 4, 1941, *ibid.*, p. 370.

53. Iriye, *Power and Culture*, pp. 28-35; Robert J.C. Butow, *Tojo and the Coming of the War*, pp. 310-63.

54. Dallek, *Roosevelt and American Foreign Policy*, pp. 304-9.

55. Lowe, *Great Britain and the Origins of the Pacific War*, pp. 248-50, 269-74; Woodward, *British Foreign Policy in the Second World War* 2:134-36; 178-80; Halifax to Foreign Office, Dec. 1 and 4, 1941, PREM 3 156/5.

56. Gary R. Hess, *America Encounters India*, pp. 24-32.

57. The extent to which American and Japanese wartime objectives tended to converge is explored fully by Akira Iriye in *Power and Culture*.

## 3. Planning for Decolonization in Southeast Asia, 1942–1943

1. Elliot Roosevelt, *As He Saw It*, pp. 115-16.

2. "The Post Singapore War in the East," *Washington Post*, Feb. 21, 1942.

3. Akira Iriye, *Across the Pacific*, pp. 3-32, 156-60; James C. Thomson, Peter W. Stanley, and John Curtis Perry, *Sentimental Imperialists*, pp. 1-60, 162-202; William L Neumann, *American Encounters Japan*, pp. 228-55.

4. Buck speech of February 1942, quoted in Christopher Thorne, *Allies of a Kind*, p. xxiii.

5. Ruth B. Russell, *A History of the United Nations Charter*, pp. 11-15, 32-43, *et passim.*

6. U.S. *Department of State Bulletin*, (May 30, 1942), 6:488.

7. William Roger Louis, *Imperialism at Bay*, pp. 30-32, 51-52, 88-117; Thorne, *Allies of a Kind*, pp. 175-76, 279-80, 340-41.

8. Louis, *Imperialism at Bay*, pp. 3-5; Foster Rhea Dulles and Gerald Ridinger, "The Anti-Colonial Policies of Franklin D. Roosevelt," pp. 1-18; Lowell Young, "Franklin D. Roosevelt and Imperialism," pp. 295-308.

9. Samuel I. Rosenman, *The Public Papers and Addresses of Franklin D. Roosevelt* 3:118.

10. Memorandum of Conference at White House (Cross), June 1, 1942, *FRUS 1942* 3:578-81.

11. James MacGregor Burns, *Soldier of Freedom*, pp. 606-11; Gaddis Smith, *American Diplomacy*, pp. 8-12, 91; William L. Neumann, *After Victory*, pp. 52-55.

12. On general Anglo-American relations over colonialism in the early stage of the war, see Louis, *Imperialism at Bay*, pp. 121-74.

13. Thorne, *Allies of a Kind*, p. 219.

14. Hornbeck to Welles, March 27, 1942, DOS: 740.0011 PW/2232.

15. Herbert Feis, *Churchill, Roosevelt, Stalin*, p. 41 n.

16. Memorandum of Conversation (Hull), June 5, 1942, DOS: 856D.00/153; Netherlands Foreign Office to Dept. of State, Aug. 8, 1942, DOS: 856D.00/155.

17. Pacific War Council, July 21, 1943, FDR Papers, Map Room Files Box 168; Thorne, *Allies of a Kind*, p. 219; Louis, *Imperialism at Bay*, pp. 29-30; Gaddis Smith, *American Diplomacy*, p. 92.

18. William L Langer, *Our Vichy Gamble*, pp. 212-26, 352-81.

19. Thorne, *Allies of a Kind*, p. 218; Burns, *Roosevelt: Soldier of Freedom*, pp. 319-23.

20. Robert O. Paxton, *Vichy France*, pp. 57-59, 69, 80-84 *et passim*.

21. Welles to Roosevelt, April 19, 1942, appended to Pacific War Council, April 19, 1942, FDR Papers, Map Room Files Box 168.

22. For overviews of the Anglo-American differences over India in 1942 see: Gary Hess, *American Encounters India*, pp. 33-88 and Thorne, *Allies of a Kind*, pp. 233-51. See also: Pacific War Council, July 29 and August 12, 1942, FDR Papers, Map Room Files Box 168, for some of Roosevelt's reflections on the Indian situation.

23. *Department of State Bulletin* (July 25, 1942), 7:642.

24. Cordell Hull, *Memoirs*, 2:1484-85; Campbell to Cadogan, Aug. 6, 1942, G 44/1, no. 3538, FO 115; Winant to Eden, July 25, 1942, FO 371/3707.

25. *New York Times*, Oct. 27, 1942.

26. Harley Notter, *Postwar Foreign Policy Preparation*, pp. 63-84; Fifield, *Americans in Southeast Asia*, pp. 22-23; Tongdhummachart, "American Policy in Southeast Asia," pp. 34-36; Kenneth Landon, "Southeast Asia and the United States Foreign Policy," pp. 267-71.

27. Berle to Welles, Feb. 17, 1942, Berle Papers, Box 73; Berle to Hamilton, Feb. 28, 1942, *ibid.*; Hornbeck to Welles and Hull, May 6, 1942, DOS: 740.0011 PW2409 1/2; Welles to Gauss, March 25, 1942, *FRUS 1942: China*, p. 730; Gauss to Hull, March 28, 1942, *FRUS1942: China*, pp.738-39.

28. Territorial Committee Minutes, April 11, 1942, DOS: Notter, Box 59. The subcommitte minutes of March 7 (organizational meeting) and March 28, 1942 are useful for background on the colonial discussions. When the dependent areas issue was raised at the March 28 meeting, Pasvolsky suggested that the United States could probably exert greater influence in Africa than in Asia. Bowman concurred that Africa would be the foremost postwar dependent area problem. Berle questioned the practicality of discuss-

ing the future of the colonies in view of the unwillingness of the European nations to accept any outside interference. Territorial Committee Minutes, March 7 and March 28, 1942, DOS: Notter, Box 59.

29.*Ibid.*

30. *Ibid.*

31.Notter, *Postwar Foreign Policy Preparation,* p. 96.

32. Political Problems Subcommittee Minutes, Aug. 1, 1942, DOS: Notter, Box 55; Gauss to Hull, Aug. 3, 1942, *FRUS: 1942 China,* pp. 735-37.

33. Political Problems Subcommittee Minutes, Aug. 1 and 8, 1942, DOS: Notter, Box 55.

34. Political Problems Subcommittee Minutes, Nov. 14, 1942, DOS: Notter, Box 55; Political Subcommittee Documents 118 and 123, DOS: Notter, Box 54; Louis, *Imperialism at Bay,* pp. 91-92.

35. Hull, *Memoirs,* 2:1638; Louis, *Imperialism at Bay,* pp. 175-76, 182-86.

36. Hull to Roosevelt, Nov. 17, 1942, DOS: Notter, Box 13; Russell, *History of UN Charter,* pp. 84-86.

37. Draft of Joint Declaration of Colonial Policy submitted by British Embassy to Department of State, Feb. 4, 1943, DOS: Notter, Box 13.

38. Draft United Nations Declaration of National Independence, March 9, 1943, Taussig Papers, Box 77; Memorandum by Leo Pasvolsky, March 9, 1943, *ibid.,* Box 59.

39. Eden to Halifax, May 26, 1943, FO 371/35311; War Cabinet Minutes Conclusions 53 (43), April 13, 1943, CAB 65/34; Louis, *Imperialism at Bay,* pp. 243-58.

40. Hull to Leahy, Jan. 20, 1942, *FRUS 1942* 2:123-24; Leahy to Hull, Jan. 27, 1942, *ibid.,* p. 124.

41. Joint Chiefs of Staff Minutes, Jan. 7, 1943, *FRUS: The Conferences at Washington, 1941-42 and Casablanca, 1943,* pp. 514; David H. White, Jr., "The United States and Indochina," pp. 15-36.

42. Pacific War Council, Dec. 9, 1942, FDR Papers, Map Room Files Box 168; Pacific War Council, May 23, 1942, *ibid.*

43. Notes on Meeting with President, Feb. 22, 1943, DOS: Notter, Box 54. While Roosevelt pursued his Indochina objective independently of the State Department, his conversation with planning personnel encouraged Bowman, who was among those present on February 22, to consider the Indochina issue in the Territorial Subcommittee. In addition, a report prepared for that subcommittee by Melvin Knight argued that Indochina was of no benefit to France economically or commercially. There was some discussion, although not clearly focused, in the subcommittee on the question of whether the United States could insist upon treating a French colony differently from those of other European nations. Territorial Committee Minutes, Feb. 26 and March 5, 1943, DOS: Notter, Box 59.

44. Foreign Office Minutes, Jan. 12, 1943 and Minute by Barclay, Jan. 27, 1943, Minute by Halifax, Feb. 4, 1943, G 44/1, FO 115; Thorne, *Allies of a Kind,* pp. 217-18.

45. Burns, *Roosevelt: Soldier of Freedom,* p. 287.

46. Memorandum of Conversation (Hull), March 27, 1943, *FRUS 1943* 3:36-38; Anthony Eden, *The Memoirs of Anthony Eden,* pp. 436-38; Hull, *Memoirs,* 2:1595-96.

47. Record of Conversation, March 24, 1943, FO 371/35917; Hess, *America Encounters India,* pp. 76-77, 106-7.

48. Pacific War Council, March 17, 1943, FDR Papers, Map Room Files Box 168.

49. Louis, *Imperialism at Bay,* pp. 225-27; E. Roosevelt, *As He Saw It,* pp. 74-86; Milton Viorst, *Hostile Allies,* pp. 142-43; Territorial Committee Document 262, March 2, 1943; DOS: Inter-Intra Committee, Box 88 D.

50. Territorial Committee Document 309, Oct. 29, 1943, DOS: Notter, Box 70.

51. Territorial Committee Minutes, Nov. 5, 1943, DOS: Notter, Box 59.

52. *Ibid.;* Territorial Committee Minutes, Nov. 11, 1943; DOS: Notter, Policy Summary H 105 Indochina: Postwar Status; DOS: Notter, Box 154.

53. Territorial Comm. Document 428: Future Status of Indochina, Nov. 16, 1943, DOS: Notter, Box 65.

54. Memorandum: General Summary of Military, Economic and Political Situation in French Indochina (Reed), Aug. 14, 1942, DOS: 851G.00/76; Memorandum, Division of Far Eastern Affairs, Sept. 14, 1942, DOS: 851G.00/77; Vincent to Berle, Nov. 2, 1943, *FRUS 1943: China,* pp. 885-86.

55. Ronald Spector, "'What the Local Annamites are Thinking'" 741-51; Atcheson to Hull, July 21, 1942, DOS: 851G.00/88.

56. Pacific War Council, July 21, 1943, FDR Papers, Map Room Files Box 168.

57. Minutes by Hudson and Clarke, July 26, and Aug. 11, 1943, FO: 371/35930; Brief for Cadogan, Nov. 22, 1943, FO 371/35935.

58. Minute by Clarke, Oct. 15, 1943, FO 371/35930; Record of Conversations between Clarke and Hornbeck, Oct. 14-15, 1943, FO 381/35927; Report of Hornbeck on London Trip, Oct. 28, 1943, DOS: Notter, Box 79.

59. Notes on Meeting with President, Oct. 5, 1943, DOS: Notter, Box 54; Hull, *Memoirs,* 2:1596.

60. Chinese Summary Record of Roosevelt-Chiang Meeting, Nov. 23, 1943, *FRUS: The Conferences at Cairo and Teheran 1943,* pp. 323-25; E. Roosevelt, *As He Saw It,* p. 165; Press Conference of Feb. 23, 1945, in Samuel I. Rosenman, *Public Papers and Addresses of Franklin D. Roosevelt* 13:562-63; Theodore White, *The Stillwell Papers,* p. 253.

61. Bohlen Minutes of Roosevelt-Stalin Meeting, Nov. 28, 1943, *FRUS: Conferences at Cairo and Teheran,* pp. 482-86.

62. Deputy Prime Minister to Churchill, Nov. 30, 1943, PREM 3/178/2.

63. Churchill to Deputy Prime Minister, Dec. 1, 1943, PREM 3/178/2.

## 4. United States'–European Differences Over Postwar Southeast Asia, December 1943–October 1944

1. On general military strategy in Southeast Asia, see Christopher Thorne, *Allies of a Kind,* pp. 405-416, 450-55.

2. *Ibid.,* pp. 300-1; Roosevelt to Churchill, June 30, 1943 in Francis L. Lowenheim, Harold D. Langley and Manfred Jonas, eds., *Roosevelt and Churchill,* pp. 349-50; Churchill to Roosevelt, July 3, 1943, *ibid.,* pp. 350-51; Roosevelt to Churchill, July 9, 1943, *ibid.,* 353-54; Vice-Admiral the Earl Mountbatten of Burma, *Report to the Combined Chiefs of Staff,* pp. 5-7.

3. Atcheson to Hull, Sept. 22, 1943, DOS: 800.0146/170; Atcheson to Hull, Sept. 16, 1943, DOS: 800.0146/164; Atcheson to Hull, Sept. 17. 1943, DOS: 800.0146/200; Memorandum, Division of Far Eastern Affairs, Oct. 22, 1943, DOS: 800.0146/170; Gauss to Hull, Nov. 10, 1943, DOS: 800.0146/226; Memorandum, Division of Political Studies, Nov. 13, 1943, DOS: 800.0146/170; Hornbeck to Hull, Jan. 5, 1944, DOS: 851G.01/45; Gauss to Hull, Jan. 5, 1944, DOS: 851G.00/96.

4. Memorandum by Davies, Nov. 22, 1943, *FRUS: Conferences at Cairo and Teheran*, pp. 371-72; Hull to Merrell, Nov. 26, 1943, DOS: 740.0011PW/3513; Merrell to Hull, Nov. 29, 1943, DOS: 740.0011PW/3565; Hull to Merrell, March 27, 1944, DOS: 740.0011PW/3589.

5. Memorandum of Conversation by Berle, Oct. 21, 1943. *FRUS 1943: China*, pp. 883-84.

6. Berle to Stettinius, Oct. 22, 1943, *FRUS 1943: China*, pp. 884-85; Stettinius to Roosevelt, Nov. 8, 1943, *FRUS 1943: China*, p. 886; Roosevelt to Stettinius, Nov. 9, 1943, *FRUS 1943: China*, pp. 886-87; Memorandum, Division of Far Eastern Affairs, Dec. 3, 1943, DOS: 740.0011PW/3625.

7. Memorandum from Netherlands Embassy, Aug. 11, 1943, FDR Papers, Map Room Files, Box 164.

8. Minute by Clarke on London-Halifax Conversation, Dec. 3, 1943, FO 371/35910; Halifax to Eden, Nov. 22, 1943, FO 115, 3574.

9. Minute by Butler on London-Halifax Conversation, Dec. 3, 1943, FO: 371/35910; Eden to Halifax, Dec. 24, 1943, FO 115, 3574.

10. Annexure A, Allied Missions to H.Q., SACSEAC, Supplement to Report, SEAC Records, Box 1.

11. Thorne, *Allies of a Kind*, pp. 409-16.

12. Eden to Churchill, Dec. 20, 1943, FO 371/41723.

13. Churchill to Eden, Dec. 21, 1943, PREM 3/178/2.

14. Eden to Churchill, Dec. 24, 1943, PREM 3/178/2; Churchill to Eden, Dec. 25, 1943, PREM 3/178/2; Minute by Barclay, Dec. 31, 1943, FO 115, 3538; Eden to Halifax, Dec. 29, 1943, PREM 3/178/2.

15. Halifax to Eden, Jan. 4, 1944, FO 371/41723; Memorandum of Conversation, Jan. 3, 1944, *FRUS: Conferences at Cairo and Teheran*, p. 864. Following his meeting with Halifax, Hull wrote a memorandum to Roosevelt and enclosed the statement of British policy and a summary of American promises to restore French sovereignty. Hull to Roosevelt, Jan. 14, 1944, *FRUS 1944* 3:769-73.

16. Halifax to Eden, Jan. 18, 1944, FO 371/41723. Roosevelt's disparaging comments about French colonial record led to a Foreign Office review of the matter and the preparation of a statement of French contributions in Indochina. Minute by Martin to Churchill, Jan. 25, 1944, PREM 3/178/2.

17. Roosevelt to Hull, Jan. 24, 1944, *FRUS: Conferences at Cairo and Teheran*, pp. 872-73.

18. Samuel I. Rosenman, *The Public Papers and Addresses of Franklin D. Roosevelt*, 13:63-64.

19. WP (44) 111, Feb. 16, 1944, CAB 66/17.

20. WM 25 (44) 4, Feb. 24, 1944, CAB 65/41; Draft Telegram prepared by Dominion Office, ca. March 1, 1944, PREM 3/178/2.

21. Minute by Churchill, March 11, 1944, M-266/4, PREM 3.178/2; Cranborne to Churchill, March 31, 1944, PREM 3/178/2.

22. French Committee for National Liberation (Hoppenot) to Berle, Dec. 13, 1943, DOS: 740.0011PW/3630; Berle to Leahy, Jan. 5, 1944, DOS: 740.0011PW/369A; Berle to Hoppenot, Jan. 5, 1944, DOS: 740.0011PW/3630.

23. Policy Summary H-103, Feb. 7, 1944, DOS: Notter, Box 153: CAC Document 66A, Feb. 5, 1944, DOS: Notter, Box 109; Stettinius to Roosevelt, Feb. 17, 1944, DOS: 851G.01/46; Dunn to Hilldring, March 14, 1944, *FRUS 1944* 5:1205-6.

24. Milton Viorst, *Hostile Allies*, pp. 208-20, Hull to Roosevelt, Sept, 17, 1944, *FRUS 1944* 3:735-36; Hull to FDR, Sept. 21, 1944, *FRUS 1944* 3:737-38; Churchill to Roosevelt, Oct. 14, 1944, *FRUS 1944* 3:739-41; Roosevelt to Churchill, Oct. 19, 1944, *FRUS 1944* 3:741.

25. Harley Notter, *Postwar Foreign Policy Preparation*, pp. 108-23, 163-79, 208-13.

26. Kramol Tongdhummachart, "American Policy in Southeast Asia," pp. 64-68; Senate, CFR *Causes, Origins, and Lessons of the Vietnam War*, pp. 161-62.

27. Policy Summary H-92A, Jan. 10 1944, DOS: Notter, Box 153. Summaries of Plans for Southeast Asia, Jan. 31-Feb. 2, 1944, DOS: Notter, Box 153.

28. Policy Summary H-49A, DOS: Notter, Box 153.

29. Memorandum, Office of Far Eastern Affairs, Feb. 5, 1944, DOS: 856D.00/2-544.

30. Memorandum of Conversation (Dunn), Feb. 10, 1944, DOS: 856D.01/122; Policy Committee Document EUR-3, Feb. 18, 1944, DOS: Notter, Box 137; Policy Committee Minutes, Feb. 21 1944, DOS: Notter, Box 138; Hull, *Memoirs*, 2:1599; Minutes, IAC-FE, Feb. 22, 1944, DOS: Notter, Box 118; Policy Committee Document EUR-4, Feb. 24, 1944, DOS: Notter, Box 137; Policy Committee Minutes, Feb. 25, 1944, DOS: Notter, Box 138; Minutes, IAC-FE, Feb. 28, 1944, DOS: Notter, Box 117: Dunn to Hilldring, Feb. 28, 1944, *FRUS 1944* 5:1195-98. Territorial Committee Document 262 March 2, 1943, DOS: Inter-Intra Committee, Box 88 D; Territorial Committee Minutes, March 26, 1943, DOS: Notter, Box 59; Territorial Committee Minutes, Nov. 19, 1943, DOS: Notter, Box 59; Territorial Committee Document 422, DOS: Notter, Box 65.

31. Minutes, IAC-FE, Feb. 23, 1944, DOS: Notter, Box 117; Policy Summary H-103, DOS: Notter, Box 118.

32. CAC Document 89, March 1, 1944, DOS: Notter, Box 109.

33. CAC Document 114, March 13, 1944, DOS: Notter, Box 109.

34. Minutes, IAC-FE, July 3, 1944, DOS: Notter, Box 118.

35. CAC Document 239, July 1, 1944, DOS: Notter, Box 112.

36. *Ibid.*

37. *Ibid.*

38. *Ibid.* Reflecting the confusion within the adminstration over the Indochina issue, a White House memorandum prepared for Roosevelt in his July 1944 meetings with de Gaulle suggested that the President disavow any American interest in Indochina and indicate that the future of the country should be decided by France and the other Allies which did have an interest in Indochina. The Roosevelt–de Gaulle conversations did not include discussion of Indochina. Memorandum to Roosevelt, July 4, 1944, FDR Papers, PSF Box 6; Viorst, *Hostile Allies*, pp. 207-10.

39. Minutes, CTP, Feb. 8, 1944, DOS, Notter, Box 119; Minutes, CTP, Feb. 23, 1944, *ibid.*, Box 120; Minutes, CAC-FE, May 30, 1944, *ibid.*, Box 117.

40. Minutes, CDA, May 9, 1944, *ibid.*, Box 120; Minutes, CAC-FE, May 29, 1944, *ibid* ., Box 118.

41. Minutes, CDA, March 31, 1944, *ibid.*, Box 120; Minutes, IAC-FE, May 29, 1944 *ibid.*, Box 117; Minutes, CDA, June 6, 1944, *ibid.*, Box 121.

42. Notter, *Postwar Foreign Policy Preparation*, pp. 246-47.

43. Thomas M. Campbell and George C. Herring, eds., *The Diaries of Edward R. Stettinius, Jr.*, pp. 35-40.

44. *Ibid.*, pp. 52-55, 70-71; Louis, *Imperialism at Bay*, pp. 327-36; Stettinius

Report on London Conversations, *FRUS 1944* 3:20-22.

45. Russell, *History of UN Charter*, pp. 336-38; Louis, *Imperialism at Bay*, pp. 360-62.

46. Russell, *History of UN Charter*, pp. 339-40.

47. *Ibid.*, pp. 340-48; Louis, *Imperialism at Bay*, pp. 366-77; Notter, *Postwar Foreign Policy Preparation*, pp. 387, 606-7.

48. French Committee of National Liberation to Dept. of State, May 5, 1944, DOS: 740.0011PW/3907; Memorandum Division of Southwest Pacific Affairs to Hull, July 6, 1944, DOS: 740.0011PW/7644; Donovan to Roosevelt, July 10, 1944, FDR Papers, PSF Box 168; Lodge to Forrestal, Aug 19, 1944,Millis, ed., *Forrestal Diaries*, vol. l.

49. Bishop to Hull, July 26, 1944, DOS: 740.00llPW/7-2644; Bishop to Hull, July 29, 1944, DOS: 740.00llPW/7-2944; Division of Far Eastern Affairs to Hull, July 27, 1944, DOS: PSEA, Box 9; Memorandum, Office of Far Eastern Affairs to Stettinius, July 29, 1944, DOS: 740.0011PW/7-2944; Murphy to Hull, June 10, 1944, DOS: 740.0011PW/3967.

50. Memorandum by Representatives of British Chiefs of Staff, Aug. 5, 1944, JCS Files/CCS 370 France.

51. Memorandum on French Participation in War, Aug. 30, 1944, JCS/CCS 370 France.

52. Aide-Memoire, British Embassy to Dept. of State, Aug. 25, 1944, FDR Papers, Map Room Files, Box 166; Memorandum of Conversation (Matthews), Aug. 26, 1944, DOS: 740.0011PW/8-2544.

53. Memorandum of Conversation (Matthews), Aug. 29, 1944, DOS: 740.0011 PW/8-2944. Hull to Roosevelt, Aug. 26, 1944; *FRUS 1944* 3:774-75; Roosevelt to Hull, Aug. 28, 1944,*FRUS 1944* 3:774-75.

54. Gauss to Hull, July 26, 1944, DOS: 851G.00/7-2644; Langdon to Hull, Aug. 3. 1944, DOS: 851G.00/8-344.

55. Memorandum, Grew to Hull, Aug. 28, 1944, DOS: 740.0011PW/8-2544; Testimony of Moffat, U.S. Senate, CFR, *Causes, Origins, and Lessons of the Vietnam War*, pp. 163-64. In his testimony at the Senate Foreign Relations Committee hearings in 1972, Moffat indicated that the Division of Southwest Pacific Affairs strongly favored Roosevelt's plans for Indochina and hoped that he had some secret means of accomplishing the trusteeship.

56. Hull to Roosevelt, Sept. 8, 1944, DOS: 851G.01/9-844; see also Hull, *Memoirs*, 2:1600; U.S. Senate, CFR, *Causes, Origins, and Lessons of the Vietnam War*, pp. 162-63.

57. *Ibid.*

58. *Ibid.*

59. Churchill to Eden, May 21, 1944, PREM 3/180/7.

60. *Ibid.*

61. WP (44) 444, Aug. 13, 1944, CAB 66/53;WM 106 (44) 5, CAB 65/43; Record of Eden-Massigli Meeting, Aug. 24, 1944, FO 371/41719; Minute by Henderson, Sept. 7, 1944, FO 371/41724.

62. Questions Arising out of U.S. Reactions to Proposals for French Participation in the War in the Far East, Sept. 8, 1944, FO 371/41720.

63. *Ibid.*

64. Hull, *Memoirs*, 2:1601.

65. Fifield, *Americans in Southeast Asia*, pp. 86-87; Thorne, *Allies of a Kind*, pp. 219, 460-62; Martin, "Thai-American Relations in World War II," pp. 464-65; Herbert A. Fine, "The Liquidation of World War II in Thailand, pp. 65-67.

66. Martin, "Thai-American Relations in World War II," pp. 459-61; Memorandum of Conversation by Hull, Dec. 8, 1941, *FRUS 1941* 5:377-78; Dept. of State to British Embassy, Dec. 18, 1941, *FRUS 1941* 5:387-88; British Embassy to Dept. of State, Dec. 24, 1941, *FRUS 1941* 5:392-93; Dept. of State to British Embassy, *FRUS 1942* 1:913-14; Berle to Roosevelt, Jan. 5, 1942, Berle Papers, Box 67.

67. Martin, "Thai-American Relations in World War II," pp. 460-61; Fifield, *Americans in Southeast Asia*, pp. 86-87; Herbert H. Fine, "Liquidation of World War II in Thailand," p. 67; Berle to Roosevelt, Jan. 28, 1942, Berle Papers, Box 58; Berle to Hull, Jan. 28, 1942, *FRUS 1942* 1:914; Chinese Embassy to Hull, *FRUS 1942* 1:915; Dept. of State to British Embassy, Feb , 1942, *FRUS 1942* 1:916.

68. Conference of March 12, 1943, *Complete Presidential Press Conferences of Franklin D. Roosevelt*; 21:189-190 ; Welles to Roosevelt, March 6, 1943, FDR Papers, OF Box 339; Gauss to Hull, Feb. 27, 1943, *FRUS 1943: China*, pp. 13-14; Chinese Foreign Ministry to Chinese Embassy, April 18, 1942, *FRUS 1942*: China, pp. 32-33; Hull to Roosevelt, May 2, 1942, *FRUS 1942: China* pp. 37-38.

69. Chinese Summary Record of Roosevelt-Chiang Meeting, Nov. 23, 1943, *FRUS: Conferences at Cairo and Teheran*, pp. 323-25; Martin, "Thai-American Relations in World War II," pp. 462-64.

70. Minutes, Political Planning Committee, Nov. 4, 1943, DOS: Notter, Box 146; Policy Summary H-106, Nov. 27, 1943, DOS: Notter, Box 154.

71. Ballantine to Berle, Dec. 31, 1943, DOS: 892.01/12-3143.

72. Foreign Office Memorandum, Nov. 22, 1943, FO 371/35935; Memorandum by Hornbeck, Dec. 13, 1943, DOS: 892.01/12-1343; Memorandum of Conversation (Ballantine), Jan. 14, 1944; DOS: 892.01/1-1444.

73. Memorandum of Conversation (Ballantine) and attached statement, Feb. 26, 1944, DOS: 892.01/53.

74. Sansom to Ballantine, Feb. 28, 1944, FO 115/3632.

75. Stettinius to Roosevelt, March 8, 1944, Berle Papers, Box 67.

76. Ballantine to Berle, Feb. 28, 1944, DOS: 892.01/56; Policy Committee Minutes, Feb. 28, 1944, DOS: Notter, Box 138; Minutes, IAC-FE, March 7, 8, 9, 13, and 15, 1944, DOS: Notter, Box 117; Minutes, IAC-FE, March 14, 1944, DOS: Notter, Box 118; Policy Summary H-119, DOS: Notter, Box 138; Stettinius to Roosevelt, March 8, 1944, Berle Papers, Box 67.

77. Memorandum of Conversation (Berle), March 20, 1944, DOS: 892.01/55; Halifax-Berle Conversation, March 20, 1944, FO 115/3632.

78. Memorandum of Conversation (Ballantine), March 17, 1944, DOS: 892.01/54; CAC Documents 96B (March 21, 1944), 112 (March 15, 1944), and 113 (March 22, 1944), DOS: Notter, Box 109.

79. Memorandum of Conversation (Ballantine), May 30, 1944, DOS: 892.01/59; WP (44) 365, July 3, 1944, CAB 66/52; WM 89 (44), 11, July 10, 1944, CAB 65/43; Memorandum of Conversation, July 31, 1944, DOS: 892.01/7-3144.

80. Memorandum, Division of Far Eastern Affairs, Aug. 14, 1944, DOS: 892.01/8-1444; Policy Document, FE-9, Aug. 7, 1944, DOS: Notter, Box 137; Policy Committee Minutes, Aug. 11, 1944, DOS: Notter, Box 138; Sec. State to Embassy in London, Aug.

14, 1944, DOS: 892.01/8-1644; Embassy in Washington to Foreign Office, Aug. 31, 1944, FO 371/41848.

81. Winant to Hull, Sept. 8, 1944, DOS: 892.01/9-544.

82. Memorandum, Recent Policy Matters, Oct. 12, 1944, DOS: 740.0011PW/10-1244; Hull to Winant, Oct. 19, 1944, DOS: 892.01/9-544.

83. Winant to Sec. State, Nov. 24, 1944, DOS: 892.01/11-2444.

84. Thorne, *Allies of a Kind*, p. 462.

85. Minute on U.S. Policy toward Siam, Nov. 29, 1944, FO 371/41848.

86. *Ibid*.

87. Fine, "Liquidation of World War II in Thailand," pp. 67-68; Martin, "Thai-American Relations in World War II," pp. 465-66.

## 5. Toward a Limited Anticolonialism: The Final Phase of Postwar Planning, November 1944–July 1945

1. Thorne, *Allied of a Kind*, pp. 406-10, 520-22.

2. Minister of Defense to Churchill, Oct. 13, 1944, FO 371/41720; Churchill to Eden, Oct. 21, 1944, FO 371/41720; Foreign Office to SACSEA, Oct. 21, 1944, FO 371/41720; Proceedings of Conference, *FRUS: Conference at Quebec 1944*, pp. 295-98.

3. Thorne, *Allies of a Kind*, pp. 563-75; Michael Schaller, *The U.S. Crusade in China, 1938-1945*, pp. 147-75.

4. Memorandum of Conversation with Roosevelt, Jan. 2, 1945, in Millis, ed., *Stettinius Diaries*, pp. 210-12.

5. Schaller, *The U.S. Crusade in China*, pp. 176-200; Dallek, *Roosevelt and American Foreign Policy*, pp. 491-502.

6. OSS Memorandum, "Problems and Objectives of United States Foreign Policy," April 2, 1945, HST Papers, OSS Files.

7. Hull to Roosevelt, Oct. 5, 1944, FDR Papers, Map Room Files, Box 166.

8. Hull to Roosevelt, Oct. 13, 1944, *FRUS 1944* 3:776-77.

9. Buell to Hull, Oct. 5, 1944, DOS: 740.0011 PW/10-544; Buell to Hull, Oct. 6, 1944, DOS: 740.0011 PW/10-644; Hull to Roosevelt, Oct. 10, 1944, *FRUS 1944* 3:775- 76.

10. Donovan to Roosevelt, Oct. 27, 1944, FDR Papers, PSF Box 169.

11. Buell to Hull, Oct. 30, 1944, DOS: 740.0011 PW/10-3044.

12. Stettinius to Roosevelt, Nov. 2, 1944, *FRUS 1944* 3:778-79; Moffat to Stettinius, Nov. 1, 1944, DOS: 851G.00/11-144.

13. Roosevelt to Stettinius, Nov. 3, 1944, *FRUS 1944* 3:780; Hull, *Memoirs*, 2:1598.

14. Moffat to Stettinius, Nov. 10, 1944, DOS: 740.0011 PW/11-1044; Stettinius to Roosevelt, Nov. 15, 1944, FDR Papers, PSF Box 55.

15. Roosevelt to Secretaries of Navy and War, Directors of OSS and OWI, and Admiral Leahy, Nov. 17, 1944, FDR Papers, PSF Box 55.

16. Navy Dept. Staff Memorandum, Nov. 19, 1944, Leahy File-126, Marshall Papers; Stimson to Roosevelt, Nov. 24, 1944, FDR Papers PSF Box 55.

17. Caffery to Hull, Nov. 4, 1944, *FRUS 1944* 3:780-81; Stettinius to Roosevelt, Nov. 15, 1944, FDR Papers, PSF Box 55.

18. Hull to Embassy at Chungking, Nov. 6, 1944, DOS: 851G.01/11-644; Wedemeyer to Marshall, Nov. 15, 1944, FDR Papers, Map Room Files, Box 11; Roosevelt to Hurley, Nov. 16, 1944, Leahy File-105, Marshall Papers; Atcheson to Hull, Nov. 17, 1944, DOS: 740.0011 PW/11-1744.

19. Buell to Hull, Nov. 10, 1944, DOS: 740.0011 PW/11-1044.

20. Stettinius to Roosevelt, Nov. 20, 1944, FDR Papers, PSF Box 55.

21. Roosevelt to Stetinius, Nov. 24, 1944, FDR Papers, PSF Box 55. It is uncertain whether Roosevelt had read Stimson's Nov. 24 message regarding the Joint Chiefs of Staff's action on the French mission before he dispatched directive to Stettinius on that date. Roosevelt's statement was carefully worded to make clear that he and Churchill had not approved the mission.

22. British Embassy to Hull, Nov. 22, 1944, *FRUS 1944* 3:781-83.

23. Stettinius to Roosevelt, Dec. 26, 1944, FDR Papers, PSF Box 55; Stettinius to Roosevelt, Dec. 27, 1944, *FRUS 1944* 3:783-84.

24. Churchill to Eden, Oct. 11, 1944, FO 371-41720; Eden to Churchill, Oct. 8, 1944, FO 371/41720.

25. Dening to Sterndale Bennet, Oct. 14, 1944, FO 371/41724; Brief for Eden, Nov. 9, 1944, FO 371/41721.

26. Stettinius to Stimson, Dec. 11, 1944, JCS Files/CCS 370; Policy Regarding Indochina, Jan. 11, 1945, JCS Files/CCS 370.

27. Roosevelt to Sec. State, Jan. 1, 1945, *FRUS 1945* 6:293.

28. Foulds Minute, Jan. 4, 1945, FO 371/46304; Memorandum of Conversation with Roosevelt, Jan. 2, 1945, Millis, ed., *Stettinius Diaries,* pp. 210-12; Halifax to Foreign Office, Jan. 3, 1945, FO 371/46304.

29. Halifax to Foreign Office, Jan. 9, 1945, FO 371/46304. The question of approving French sabboteurs had been raised earlier with Roosevelt, the State Department having been requested to do so by the British Embassy. Roosevelt, however, had not indicated his views on the matter prior to the meeting with Halifax. Memorandum of Conversation with Halifax (Stettinius), Dec. 26, 1944, DOS: PSEA, Box 9; Matters to Discuss with President, Jan. 2, 1945, Stettinius Papers, Box 741; Stettinius to Roosevelt, Jan. 3, 1945, Stettinius Papers, Box 733; Items for Undersecretary, Jan. 9, 1945, Stettinius Papers, Box 741.

30. Halifax to Foreign Office, Jan. 9, 1945, FO 371/46304.

31. Hurley to Roosevelt, Jan. 2, 1945, FDR Papers, Map Room Files Box 11; Wedemeyer to Marshall, Dec. 29, 1944, Marshall Papers, Wedemeyer Correspondence File, (includes notation that Roosevelt had seen the message); Stettinius to Roosevelt, Dec. 1, 1944, FDR Papers, PSF Box 55.

32. Wedemeyer to Marshall, Dec. 10, 1944, Marshall Papers, Wedemeyer Correspondence File. The American view that SEAC had become the center for a coordinated effort to reestablish European imperialism was known to the British, Dutch and French. The British and Dutch made efforts to correct that impression. See Eden to Halifax, Jan. 29, 1945, FO 381/46325; Stettinius to Roosevelt, Jan. 16, 1945, FDR Papers, Box 55; Winant to Hull, Nov. 27, 1944, FDR Papers, Box 55; Stettinius to Roosevelt, Dec. 1, 1944, FDR Papers, Box 55. Relations among the European nations were not as close as the Americans suspected. As noted earlier, the British had some reservations about accepting the French mission, fearing its political implications. And the Dutch were known to complain that the British deferred their requests on the excuse that American approval was needed. Thorne, *Allies of a Kind,* pp. 600, 613-14. Subsequent SEAC operations in Indochina and the East Indies underscored stress among the European powers. Those difficulties within SEAC notwithstanding, the European nations did share important common interests in Southeast Asia which were served by SEAC.

33. Hurley to Roosevelt, Nov. 26, 1944, FDR Papers, Map Room Files, Box 11.

34. Bishop to Sec. State, Dec. 30, 1944, 2 messages, DOS 740.0011 PW/12-3044.

35. Memorandum for President, Jan. 13, 1945, Taussig Papers, Box 49; Memorandum on Roosevelt-Stanley Conversation, Jan. 16, 1945, Taussig Papers, Box 49; *Imperialism at Bay,* pp. 436-40; Moffat to Ballantine, Jan. 17, 1945, DOS: PSEA, Box 9; Pasvolsky to Roosevelt, *FRUS 1945* a:18-22.

36. Memorandum of Conversation (Stettinius), Jan. 4, 1945, DOS: 851G.00/1-145.

37. Stettinius to Roosevelt, Jan. 12, 1945, DOS: 740.0011 PW/1-1245.

38. CDA 259, Jan. 17, 1945, DOS: Notter, Box 125.

39. *Ibid.*

40. *Ibid.*

41. CDA Minutes, Jan. 16, 1945, DOS: Notter, Box 121; Russell, *History of UN Charter,* pp. 336-48, 573-81.

42. Butler Minute, July 10, 1945, FO 371/46307.

43. Donovan to Roosevelt, Dec. 4, 1944, FDR Papers, PSF Box 170; Donovan to Roosevelt, Dec. 15, 1944, *ibid.*

44. Bishop to Stettinius, Dec. 29, 1944, DOS: 740.0011 PW/12-2944; Bishop to Stettinius, Jan. 12, 1945, DOS: 892.01/1-1245.

45. Memorandum of Conversation (Landon), Jan. 18, 1945, DOS: 892.01/1-1845; Spector, *Eagle Against the Sun,* pp. 468-69; Sethachuay, "U.S.-Thailand Relations," pp. 248-96.

46. OSS (Cheston) to Dept. State (Dunn), Jan. 30, 1945, DOS: 892.01/1-3045; Ballantine to Dunn and Grew, Jan. 31, 1945, DOS: 892.01/1-3145.

47. Memorandum for President, Jan. 13, 1945, *FRUS 1945* 6:1242-44.

48. Memorandum by Ballantine, Jan. 25, 1945, *FRUS 1945* 6:1244-46; SC Document 44, DOS: Inter-Intra Comm.; SC Minutes, Jan. 31, 1945, DOS: Inter-Intra Comm.

49. IAC-FE, Jan. 16, 1945, DOS: Notter, Box 118.

50. Memorandum of Conversation (Landon), Feb. 9, 1945, DOS: 892.01/2-945; Ballantine to Dunn and Grew, Feb. 22, 1945, DOS: 892.01/2-1645; Memorandum of Conversation (Landon), Feb. 26, 1945, DOS: 892.01/2-2645; Donovan to Roosevelt, FDR Papers, PSF Box 171.

51. Hurley to Stettinius, Feb. 2, 1945, *FRUS 1945* 6:1246-47; Grew to Hurley, Feb. 6, 1945, *FRUS 1945* 6:1247-48; Hurley to Stettinius, Feb. 5, 1945, DOS: 892.01/2-545; Memorandum of Conversation (Landon), March 14, 1945, DOS: 892.01/3-1445.

52. Donovan to Roosevelt, March 12, 16, and 26, 1945, FDR Papers, PSF Box 171; Ballantine to Dunn, March 20, 1945, DOS: 892.01/3-1545; Bishop to Stettinius, March 22, 1945, DOS: 892.01/3-2245; Bishop to Stettinius, March 23, 1945, DOS: 892.01/3-2345.

53. Memorandum of Conversation (Ballantine), Feb. 21, 1945, *FRUS 1945* 6:1249-51; Dept. of State to British Embassy, March 15, 1945, *FRUS 1945* 6:1254-55; Grew to Merrell, April 28, 1945, *FRUS 1945* 6:1264-67; British Embassy to Dept. of State, April 5, 1945, *FRUS 1945* 6:1262-63; Ballantine to Cox, March 28, 1945, DOS: 892.01-3-2845; Minutes, SWNCC, March 30, 1945, DOS: SWNCC Box 1; Memorandum of Conversation (Ballantine), April 9, 1945, DOS: 892.01/4-945.

54. SWNCC Report, Feb. 1945, *FRUS 1945* 6:1248-49; Dept. of State to British Embassy, June 25, 1945, *FRUS 1945* 6:1272-75; Landon to SWNCC, June 6, 1945, DOS:

892.01/6-645; Winant to Stettinius, July 11, 1945, DOS: 892.01/7-1145; SC Minutes, June 13 and 15, 1945, DOS: Inter-Intra Comm.; Minutes, IAC-FE, June 26, 1945, DOS: Notter, Box 118; SWNCC Document 109/2, July 12, 1945, DOS: SWNCC, Box 3; SWNCC to CCS, July 12, 1945, JCS Files/CCS 092 Thailand.

55. Louis, *Imperialism at Bay,* pp. 448-53; Russell, *History of UN Charter,* pp. 510-14, 573.

56. Russell, *History of UN Charter,* pp. 540-42; Edward Stettinius, *Roosevelt and the Russians,* pp. 236-38; Robert E. Sherwood, *Roosevelt and Hopkins,* pp. 865-66; Louis, *Imperialism at Bay,* pp. 454-60. As Louis observes, Stettinius' assurances that the empire was excluded from the trusteeship plan may have led Churchill to ignore the fact that the British mandates were explicitly covered. The Foreign Office had already concluded that assimilation of the mandates within the trusteeship system was necessary.

57. Minutes of Roosevelt-Stalin Meeting, Feb. 8, 1945, *FRUS: The Conferences at Malta and Yalta,* pp. 770-71.

58. *Ibid.,* pp. 564-67.

59. *Complete Presidential Press Conferences of Franklin D. Roosevelt,* 25: 70-71.

60. Hurley to Stettinius, Jan. 31, 1945, *FRUS 1945* 6:294; French Embassy in China to U.S. Embassy in China, Jan. 20. 1945, *FRUS 1945* 6:295-96; Caffery to Stettinius, Jan. 30, 1945, *FRUS 1945* 6:667-68; Langdon to Stettinius, March 8, 1945, DOS: 851G.00/3-845; French Naval Mission to CCS, Feb. 20, 1945, JCS Files/CCS 373.11 Indo-China; Memorandum, Division of Southwest Pacific Affairs (Landon), March 2, 1945, DOS: 851G.00/3-245.

61. Memorandum of Conversation (Stettinius), March 12, 1945, DOS: 851G.00/3-1245; Memorandum of Conversation (Matthews), March 12, 1934, DOS: 851G.00/3-1245.

62. Eden to Churchill, March 11, 1945, PREM 3/178/3; SACSEAC to Foreign Office, Feb. 21, 1945, FO 371/46304.

63. SWNCC 35/d, Feb. 27, 1945, DOS: SWNCC, Box 3.

64. F. C. Jones, *Japan's New Order in East Asia,* pp. 396-98; Clarke W. Garrett, "France and Vietnam, 1940-1946," pp. 310-12.

65. Charles F. Romanus and Riley Sunderland, *Time Runs Out in CBI,* pp. 259-60; SWNCC 35/1/D, March 13, 1945 and 35/2/D, March 14, 1945, DOS: SWNCC Files, Box 3; Memorandum of Conversation (Ballantine), March 12, 1945, DOS: PSEA, Box 9. Acting Sec. State to Caffery, March 19, 1945, *FRUS 1945* 6:301; Bonnet to Stettinius, March 12, 1945, *FRUS 1945* 6:297-99; Caffery to Stettinius, March 13, 1945, *FRUS 1945* 6: 300; JSM to AMSSO, March 18 and 19, 1945, PREM 3/178/3; Churchill Minute, March 19, 1945, PREM 3/178/3. The French requests for assistance and the ensuing strains in Franco-American relations were rather fully reported, somewhat to the annoyance of the White House which believed that the French government was seeking to enlist popular sympathy in America; *New York Times,* March 15, 22, 28, 29, and 31, 1945.

66. Thomas M. Campbell and George C. Herring, eds., *Stettinius Diaries,* pp. 304-5; Stettinius to Roosevelt, March 16, 1945, House Committee on Armed Services, *United States-Vietnam Relations 1945-1967* (Book 1), I, A, 16-18; Memorandum of Conversation (Dunn), March 19, 1945, *FRUS 1945* 6:301-2; Memorandum, Bohlen to Dunn, March 19, 1945, DOS: 851G.00/3-1945; Memorandum for Secretaries of War and Navy,

March 20, 1945, JSC Files/CCS 370; JSM Washington to Prime Minister, March 20, 1945, PREM 3/178/3; SWNCC 35/9, March 24, 1945, DOS: SWNCC Files, Box 3; Fenard to CCS, March 26 and 27, 1945, JCS Files/CCS 370.

67. Caffery to Stettinius, March 24, 1945, *FRUS 1945* 6:302; Acting Secretary of State to Caffery, March 29, 1945, *FRUS 1945* 6:302; Stettinius to Bonnet, April 4, 1945, *FRUS 1945* 6:303; Stettinius to Caffery, April 19, 1945, *FRUS 1945* 6:306; Bonnet to Stettinius, April 14, 1945, *FRUS 1945* 6: 304-6; CCS 644/25, JCS Files 370 France; AMSSO/JSM Washington to COS April 5, 1945, FO 371/46306; Minutes on JSM 629, March 29, 1945, FO 381/46306; Memorandum of Conversation (Dunn), April 13, 1945, DOS: PSEA, Box 9.

By April 19, the Fourteenth Air Force had flown 67 missions with 181 sorties at French request, in addition to other air force operations in Indochina. H. A. Bryode-Maddux, April 24, 1945 DOS: 740.0011 PW/4-2445; Lovett to Matthews, April 15, 1945, DOS: 740.0011 PW/4-1545; Lincoln to Maddux, April 16, 1945, DOS: PSEA, Box 9. Bernard Fall, *The Two Viet-Nams,* pp. 54-59, provides a pertinent critique of the American response to the desperate position of the French.

68. Memorandum of Conversation, March 15, 1945, *FRUS 1945* 1:124.

69. Churchill to Roosevelt, March 17, 1945, Lowenheim, Langley, and Jonas, eds., *Roosevelt and Churchill,* P. 677; Hollis to Churchill, March 15, 1945, PREM 3/178/3.

70. Minute (Sterndale-Bennet), March 24, 1945, FO 371/46305.

71. Roosevelt to Churchill, March 22, 1945, Lowenheim, Langley, and Jonas, eds., *Roosevelt and Churchill,* pp. 682-83; Marshall to Wedemeyer, March 24, 1945, JCS Files/CCS 370 France; JSM Washington to AMSSO March 30, 1945, FO 371/46306.

72. SWNCC 35/7, March 20, 1945, DOS: SWNCC Files, Box 3; JSM Washington to AMSSO, March 24, 1945, FO 371/46305; CCS to Fenard, April 18, 1945, JCS Files/CCS 373.11 Indochina; Secretary State to Ambassador from France, April 13, 1945, *FRUS 1945* 6:306-7.

73. Hurley to Truman, May 29, 1945, HST Papers, Map Room Files; Memorandum by Assistant to President's Naval Aide, July 1945, *FRUS: The Conference of Berlin,* 1:915-21.

74. Acting Sec. State to Hurley, June 7, 1945, quoted in Allan W. Cameron, ed., *Viet-Nam Crisis,* 1:37-39; *House Committee on Armed Services, United States-Vietnam Relations, 1945-1967* (Book 1), I, A:2; Walter LaFeber, "Roosevelt, Churchill, and Indochina," p. 1294.

75. U.S. Policy with Regard to Future of Indochina, *ca.* April 5, 1945, DOS: 851G.00/4-545; Stettinius to Dunn, March 15, 1945, Stettinus Papers, Box 727; Staff Committee Minutes, March 14 and 26, 1945, Stettinius Papers, Box 235; Calendar Notes, March 16, 1945, Stettinius Papers, Box 244; Memorandum of Conversation, April 3, 1945, Taussig Papers, Box 49.

76. U.S. Policy with Regard to Future of Indochina, *ca.* April 5, 1945, DOS: 851G.00/4-545.

77. *Ibid.*

78. On the afternoon of Roosevelt's death in Warms Springs, Georgia, Taussig met with Eleanor Roosevelt at the White House in an effort to have her intercede with the President on behalf of keeping the general trusteeship proposal of the State Department on the agenda at the United Nations Conference. Military and naval officers, sup-

ported by European Affairs officials at the State Department, seemed determined to delay consideration. Taussig lamented that Stettinius was not providing leadership on the matter. Eleanor Roosevelt, who had strong anticolonial convictions, agreed to support Taussig's concerns. Memorandum of Conversation by Taussig, April 12, 1945, Taussig Papers, Box 49.

I speculated on the trusteeship for Indochina in "Franklin Roosevelt and Indochina," p. 365-68. See also Arthur M. Schlesinger, Jr., *The Bitter Heritage*, p. 23; La Feber, "Roosevelt, Churchill, and Indochina," pp. 1277-95.

In 1954, Dean Acheson, Averill Harriman, and Herbert Feis discussed their recollections about Roosevelt's Indochina policy. All recalled his frequent comments on the subject and determination to prevent a French restoration. Achson and Harriman, neither of whom was closely involved in policy formulation for the area in early 1945, observed as well a sense of State Department uncertainty about the disposition of the Indochina question at the time of Roosevelt's death. Princeton Seminar, May 15, 1954, Acheson Papers.

79. SWNCC Minutes, April 13, 1945, SWNCC Minutes Box 1/1, Marshall Library; Matthews to Dunn, April 20, 1945, DOS: 851G.00/4]2045; Testimony by Moffat, May 11, 1972, U.S. Senate, CFR, *Causes, Origins, and Lessons of the Vietnam War*, pp. 165-67. The recollections of Kenneth Landon express the sense of identity which State Department officers with responsibility for Southeast Asia had with Roosevelt's trusteeship plan. Landon, "Southeast Asia and U.S. Foreign Policy," pp. 269-70.

80. Leahy to Stettinius, March 30, 1945, and Leahy to Stettinius, April 5, 1945, JCS Files/CCS 370 France. These files provide, as do many other sources of early 1945, evidence of the Joint Chiefs' interest in accepting French assistance in Asia, the general inclination of the Department of State to endorse such proposals, but they reveal the understanding in both agencies that Roosevelt's approval was necessary on any matters affecting Indochina.

81. SACSEAC to Foreign Office, April 11, 1945, FO 371/46306; Churchill to Roosevelt, April 11, 1945, FDR Papers, Map Room Files, Box 23; Truman to Churchill, April 14, 1945, HST Papers, Map Room Files.

82. Ismay to Churchill, April 19, 1945, PREM 3/178/3.

83. JSM Washington to AMSSO, April 22, 1945, FO 371/46306; CCS 64/24, April 22, 1945, JCS Files/CCS 370 France.

84. JCS 1200/14, JCS Files/CCS 370 France.

85. Memorandum of Conversation (Wallner), May 3, 1945, Stettinius Papers, Box 313.

86. Grew to Caffery, May 19, 1945, *FRUS 1945* 6:307.

87. Grew to Dunn, April 23, 1945, DOS: 851G.00/4-2345; SC Minutes, April 24, 1945, DOS: Inter-Intra Comm.; Moffat Testimony, May 11, 1972, U.S. Senate, CFR, *Causes, Origins, and Lessons of the Vietnam War*, pp. 167-68; Memo for President, May 9, 1945, DOS: 851G.00/5-945; Memorandum of Conversation with Eleanor Roosevelt (Taussig), April 12, 1945, Taussig Papers, Box 49; Marshall to Gen. Hull, May 3, 1945, Marshall Papers, Box 2; Marshall to Stimson, May 11, 1945, Marshall Papers, Box 89-A; Memorandum on French Units in Far East, May 30, 1945, Marshall Papers, Box 2; Grew to Truman, May 16, 1945, *FRUS 1945* 6:307-9; Matthews to SWNCC, May 23, 1945, *FRUS 1945* 6:309-11; Memorandum of Conversation, May 31, 1945, *FRUS 1945* 6:311; SWNCC 35/11, May 25, 1945, DOS: SWNCC Box 3; Memorandum of Conversation

(Phillips), May 19, 1945, DOS: PSEA Box 9; French Military Mission in U.S. to U.S. Chief of Staff, May 29, 1945, JCS Files/CCS 370 France; Memorandum of Conversation (Grew), May 31, 1945, DOS: 740.0011 PW/5-3145.

88. Memorandum to Truman, May 9, 1945, DOS: 851G.00/5-945. David H. White, "The American Perspective on Indochina: The Department of State, 1942–1945" (American Historical Association Convention, December 1978, San Francisco), provides a useful summary of State Department consideration of the Indochina issue.

89. Russell, *History of the UN Charter,* pp. 581-89, 808-42; Stettinius, Stimson and Forrestal to Truman, April 18, 1945, *FRUS 1945* 1:350-61; WM 38 (45) 1, April 3, 1945, CAB 65; WM 42 (45) 7, April 12, 1945, CAB 65; Ickes to Roosevelt, April 5, 1945, Taussig Papers, Box 77; Stettinius to Roosevelt, April 9, 1945, *FRUS 1945* 1:211-14; Millis, ed., *Forrestal Diaries,* pp. 37-38, 2:279, 283-87, 293-301.

90. Russell, *History of UN Charter,* pp. 808-10.

91. Draft Arrangements for Trusteeship, April 20, 1945, Taussig Papers, Box 67.

92. Russell, *History of UN Charter,* pp. 830-33; Draft Proposals for Trusteeship, April 26, 1945, *FRUS 1945,* 1:459-60; Minutes, 34th Meeting of U.S. Delegation, May 9, 1945, *ibid.,* pp. 654-57; Minutes, 50th Meeting of U.S. Delegation, May 22, 1945, *ibid.,* 837-47; Minutes, 64th Meeting of U.S. Delegation, June 5, 1945, *ibid.,* 1160-71; Minutes, 66th Meeting of U.S. Delegation, June 8, 1945, *ibid.,* 1197-1211; Minutes, 67th Meeting of U.S. Delegation, June 9, 1945, *ibid.,* pp. 1222-36; Minutes, 70th Meeting of U.S. Delgation, June 13, 1945, *ibid.,* pp. 1273-80; Ickes to Stettinius, June 26, 1945, *FRUS 1945* 1:1430; Taussig to Fortas, June 9, 1945, Taussig Papers, Box 67; WM 61 (45) 3, May 14, 1945, CAB 65.

93. Trusteeship Questions, June 2, 1945, Taussig Papers, Box 67.

94. Louis, *Imperialism at Bay,* pp. 534-40; Taussig to Stettinius, May 16, 1945, Taussig Papers, Box 67; Minutes, 44th Meeting of U.S. Delegation, May 17, 1945, *FRUS 1945* 1:778-90; Minutes, 45th Meeting of U.S. Delegation, May 18, 1945, *FRUS 1945* 1:790-99; Stimson and Forrestal to Stettinius, June 26, 1945, *FRUS 1945* 1:1430-31; Statement on U.S. Policy toward Dependent Peoples, May 18, 1945, Taussig Papers, Box 59; Draft Report on Dependent Territories, June 4, 1945, Taussig Papers, Box 66; Revised U.S. Redrafts, June 5 and 12, 1945, Taussig Papers, Box 67; Ickes to Stettinius, June 8, 1945, Taussig Papers, Box 67; Taussig to Stassen, June 13, 1945, Taussig Papers, Box 67; Memo for U.S. Delegation, *ca.* June 10, 1945, Taussig Papers Box 67; Memorandum of Conversation with Hickerson, June 7, 1945, Taussig Papers, Box 77; Memorandum of Conversation with Romulo, June 11, 1945, Taussig Papers, Box 77.

95. Russell, *History of UN Charter,* p. 1047.

96. On the latter point, see Louis, *Imperialism at Bay,* pp. 116-17.

97. Hurley to Truman, May 29, 1945, Truman Papers, May Room Files; SC Minutes, DOS: Inter-Intra Comm; MacLeish to Grew, June 4, 1945, DOS: 851G.01/6-45. Hurley's memorandum encouraged an extensive review of Indochina policy developments: Memorandum by Assistant to President's Naval Aide to Leahy and Truman, July 1, 1945, *FRUS: The Conference at Berlin,* 1:915-21.

98. Minute (Foulds), May 22, 1945, FO 371/46307; SWNCC 138/1, June 13, 1945, DOS: SWNCC Box 3; SWNCC to Stettinius, DOS: 740.0011 PW/6-346; SWNCC Minutes, June 18, 1945, SWNCC Minutes Box 1, Marshall Library; Grew to Forrestal, June 23, 1945, JCS Files/CCS 383.21 Indo China; JCS Meeting July 16, 1945, JCS File/ CCS 370 France; Memorandum of Conversation (Grew), June 13, 1945, DOS: 740.0011

PW/6-1345; CCS to French and Dutch Representatives, July 19, 1945, DOS: 740.0011 PW/7-2445.

99. Memorandum by U.S. Chiefs of Staff, July 17, 1945, *FRUS 1945: Conference of Berlin* 2:1313-15; CCS to SACSEAC, *FRUS 1945:* pp. 1469-71; CCS to French Military Mission, July 19, 1945, JCS Files/CCS 370; Mountbatten, *Report to the Combined Chiefs of Staff,* pp. 181-82.

## 6. The Nationalist Revolutions in Indonesia and Indochina, 1945–1947

1. Department of State *Bulletin* (Oct. 21, 1945), 13:646.

2. Hurley to Truman, Nov. 26, 1945, HST Papers, OF 292.

3. Yost to Byrnes, Dec. 13, 1945, *FRUS 1945* 6:1389-90.

4. PR 36 "U.S. Policy towards the Netherlands Indies and Indochina," Dec., 1945, DOS: Notter, Box 119A.

5. Southeast Asian Affairs Draft Memo, Dec. 18, 1945, DOS: Notter, Box 119A.

6. Fifield, *Americans in Southeast Asia,* pp. 70-71; JCS to Commanding General, US Forces CBI, Sept. 14, 1945, JCS: CCS 092 Thailand; SWNCC Memorandum, Aug. 23, 1945, JCS: CCS 092 Thailand; U.S. Participation in SEAC, Oct. 17, 1945, JCS: CCS 092 Thailand.

7. Mountbatten, *Report to the Combined Chiefs of Staff,* pp. 183-86; Mountbatten, *Post-Surrender Tasks,* pp. 282-85.

8. Jan Pluvier, *South East Asia from Colonialism to Independence,* pp. 359-62.

9. Josef Silverstein, "The Importance of the Japanese Occupation of Southeast Asia," pp. 1-12; Benedict R.O'G. Anderson, "Japan: The Light of Asia," pp. 13-15.

10. George S. Kanahele, "The Japanese Occupation of Indonesia," pp. 1-115, 235-43; Bernard Dahm, *Sukarno,* pp. 285-90; F.C. Jones, *Japan's New Order,* pp. 370-79; Willard H. Elsbree, *Japan's Role,* pp. 96-132; Herbert Feith, *The Decline of Constitutional Democracy in Indonesia,* pp. 5-11; Anderson, "Japan: The Light of Asia," pp. 17-27.

11. Benedict R. O'G. Anderson, *Some Aspects of Indonesian Politics under the Japanese Occupation,* pp. 94-126; Dahm, *Sukarno,* pp. 225-49; Jones, *Japan's New Order,* pp. 380-81.

It has been argued that the wartime American policy was consistently hostile to the Dutch position in the East Indies. According to such an interpretation, the United States ignored the colonial reform promised by Dutch officials, failed to respond to Dutch requests for assistance in transporting troops, and transferred the East Indies to the SEAC command fully aware that Mountbatten lacked adequate shipping and troops. As a result, the United States was responsible for the political vacuum which enabled Sukarno to proclaim Indonesian independence. See Wolthuis, "U.S. Foreign Policy towards the Netherlands Indies, 1941-1945," pp. 381-431 *et passim.*

12. Huynh Kim Khanh, "The Vietnamese August Revolution Reinterpreted," pp. 770-71.

13. *Ibid.,* pp. 772-74; Joseph Buttinger, *Vietnam,* 1:225-26, 269-77; Bernard B. Fall, *The Two Viet-Nams,* pp. 61-65.

14. Khanh, "Vietnamese August Revolution Reinterpreted," pp. 768-82; Fall, *Two Viet-Nams*, pp. 60-64.

15. Pluvier, *South-East Asia from Colonialism to Independence*, pp. 363-64; Buttinger, *Vietnam*, 1:292-99; Khanh, "Vietnamese August Revolution Reinterpreted," pp. 761-62, 778-79.

16. King C. Chen, *Vietnam and China*, pp. 90-97; Chester Cooper, *The Lost Crusade*, pp. 25-26; Charles Fenn, *Ho Chi Minh: A Biographical Introduction*, pp. 72-80; Jean Lacouture, *Ho Chi Minh*, pp. 266-69; Robert Shaplen, *The Lost Revolution*, pp. 33-36; Edgar O'Ballance, *The Indo-China War, 1945-1954*, pp. 47-49; Report of Field Mission of Capt. Phelan to HQ, China Theater, Oct. 17, 1945, DOS: 851 G.00/10-1745; Archimedes L.A. Patti, *Why Vietnam?* pp. 45-58.

17. Fenn, *Ho Chi Minh*, pp. 80-83; Chen, *Vietnam and China*, pp. 102-4; U.S. Senate CFR, *The United States and Vietnam, 1944-1947*, p. 3; U.S. Senate, CFR, *Causes, Origins, and Lessons of the Vietnam War*, pp. 243-57.

18. Report No 1 Deer Mission, July 17, 1945, U.S. Senate, CFR, *Causes, Origins, and Lessons of the Vietnam War*, pp. 244-47.

19. Thomas to Wampler, July 20, 1945, *ibid.*, p. 248. Some intelligence reports from Indochina in July-August 1945 that recognized the strength of the Viet Minh and extent of anti-French sentiment, also anticipated considerable Chinese influence over Vietnamese nationalism. Military Intelligence Research Project, No. 2428, July 25, 1945, DOS: 740.0011 PW/7-2645; Donovan to Truman, Aug. 21, 1945, HST Papers, OSS Files.

20. Lacouture, *Ho Chi Minh*, p. 271; Paul Mus, *Viet-Nam*, pp. 307-8.

21. Representative of the French viewpoint are: G. Sabattier, *Le Destin de L'Indochine*, pp. 336-38; Michel Deveze, *Le France d'Outre-Mer*, pp. 212-14; Jean Sainteny, *Histoire d'une Paix Manquée*, pp. 62-70, 94-95, 124-27; Jean Chesneaux, *The Vietnamese Nation*, pp. 158-67, 219; Phillippe Devillers, *Historie de Viêt-Nam de 1940 a 1952*, pp. 116, 133, 149-51, 202-3, 382; Paul Isoart, *Le Phénomène National Vietnamien*, pp. 329, 340-41, 349; Lucien Bodard, *The Quicksand War*, p. 221.

On the "lost opportunity" viewpoint see: Harold Isaacs, *No Peace for Asia*; Shaplen, *Lost Revolution*, pp. 28-35; Cooper, *Lost Crusade*, pp. 49-50; Chen, *Vietnam and China*, pp. 335-36; Fenn, *Ho Chi Minh*, pp. 83-85.

22. Langdon to Byrnes, Aug. 16, 1945, DOS: 851G.00/8-1645.

23. Report of Deer Mission, Sept. 17, 1945, U.S. Senate, CFR, *Causes, Origins, and Lessons of Vietnam War*, pp. 258-64; Chen, *Vietnam and China*, pp. 27-41; Buttinger, *Vietnam* 1:343-44; Shaplen, *Lost Revolution*, pp. 28-30; Bert Cooper, John Killigrew, and Norman LaCharite, *Case Studies in Insurgency and Warfare*, pp. 106.

24. Hurley to Byrnes, Aug. 13, 1945, *FRUS 1945* 7:498-99.

25. Byrnes to Caffery, Aug. 14, 1945, *FRUS 1945* 7:499-500; Hurley to Byrnes, Aug. 17, 1945, *FRUS 1945* 7:503.

26. Donovan to Byrnes, Aug. 22, 1945, U.S. House, CAS, *United States-Vietnam Relations 1945-1967* (Book 1), I-C, pp. 66-68; Sabattier, *Le Destin de L'Indochine*, pp. 335; Sainteny, *Histoire d'une Paix Manquée*, pp. 63-77; Fall, *Two Viet-Nams, pp. 68-70*; Buttinger, *Vietnam*, 1:339-40; Donald Lancaster, *The Emancipation of French Indochina*, pp. 124-25; Patti, *Why Viet Nam?* pp. 151-60.

27. Shaplen, *Lost Revolution*, pp. 41-42.

28. Donovan to Truman, Aug. 22, 1945, HST Papers, OSS Files, U.S. Senate, CFR, *The United States and Vietnam, 1944-1947*, p. 11.

29. DRV Declaration of Independence, Sept. 2, 1945, Allen W. Cameron, ed. *Vietnam Crisis,* 1:52-54; Bernard Fall, "The Political Development of Viet-Nam," pp. 6-11.

30. Decisions of the National Congress of the Indochinese Communist Party, Aug. 13-15, 1945, Democratic Republic of Vietnam, *Breaking Our Chains,* pp. 66-67.

31. Fenn, *Ho Chi Minh,* p. 83; Chen, *Vietnam and China,* p. 108.

32. Chen, *Vietnam and China,* p. 114

33. Chen, *Vietnam and China,* p. 115-54; *New York Times,* Sept. 17-19, 1945; Buttinger, *Vietnam,* 1:337-63; Cooper, Killigrew and LaCharite, *Case Studies in Insurgency and Warfare,* p. 109, O'Ballance, *Indo-China War,* pp. 55-56; Ellen J. Hammer, *The Emergence of Viet Nam,* p. 31; Patti, *Why Viet Nam?* pp. 343-62.

34. Chen, *Vietnam and China,* pp. 118-27; Charles de Gaulle, *War Memoirs,* p. 261.

35. Frank S. V. Donnison, *British Military Administration in the Far East,* pp. 404-7; Mountbatten, *Post-Surrender Tasks,* pp. 285-88.

36. Affidavit of Blueschel, Oct. 13, 1945, U.S. Senate, CFR, *Causes, Origins, and Lessons of the Vietnam War,* pp. 286-91; Investigation of Death of Dewey, Oct. 25, 1945, *ibid.,* pp. 296-98; Report OSS Detachment 404, Sept. 30, 1945, *ibid.,* pp. 283-84; Testimony of White and Moffat, May 11, 1972, *ibid.,* pp. 183-84; Lancaster, *Emancipation of Indochina,* pp. 132-33; SAC SEAC (Dening) to Foreign Office, Sept. 21, 1945, FO 371/ 46308.

37. U.S. House, CAS, *United States and Vietnam, 1944-1947,* pp. 4-6; Lacouture, *Ho Chi Minh,* pp. 268-72; Buttinger, *Vietnam,* 1:340-41; Shaplen, *Lost Revolution,* pp. 4-43; Chen, *Vietnam and China,* pp. 116-17; Sainteny, *Histoire d'une Paix Manquee,* pp. 124-27.

38. Donovan to Truman, Sept. 5, 1945, HST Papers, OSS Files; Donvan to Truman, Sept. 17, 1945, HST Papers; Sprouse to Byrnes, Sept. 27, 1945, DOS: 851G.00/9-2745; OSS, China Theater, SI Branch, APC 627, Sept. 19, 1945, U.S. Senate, CFR, *Causes, Origins, and Lessons of the Vietnam War,* pp. 304-5; Testimony of White and Moffat, May 11, 1972, *ibid.,* p. 188; U.S. Senate, CFR, *United States and Vietnam, 1944-47,* pp. 5-6; Shaplen, *Lost Revolution,* p. 42; Buttinger, *Vietnam,* 1:43.

39. OSS, China Theater, SI Branch, APC 627, Sept. 19, 1945, U.S. Senate, CFR, *Causes, Origins, and Lessons of the Vietnam War,* pp. 306-7.

40. OSS, China Theater, SI Branch, APC 627, Sept. 20, 1945, U.S. Senate, CFR, *Causes, Origins, and Lessons of the Vietnam War,* pp. 308-11; Political Information Report: Indochina, Oct. 17, 1945, *ibid.,* pp. 312-26.

41. Donovan to Truman, Sept. 27, 1945, HST Papers, OSS Files; Donovan to Truman, Sept. 28, 1945, *ibid.*

42. Report by Hale, Oct. 2, 1945, U.S. Senate, CFR, *United States and Vietnam, 1944-1947,* pp. 23-31.

43. Cheston to Truman, Sept. 25, 1945, HST Papers, OSS Files; Robertson to Byrnes, Nov. 8, 1945, DOS: 851G.00/11-845; Robertson to Byrnes, Oct. 18, 1945, DOS: 851G.00/10-1845; Sprouse to Byrnes, Oct. 24, 1945, DOS: 851G.00/12-2445; Ho Chi Minh to Truman via Kunming, Oct. 17, 1945, Oct. 24, 1945, U.S. House, CAS, *United States-Vietnam Relations 1945-1967,* Book 1, I-C, 73-74, 80-81; Smyth to Byrnes, Nov. 26, 1945, U.S. House, CAS, *United States-Vietnam Relations,* pp. 89-90; Robertson to Byrnes, Nov. 23, 1945, *ibid.,* pp. 87-88; U.S. Senate, CFR, *United States and Vietnam, 1944-1947,* pp. 5-12.

44. Testimony of Moffat and White, May 11, 1972, U.S. Senate, CFR, *Causes, Origins, and Lessons of the Vietnam War,* pp. 187-88, 201-2. Officers in the Division of European affairs questioned the propriety of the Army and the OSS in transmitting messages from the DRV and took the initiative in establishing the practice of filing and not acknowleding such messages. Memorandum by Division of European Affairs (Bonbright), Dec. 5, 1945, DOS: 851G.00/10-2245.

45. Bishop to Byrnes, Byrnes to Bishop, Aug. 29, 1945, Allen W. Cameron, ed., *Vietnam Crisis* 1:51-52; Acheson to Robertson, Oct. 5, 1945, *FRUS 1945* 6:313; de Gaulle, *War Memoirs,* pp. 242-43.

46. Memorandum of Conversation (Moffat), Aug. 14, 1945, DOS: 851G.00/8-1845; Caffery to Byrnes, Sept. 14, 1945, DOS: 851G.00/9-1445; Sterndale-Bennett to Price, Sept. 25, 1945, FO 371/46308; Price to Sterndale-Bennett, Oct. 1, 1945, FO 371/46308; Extract DO (45) 7th Meeting, Oct. 5, 1945, PREM 8/63.

47. Memorandum of Conversation (Vincent), Sept. 24, 1945, *FRUS 1945* 6:313; Caffery to Byrnes, Oct. 12, 1945, *FRUS 1945* 6:314; Mountbatten, *Post-Surrender Tasks,* p. 288.

48. Caffery to Byrnes, Aug. 16, 1945, *FRUS 1945* 4:703-5.

49. Caffery to Byrnes, Sept. 1, 1945, DOS: 851G.01/9-1445; Memorandum of Conversation (Dunn), Aug. 29, 1945, *FRUS 1945* 7: 540-42.

50. Byrnes to Hurley, Aug. 31, 1945, *FRUS 1945* 7:513; French Military Mission to CCS, Aug. 27, 1945, JCS Files/CCS 370 France; CCS to French Military Mission, JCS Files/CCS 370; Caffery to Byrnes, Sept. 13, 1945, DOS: 851G/009-1345; Caffery to Byrnes, Sept. 22, 1945, DOS: 851G.00/9-2245; Memorandum of Conversation by Bonbright, DOS: 851G.00/9-1745; Sainteny, *Histoire d'une Paix Manquee,* p. 100; *New York Times,* Oct. 5, 1945.

51. Donovan to Truman, Aug. 30, 1945, HST Papers, OSS Files; Donovan to Truman, Aug. 31, 1945, *ibid.;* Oakes to Byrnes, Sept. 6, 1945, DOS: 851G.00/9-645; Byrnes to New Delhi Mission, Sept. 22, 1945, DOS: 851G.00/9-645.

52. Vincent to Acheson, Sept. 28, 1945, DOS: 851G.00/9-2845; Bonbright to Acheson, Sept. 29, 1945, DOS: 851G.00/9-2945; Bonbright to Acheson, Oct. 2, 1945, DOS: 851G.00/10-245.

53. U.S. Senate, CFR, *United States and Vietnam 1944-1947,* pp. 6-7; Lacouture, *Ho Chi Minh,* pp. 271-72.

54. Report by Hale, Oct. 1945, U.S. Senate, CFR, *United States and Vietnam 1944-1947,* p. 32

55. Smyth to Byrnes, Nov. 26, 1945, U.S. House, CAS, *United States-Vietnam Relations 1945-1967* (Book 1), I-C, pp. 89-92.

56. Testimony of White, May 11, 1972, U.S. Senate, CFR, *Causes, Origins, and Lessons of the Vietnam War,* pp. 144-55; U.S. Senate, CFR, *United States and Vietnam, 1944-1947,* pp. 11-12.

57. U.S. Senate, CFR, *United States and Vietnam 1944-1947,* p. 5.

58. Memorandums of Conversations with Nordlinger, Patti, Garden by Sharp, Dec. 5, 1945, DOS: 851G.00/12-545.

59. Report by Hale, Oct. 16, 1945, U.S. Senate, CFR, *United States and Vietnam, 1944-1947,* pp. 23-36. In early December, the State Department also received a lengthy report from Foreign Service Officer, Charles Millett, who had been in Hanoi two months earlier. Millett was notably less favorably disposed toward the Viet Minh than

his American colleagues and stressed, among other points, divisions within the ranks of Vietnamese nationalists. Butrick to Byrnes, Dec. 1, 1945, DOS: 851G.00/12-1245. Memorandum of Conversation (Cady), Dec. 12, 1945, DOS: 851G.00/12-1245.

60. Memorandum of Conversation (Sharp), Jan. 30, 1946, *FRUS 1946* 8:15-20. Gallagher's views were summarized for higher officers; Vincent to Acheson, Feb. 8, 1946, DOS: 851G.01/2846. Before leaving Indochina, Gallagher had been instrumental in resolving a disagreement between the French and Chinese, which had led to Viet Minh organized protests and boycotts, over the validity, distribution, and exchange rate of the Vietnamese currency. It seemed to the French that, as in other matters, Gallagher had been preferential toward the Viet Minh. Chen, *Vietnam and China,* pp. 137-39.

61. Robert J. McMahon, "Anglo-American Diplomacy and the Reoccupation of the Netherlands Indies," pp. 7-14; David Wehl, *The Birth of Indonesia,* pp. 43-44; Mountbatten, *Post-Surrender Tasks,* pp. 289-93; Dahm, *Sukarno,* pp. 323-25; Hornbeck to Byrnes, Oct. 5, 1945, DOS: 856D.01/10-545; Hornbeck to Byrnes, Nov. 8, 1945, *FRUS 1945* 6:1172-73.

62. Memorandum, Division of Northern European Affairs (Cumming), Oct. 8, 1945, *FRUS 1945* 6: 1158-63; Memorandum of Conversation, Oct. 10, 1945, *FRUS 1945* 6:1163-64; Memorandum of Conversation (Moffat), Oct. 18, 1945, *FRUS 1945* 6: 1165-67; Donovan to Truman, Sept. 26, 1945, HST Papers, OSS Files; Foote to Byrnes, Oct. 25, 1945, DOS: 856E.00/1-2545; Gallman to Byrnes, Oct. 15, 1945, DOS: 856E.00/10-1545; Summary of War Dept. Cable from Kandy, Sept. 29, 1945, DOS: 856D.01/9-2945.

63. Memorandum of Conversation (Vincent), Oct. 22, 1945, *FRUS 1945* 6:1167-68; Sukarno to Truman, Oct. 25, 1945, DOS: 856E.00/10-2645; Foote to Byrnes, Oct. 26, 1945, DOS: 856E.00/10-2645; Byrnes to Foote, Oct. 31, 1945, DOS: 856E.00/10-2845.

64. Benedict R.O'G. Anderson, *Java in a Time of Revolution,* pp. 180-95.

65. McMahon, "Anglo-American Diplomacy," pp. 16-17; Byrnes to Winant, Oct. 13, 1945, *FRUS 1945* 6:1164; Vincent to Acheson, Oct. 10, 1945, DOS: PSEA, Box 11; Memorandum, Northern European Affairs to Southeast Asian Affairs, Nov. 27, 1945, DOS: PSEA, Box 11; Memorandum by Moffat, Dec. 18, 1945, DOS: PSEA, Box 11; Hornbeck to Byrnes, Dec. 10, 1945, 856E.00/12-1045; Byrnes to Yost, Dec. 15, 1945, DOS: 856E.00/12-1245; *New York Times,* Jan. 1, 1946.

66. Memorandum of Conversation (Moffat), Nov. 8, 1945, *FRUS 1945* 6:1170-72; Winant to Byrnes, Nov. 7, 1945, *FRUS 1945* 6:1168-69.

67. Byrnes to Winant, Nov. 20, 1945, *FRUS 1945* 6:1173; Vincent to Byrnes, Nov. 14, 1945 DOS: PSEA, Box 12; Feith, *Decline of Constitutional Democracy,* pp. 8-9.

68. Winant to Byrnes, Dec. 1, 1945, *FRUS 1945* 6:1175; Memorandum of Conversation (Moffat), Dec. 6, 1945, *FRUS 1945* 6:1178-80; Memorandum of Conversation (Byrnes), Dec. 10, 1945, *FRUS 1945* 6: 1181; Acheson to Foote, Dec. 19, 1945, *FRUS 1945* 6:1182-83; Memorandum of Conversation (Cady), DOS: 856E.00/12-145; Vincent to Hickerson, Dec. 11, 1945, *DOS:* 856E.00/12-1145; *New York Times,* Dec. 20, 1945; Rajendra Singh, *Post-War Occupation Forces,* pp. 224-32.

69. Mountbatten, *Post-Surrender Tasks,* pp. 308-12.

70. Memorandum of Conversation (Vincent), Feb. 7, 1946, *FRUS 1946* 8:804-6; Alistair M. Taylor, *Indonesian Independence,* p. 384.

71. Hornbeck to Byrnes, March 8, 1946, DOS: 856D.00/3-846; Harriman to Byrnes, Nov. 19, 1945, DOS: 856E.00/11-1945; Harriman to Byrnes, Dec. 10, 1945, DOS: 856E.00/12-1045; Harriman to Byrnes, Jan. 5, 1946, DOS: 856E.00/1-546; Council of

Foreign Ministers Summary Minutes, Dec. 16, 1945, HST Papers, PSF: Foreign Affairs, Box 177; *New York Times,* Nov. 5, 1945; McVey, *The Soviet View of the Indonesian Revolution,* pp. 1-16.

72. Pluvier, *Southeast Asia from Colonialism to Independence,* pp. 420-23; Anderson, *Java in a Time of Revolution,* pp. 405-9.

73. Robert J. McMahon, *Colonialism and Cold War,* pp. 114-36; Pluvier, *Southeast Asia from Colonialism to Independence,* pp. 409-13, 427-30; Record of Meeting, Dec. 27, 1945, PREM 8/71; Record of Meeting, April 12, 1946, PREM 81/263; Cabinet Conclusions 78 (46) 3, Aug. 14, 1946, CAB 128/6.

74. Byrnes to Hornbeck, Jan. 24, 1946, *FRUS 1946* 8:801; Foote to Byrnes, Feb. 17, 1946, *FRUS 1946* 8:811; Foote to Byrnes, March 8, 1946, *FRUS 1946* 8:813-14; Foote to Byrnes, July 10, 1946, *FRUS 1946* 8:832-33; Foote to Byrnes, Sept. 17, 1946, *FRUS 1946* 8:844; Foote to Byrnes, Dec. 30, 1945, DOS: 856E.00/12-3045; Foote to Byrnes, Jan. 29. 1946, DOS: 856E.00/1-2946; Foote to Byrnes, Feb. 1, 1946, DOS: 856E.00/2-146; Foote to Byrnes, July 12, 1946, DOS: 856E.00/7-1246.

75. Memorandum of Conversation (Lacy), May 15, 1946, DOS: 856E.00/5-1546; Memorandum of Conversation (Wolfe), Feb. 14, 1946, DOS: 856E.00/2-1446; Memorandum of Conversation (Lacy), June 28, 1946, DOS: 856E.00/6-2846.

76. Acheson to Hornbeck, Aug. 5, 1946, *FRUS 1946* 8:840; Foote to Byrnes, Oct. 21, 1946, *FRUS 1946* 8:849-51; Harriman to Byrnes, March 28, 1946, DOS: 856E 00/3-2846; Harriman to Byrnes, April 19, 1946, DOS: 856E.00/4-1946; Smith to Byrnes, April 25, 1946, DOS: 856E.00/4-2546; Smith to Byrnes, June 12, 1946, DOS: 856E.00/7-1746; Smith to Byrnes, July 31, 1946, DOS: 856E.00/7-3146; Memorandum of Conversation (Hickerson), Aug. 15, 1946, DOS: 856D.00/8-1546; Byrnes to Hornbeck, Sept. 20, 1946, DOS: 856E.00/9-2046; Foote to Byrnes, Oct. 23, 1946, DOS: 856E.00/10-2346; Memorandum of Conversation (Lacy), Oct. 31, 1946, DOS: 856D.00/10-3146.

77. Vincent to Hickerson to Acheson, Nov. 27, 1946, *FRUS 1946* 8:853-55; Acheson to Hornbeck, Nov. 19, 1946, *FRUS 1946* 8:852-53.

78. JCS 1200/16; Policy in Indochina, Jan. 28, 1946, JCS Files/CCS France; Memo to British Chiefs of Staff, Dec. 21, 1945, JCS Files/CCS France; Irving, *The First Indochina War,* pp. 13-17; Mountbatten, *Post-Surrender Tasks,* pp. 289-98; Singh, *Post-War Occupation,* pp. 204-6; John T. McAlister, Jr., *Vietnam,* pp. 202-16; COS (46), Feb. 20, 1946, FO 371/54046; JP (46) 30 (Final) Feb. 19, 1946, FO 371/54046.

79. Ellen J. Hammer, *The Struggle for Indochina,* pp. 142-46; Shaplen, *Lost Revolution,* pp. 45-46; McAlistair, *Vietnam,* pp. 238-39; Chen, *Vietnam and China,* pp. 123-30; Fall, "Political Development of Vietnam," pp. 17-20.

80. JSM (Washington) to Cabinet Officers, March 13, 1946, FO 371/53960; Chen, *Vietnam and China,* pp. 132-46.

81. Smyth to Byrnes, Feb. 13, 1946, U.S. House, CAS, *United States-Vietnam Relations, 1945-1967* (Book 1), I-C, 93-94; U.S. Senate, CFR, *United States and Vietnam, 1944-1947,* pp. 11-12; Landon to Byrnes, undated (*ca.* Jan. 27, 1946), *FRUS 1946* 8:20-21; Byrnes to Landon, Jan. 28, 1946, *FRUS 1946* 8:15; Landon to Byrnes, Feb. 5, 1946, *FRUS 1946* 8:23-24; Landon to Vincent, Jan. 24, 1946; DOS: 851G.00/1-2446.

A few days prior to Ho's January 18 appeal to Truman, the *New York Times* carried a story on Ho's interest in securing United Nations intervention and his willingness to cooperate with France provided independence was acknowledged. Ho was described as the "mystery man of the Annamite revolutionary movement." *New York Times,* Jan. 13, 1946.

82. Landon to Byrnes, Feb. 16, 1946, *FRUS 1946* 8:25-26; DRV to Governments of US, UK, USSR and France, Feb. 18, 1946, U.S. House, CAS, *United States-Vietnam Relations 1945-1967* (Book 1), I-C, 98-100; Landon to Moffat, Feb. 19, 1946, DOS: 851G.00/2-1946; Ho Chi Minh to Landon, Feb. 20, 1946, DOS: 851G.00/2-2046; Kenneth Landon, "Southeast Asia and US Foreign Policy," pp. 272-74.

83. Landon to Byrnes, *ca.* Feb. 25, 1946, *FRUS 1946* 8:26-27.

84. *Ibid.;* U.S. Senate, CFR, *United States and Vietnam 1944-1947,* pp. 10-11. At the Foreign Office, the Vietnamese appeals for United Nations intervention elicited the following minutes: "The Annamites have a fairly strong case against the French. It is not impressively stated in these documents. . . . They are not to be despised as propaganda nevertheless. Fortunately they do not require an answer." Minutes on "Indochina's Political Problems," Feb. 16, 1946, FO 371/53958.

85. Hammer, *Struggle for Indochina,* pp. 157-59.

86. *Ibid.,* pp. 150-55; Shaplen, *Lost Revolution,* pp. 43-44; Irving, *First Indochina War,* pp. 17-22; McAlistair, *Vietnam,* pp. 282-84; Chen, *Vietnam and China,* pp. 147-48; O'Ballance, *Indo-China War,* pp. 65-66.

87. Sainteny, *Histoire D'Une Paix Manquée,* p. 167.

88. Byrnes to Certain Officers, April 18, 1946, *FRUS 1946* 8:36; Smyth to Byrnes, March 30, 1946, DOS 851G.00/3-3046; Cooper to Foreign Office, April 3, 1946, FO 371-53962; Chen, *Vietnam and China,* pp. 148-49.

89. Hammer, *Struggle for Indochina,* pp. 159-62; Shaplen, *Lost Revolution,* pp. 11-13; Irving, *First Indochina War,* pp. 22-23.

90. Reed to Byrnes, April 27, 1946, *FRUS 1946* 8:37-38; Reed to Byrnes, *FRUS 1946* 8:39; U.S. Senate, CFR, *United States and Vietnam, 1944-1947,* p. 12.

91. Acheson to Certain Officers, April 30, May 1, 13, and 14, 1946 *FRUS 1946* 8:38-39, 41-42; O'Sullivan to Byrnes, May 8, 1946, DOS: 851G.00/5-846; O'Sullivan to Byrnes, May 28 1946, DOS: 851G.00/5-2846.

92. Reed to Byrnes, March 14, 1946, *FRUS 1946* 8:33; Memoranda of Conversations (Moffat), March 26 and May 9, 1946, *FRUS 1946* 8:33-34, 40; Byrnes to Bonnet, April 10, 1946, *FRUS 1946* 8:34-35; O'Sullivan to Byrnes, April 18, 1946, *FRUS 1946* 8:35-36; O'Sullivan to Byrnes, April 22 and May 1, 1946, *FRUS 1946* 8:36-39; Acheson to Marshall, May 15, 1946, *FRUS 1946* 8:42-43; Smyth to Byrnes, May 22, 1946, *FRUS 1946* 8:45; State Dept. to French Embassy, July 2, 1946, *FRUS 1946* 8:47-48; War Dept.Intelligence Dissemination, A-65963, March 6, 1946, U.S. Senate, CFR, *Causes, Origins, Lessons of Vietnam War,* pp. 331-32; Chen, *Vietnam and China,* pp. 143-45; O'Ballance, *Indo-China War,* pp. 68-73.

93. Shaplen, *Lost Revolution,* pp. 13-14; Hammer, *Struggle for Indochina,* pp. 165-72.

94. Caffery to Byrnes,June 28, July 7, and Aug. 2, 1946, *FRUS1946* 8:47-50; Reed to Byrnes, Aug. 6 and 8, 1946, *FRUS 1946* 8:50-51; Byrnes to Reed, July 19, 1946, DOS: 851G.00/7-1946; O'Sullivan to Byrnes, July 26, 1946, DOS: 851G.00/7-2646; O'Sullivan to Byrnes, July 29, 1946, DOS: 851G.00/7-2946; Reed to Byrnes, Aug. 3, 1946, DOS: 851G.00/8-346.

95. Moffat to Vincent, Aug. 9, 1946, *FRUS 1946* 8:52-54.

96. Caffery to Byrnes, Sept. 11, 1946, *FRUS 1946* 8:58.

97. Caffery to Byrnes, Sept. 12, 1946, U.S. House, CAS, *United States-Vietnam Relations 1945-1967* (Book 1), I-C, pp. 102-4.

98. Shaplen, *Lost Revolution,* pp. 46-47; Irving, *First Indochina War,* pp. 23-28;

Chen, *Vietnam and China,* pp. 149-50; Hammer, *Struggle for Indochina,* pp. 172-74; *New York Times,* Sept. 16, 1946.

99. Chen, *Vietnam and China,* pp. 157-59; Hammer, *Struggle for Indochina,* pp. 175-81; Shaplen, *Lost Revolution,* pp. 49-51.

100. Hammer, *Struggle for Indochina,* pp. 183-89; O'Ballance, *Indo-China War,* pp. 74-77.

101. O'Sullivan to Byrnes, Nov. 23, 1946, DOS: 851G.00/11-2346; O'Sullivan to Byrnes, Nov. 29, 1946, DOS: 851G.00/11-2946; O'Sullivan to Byrnes, Dec. 1, 1946, DOS: 851G.00/12-146; O'Sullivan to Byrnes, Nov. 30, 1946, *FRUS 1946* 8:64; Caffery to Byrnes, Dec. 3 and 4, 1946, *FRUS 1946* 8:65-66.

102. Reed to Byrnes, Dec. 6, 1946, *FRUS 1946* 8:69-70; Letters from Moffat to his wife during visit to Hanoi, Dec. 1946, U.S. Senate, CFR, *United States and Vietnam, 1944-1947,* pp. 36-44.

103. Acheson to Reed, Dec. 5, 1946, *FRUS 1946* 8:67-69.

104. Minute by Allen, Nov. 29, 1946, FO 371/53969; Graves to Foreign Office, Dec. 4, 1946, FO 371/53969; Reed to Byrnes, Dec. 15, 1946, DOS: 851G.00/12-1546; Byrnes to Certain Missions, Dec. 17, 1946, *FRUS 1946* 8:72-73.

105. Memoranda of Conversations (Landon), Dec. 5 and 16, 1946, *FRUS 1946* 8:70, 73; Caffery to Byrnes, Dec. 7 and 21, 1946, *FRUS 1946* 8:70, 75; O'Sullivan to Byrnes, Dec. 16, 1946, *FRUS 1946* 8:71-72; Reed to Byrnes, Dec. 19, 1946, *FRUS 1946* 8:73; Foote to Byrnes, Dec. 19, 1946 *FRUS 1946* 8:74; Memorandum of Conversation (Landon), Dec. 5, 1946, DOS: PSEA Box 9; O'Sullivan to Byrnes, Dec. 6, 1946, DOS: 851G.00/12-546; Reed to Byrnes, Dec. 18, 1946, DOS: 851G.00/12-1846.

106. Vincent to Acheson, Dec. 23, 1946, *FRUS 1946* 8:75-77; Byrnes to Caffery, Dec. 24, 1946, *ibid.,* pp. 77-78.

107. Reed to Byrnes, Dec. 22 (24?), 1946, *FRUS 1946* 8:78-79; Josselyn to Byrnes, Jan. 7, 1947, *FRUS 1947* 6:54-55; O'Sullivan to Byrnes, Jan. 6, 1947, *FRUS 1947* 6:54; Memorandum of Conversation (Landon), Dec. 24, 1946, DOS: PSEA, Box 9; O'Sullivan to Byrnes, Dec. 23, 1946, DOS: 851G.00/12-2346.

On Jan. 7, 1947, the American mission in Bangkok transmitted to Washington appeals from Vietnamese, Cambodian, and Laotian representatives for United Nations intervention. The State Department subsequently instructed Bangkok to return the documents and declined to bring the appeals before the Security Council. Stanton to Byrnes, Jan. 7, 1947, *FRUS 1947* 6:56-57; Byrnes to Stanton, Jan. 8, 1947, DOS: 851G.00/1-747.

108. Vincent to Acheson, Jan. 8, 1947, *FRUS 1947* 6:58-59.

109. *Ibid.* At about this time, French officials began blaming the United States for France's problems in Indochina, asserting that Roosevelt's policies and the actions of the OSS had undermined French authority. For instance, the French chargé at Bangkok took such a line with American officials who sought to express concern over the deteriorating situation in Indochina. Stanton to Byrnes, Jan. 9, 1947, DOS: 851G.00/1-947.

110. Landon to Vincent, Jan. 14, 20, and 21, 1947, DOS: PSEA, Box 9: Gallman to Marshall, Jan. 21, 1947, *FRUS 1947* 6:64-65.

111. Marshall to Caffery, Feb. 3, 1947, *FRUS 1947* 6:67-68.

112. O'Sullivan to Byrnes, Nov. 1, 4, and Dec. 23, 1946, *FRUS 1946* 8:62-63, 77; Reed to Byrnes, Sept. 4, 9, and Dec. 2, 1946, *FRUS 1946* 8:57, 66; Acheson to Reed, Oct. 9, 1946, *FRUS 1946* 8:61; Strategic Service Unit, War Dept., Intelligence Dissemination

nos. A-66610 and 66643, March 26, 1946, U.S. Senate, CFR, *Causes, Origins, and Lessons of Vietnam War*, pp. 337-38; Memorandum of Conversation (Ogburn), Nov. 5, 1946, DOS: 851G.00/11-1546; O'Sullivan to Byrnes, Sept. 14, 1946, DOS: 851G.00/9-1446; Caffery to Byrnes, Sept. 16, 1946, DOS: 851G.00/9-1646; Millett to Byrnes, March 8, 1946, DOS: 851G.00/3-846; Southeast Asia Weekly Review (Ogburn), Oct. 2, 1946, DOS: PSEA, Box 9.

113. Paper, "Ho Chi Minh" (early 1946), DOS: PSEA, Box 9.

114. O'Sullivan to Byrnes, Dec. 3, 1946, *FRUS 1946*, 8:64-65; Reed to Byrnes, Sept. 17, 1946, *FRUS 1946* 8:59; Caffery to Byrnes, Nov. 29, 1946, *FRUS 1946* 8:63; Caffery to Byrnes, Dec. 13, 1946, 851G.00/12-1346; Reed to Byrnes, Aug. 31, 1946, DOS: 851G.00/3-3146; O'Sullivan to Byrnes, Dec. 3, 1946, U.S. Senate, CFR, *United States and Vietnam 1944-1947*, p. 14; Memorandum of Conversation (Ogburn), DOS: PSEA, Box 9; Vincent to Acheson, Oct. 21, 1946, DOS: PSEA, Box 9.

115. Kennan to Byrnes, Sept. 26, 1945, DOS: 851G.01/9-2645; Smith to Marshall, Jan. 7, 1947, DOS: 851G.00/1-747; Smith to Marshall, Jan. 13, 1947, DOS: 851G.00/1-1347; Smith to Marshall, Jan. 28, 1947, DOS:851G.0/12847; Charles B. McLane, *Soviet Strategies in Southeast Asia*, pp. 266-70.

116. Pluvier, *Southeast Asia from Colonialism to Independence*, pp. 413-18.

117. Acheson to Benton, March 12, 1947, *FRUS 1947* 6:905.

118. McMahon, *Colonialism and Cold War*, pp. 142-48.

119. Acheson to Hornbeck, Nov. 19, 1946, *FRUS 1946* 8:852-53; Memorandum of Conversation (Acheson), Nov. 27, 1946, *FRUS 1946* 8:855-56. The State Department had also maintained its vigilence against American supplies being used against the Indonesians. Memorandum of Conversation (Lacy), Feb. 7, 1947, HST Papers, OF Box 4; Acheson to Forrestal, Dec. 10, 1946, DOS: PSEA, Box 11; Draft letter, State Dept. to Netherlands Embassy, Feb. 21, 1947, DOS: PSEA, Box 11.

120. Foote to Byrnes, Dec. 2, 1946, *FRUS 1946* 8:745-58; Foote to Marshall, Jan. 9, 13, 23, and April 8, 1947, *FRUS 1947*, 6:891-96; Acheson to Embassy in Netherlands, April 9, 18, 23, 1947, *FRUS 1947* 6:916-19; Acheson to Foote, April 3, 1947, *FRUS 1947* 6:912; Benton to Marshall, April 5, 1947, *FRUS 1947* 6:914; Foote to Marshall, Jan. 14, 1947, DOS: 856E.01/4-847; Memorandum of Conversation (Lacy), April 14, 1947, DOS: 856E.01/4-847; Foote to Marshall, April 16, 1947, DOS: 856E.01/4-1647; Foote to Marshall, July 2, 1947, DOS: 856E.01/7-347.

121. Marshall to Embassy in Netherlands, May 16, 1947, *FRUS 1947* 6:924-26.

122. Baruch to Marshall, May 10, 1947, *FRUS 1947* 6:921-22; Marshall to Foote, May 22, 1947, DOS: 856E.00/5-1047; Memorandum of Conversation (Moffat), May 22, 1947, DOS: 856D.00/5-1047; Marshall to Baruch, May 26, 1947, DOS: 856E.01/5-2647; Hillenkoetter (CIA) to Truman, May 23, 1947, Marshall Papers, Leahy File.

123. Benton to Marshall, March 26, 1947, *FRUS 1947* 6:911; Foote to Marshall, May 17, 23, and 28, 1947, *FRUS 1947* 6:926-27, 929-30.

124. Memorandum by Cumming and Moffat, April 17, 1947, *FRUS 1947* 6:917-18.

125. Baruch to Marshall, June 3, 1947, *FRUS 1947* 6:934-36; Douglas to Marshall, May 29 and June 4, 1947, *FRUS 1947* 6:931, 938-39; Foote to Marshall, June 13, 1947, *FRUS 1947* 6:947-48; Acheson to Foote, June 5, 1947, *FRUS 1947* 6:941-42; British Embassy to Dept. of State, June 4, 1947, *FRUS 1947* 6:939-40; Memoranda of Conversations (Schnee), May 29 and June 6, 1947 *FRUS 1947* 6:924-25; 6:924-25, 932-33; Foote to Marshall, May 31, 1947, DOS: 856E.00/5-3147; Matthews and Vincent to Acheson,

June 5, 1947, DOS: 856D.00/7-547; Memorandum of Conversation (Schnee), June 6, 1947, DOS: 856E.01/6-647; Foote to Marshall, June 7, 1947, DOS: 856E.00/6-747.

126. Memorandums by Marshall, June 16 and 17, 1947, *FRUS 1947* 6:948-50; Marshall to Baruch, June 17, 26, and 28, 1947, *FRUS 1947* 6:950, 960-62; Baruch to Marshall, June 18, 28 and 29, 1947, *FRUS 1947* 6:951-52; 936-67; Marshall to Foote, June 17 and 26 and July 3, 1947 *FRUS 1947* 6:950-51, 959-60, 971-72; Foote to Marshall, June 19, and 30, 1947, *FRUS 1947* 6:952-53, 967-68; Memorandum of Conversation (Moffat), June 20, 1947, *FRUS 1947* 6:953-54; Morgan to Matthews, July 8, 1947, *FRUS 1947* 6:972-73; Memorandum by Moffat, July 8, 1947, DOS: PSEA, Box 12; Foote to Marshall, July 3, 1947, DOS: 856D.99/7-347; Memorandum of Conversation (Allison), June 15, 1947, DOS: 856E.00/6-1547; Vincent to Carter, June 16, 1947, DOS: 856E.00/6-1647; Vincent and Hickerson to Marshall, June 16, 1947, DOS: 856E.00/6-1647.

127. Memorandum of Conversation (Landon), July 9, 1947, *FRUS 1947* 6:974; Matthews to Marshall, July 1, 1947, DOS: 856E.01/6-2947; Vincent to Armour, July 9, 1947, DOS: 856E.00/7-847; Nolting to Dupuy and Metze, July 1, 1947, DOS: PSEA, Box 12: Landon to Vincent, July 18, 1947, DOS: PSEA, Box 12.

128. Marshall to Baruch, July 17, 1947, *FRUS 1947* 6:977-78; Baruch to Marshall, July 20, 1947, 6:982-83 *FRUS 1947;* Memorandum of Conversation (Armour), July 20, 1947, *FRUS 1947* 6:981.

## 7. The United States' Model: Decolonization in the Philippines

1. *New York Times,* Dec. 29, 1941. On the Japanese conquests, see Ronald Spector, *Eagle Against the Sun,* pp. 106-19.

2. Sayre to Hull, Dec. 15, 1941, *FRUS 1942*, 1:882-83; Hull to Steintorf, Dec. 15, 1941, *FRUS 1942*, 1:883; MacArthur to Adams, Jan. 28, 1942, *FRUS 1942*, 1:888-90; Donovan to Roosevelt, Jan. 5, Feb 19 and 21, 1942, FDR Papers, PSF Box 163; Sayre to Roosevelt, Jan. 26, 1942, FDR Papers, PSF Box 64.

3. Quezon to Roosevelt, in MacArthur to Adams, Jan. 28, 1942, *FRUS 1942* 1:888-90; Stimson to Roosevelt, Jan. 30, 1942, *FRUS 1942* 1:89-91; Teodora A. Agoncillo, *The Fateful Years,* 2:892-98.

4. Quezon to Roosevelt, Feb 8 and 10, 1942, *FRUS 1942* 1:894-96.

5. Quezon to Roosevelt, Feb 8 and 10, 1942, *FRUS 1942* 1:894-96; David V. DuFault, "Francis B. Sayre," pp. 415-40.

6. JCS Meeting, Feb. 9, 1942, JCS Files, CCS 371; Marshall to MacArthur, Feb. 9, 1942, *FRUS 1942* 1:897-98; Gerow to Adams, Feb. 11, 1942, *FRUS 1942* 1:899-900; MacArthur to Marshall, Feb 12, 1942, *FRUS 1942* 1:900.

7. Friend, *Between Two Empires,* pp. 211-28; Fifield, *Americans in Southeast Asia,* pp. 11-13.

8. Memorandum by Berle, Jan 19, 1942, Berle Papers, Box 58; Marshall to MacArthur, Feb. 2, 1942, *FRUS 1942* 1:893; Davies to Welles, April 7, 1942, DOS: 811.B.01/469; Welles to Hornbeck, DOS:811.B.01/469; Hamilton to Hornbeck, April 14, 1942, DOS: 811.B.01/470; Hester to Frank, July 19, 1943, Department of Interior Records (National Archives),CCF:3691; Milton W. Meyer, *A Diplomatic History of the Philippine Republic,* pp. 24-25.

Sayre resigned as High Commissioner in June 1942 and was not replaced; the functions of that office were transferred for the course of the war to the Secretary of Interior Harold Ickes. Roosevelt to Ickes, May 27, 1942, FDR Papers, PSF; Ickes to Roosevelt, FDR Papers, OF 400, Box 39, Roosevelt to Hull, June 9, 1942, FDR Papers,

PSF Box 75; Roosevelt to Sayre, June 30, 1942, FDR Papers, OF 400, Box 39; Hull to Roosevelt, July 24, 1942, FDR Papers, OF 400, Box 39; Roosevelt to Ickes, Sept. 16, 1942, FDR Papers, OF 400, Box 39; Quezon to Ickes, June 20, 1942, *FRUS 1942* 1:908-9; Roosevelt to Hull, July 23, 1942, *FRUS 1942* 1:909-10.

9. Berle to Roosevelt, April 16, 1942, Berle Papers, Box 67; Welles to Roosevelt, April 17, 1942, *FRUS 1942* 1:903-04; Roosevelt to Hull, April 22, 1942, *FRUS 1942* 1:906; Hull to Quezon, June 13, 1942, *FRUS 1942* 1:908; Minutes of Pacific War Council, June 7, 1942, FDR Papers, Map Room Files 168.

10. Agoncillo, *Fateful Years*, 2:786-91; Friend, *Between Two Empires*, pp. 229-30; Quezon to MacArthur, May 2, 1943, Douglas MacArthur Papers; Memorandum of Conversation (Welles), Feb 9, 1943, DOS: 811.B.01/476; Ickes to Roosevelt, Feb. 25, 1943, Interior Files, CCF 1937-53, Box 3691; Quezon to Welles, May 3, 1943, DOS: 811B.001/141.

11. Friend, *Between Two Empires*, pp. 234-37; Agoncillo, *Fateful Years*, 2:794-819; Memorandum, Division of Far Eastern Affairs, June 7, 1943, DOS: 811.B./00/613; Memorandum of Conversation (Lockhart), Nov. 4, 1943, DOS: 811B.01/623; Memorandum of Conversation (Long), Nov. 8, 1943, DOS: 811B.00/153; Ickes to Roosevelt, Sept. 1, 1943, DOS: 811.B.01/482; Hull to Roosevelt, Sept. 8, 1943, DOS: 811B.01/482; Stimson to MacArthur, Oct. 27, 1943, MacArthur 1941-45 File, George C. Marshall Papers; Kromer to Chiefs of Staff, Aug. 31, 1943, Map Room Files, Box 99, FDR Papers; *Congressional Record*, 78th Cong., 1st Sess., pp. 9205, 9307 -9, 9352-56, 9376-96.

12. *New York Times*, Aug. 13, 1943.

13. *Congressional Record*, 78th Cong., 1st Sess., pp. 8121, 8173, 9040, 10489, 10564, 7812-13; *Congressional Record*, 78th Cong., 2d Sess., pp. 4836, 6207-8, 6248; Roosevelt Press Conference, March 24, 1944, *Presidential Press Conferences of Franklin D. Roosevelt* (New York: DaCapo Press, 1972), 23: 109-10; *Washington Post*, Sept 30, 1943; Leahy to Roosevelt, Jan. 1, 1944, Leahy File 126, Marshall Papers; Hester to Fortas, Nov. 5, 1943, Interior Files, Fortas Records-Box 9; Marshall to MacArthur, Nov.1, 1943, MacArthur 1941-45 File, Marshall Papers; Ickes to Roosevelt, Sept. 1, 1943 and Hull to Roosevelt, Sept. 8, 1943, DOS: 811.B.01/482; Memorandum of Conversation (Hiss), Sept. 23, 1943, Hornbeck to Hull, Sept. 25, 1943, Memorandum by Lockhart, Oct. 1, 1943, Memorandum by Long, Oct. 2, 1943, and Lockhart to Stettinius, Oct. 8, 1943, DOS: 811.B.01/623; Fortas to Lockhart, Sept. 27, 1943, DOS: 811.B.01/624; Memorandum of Conversation (Hiss), Oct. 6, 1943, DOS: 811B.00/145; Memorandum of Conversation (Hawkins), Oct. 29, 1943, DOS: 811.B.00/156.

14. Steintorf to Grew, Oct. 10, 1944, DOS: 811B.00/10-1044; Stimson to Ickes, Oct. 5, 1944, FDR Papers, PSF Box 64; Memorandum of Conversation, July 19, 1944, MacArthur Papers, RG 4 USAFPAC Correspondence-Philippine Govt.

15. Friend, *Between Two Empires*, pp. 173-82, 232-41; David Steinberg, *Philippine Collaboration in World War II*, pp. 71-98; David Steinberg, "The Philippine 'Collaborators'" pp. 67-70; Garel A. Grunder and William Livezey, *The Philippines and the United States*, pp. 255-58; Elmer Lear, *The Japanese Occupation of the Philippines* pp. 18-29, 222-38 *et passim.*; Pluvier, *Southeast Asia from Colonialism to Independence*, pp. 228-34. The Japanese perspective on the independence issue is explored by Iriye, *Power and Culture*, pp. 112-19.

16. Quezon to Roosevelt, July 18, 1944, FDR Papers, OF 400; Agoncillo, *Fateful Years*, 2:909-17.

17. Angoncillo, *The Fateful Years*, 2:763-77; Pluvier, *Southeast Asia from*

*Colonialism to Independence,,* pp. 5-11; Hartendorp, *The Japanese Occupation of the Philippines,* 2:640-45; Meyer, *Diplomatic History of Philippine Republic,* pp. 55-58; JCS Staff Plan for Recapture of Luzon, May 20, 1944, JCS Files/CCS 381 Philippine Islands.

18. Steinberg, *Philippine Collaboration,,* pp. 122-23; Steinberg, "Philippine 'Collaborators'," p. 74; *New York Times,* March 17, 1946.

19. Steinberg, "Philippine 'Collaborators'," pp. 71-74; Friend, *Between Two Empires,* pp. 247-53; Hartendorp, *Japanese Occupation of Philippines,* 2:635-37; Steintorf to Stettinius, May 2, 1945, DOS: 811.B.00/5-245; Steintorf to Stettinius, June 8, 1945, DOS: 811.B.00/6-845; Vinson to Truman, Aug. 30, 1945, HST Papers, PSF Foreign Affairs File-Box 185; Memorandum of Conversation (Taussig), Jan. 25, 1945, Taussig Papers, Box 49.

20. Roosevelt Press Conference, April 5, 1945, *Press Conferences of Roosevelt,* 25: 113-14, SC Document 64, Feb. 24, 1945, DOS: Inter-Intra; Staff Comm. Minutes, Feb. 26, 1945, DOS: SC; Ickes to Roosevelt, March 22 and April 6, 1945, FDR Papers OF 400-Box 39, Stettinius to Steintorf, April 13, 1945 and Steintorf to Stettinius, April 14, 1945, DOS: 811.B.01/4-1345; Steintorf to Stettinius, March 21, 1945, *FRUS 1945,* 6:1195-96.

21. Truman Statement, May 5, 1945, *FRUS 1945* 6:1199-1200; Memorandum on Meeting, April 17, 1945, HST Papers, PSF Foreign Affairs File-Box 185; Osmena to Truman, May 3, 1945, HST Papers; Stettinius to Truman, April 19, 1945, Stettinius Papers, Box 734.

22. *New York Times,* July 1, 1944.

23. George E. Taylor, *The Philippines and the United States,* pp. 108-18; Hartendorp, *Japanese Occupation of Philippines,* 2:637-42; Steinberg, "Philippine 'Collaborators'," pp. 68-71; Memorandum of Conversation (Steintorf), Dec. 6, 1944, DOS: 740. 0011PW/12-644; Mills to Lockhart, June 19, 1945, DOS: 811.B.00/5-545.

24. Steintorf to Byrnes, Aug 13, 1945, *FRUS 1945,* 6:1231-32; Acheson to Steintorf, Sept. 10, 1945, *FRUS 1945* 6:1233; Ickes to Osmena, Sept. 11, 1945, *FRUS 1945* 6:1233-34; Steintorf to Byrnes, Sept. 5, 1945, and Ballantine to Acheson, Sept. 7, 1945, DOS: 811B.00/9-545.

25. Osmena to Ickes, Sept. 12, 1945, *FRUS 1945,* 6:1234-35; Steintorf to Byrnes, Sept. 15, 1945, *FRUS 1945,* 6:1235.

26. Steinberg, *Philippine Collaboration,* pp. 125-26; Steintorf to Byrnes, Sept. 17, 1945, DOS: 811B.00/9-1745; Steintorf to Byrnes, Sept. 19, 1945, DOS: 811B.00/9-1945; David Bernstein, *The Philippine Story,* pp. 210-12.

27. McNutt and Fortas to Truman, Sept. 29, 1945, Rosenman Papers, Philippine Folder.

28. Fortas to Ickes, Oct. 1, 1945, Interior Files, CCF-3692.

29. Hasset to Latta, Aug. 20, 1945, HST Papers, OF 1055; Fortas to Truman, Sept. 12, 1945, *ibid.;* Ickes to Truman, Nov. 7, 1945, *ibid.;* McNutt to Truman, Nov. 13, 1945, *ibid.;* Truman to Osmena, Nov. 14, 1945, *ibid.;* Truman to Clark, Oct. 25, 1945, *ibid.;* Gardner to Ickes, Nov. 8 and 16, 1945, Gardner Papers, Philippines Folder; Memorandum of Conversation (Mill), Nov. 2, 1945 DOS: 811B.01/11-245; Steinberg. *Philippine Collaboration,* pp. 127-28; *Congressional Record,* 79th Congress, 1st Sess., pp. 10893, 11470, 12136.

30. I. George Blake, *Paul V. McNutt,* pp. 227-373; Ickes to Roosevelt, Feb. 6, 1945, FDR Papers, Map Room Box 21; Philips to Stettinius, May 9, 1945, *FRUS 1945*

6:1200-01; Memorandum by Lockhart, April 21, 1945, *FRUS 1945* 6:1197-99; Memorandum on Philippines, May 1, 1945, Marshall Papers, Philippine File; Ickes to Truman, July 17, 1945, Interior Files, CCF-3692; DuFault, "Francis B. Sayre," pp. 449-61.

31. Blake, *Paul V. McNutt,* pp. 348-50; Lockhart to Acheson, Dec. 26, 1945 and Moffat to Acheson, Dec. 27, 1945, DOS: 811B.01/12-2645; Acheson to Lockhart, Jan. 2, 1945, DOS: 811B.01/1-246; Steintorf to Byrnes, Jan. 11, 1946, DOS: 81B.01/1-1146; Grunder and Livezey, *Philippines and the United States,* pp. 248-49; Patricio R. Minot, "Paul V. McNutt," pp. 149-81.

32. Steinberg, *Philippine Collaboration,* pp. 132-34; Clark to Truman, March 1, 1946, HST Papers, PSF-Box 185.

33. Clark to Truman, March 1, 1946, and Patterson to Truman, March 4, 1946, HST Papers, PSF-Box 185.

34. MacArthur to Clark and Patterson, March 3, 1946, MacArthur Papers, RG 9 Messages, Blue Binder Series-War Crimes. A copy of MacArthur's message was attached to the Patterson-Truman memorandum of April 4, 1946.

35. Steinberg, *Philippine Collaboration,* pp. 139-63; MacArthur to Patterson, Dec. 14, 1946, MacArthur Papers, RG 9 Messages, Blue Binder Series-Philippine Islands; Roxas to MacArthur, July 3, 1946, *ibid.*

36. Hartendorp, *Japanese Occupation of Philippines,* 2:637-47; Steinberg, *Philippine Collaboration,* pp. 128-30; Steinberg, "Philippine 'Collaborators'," pp. 74-77; Friend, *Between Two Empires,* pp. 254-58.

37. Blake, *McNutt,* pp. 352-60; USAF-Pacific to USNR Liaison Officer, July 17, 1945, DOS: 896.00/7-1745; Steinberg, "Philippine 'Collaborators'," pp. 75-76.

38. Steinberg, *Philippine Collaboration,* pp. 143-44.

39. Friend, *Between Two Empires,* p. 252; Meyer, *Diplomatic History,* pp. 4-6; Mulligan to Tydings, Sept. 28, 1945, Tydings Mission File, Jones Papers; Osmena to Truman, Nov. 9, 1945, HST Papers, PSF-Box 185; *Congressional Record,* 78th Cong., 1st Sess., pp. 10526-528, 10570, 10602, 10795; *Congressional Record,* 78th Cong., 2d Sess., pp. 6208-11, 6248, 6683.

40. Grew to Roosevelt, March 20, 1945, *FRUS 1945* 6:1216-17; Sec. State Staff Comm., March 20 and April 10, 1945, DOS: SC; Meyer, *Diplomatic History,* pp. 9-10.

41. Meyer, pp. 10-11; Legarda and Garcia, "Economic Collaboration," pp. 132-33; Byrnes to Truman, ca. Oct. 1945, HST Papers, PSF-Foreign Affairs Files; Byrnes to Truman, Nov. 8, 1945, HST Papers, OF 1055; Osmena to Truman, Nov. 8, 1945, HST Papers, PSF Box 185; Byrnes to Hawes, Nov. 26, 1945, *FRUS 1945* 6:1219-20.

42. Anderson to Truman, Jan. 7, 1946, *FRUS 1946* 8:861-63; McNutt to Ely, Jan. 18, 1946, *FRUS 1946* 8:863-66; Byrnes to Truman, Jan. 28, 1946, *FRUS 1946* 8:868-89; Meyer, *Diplomatic History,* pp. 11-12; Blake, *McNutt,* pp. 350-63; Minot,"McNutt," pp. 140-49; *Congressional Record,* 79th Cong., 2d Sess., pp. 2753-54, 2758-60, 2760-64, 2824-56, 3533-40, 3985-87.

43. *Congressional Record,* 79th Cong., 1st Sess., p. 11466.

44. *Ibid.,* pp. 11469, 11785, 11036-38; *Congressional Record,* 79th Cong., 2d Sess., pp. 3435-50, 3987, 4038-39, 4266.

45. McNutt to Truman, April 23, 1946, HST Paperss, White House Bill File; Friend, *Between Two Empires,* pp. 258-61; Minot, "McNutt," pp. 108-39; Meyer, *Diplomatic History,* pp. 6-10; McNutt to Truman, Dec. 11, 1945, HST Papers, PSF Box 185.

46. Wallace to Truman, April 19, 1946, HST Papers, OF 1055; Byrnes to Truman,

April 20, 1946, HST Papers, White House Bill File; Appleby to Latta, April 26, 1946, HST Papers; Smith to Latta, April 29, 1946, HST Papers; Byrnes to Truman, April 18, 1946, *FRUS 1946* 8:873-75.

47. Steintorf to Byrnes, April 24, 1946, DOS: 811B.01/4-2446; *Manila Daily Bulletin*, April 16, 1946; *Nation*, June 1, 1946, p. 643; *Manila Chronicle*, June 22, 1946; David Wurfel, "Problems of Decolonization," in Frank H. Golay, ed., *The United States and the Philippines*, pp. 149-52; Grunder and Livezey, *Philippines and United States*, pp. 262-64; Legarda and Garcia, "Economic Collaboration," pp. 133-34; Sung Yong Kim, *United States-Philippine Relations*, pp. 3-8; Teodora V. Cortes, "Interaction Patterns," pp. 113-39.

48. Fifield, *Diplomacy of Southeast Asia*, pp. 63-64; Meyer, *Diplomatic History*, pp. 13-15; Kim, *United States-Philippine Relations*, pp. 4-6; Memorandum by Fetter, May 14, 1946, *FRUS 1946* 8:878-79.

49. Meyer, *Diplomatic History*, pp. 15-16; Grew to Truman, May 3, 1945, HST Papers, PSF Box 185; Forrestal to Truman, ca. May 1945, HST Papers, PSF Box 185; Stimson to Truman, May 14, 1945, HST Papers, PSF Box 185; Stettinius to Truman, April 22, 1945, Stettinius Papers, Box 734; Stimson to Truman, May 11, 1945, Marshall Papers, Box 96-A; SWNCC Minutes, May 2, 1946, DOS: SWNCC Box 1, SWNCC Summary Actions and Decision, Series 38, DOS: SWNCC Box 3; SWNCC Summary Actions and Decisions, Series 276, DOS: SWNCC Box 4; Memorandum of Conversation (Grew), May 14, 1945, *FRUS 1945* 6:1207-9.

50. Memorandum by Vincent, June 6, 1946, *FRUS 1946* 8:880-81; State Dept. Memorandum, June 14, 1946, *FRUS 1946* 8:885-86; Acheson to McNutt, July 2, 1946, *FRUS 1946* 8:895; Entry of July 5, 1946, Millis, ed., *Forrestal Diaries*, 5:1126-27; *Congressional Record*, 79th Cong., 2d Sess., pp. 6704, 6966-68, 7045, 8298; Meyer, *Diplomatic History*, p. 17.

51. Meyer, pp. 58-60.

52. All-India Congress Committee, *Congress Bulletin*, Aug. 3, 1946.

53. Meyer, *Diplomatic History*, pp. 48-53.

54. McNutt to Truman, July 3, 1946, Jones Papers, War Damage and Rehabilitation File; Roxas to Truman, July 3, 1946, Jones Papers; Memorandum to Truman, Aug. 20, 1946, HST Papers, PSF Box 185; McNutt to Ely, July 14, 1946, *FRUS 1946* 8:883-84; McNutt to Byrnes, Sept. 14, 1946, *FRUS 1946* 8:916-17; Clayton to McNutt, Sept. 17, 1946, *FRUS 1946* 8:918; Byrnes to McNutt, Dec. 30, 1946, *FRUS 1946* 8:942; McNutt to Byrnes, Dec. 31, 1946, *FRUS 1946* 8:942-43.

55. McNutt to Byrnes, Sept. 16, 1946, *FRUS 1946* 8:917; McNutt to Byrnes, Sept. 25, 1946, *ibid.*, p. 919; McNutt to Byrnes, Sept. 30, 1946, *ibid.*, p. 920; Acheson to McNutt, Oct. 15, 1946, *ibid.*, pp. 921-22; McNutt to Byrnes, Sept. 7, 1946, *ibid.*, pp. 907-9; Memorandum of Conversation (Ely), Nov. 19, 1946, *ibid.*, p. 932; Davies to Byrnes, Nov. 27, 1946, *ibid.*, p. 933; McNutt to Byrnes, Nov. 7, 1946, *ibid.*, p. 924; McNutt to Byrnes, Nov. 10, 1946, *ibid.*, p. 926.

56. Patterson to Byrnes, Nov. 29, 1946, *FRUS 1946* 8:934-35; Memorandum by Byrnes, Dec. 1, 1946, *ibid.*, p. 935; McNutt to Byrnes, Dec. 23, 1946, *ibid.*, pp. 939-40; Patterson to Byrnes, Dec. 27, 1946, *ibid.*, pp. 940-41; Acheson to McNutt, Jan. 14, 1947, *FRUS 1947* 6:1102-3; SWNCC Summary Actions and Decisions, 340 Series, DOS: SWNCC Box 4; Meyer, *Diplomatic History*, pp. 41-48; Fifield, *Diplomacy of Southeast Asia*, pp. 62-63; Kim, *United States-Philippine Relations*, pp. 407; Vincent to Acheson, Nov. 20, 1946, DOS: 896.00/11/2046; Cortes, "Interaction Patterns," pp. 67-108.

57. Hernando J. Abaya, *Betrayal in the Philippines*, pp. 21-150, 175-223, 255-70; Bernstein, *Philippine Story*, pp. ix-xii, 203-70; Taylor, *Philippines and the United States*, pp. 109-115; Friend, *Between Two Empires*, pp. 252-53.

58. McNutt to Byrnes, Sept. 8, 1946, *FRUS 1946* 8:909-10; Edelstein to Byrnes, Aug. 24, 1946, DOS: 896.00/9-446; Davies to Byrnes, Sept. 4, 1946, DOS: 896.00/9-446.

## 8. The Emergence of United States' Influence in Thailand, Burma, and Malaya, 1945–1948

1. Byrnes to Winant, Aug. 15, 1945, *FRUS 1945* 6:1278-79; State Dept. Memo Aug. 18, 1945, *FRUS 1945* 6:1281-82; British Embassy to State Dept., *FRUS 1945* 6:1283-90; State Dept. to British Embassy, Aug. 31, 1945, *FRUS 1945* 6:1296-1303; SWNCC 177, Aug. 23, 1945, JCS Files/CCS 092 Thailand S.1; Landon to SWNCC, DOS: 892.01/8-2345; Fine, "Liquidation of World War II in Thailand," pp. 71-72.

2. Fine, "Liquidation of World War II in Thailand," pp. 73-75; Merrell to Byrnes, Sept. 6, 1945, *FRUS 1945* 6:1305-6; Memorandum of Conversation (Moffat), Sept. 6, 1945, *FRUS 1945* 6:1306-7; Sansom to Moffat, Sept. 6, 1945, *FRUS 1945* 6:1307-8; Winant to Byrnes, Sept. 6, 1945, *FRUS 1945* 6:1308; British Embassy to State Dept., Sept. 8, 1945, *FRUS 1945* 6:1309-14; British Embassy to State Dept., Sept. 10, 1945, *FRUS 1945* 6:1316-22; State Dept. to British Embassy, Sept. 19, 1945, *FRUS 1945* 6:1323-30; Donovan to Truman, Sept. 6, 1945, HST Papers, OSS Files; Cheston to Truman, Sept. 10, 1945, HST Papers, OSS Files; US Army Liaison Kandy to CG, US Forces, I-B Theater, Sept. 7, 1945; CG, US Forces, I-B Theater to CG, SEAC, Sept. 8, 1945, JSC Files/CCS 092 Thailand S.2; US Army Liaison Kandy to War Dept., Sept. 9, 1945, *ibid.*

3. Yost to Byrnes, Sept. 24, 1945, *FRUS 1945* 6:1332-33; Yost to Byrnes, Sept. 26, 1945, *FRUS 1945* 6:1339; British Embassy to State Dept., Sept. 29, 1945, *FRUS 1945* 6:1342-46; Acheson to Winant, Oct. 2, 1945, *FRUS 1945* 6:1348; State Dept. to British Embassy, Oct. 9, 1945, *FRUS 1945* 6:1352-55; Vincent to Acheson, Oct. 31, 1945, *FRUS 1945* 6:1363-64; Byrnes to Yost, Dec. 31, 1945, *FRUS 1945* 6:1413-14; State Dept. to British Embassy, Oct. 25, 1945, *FRUS 1945* 6:1360-63; Cheston to Truman, Sept. 25, 1945, HST Papers, OSS Files; Fine, "Liquidation of World War II in Thailand," pp. 74-78.

4. Yost to Byrnes, Nov. 23, 1945, DOS: 892.01/11-2345; Yost to Byrnes, Nov. 24, 1946, DOS: 892.01/11-2445; Yost to Byrnes, Dec. 13, 1945, *FRUS 1945* 6:1388-90.

5. British Embassy to State Dept., Nov. 12, 1945, *FRUS 1945* 6:1367-69; State Dept. to British Embassy, Nov. 23, 1945, *FRUS 1945* 6:1371-73; State Dept. to British Embassy, Nov. 29, 1945, *FRUS 1945* 6:1377-80; Memorandum of Communication to British Embassy, Nov. 29, 1945, *FRUS 1945* 6:1381; Fine, "Liquidation of World War II in Thailand," pp. 78-81.

6. British Embassy to State Dept., Dec. 10, 1945, *FRUS 1945* 6:1385-86; Acheson to Yost, Dec. 13, 1945, *ibid.*, p. 1390; Acheson to Winant, Dec. 13, 1945, *ibid.*, pp. 1391-97; Yost to Brynes, Dec. 14, 1945, *ibid.*, p. 1397; Acheson to Mallon, Dec. 14, 1945, *ibid.*, p. 1398; Yost to Brynes, Dec. 15, 1945, *ibid.*, pp. 1398-99.

7. British Embassy to State Dept., Dec. 18, 1945, *FRUS 1945* 6:1400; Winant to Brynes, Dec. 18, 1945, *FRUS 1945* 6:1401; Acheson to Winant, Dec. 19, 1945, *FRUS 1945* 6:1404; Acheson to Yost, Dec. 22, 1945, *FRUS 1945* 6:1406-7; Fine, "Liquidation of World War II in Thailand," pp. 80-82.

8. Pluvier, *Southeast Asia from Colonialism to Independence,* pp. 405-7; Russell H. Fifield, *Americans in Southeast Asia,* pp. 92-93.

9. Byrnes to Bonnet, Oct. 1, 1945, *FRUS 1945* 6:1346; Siamese Legation to State Dept., Oct. 15, 1945, *ibid.,* p. 1356-57; Memorandum by Moffat, Oct. 16, 1945, *ibid.,* pp. 1358-60; Brynes to Yost, Jan. 2, 1946, *FRUS 1946* 8:978-80.

10. Caffery to Byrnes, May 11, 1946, *FRUS 1946* 8:1000-1; Yost to Byrnes, May 24, 1946, *ibid.,* pp. 1002-3; Pridi to Truman, May 27, 1946, *ibid.,* p. 1005; French Embassy to State Dept., June 3, 1946, *ibid.,* p. 1010-13; Truman to Pridi, June 7, 1946, *ibid.,* p. 1016; Byrnes to Caffery, June 8, 1946, *ibid.,* pp. 1016-18; Memorandum of Conversation (Moffat), June 11, 1946, *ibid.,* pp. 1018-20; Harriman to Byrnes, June 14, 1946, *ibid.,* pp. 1022-23; Acheson to Harriman, June 22, 1946, *ibid.,* p. 1024; Acheson to Johnson, June 22, 1946, *ibid.,* pp. 1026-27; Byrnes to Harriman, July 19, 1946, *ibid.,* pp. 1036-37; Acheson to Truman, July 31, 1946, *ibid.,* pp. 1045-46.

11. Memorandum of Conversation (Moffat), Aug. 19, 1946, *FRUS 1946* 8:1066-67; Memorandum of Conversation (Moffat), Aug. 28, 1946, *ibid.,* pp. 1072-74; Acheson to Caffery, Aug. 30, 1946, *ibid.,* p. 1075; Memorandum of Conversation (Moffat), Oct. 1, 1946, *ibid.,* pp. 1078-80.

12. Memorandum of Conversation (Moffat), Oct. 2, 1946, *FRUS 1946* 8:1080-81; Stanton to Byrnes, Oct. 17, 1946, *FRUS 1946* 8:1088-92; Stanton to Byrnes, Dec. 17, 1946, *FRUS 1946* 8:1104-5. Shortly after completing his tour of duty in Thailand, Stanton wrote his memoirs; see Edwin F. Stanton, *Brief Authority; Excursions of a Common Man in an Uncommon World.* Although half of the book is devoted to his mission in Bangkok, there is little discussion on American policy and problems.

13. Yost to Byrnes, April 26, 1946, DOS: 892.00/4-2646; David A. Wilson, "Thailand," p. 21-22.

14. *Ibid.,* pp. 22-24; Fifield, *Diplomacy of Southeast Asia,* pp. 243-45; Yost to Byrnes, June 5, 1946, DOS: 892.00/6-546.

15. Byrnes to Stanton, April 4, 1947, DOS: 892.00/3-2747; Stanton to Marshall, April 8, 1947, DOS: 892.00/4-847; Stanton to Marshall, April 10, 1947, DOS: 892.00/4-1047; Marshall to Stanton, April 17, 1947, DOS: 892.00/4-1047; Stanton to Marshall, April 19, 1947, DOS: 892.00/4-1947; Smith to Marshall, Jan. 16, 1947, DOS: 892.00/1-1647; Acheson to Yost, Feb. 5, 1947, DOS: 892.00/2-547; Stanton to Marshall, July 2, 1947, DOS: 892.00/7-2747.

16. Fifield, *Americans in Southeast Asia,* pp. 98-100; Marshall to Stanton, Nov. 10, 1947, DOS: 892.00/11-947; Memorandum of Conversation (Landon), Nov. 10, 1947, DOS: 892.00/11-1047; Butterworth to Lovett, Nov. 11, 1947, DOS: 892.00/11-1147; Memorandum of Conversation (Lacy), Nov. 11, 1947, DOS: 892.00/11-1147; Memorandum of Conversation (Landon), Nov. 12, 1947, DOS: 892.00/11-1247; Stanton to Marshall, Nov. 13, 1947, DOS: 892.00/11-1347; Marshall to Stanton, Nov. 14, 1947, DOS: 892.00/11-1347; Memorandum of Conversation (Faus), Nov. 18, 1947, DOS: 892.00/11-1847; Stanton to Marshall, Nov. 19, 1947, DOS: 892.00/11-1947; Landon to Butterworth, Nov. 25, 1947, DOS: 892.00/11-2447; Memorandum of Conversation (Landon), Dec. 8, 1947, DOS: 892.00/12-847; Douglas to Marshall, Dec. 9, 1947, DOS: 892.00/12-947; Stanton to Marshall, Dec. 11, 1947, DOS: 892.00/12-1147; Stanton to Marshall, Dec. 18, 1947, DOS: 892.00/12-1847; Lovett to Stuart, Dec. 29, 1947, DOS: 892.00/12-2947.

17. Lovett to Stanton, April 9, 1948, DOS: 892.00/4-848; Stanton to Marshall, April 11, 1948, DOS: 892.00/4-1048; Lovett to Stanton, April 12, 1948, DOS: 892.00/

4-848; Marshall to Stanton, April 13, 1948, DOS: 892.01/4-1348; Stanton to Marshall, April 16, 1948, DOS: 892.01/4-1748; Lovett to Stanton, April 21, 1948, DOS: 892.00/4-1748; Landon to Butterworth, April 22, 1948, DOS: 892.01/4-2248; Memorandum of Conversations (Stanton), July 29, 1948, DOS: 892.01/7-2948; Reed to Butterworth, Aug. 13, 1948, DOS: 892.01/8-1248; Donald E. Neuchterlein, *Thailand and the Struggle for Southeast Asia*, pp. 52-58.

18. Legation at Bangkok to Foreign Office, Dec. 6, 1948, FO 371/54422; Stanton to Marshall, March 5, 1947, DOS: 892.00/33-547; Agreement with Siam on Sale of Surplus American Property, *FRUS 1946* 8:1108-9; Minute by Anderson, Nov. 19, 1946, FO 371/54422.

19. John F. Cady, *Modern Burma*, pp. 427-84; Frank N. Trager, ed., *Burma*, pp. 1-25; Dorothy Guyot, "The Burma Independence Army"; Jones, *Japan's New Order*, pp. 352-90.

20. Donovan to Roosevelt, Dec. 19, 1941, FDR Papers, PSF Box 163; Donovan to Roosevelt, Feb. 28, 1942, FDR Papers, PSF Box 163; Memorandum by Murray, Dec. 31, 1941, DOS: 740.0011PW/1764; Schnare to Hull, Feb. 9, 1942, DOS: 740.0011PW 1850; Memorandum to Alling, March 17, 1942, DOS: 845C.00/56; Gauss to Hull, April 9, 1942, DOS: 845C.00/59; Gauss to Hull, Aug. 12, 1942, *FRUS 1942: China*, pp. 127-29.

21. Roosevelt to Churchill, April 16, 1942, cited in Thorne, *Allies of a Kind*, p. 6; Louis, *Imperialism at Bay*, p. 108.

22. Thorne, Allies of a Kind, pp. 345-46, 608-09; Cady, *Modern Burma*, pp. 485-511.

23. WM Conclusions, 54 (43) 3, April 14, 1943, CAB 65; WM 61 (45) 6, May 14, 1945, *ibid.*; Hull to Merrell, April 12, 1944, DOS: 845 C.01/13B; Merrell to Hull, June 1, 1944, DOS: 845C.01/14; Merrell to Hull, June 9, 1944, DOS: 845C.01/15; Memorandum by Berry, Aug. 17, 1944, DOS: 845C.01/15; Merrell to Hull, Aug. 22, 1944, DOS: 845C.00/8-2244; Langdon to Hull, Aug. 31, 1944, DOS: 845C.00/8-3144; Memorandum by Hall, Jan. 19, 1945, DOS: 845C.00/1-1945; Memorandum of Conversation (Sharp), April 19, 1945, DOS: 845C.00/4-1945; Winant to Stettinius, May 26, 1945, DOS: 845C.00/5-2645; Merrell to Stettinius, May 30, 1945, DOS: 845C.00/5-3045; Donovan to Stettinius, May 21, 1945, DOS: 845C.01/5-2145; Gatewood to Lovett, June 28, 1945, DOS: 845C.01/6-2845; Donovan to Lovett, July 1, 1945, DOS: 845C.01/7-145.

24. Cady, *Modern Burma*, pp. 499-504; Mountbatten, *Report to the Combined Chiefs of Staff*, pp. 144-45, 200-3.

25. Cady, *Modern Burma*, pp. 517-39; Thorne, *Allies of a Kind*, pp. 684-86.

26. Gatewood to Byrnes, July 10, 1945, DOS: 740.0011PW/ 7-1045; Cady to Berry, Aug. 1, 1945, DOS: 845C.01/8-145; Merrell to Byrnes, Aug. 24, 1945, DOS: 845C.01/8-2445; Memorandum of Conversation (Cady), DOS: 845C.00/11-645; Abbey to Byrnes, Nov. 21, 1945, DOS: 845C.00/11-2145; Henderson to Acheson, Dec. 10, 1945, DOS: 845C.00/12-745; Abbey to Byrnes, Jan. 25, 1946, DOS: 845C.00/1-2546; CIB, April 15, 1946, DOS: Inter-Intra Comm., Box 13.

27. Abbey to Byrnes, April 22, 1946, *FRUS 1946* 8:1-3.

28. Abbey to Byrnes, May 4, 1946, DOS: 845C.00/5-446; Abbey to Byrnes, May 13, 1946, DOS: 845C.00/5-1346; Abbey to Byrnes, June 1, 1946, DOS: 845C.01/6-146; Cady to Minor and Berry, June 10, 1946, DOS: 845C.01/6-1046; Abbey to Byrnes, July 5, 1946, DOS: 845C.00/7-546; Flood to Byrnes, Aug. 13, 1946, DOS: 845C.00/8-1345; Packer to Byrnes, Sept. 20, 1946, DOS: 845C.00/9-2046.

29. Acheson to Gallman, Nov. 8, 1946, *FRUS 1946* 8:6-7; Acheson to Packer, Nov.

15, 1946, *FRUS 1946* 8:7; Acheson to Gallman, Dec. 10, 1946, *FRUS 1946* 8:10; Byrnes to Gallman, Dec. 17, 1946, *FRUS 1946* 8:11-12; Byrnes to Packer, Dec. 20, 1946, *FRUS 1946* 8:12-13; Byrnes to Packer, Dec. 24, 1946, *FRUS 1946* 8:13; Packer to Byrnes, Dec. 16, 1946, DOS: 851C.00/13-1646.

30. Cady, *Modern Burma,* pp. 541-58; Josef Silverstein, "Burma," pp. 85-86; Packer to Byrnes, Nov. 30, 1946, *FRUS 1946* 8:8-10; Byrnes to Stuart, Dec. 16, 1946, *FRUS 1946* 8:11; Gallman to Marshall, Jan. 22, 1947, *FRUS 1947* 6:3-4; British Embassy to State Dept., Jan. 22, 1947, *FRUS 1947* 6:4-5; State Dept. to British Embassy, Jan. 23, 1947, *FRUS 1947* 6:5; Marshall to Gallman, Jan. 29, 1947, *FRUS 1947* 6:11.

31. Henderson to Marshall, Feb. 10, 1947, *FRUS 1947* 6:16-17.

32. Byrnes to Packer, Feb. 11, 1947, *FRUS 1947* 6:17-18; Gallman to Marshall, Feb. 12, 1947, *FRUS 1947* 6:18-19; Packer to Marshall, June 10, 1947, *FRUS 1947* 6:30-32; Packer to Marshall, July 2, 1947, DOS: 845C.00/7-247.

33. Cady, *Modern Burma,* pp. 554-57; Packer to Marshall, April 19, 1947, *FRUS 1947* 6:22; Marshall to Truman, May 28, 1947, *FRUS 1947* 6:23-24; Memorandum of Conversation (Packer), May 28, 1947, *FRUS 1947* 6:25-28; Packer to Marshall, June 3, 1947, DOS: 845C.00/6-347.

34. Cady, *Modern Burma,* pp. 557-77; Trager, ed., *Burma, Japanese Military Administration,* pp. 22-25; Josef Silverstein, "Political Thought in Burma," pp. 78-90.

35. Packer to Marshall, Aug. 4, 1947, *FRUS 1947* 6:40-41; Packer to Marshall, Sept. 19, 1947, *FRUS 1947* 6:44; Packer to Marshall, Nov. 13, 1947, *FRUS 1947* 6:47; Lovett to Packer, Dec. 19, 1947, *FRUS 1947* 6:47-49; Gallman to Marshall, Jan. 29, 1947, *FRUS 1947* 6:11-13; Dahl to Hare, Nov. 10, 1947, DOS: 845C.00/11-1047; Packer to Marshall, Nov. 11, 1947, DOS: 845C.00/11-1147; Acly to Marshall, Nov. 13, 1947, DOS: 845C.00/11-1347; Douglas to Marshall, Nov. 20, 1947, DOS: 845C.00/11-2047; Acly to Marshall, Dec. 3, 1947, DOS: 845C.00/12-447; Packer to Marshall, Aug. 2, 1947, DOS: 845C.00/8-247; Acly to Marshall, Dec. 20, 1947, DOS: 845C.00/12-2047; Smith to Marshall, Feb. 3, 1947, DOS: 845C.00/2-347; Smith to Marshall, Feb. 4, 1947, DOS: 845C.00/2-447.

36. Frank Trager, "Historical Perspectives on Independent Burma," pp. 71-91; Frank Trager, "Burma's Foreign Policy," pp. 90-102; William C. Johnstone, *Burma's Foreign Policy,* pp. 42-47.

37. Huddle to Marshall, March 20, 1948, DOS: 845C.00/ 3-2049; Huddle to Marshall, March 21, 1948, DOS: 845C.00/ 3-3148; Douglas to Marshall, April 2, 1948, DOS: 845C.00/4-248; Huddle to Marshall, April 12, 1948, DOS: 845C.00/4-1248; Huddle to Marshall, April 16, 1948, DOS: 845C.00/4-1648.

38. Huddle to Marshall, May 28, 1948, DOS: 845C.00/6-2748.

39. Huddle to Marshall, June 4, 1948, DOS: 845C.00/6-348; Donovan to Marshall, Sept. 15, 1948, DOS: 845C.00/9-1448; Memorandum of Conversation (Sparks), Sept. 21, 1948, DOS: 845C.00/9-2148; Acly to Marshall, Oct. 18, 1948, DOS: 845C.00/ 10-1848; Memorandum of Conversation (Lacy), July 27, 1948, DOS: 845C.00/7-2748; State Dept. to Marshall, Oct. 18, 1948, DOS: 845C.00/10-1848; Memorandum of Conversation (Parsons), Oct. 21, 1948, DOS: 845C.00/10-2148.

40. Acly to Marshall, Dec. 7, 1948, DOS: 845C.00/12-748; Memorandum of Conversation (Usher), Jan. 14, 1949, DOS: 845C.00/1-1449.

41. Landon to Vincent, March 14, 1946, DOS: 890.00/3-1446.

42. Sodhy, "Passage of Empire," pp. 120-30.

43. *Ibid.*, pp. 131-50; Anthony Short, *The Communist Insurrection in Malaya*, pp. 3-35 *et passim.*

## 9. The Indonesian Revolution, 1947-1949: The Fulfillment of Anticolonialism

1. Pluvier, *Southeast Asia from Colonialism to Independence*, pp. 434-36; Wolf, *Indonesian Story*, p. 49; Hudson, "Australia and Indonesian Independence," pp. 226-39; Grady to Marshall, July 23, 1947, DOS: 856E.00/7-2344; Flexer to Marshall and Patterson to Marshall, July 24, 1947, DOS: 856E.00/7-2447; Wilson to Marshall and Flexer to Marshall, July 25, 1947, DOS: 856E.00/7-2547; Smith to Marshall, July 26, 1947, DOS: 856E.00/7-2647; Grady to Marshall, July 27, 1947, DOS: 856E.00/7-2747; Minnigerode to Marshall, July 28, 1947, DOS: 856E.00/7-2847; Thompson to Marshall, July 29, 1947, DOS: 856E.00/7-2947; Smith to Marshall, MacDonald to Marshall, Grady to Marshall, July 30, 1947, DOS: 856E.00/7-3047; Service to Marshall, July 31, 1947, DOS: 856E.00/7-3147; Smith to Marshall, Aug. 2, 1947, DOS: 856E.00/8-247; Mallon to Marshall, Aug. 3, 1947, DOS: 856E.00/8-247; Smith to Marshall, Aug. 5, 1947, 856E.00/8-547; Wadsworth to Marshall, Aug 11, 1947, DOS: 856E.00/8-1147; McVey, *Soviet View of Indonesian Revolution*, pp. 21-22.

2. Grady to Marshall, July 29, 1947, DOS: 856E.00/7-2947; Grady to Marshall, July 23 and 26, 1947, *FRUS 1947* 6:985, 990-91; Charles Wolf, Jr., "Hornet's Nest in Indonesia," *Nation*, Aug. 2, 1947, pp. 124-25.

3. Memorandum of Conversation (Morgan) and British Embassy to Department of State, July 24, 1947, *FRUS 1947* 6:986-89; Baruch to Marshall, July 21, 1947, DOS: 856E.00/7-2147; Douglas to Marshall, July 24, 1947, DOS: 856E.00/7-2447; Douglas to Marshall and Foote to Marshall, July 25, 1947, DOS: 856E.00/7-2547; Marshall to Douglas, July 26, 1947, DOS: 856E.00/7-2647.

4. Moffat to Thorpe, July 24, 1947, HST Papers, OF Box 4; Vincent to Lovett, Villard to Bohlen, and Memorandum by Bohlen, July 29, 1947, *FRUS 1947* 6:993-96; Marshall to Truman, July 30, 1947, *FRUS 1947* 6:997.

5. Memorandum of Conversation (Armour), July 30, 1947, *FRUS 1947* 6:997-98; Baruch to Marshall, July 31, 1947, *FRUS 1947* 6:1001-02; Marshall to Baruch, Aug. 1, 1947, *FRUS 1947* 6:1004; Foote to Marshall, Aug. 1, 1947, *FRUS 1947* 6:1004-6; Memorandum of Conversation (Lovett), Aug. 2, 1947, *FRUS 1947* 6:1006-8; Foote to Marshall, Aug. 6, 7, and 8, 1947, *FRUS 1947* 6:1015-19; Memorandum of Conversation (Ringwalt), Aug. 8, 1947, DOS: PSEA Box 12.

6. Foote to Marshall, Aug. 12, 14, 17, and 19, 1947, *FRUS 1947* 6:1022-29, 1034-37; Lovett to Foote, Aug. 19, 1947, *FRUS 1947* 6:1037; Foote to Marshall, July 29, 1947, DOS: 856E.00/7-2947.

7. Johnson to Marshall, Aug. 16, 1947, *FRUS 1947* 6:1033-34; Memorandum of Conversation (Landon), Aug. 20, 1947, *FRUS 1947* 6:1037-39; Lovett to Baruch, Aug. 21, 1947, *FRUS 1947* 6:1039-42; Lovett to Foote, Aug. 27, 1947, *FRUS 1947* 6:1042-43; Memorandum by Lovett, Aug. 28, 1947, *FRUS 1947* 6:1043; Landon to Marshall, Aug. 22, 1947, DOS: 856E.00/8-547; Lewis to Marshall, Aug. 21, 1947, DOS: 856E.00/8-2147.

8. Marshall to Johnson, Aug. 8, 1947, *FRUS 1947* 6:1020-21; Grady to Marshall, Aug. 9, 1947, DOS: 856E.00/8-947; Memorandum of Conversation (Penfield), Aug. 1, 1947, DOS: PSEA Box 13; George M. Kahin, *Nationalism and Revolution in Indonesia*,

pp. 215-17; Taylor, *Indonesian Independence and the United Nations,* pp. 388-94; Wolf, *Indonesian Story,* pp. 138-43.

9. Foote to Marshall, Sept. 22, 1947, *FRUS 1947* 6:1051-52; Lovett to Austin, Oct. 10, 1947, *FRUS 1947* 6:1053; Livengood to Marshall, Oct. 11, 1947, *FRUS 1947* 6:1053-54; Marshall to Lovett, Oct. 21, 1947, *FRUS 1947* 6:1059-60; Austin to Marshall, Oct. 25, 1947, *FRUS 1947* 6:1060-63; Memorandum of Conversation Landon, Oct. 13, 1947, DOS: 856E.00/10-1347; Memorandum of Conversation (Lacy), Oct. 18, 1947, DOS: PSEA, Box 13; Memorandum "Netherlands East Indies" Oct. 21, 1947, *DOS: PSEA,* Box 12; Taylor, *Indonesian Independence and the United Nations,* pp. 385-86.

10. Memorandum of Conversation by Marshall, Sept. 8, 1947, *FRUS 1947* 6:1048-51; Livengood to Marshall, Oct. 29, 31, Nov. 7, 13, and 17, 1947, *FRUS 1947* 6:1063-74; Lovett to Livengood, Nov. 18, 1947, *FRUS 1947* 6:1074; Baruch to Marshall, Sept. 6, 1947, DOS: 856E.00/9-647; Foote to Marshall, Sept. 16, 1947, DOS: 856E.00/9-1647; Livengood to Marshall, Sept. 17, 1947, DOS: 856E.00/9-1747; Davies-Penfield Memorandum, Sept. 5, 1947, DOS: PSEA Box 13; Kahin, *Nationalism and Revolution in Indonesia,* pp. 220-22.

11. Livengood to Marshall, Dec. 1, 4, and 6, 1947, *FRUS 1947* 6:1075-81.

12. Lovett to Livengood, Dec. 19, 1947, *FRUS 1947* 6:1084-85.

13. Livengood to Marshall, Dec. 13 and 20, 1947, *FRUS 1947* 6:1082-83, 1085-89; Livengood to Marshall, Dec. 23, 1947, DOS: 856E.00/12-2347; Kahin, *Nationalism and Revolution in Indonesia,* pp. 222-25; McMahon, *Colonialism and Cold War,* pp. 195-205.

14. Lovett to Livengood, Dec. 31, 1947, *FRUS 1947* 6:1099-1101.

15. Livengood to Marshall, Jan. 5, 6, 7, 9, 10, 12, and 19, 1948, *FRUS 1948* 6:57-67, 69-76, 78-79; Marshall to Livengood, Jan. 7 and 10, 1948, *FRUS 1948* 6:68, 72; Memorandum of Conversation (Hulley), Jan. 6, 1948, *FRUS 1948* 6:64-65; Marshall to Netherlands Embassy, Jan. 9, 11, and 13, 1948, *FRUS 1948* 6:70-71, 75, 77; Bonsal to Marshall, Jan. 12, 1948, DOS: 856E.00/1-1248; Kahin, *Nationalism and Revolution in Indonesia,* pp. 226-28.

16. Louis Fischer, *The Story of Indonesia,* p. 103.

17. Kahin, *Nationalism and Revolution in Indonesia,* pp. 239-46; Taylor, *Indonesian Independence and the United Nations,* pp. 400-8.

18. Lovett to Livengood, Jan. 23, 1948, *FRUS 1948* 6:81; Memorandum of Conversation by Armour, Jan. 29, 1948, *FRUS 1948* 6:85-86; Memorandum of Conversation by Lacy, Feb. 4, 1948, *FRUS 1948* 6:88-89; Rusk-Hickerson-Butterworth to Marshall, Feb. 10, 1948, *FRUS 1948* 6:91-94; Livengood to Marshall, Feb. 20, 24, 26, March 2, 4, 10, 25, and April 6, 8, 10, 11, 16, 26, 28, 30, 1948, *FRUS 1948* 6:99-105, 107-8; 113-17; 127-28; 133-36; 143-48, 157-61; Lovett to Livengood, March 5, and April 19, 1948, *FRUS 1948* 6:114, 148-49; Baruch to Marshall, March 2, 1948, *FRUS 1948* 6:109-11; Marshall to Austin, *FRUS 1948* 6:108; Gallman to Marshall, Feb. 19, 1948, DOS: 856E.00/5-1248.

19. Marshall to Livengood, April 30 and May 7, 1948, *FRUS 1948* 6:161-64; Livengood to Marshall, May 11, 1948, *FRUS 1948* 6:168-69; Memorandum of Conversation (Nolting), May 12, 1948, DOS: 856E.00/5-1248.

20. Livengood to Marshall, May 10, 21, 25, 28, 29, 31 and June 1, 3, 1948, *FRUS 1948* 6:164-68, 178-83, 185-86, 189-91, 199-207, 210-13; Lovett to Livengood, May 27 and 31, 1948, *ibid.,* pp. 186-87, 198.

21. DuBois to Marshall, June 5, 1948, *FRUS 1948* 6:218-23; Livengood to Marshall, June 6 and 7, 1948, *ibid.,* pp. 223-28.

22. Marshall to Livengood, June 8, 1948, *FRUS 1948* 6:229-31; Livengood to Marshall, June 11, 1948, *ibid.,* pp. 234-37.

23. Memorandum of Conversation (Lacy), June 11, 1948, DOS: 856E.00/6-1148; Butterworth to duBois, June 8, 1948, DOS: 501BC Indonesia/8-548; Baruch to Marshall, June 12, 1948, *FRUS 1948* 6:237-38; Marshall to Livengood, June 12, 1948, *FRUS 1948* 6:239-40.

24. Livengood to Marshall, June 16 and 18, 1948, *FRUS 1948* 6:250-51, 253-55; Memorandum of Conversation (Lovett), June 14, 1948, *FRUS 1948* 6:234-35; Livengood to Marshall, June 14, 1948, DOS: 856E.00/6-1448; Baruch to Marshall, June 14, 1948, DOS: 856E.00/6-1448; Andrew Roth, "Jokja Journal," *Nation,* June 26, 1948, pp. 715-17; Kahin, *Nationalism and Revolution in Indonesia,* pp. 248-49.

25. Livengood to Marshall, June 12, 16, 23, 25, 28, and 30, 1948, *FRUS 1948* 6:240-43, 248-50, 261-62, 267-73, 275-77; Marshall to Livengood, June 14, 16, and 25, 1948, *FRUS 1948* 6:245-46, 251-52, 269-70; Marshall to Embassy in Netherlands, June 24, 1948, *FRUS 1948* 6:266; Memorandum of Conversation (Scott), June 23, 1948 *FRUS 1948* 6:262; Andrew Roth, "American Flipflop in Indonesia," *Nation,* July 10, 1948, pp. 39-41; Taylor, *Indonesian Independence and the United Nations,* pp. 393-95.

26. Kahin, *Nationalism and Revolution in Indonesia,* pp. 249-55; McMahon, *Colonialism and Cold War,* pp. 219-33.

27. Marshall to Livengood, July 6, 23, 1948, *FRUS 1948* 6:277, 288-89; Livengood to Marshall, July 10, 16, 21, 26, and 28, 1948, *FRUS 1948* 6:278-79, 283-93; Memorandum of Conversation (Butterworth), July 27, 1948, *FRUS 1948* 6:290-91; Memorandum of Conversation (Lacy), July 21, 1948, *FRUS 1948* 6:285; Memorandum of Conversation (Lovett), July 12, 1948, *FRUS 1948* 6:282-83; Memorandum for Lovett, July 12, 1948, *FRUS 1948* 6:279-81; Memorandum of Conversation (Reed), July 7, 1948, *FRUS 1948* 6:277-78; Memorandum of Conversation (Reed), July 21, 1948, DOS: 856E.00/7-2248; Reed to Butterworth, July 22, 1948, DOS: 856E.00/7-248; Memorandum of Conversation (Sparks), July 23, 1948, DOS: 856E.00/7-2348; Marshall to Livengood, Aug. 3, 1948, DOS: 856E.00/8-248; Acly to Marshall, Aug. 9, 1948, DOS: 856E.01/8-948.

28. Netherlands Embassy to Dept. of State, July 9, 1948, DOS: 856E.00/7948; Memorandum of Conversation (Nolting), Aug. 3, 1948, DOS: 856E.00/8-348; Memorandum of Conversation (Butterworth), Aug. 2, 1948, *FRUS 1948* 6:296-97; Memorandum of Conversation (Reed), DOS: PSEA Box 12.

29. Memorandum of Conversation (Lacy), Aug. 12, 1948, DOS: 856E.01/8-1248; Baruch to Marshall, July 24, 1948, DOS: 856E.00/7-2448; Livengood to Marshall, Aug. 15, 1948, *FRUS 1948* 6:299-302.

30. Livengood to Marshall, Aug. 26, 1948, DOS: 856E.00/8-2648; Livengood to Marshall, Aug. 19 and 22, 1948, *FRUS 1948* 6:303-06.

31. Reed to Benninghoff, Aug. 27, 1948, DOS: 856E.00/8-2748.

32. Livengood to Marshall, Aug. 16, 26, 28, 31 and Sept. 1, 1948, *FRUS 1948* 6:302-3, 306-12, 314-15.

33. Barco to Rusk, Sept. 3, 1948, *FRUS 1948* 6:318-22; Marshall to Livengood, Sept. 8, 9, 10, 13, 14, and 20, 1948, *FRUS 1948* 6:325-31, 335, 339, 355-56; Livengood to Marshall, Sept. 7, 11, 13-18, and 21, 1948, *FRUS 1948* 6:322-24, 333-43, 351-53, 359-60; Baruch to Marshall, Sept. 10 and 13, 1948, *FRUS 1948* 6:331-32, 337-38; Memorandum of Conversation (Marshall), Sept. 17, 1948, *FRUS 1948* 6:343-45; Memorandum of Conversation (Lovett), Sept. 17, 1948, *FRUS 1948* 6:345-47; Memorandum of Conversation (Far Eastern Affairs), Sept. 17-18, 1948, *FRUS 1948* 6:347-50; Memorandum of Conversation

(Lovett), Sept. 14, 1948, DOS: 856D.00/9-1448; Baruch to Marshall, Sept. 15, 1948, DOS: 856E.00/9-1548; Memorandum of Conversation (Ogburn), Sept. 15, 1948, DOS: 856E.01/9-1548; Baruch to Marshall, Sept. 17, 1948, DOS: 856E.01/9-1648; Memorandum of Conversation (Hickerson), Sept. 21, 1948, DOS: 856D.00/9-2148.

34. Memorandum for Lovett, Sept. 23, 1948, *FRUS 1948* 6:364-65; Graham to Marshall, Sept. 16, 1948, DOS: 856D.00/9-1648.

35. McVey, *Soviet View of Indonesian Revolution,* pp. 39-80; *New York Times,* Sept. 17, 1948; Kahin, *Nationalism and Revolution in Indonesia,* pp. 255-58, 300-02; S.N. Aidit, *Communist Party of Indonesia,* pp. 31-35; S.N. Aidit, *Problems of the Indonesian Revolution,* pp. 81-89; Livengood to Marshall, Sept. 20, 28, and Oct. 4, 1948, *FRUS 1948* 6:353-55, 357-59, 379, 382; Lovett to Livengood, Sept. 27, Oct. 1, 7, and 28, 1948, *FRUS 1948* 6:378-79, 381-82, 390, 438-39; Livengood to Marshall, Sept. 20, 1948, DOS: 856E.00/9-2048; Reed to Butterworth, Sept. 24, 1948, DOS: 856D.00/9-2448; Marshall to Livengood, Oct. 8, 1948, DOS: 856E.01/10-848; Livengood to Marshall, Oct. 12, 1948, DOS: 856D.00/10-1248.

36. Livengood to Marshall, Sept. 25, Oct. 10 and Oct. 13, 1948, *FRUS 1948* 6:371-72, 402-5, 416-18; Lovett to Livengood, Sept. 29, Oct. 6, 11, 12, and 13, 1948, *FRUS 1948* 6:380, 388-89, 406-7, 409-10, 412-14; Baruch to Marshall, Sept. 26, Oct. 10, 12, and 13, 1948, *FRUS 1948* 6:376, 400-1, 410-11, 415-16; Lovett to Baruch, Oct. 9 and 10, 1948, *FRUS 1948* 6:399, 401; Marshall to Lovett, Oct. 13, 1948, *FRUS 1948* 6:414-15; Memorandum of Conversation (Reed), Sept. 24, 1948, *FRUS 1948* 6:369-71; Hulley to Hickerson-Butterworth, Sept. 24, 1948, DOS: 856D.00/9-2448.

37. Livengood to Marshall, Oct. 14, 19, 23, 29, Nov. 1 and 4, 1948, *FRUS 1948* 6:418-19, 421-34, 439-41, 446-49, 452-53.

38. Lovett to Livengood, Nov. 5, 1948, *FRUS 1948* 6:457-65.

39. Livengood to Marshall, Nov. 6, 11, 19, Dec. 2, 3, and 5, 1948, *FRUS 1948* 6:465-67, 481-84, 493-94, 506-9, 511-12, 520-26; Lovett to Livengood, Dec. 3 and 4, 1948, *ibid.,* pp. 512-14, 517; Lovett to Hague Embassy, Nov. 10, 1948, *ibid.,* p. 478; Lovett to Paris Embassy, Nov. 17, 1948, *ibid.,* pp. 488-89.

40. Steere to Marshall, Dec. 18, 1948, *FRUS 1948* 6:573-74; Lovett to Livengood, Dec. 6, 13, 14, and 18, 1948, *FRUS 1948* 6:527-29, 552, 558-59, 574-76; Livengood to Marshall, Dec. 14, 1948, *FRUS 1948* 6:555-58; Steere to Marshall, Dec. 7, 10, and 16, 1948, *FRUS 1948* 6:530-31, 542-43, 565-66; Dept. of State to Netherlands Embassy, Dec. 7, 1948, *FRUS 1948* 6:531-35; Memorandum for Lovett, Dec. 13, 1948, *FRUS 1948* 6:550-52; Memorandum of Conversation (Lacy), Dec. 7, 1948, DOS: 856D.00/12-748; Memorandum of Conversation (Butterworth), Dec. 15, 1948, DOS: 856D.00/12-1548; Memorandum of Conversation (Lovett), Dec. 20, 1948, DOS: 856D.00/12-1748; Memorandum of Conversation (Butterworth), Dec. 9, 1948, DOS: 856D.00/12-948; Memorandum of Conversation (Reed), DOS: 856D.00/12-848; Indian Embassy to Department of State, Dec. 17, 1948, DOS: PSEA Box 12; Kahin, *Nationalism and Revolution in Indonesia,* pp. 332-36.

41. Raymond E. Stannard, "The Role of American Aid," pp. 1-6; Fischer, *Story of Indonesia,* pp. 118-22; *New York Times,* Dec. 25, 1948; McMahon, *Colonialism and Cold War,* pp. 251-59; Lockett to Marshall, Dec. 21, 1948, DOS: 856D.00/12-2148; Doolittle to Marshall, Dec. 21, 1948, DOS: 856D.00/12-2148; Lewis to Marshall, Stanton to Marshall, Cole to Marshall, Ispahani to Marshall, and Derry to Marshall, Dec. 23, 1948, DOS: 856D.00/12-2348; Lockett to Marshall, Jan. 3, 1949, DOS: 856D.00/1-349.

42. Memoranda of Conversations (Lovett), Dec. 20 and 24, 1948, *FRUS 1948*

6:587-92, 602-3; Lovett to Jessup, Dec. 18, 19, 23, 1948, *FRUS 1948* 6:577-78, 585-86, 597-600; Lovett to Livengood, Dec. 20, 1948, *FRUS 1948* 6:592-93; Lovett to London Embassy, Dec. 24, 1948, *FRUS 1948* 6:603; Douglas to Marshall, Dec. 20, 1948, DOS: 856D.00/12-2047; Memorandum of Conversation (Sparks), Dec. 22, 1948, DOS: PSEA Box 12; Lovett to Hoffman, ca. Dec. 20, 1948, and Hoffman to Van Kleffens, Dec. 22, 1948, DOS: PSEA, Box 11.

43. Lovett to Jessup, Dec. 24 and 27, 1948, *FRUS 1948* 6:603-04, 608; Baruch to Marshall, Dec. 24, 26, and 29, 1948, *FRUS 1948* 6:604-6, 613; Holmes to Marshall, Dec. 25, 1948, *FRUS 1948* 6:605; Lovett to Paris Embassy, Dec. 26, 1948, *FRUS 1948* 6:606-7; Caffery to Marshall, Dec. 27, 1948, *FRUS 1948* 6:607-8, 611-12; Soemitro Djojohadikoesoemo to Lovett, Dec. 27 and 28, 1948, *FRUS 1948* 6:609-11; Lovett to Moscow Embassy, Dec. 30, 1948, *FRUS 1948* 6: 613-16; Baruch to Marshall, Dec. 30, 1948, DOS: 856D.00/12-3048; Memorandum of Conversation (Allison), Dec. 24, 1948, DOS: 856D.00/12-2448; Kahin, *Nationalism and Revolution in Indonesia*, pp. 339-42.

44. Lovett to Certain Officers, Dec. 31, 1948, *FRUS 1948* 6:717-20; Memorandum of Conversation (Ogburn), Jan. 12, 1949 and Lewis to Marshall, Jan. 12, 1949, DOS: 856D.00/1-1249.

45. Livengood to Marshall, Jan. 3, 1949, *FRUS 1949* 7:119-21; Lovett to Austin, Jan. 6, 1949, *ibid.,* pp. 131-32; Butterworth to Bohlen, Jan. 7, 1949, *ibid.,* pp. 136-37; Memorandum of Conversation (Lovett), Jan. 11, 1949, *ibid.,* pp. 139-41.

46. Lovett to Manila Embassy, Jan. 11, 1949, *FRUS 1949* 7:141; Jessup to Lovett, Jan. 12, 1949, *ibid.,* pp. 144-48.

47. Jessup to Marshall, Jan. 17, 18, and 26, 1949, *FRUS 1949* 7:161-66, 171-72, 194-95; Kirk to Marshall, Jan. 18, 1949, *FRUS 1949* 7:170; Kirk to Acheson, Jan. 22, 1949, *FRUS 1949* 7:188; Baruch to Acheson, Jan. 20, 1949, *FRUS 1949* 7:179-83; Austin to Marshall, Jan. 19, 1949, *FRUS 1949* 7:175-76; Netherlands Embassy to Dept. of State, Jan. 17, 1949, *FRUS 1949* 7:157-61; Memorandum of Conversation by Bancroft, Jan. 18, 1949, *FRUS 1949* 7:169-70; Memorandum by Rusk, Jan. 18, 1949, *FRUS 1949* 7:168-69; Memorandum of Conversation (Acheson), Jan. 22, 1949, Acheson Papers, Box 64; Acheson to Hague Embassy, Jan. 28, 1949, DOS: 856D.00/1-2749; Holmes to Acheson, Jan. 28, 1949, DOS: 856D.00/1-2849; Taylor, *Indonesian Independence and the United Nations,* pp. 394-98.

48. *Ibid.,* pp. 386-88; Kahin, *Nationalism and Revolution in Indonesia,* pp. 342-45, 389-403.

49. Acheson to Hague Embassy, Jan. 31 and Feb. 5, 1949, *FRUS 1949* 7:197; 208; Livengood to Acheson, Feb. 2, 1949, *FRUS 1949* 7:200-1; Austin to Acheson, Feb. 4, 1949, *FRUS 1949* 7:206-7; Baruch to Acheson, Feb. 4, 1949, *FRUS 1949* 7:206; Kird to Acheson, Feb. 9, 1949, *FRUS 1949* 7:212-23; Reed to Butterworth, Feb. 9, 1949, DOS: 856E.00/2-949; Kahin, *Nationalism and Revolution in Indonesia,* pp. 404-5.

50. Memorandum of Conversation (Butterworth), Feb. 11, 1949, *FRUS 1949* 7:225-26; Douglas to Acheson, Feb. 18, 1949, *ibid.,* pp. 242-43; Dept. of State to Netherlands Embassy, Feb. 23, 1949, *ibid.,* 246-47; Baruch to Acheson, Feb. 23, 1949, *ibid.,* pp. 247-48; Acheson to Livengood, Feb. 16 and 26, 1949, *ibid.,* pp. 233-35; Livengood to Acheson, Feb. 22, 25, 26, 27 and March 1, 1949, *ibid.,* pp. 244-46, 259-60, 262-65, 269-78.

51. Livengood to Acheson, March 27, 29, and 30, 1949, *FRUS 1949* 7:348-50, 353-55.

52. Kahin, *Nationalism and Revolution in Indonesia,* pp. 415-17.

53. McMahon, *Colonialism and Cold War,* pp. 279-81.

54. Baruch to Acheson, March 17 and 22, 1949, *FRUS 1949* 7:324, 338-39; Austin to Acheson, March 21 and 22, 1949, *FRUS 1949* 7:332-38; Memorandum by Rusk, March 21, 1949, *FRUS 1949* 7:331-32; Van Kleffens to Acheson, March 18, 1949, *FRUS 1949* 7:325-30; Dept. of State to Indian Embassy, March 2, 1949, *FRUS 1949* 7:287-88; Henderson to Acheson, March 16, 1949, *FRUS 1949* 7:323; Memorandum of Conversation (Sparks), March 29, 1949, Acheson Papers, Box 64; Pakistan Embassy to Dept. of State, March 3, 1949, and Memorandum by Lacy, Feb. 18, 1949, DOS: PSEA Box 12; Kahin, *Nationalism and Revolution in Indonesia,* pp. 413-14.

55. PPS Report, March 29, 1949, DOS: PPS Files Box 2.

56. Memorandum of Conversation (Acheson), March 31, 1949, Acheson Papers, Box 64.

57. Acheson to Livengood, April 2, 1949, *FRUS 1949* 7:355-57.

58. Livengood to Acheson, April 3, 12, 14, 21, 24-28, and May 1, 4-6, 1949, *FRUS 1949* 7:359-61, 366-72, 386-93, 400-7; Taylor, *Indonesian Independence and the United Nations,* pp. 408-10; J. Foster Collins, "The United Nations and Indonesia," pp. 115-20.

59. Taylor, *Indonesian Independence and the United Nations,* pp. 397-99.

## 10. The Vietnamese Revolution: The Evolution of the Commitment to France, 1947–1950

1. Colbert, "The Road Not Taken," pp. 608-28; Marshall to Certain Officers, Jan. 29, 1948, *FRUS 1948* 6:19; Grady to Marshall, Feb. 19, 1948, DOS: 851G.00/2-1948.

2. Irving, *First Indochina War,* pp. 37-80.

3. Weekly Review, July 1, 1947: French-Vietnamese Conflict, DOS: PSEA Box 9.

4. *Ibid.*

5. Marshall to Reed, July 17, 1947, *FRUS 1947* 6:117-18; O'Sullivan to Marshall, July 3, 19 and 21, 1947, *FRUS 1947* 6:108-9, 120-23; Reed to Marshall, July 24, 1947, *FRUS 1947* 6:123-26; Caffery to Marshall, June 3, 1947, DOS: 851G.00/6-347.

6. Landon to Butterworth, Nov. 18, 1947, DOS: 856D.00/11-1847.

7. *Ibid.*

8. Minute by Street, Nov. 6, 1947, FO 371/63457; Drumright to Whitteridge, Oct. 31, 1947, and Southeast Asia Dept. Note on Ho Chi Minh, Aug. 1947, FO 371/63457; Landon to Vincent, July 28, 1947, DOS: PSEA Box 9; Reed to Marshall, May 7, 1948, DOS: 851G.00/6-748.

9. Lacy to Penfield, Feb. 17, 1948, DOS: PSEA Box 9; Memorandum of Conversation (Butterworth), March 17, 1948, DOS: 851G.00/3-1758; Abbott to Marshall, Nov. 5, 1948, *FRUS 1948* 6:54-55; Marshall to Nanking Embassy, July 2, 1948, *FRUS 1948* 6:28-29.

10. Reed to Marshall, Sept. 15, 1947, *FRUS 1947* 6:137-38.

11. O'Sullivan to Marshall, Sept. 24, 1947, *FRUS 1947* 6:140-41; Reed to Marshall, Sept. 27, 1947, *ibid.,* pp. 141-42.

12. Caffery to Marshall, Oct. 28, 1947, *FRUS 1947* 6:145-46; Landon to Butterworth, Oct. 24, 1947 and Memorandum: French Military Capability (ca. Oct. 1947), DOS: PSEA, Box 9.

13. Butterworth to Hickerson, April 29, 1948, DOS: PSEA, Box 9; Memorandum

of Conversation (Lacy), Feb. 21, 1948, *FRUS 1948* 6:20; Memorandum of Conversation by Stanton, Feb. 24, 1948, *FRUS 1948* 6:21-23; Memorandum of Conversation (Landon), Feb. 24, 1948, DOS: 851G.00/2-2448.

14. Abbott to Marshall, June 30, 1948, DOS: 851G.01/6-3048.

15. Reed to Marshall, June 14, 1947, *FRUS 1947* 6:103-5.

16. Reed to Marshall, July 11, 1947, *FRUS 1947* 6:110-16; Wallner to Lacy, Feb. 12, 1948 and Butterworth to Hickerson, May 25, 1948, DOS: PSEA Box 9; Memorandum of Conversation (Moffat), April 11, 1947, DOS: 851G.01/4-1147; Reed to Marshall, June 9, 1947, DOS: 851G.00/6-947; O'Sullivan to Marshall, July 10, 1947, DOS: 851G.00/7-1047; Reed to Marshall, June 27, 1947, DOS: 851G.00/6-2747; O'Sullivan to Marshall, June 21, 1947, DOS: 851G.00/6-2147; Rendall to Marshall, Jan. 24, 1948, DOS: 851G.00/1-2448; Reed to Marshall, Jan. 13, 1948, DOS: 851G.00/1-1348; Riddick to Marshall, Aug. 12, 1948, DOS: 851G.01/8-1248.

17. Rendall to Marshall, June 8, 1948, DOS: 851G.01/6-848; Rendall to Marshall, June 7, 1948, DOS: 851GT.01/6-748; Rendall to Marshall, June 9, 1948, DOS: 851G.01/6-948.

18. Marshall to Paris Embassy, July 3, 14, and Aug. 30, 1948, *FRUS 1948* 6:29-30, 33, 40; Caffery to Marshall, July 9, 1948, *ibid.,* pp. 31-33; Marshall to Abbott, Aug. 27, 1948, *ibid.,* p. 38; Abbott to Marshall, Aug. 28 and Sept. 7, 1948, *ibid.,* pp. 39-42.

19. Memorandum of Conversation (Lacy), May 10, 1948, DOS: 851G.01/5-1048.

20. Policy Statement on Indochina, Sept. 27, 1948, *FRUS 1948* 6:43-49.

21. Acheson to Paris Embassy, Feb. 25, 1949, *FRUS 1949* 7:8-9.

22. Caffery to Acheson, March 6 and 16, 1949, *FRUS 1949* 7:9-10, 12-14.

23. Reed to Butterworth, April 14, 1949, DOS: 851G.00/4-1449.

24. Abbott to Acheson, May 6, 1949, *FRUS 1949* 7:22-23; Memorandum of Conversation (Landon), March 2, 1948, DOS: 851G.00/3-248; Memorandum of Conversation (Landon), April 14, 1948, DOS: 851G.00/4-1448.

25. Bruce to Acheson, May 24 and June 2, 1949, *FRUS 1949* 7:32-33, 36-38; Memorandum of Conversation (Ogburn), *ibid.,* pp. 27-28.

26. Acheson to Paris Embassy, June 6 and 16, 1949, *FRUS 1949 7:38-45, 56-57:* Bruce to Acheson, June 13, 1949, *ibid.,* pp. 45-46; Abbott to Acheson, June 10, 1949, *ibid.,* pp. 45.

27. Lovett to Certain Officers, June 14, 1949, *FRUS 1949* 7:53-54; Douglas to Acheson, June 15, 1949, *FRUS 1949* 7:55-56; Henderson to Acheson, June 17 and 21, 1949, *FRUS 1949* 7:57-58, 61-62; Stanton to Acheson, June 17, 1949, *FRUS 1949* 7:58-59; Memorandum of Conversation (Landon), June 21, 1949, *FRUS 1949* 7:62-63; Memorandum of Conversation (Ogburn), June 23, 1949, DOS: 851G.01/6-2149.

28. Ogburn to Reed and O'Sullivan, June 28, 1949, DOS: PSEA, Box 9.

29. *Ibid.*

30. Abbott to Acheson, Sept. 8, 1949, *FRUS 1949* 7:75; Acheson to Abbott, July 1949, *FRUS 1949* 7:70; Indochina Policy Study, August 1949, DOS: PSEA, Box 9; Lockett to Acheson, Aug. 5, 1949, DOS: 851G.01/8-549; Reed to Jessup, Aug. 22, 1949, DOS: 851G.00/8-2249; Gibson to Acheson, July 8, 1949, DOS: 851G.01/7-849.

31. Bruce to Acheson, July 6, 1949, DOS: 851G.01/7-649; Bruce to Acheson, July 22, 1949, DOS: 851G.01/7-2249; Abbott to Acheson, Aug. 26, 1949, DOS: 851G.01/8-2649; Gibson to Acheson, June 29, 1949, DOS: 851G.01/6-2949; Gibson to Acheson, Oct. 20, 1949, DOS: 851G.00/10-2149; Gibson to Acheson, Oct. 21, 1949, DOS: 851G.00/10-2149;

Gibson to Acheson, Oct. 26, 1949, DOS: 851G.00/10-2649.

32. Andrew Roth, "Asia's Tito?" *Nation,* Sept. 10, 1949, p. 244; Roth, "Night Club Emperor," *Nation,* Sept. 10, 1949, pp. 247-60.

33. Memorandum of Conversation (Butterworth), Sept. 9, 1949, *FRUS 1949* 7:76-79; Holmes to Acheson, Sept. 9, 1949, *ibid.,* pp. 79-80.

34. Memorandum of Conversations (O'Sullivan), Sept. 28, 1949, *FRUS 1949* 7:83-89.

35. Butterworth to Acheson, Oct. 20, 1949, *FRUS 1949* 7:92-94; Henderson to Acheson, Sept. 14, 1949, DOS: 851G.01/9-1449; Abbott to Acheson, Sept. 23, 1949, DOS: 851G.01/9-2349; Stanton to Acheson and Donovan to Acheson, Oct. 6, 1949, DOS: 851G.01/10-649.

36. Reed to Butterworth, Nov. 7, 1949, DOS: PSEA, Box 9.

37. Memorandum of Conversation (Reed), Nov. 28, 1949, DOS: 851G.01/11-2849.

38. Acheson to Paris Embassy, Dec. 1, 1949, *FRUS 1949* 7:101-2.

39. Bruce to Acheson, Dec. 11, 1949, *FRUS 1949* 7:105-10.

40. Bruce to Acheson, Nov. 21, 1949, *FRUS 1949* 7:97; Holmes to Acheson, Dec. 5, 1949, DOS: 851G.01/12-549; Abbott to Acheson, Dec. 6, 1949, DOS: 851G.00/12-649.

41. Acheson to Abbott, Dec. 19, 1949, DOS: 851G.00/12-1949; Gibson to Acheson, Dec. 22, 1949, DOS: 851G.00/12-2249.

42. Abbott to Acheson, Dec. 24, 1949, DOS: 851G.01/12-2449; Abbott to Acheson, Dec. 27, 1949, *FRUS 1949* 7:114.

43. Fifield, *Americans in Southeast Asia,* pp. 142-45; Colbert, "Road Not Taken," pp. 608-28; Record of NSC Meeting, Dec. 30, 1949, U.S. House, CAS, *United States-Vietnam Relations 1945-1967* (Book 1), I: A-56 to A-58.

44. NCS 48-1, Dec. 23, 1949, U.S House, CAS, *United States-Vietnam Relations, 1945-1967,* (Book 1), II: A-45.

45. Acheson to Stanton, Dec. 23, 1949, *FRUS 1949* 7:113.

46. Stanton to Acheson, Dec. 28, 1949, *FRUS 1949* 7:115; Acheson to Manila Embassy, Jan. 7, 1950, *FRUS 1950* 6:691-92; Henderson to Acheson, Jan. 7, 1950, *FRUS 1950* 6:692-93; Cochran to Acheson, Jan. 11, 1950, *FRUS 1950* 6:693; Stanton to Acheson, Jan. 12, 1950, *FRUS 1950* 6:693-94.

47. Acheson to Stanton, Jan. 17, 1950, *FRUS 1950* 6:697.

48. Bruce to Acheson, Jan. 13, Feb. 3 and 6, 1950, *FRUS 1950* 6:694-95, 719, 721; Memorandum of Conversation (Acheson), Feb. 3, 1950, *ibid.,* p. 719.

49. Bruce to Acheson, Jan. 31, 1950, *FRUS 1950* 6:704-5; *New York Times,* Feb. 1-2, 1950.

50. Acheson to London Embassy, Jan. 30, 1950, *FRUS 1950* 6:703-4; Acheson to Truman, Feb. 2, 1950, *ibid.,* pp. 716-17.

51. Memorandum of Conversation (Merchant), Feb. 16, 1950, *FRUS 1950* 6:733.

52. Yost to Perkins, Jan. 31, 1950, *FRUS 1950* 6:710-11; Bruce to Acheson, Feb. 22, 1950, *ibid.,* pp. 739-43; Report to NSC, Feb. 27, 1950, *ibid.,* pp. 744-47; Merchant to Acheson, March 7, 1950, *ibid.,* pp. 749-51; Marshall to Acheson, April 14, 1950, *ibid.,* pp. 780-85; Truman to Acheson, May 1, 1950, *ibid.,* p. 791.

53. Memorandum by Gullion, Dec. 7, 1949, *FRUS 1950* 6:700-2; Abbott to Acheson, Jan. 29, 31 and Feb. 9, 1950, *ibid.,* pp. 702-3, 705-7, 725-26; Bohlen to Acheson, Feb. 16, 1950, *ibid.,* pp. 734-35; Memorandum of Conversation at Quai d'Orsay, March

13, 1950, *ibid.,* pp. 754-57; Gullion to Acheson, March 18 and April 8, 1950, *ibid.,* pp. 762-63, 773-76; Memorandum by Gibson, March 14, 1950, *ibid.,* pp. 759-61; Acheson to Paris Embassy, March 29, 1950, *ibid.,* pp. 768-71.

54. U.S. House, CAS, *United States-Vietnam Relations, 1945-1967* (Book 1), II: A-1 to A-3, A-35; Joseph M. Siracusa, "The United States, Vietnam, and the Cold War," pp. 82-101.

## 11. The Redefinition of United States' Policy, 1949-1950

1. On the review of American East Asian Policy in 1949-50, see Warren I. Cohen, "Acheson, His Advisers, and China, 1949-1950," pp. 13-52; John Lewis Gaddis, "The Strategic Perspective," pp. 61-118; Thomas H. Etzold, "The Far East in American Strategy, 1948-1951," pp. 102-26; William S. Borden, *The Pacific Alliance;* Michael Schaller, "Securing the Great Crescent" 392-414; Russell Buhite, *Soviet-American Relations in Asia, 1945-1954,* pp. 37-66, 186-235; Andrew J. Rotter, "The Big Canvas," pp. 193-386; Fifield, *Americans in Southeast Asia,* pp. 130-56; Robert M. Blum, *Drawing the Line;* John Lewis Gaddis, *Strategies of Containment,* pp. 89-126.

2. PPS Paper 'U.S. Policy Toward Southeast Asia" (March 29, 1949), DOS: PPS Files, Box 2; PPS Minutes, March 25 and 29, 1949, DOS: PPS, Box 32.

3. PPS Paper "U.S. Policy Toward Southeast Asia" (March 29, 1949), DOS: PPS Files, Box 2.

4. *Ibid.*

5. U.S. House, CAS,-*Vietnam Relations, 1945-1967* (Book 1), I, A-56 to A-58; PPS 51, May 19, 1949, DOS:PPS Files, Box 2. On growing Soviet interest in Southeast Asia, see Yano Toru, "Who Set the Stage for the Cold War in Southeast Asia?" pp. 321-37, and Tanigawa Yoshihiko, "The Cominform and Southeast Asia," pp. 362-77; McVey, *The Calcutta Conference and the Southeast Asia Uprisings.*

6. Department of State, *American Foreign Policy, 1950-1955 Basic Documents* (Washington, D.C.: GPO, 1957), 2:2318-19.

7. The text of NSC-68, "A Report to the National Security Council by the Executive Secretary on United States Objectives and Programs for National Security, April 14, 1950," was printed in *Naval War College Review* (May-June 1975), pp. 51-107.

8. *Ibid,* p. 76.

9. *Ibid.,* pp. 76-77.

10. Schaller, "Securing the Great Crescent," pp. 392-414; Borden, *The Pacific Alliance,* pp. 3-17, 103-42.

11. Rotter, "The Big Canvas," pp. 84-132.

12. Meyer, *Diplomatic History of Philippine Republic,* p. 69; SWNCC Summary Actions Series 276, April 14, 1947-June 6, 1948, DOS: SWNCC, Box 4; SWNCC Summary Actions Series 340, May 16-June 20, 1947, DOS: SWNCC, Box 4; Manila Embassy to Marshall, May 13, 1947, DOS: 896.24/5-1347; Marshall to Manila Embassy, Nov. 17, 1947, *FRUS 1947* 6:1117-120; Memorandum of Conversation (Mill), Dec. 11, 1947, *FRUS 1947* 6:1122-24; O'Neal to Marshall, Dec. 20, 1947, *FRUS 1947* 6:1124-25; Truman to Marshall, July 14, 1948, *FRUS 1948* 6:627-28; Lovett to Embassy, Oct 2 and 29, 1948, *FRUS 1948* 6:634-35, 638-39; Lockett to Marshall, Oct. 20 and 25, 1948, *FRUS 1948* 6:636-38.

13. Lockett to Marshall, Aug. 18 and Sept. 13, 1948, *FRUS 1948* 6:632-34; Truman to Roxas, Aug. 25, 1947, *FRUS 1947* 6:1114-15; Lockett to Marshall, May 13, 1948, DOS: 896.0/5-1348; Lockett to Marshall, May 14, 1948, DOS: 896.00/5-1448; Lockett to

Marshall, Aug. 13, 1948, DOS: 896.00/8-1348; Lockett to Marshall, Aug. 18. 1948, DOS: 896.00/8-1848; Lockett to Marshall, Sept. 7, 1948, DOS: 896.00/9-748; Meyer, *Diplomatic History of Philippine Republic*, pp. 55-56, 85-88; Fifield, *Americans in Southeast Asia*, pp. 77-78; David Wurfel, "Philippines," pp. 699-700; David Wurfel, "The Bell Report and After," pp. 302-3.

14. Memorandum of Conversation, April 25, 1949, Acheson Papers, Box 64.

15. Fifield, *Americans in Southeast Asia*, pp. 78-79; David Wurfel, "Bell Report and After," pp. 395-442; Robert A. Smith, *Philippine Freedom*, pp. 119-22; Chapin to Acheson, April 7, 1950, *FRUS 1950* 6:1433-38.

16. U.S. Policy Toward Philippines (1949), HST Papers, WHCF-Box 36.

17. *Ibid.;* McFall to Conally, April 17, 1950, *FRUS 1950* 6:1438-40.

18. Acheson to Truman, Feb. 2, 1950, *FRUS 1950* 6:1403-11; Cowen to Acheson, Jan. 8 and 17, 1950, *FRUS 1950* 6:1399-1402; Acheson to Cowen, Feb. 3, 1950, *FRUS 1950* 6:1411; Memorandum of Conversation (Acheson), Feb. 4, 1950, pp. 1412-16; Memorandum of Conversation (Ely), Aug. 9, 1949, *FRUS 1949* 7:597-99; Memorandum of Conversation (Melby), Dec. 28, 1949, DOS: PSEA Box 17; Meyer, *Diplomatic History of Philippine Republic*, pp. 89-104.

19. Butterworth to Acheson, March 23, 1950, *FRUS 1950* 6:1423-25; Lacy to Rusk, March 30, 1950, *FRUS 1950* 6:1428-32; Acheson to Cowen, March 24, 1950, *FRUS 1950* 6:1425-27; Butterworth to Truman, Aug. 5, 1949, HST Papers, WHCF-Box 36.

20. Acheson to Truman, April 20, 1950, *FRUS 1950* 6:1440-44.

21. Acheson to Cowen, May 6 and 26, 1950, *FRUS 1950* 6:1444-45 and 1452-53; Cowen to Acheson, May 6, 8, 12 and June 1, 1950, *ibid.,* pp. 1445-50, 1453-56; Rusk to Webb, May 17, 1950, *ibid.,* pp. 1450-51; Acheson to Truman, June 1, 1950, *ibid.,* pp. 1456-57; Quirino to Truman, June 8, 1950, *ibid.,* pp. 1459-60.

22. Cady, *History of Modern Burma,* pp. 578-99; Johnstone, *Burma's Foreign Policy,* pp. 50-51; Acly to Acheson, Feb. 1, 1949, DOS: 845.C.00/2-149; Acheson to Acly, Feb. 4, 1949, DOS: 845C.00/2-149; Henderson to Acheson, Feb. 8, 1949, DOS: 845C.00/2-849; Acheson to Douglas, Feb. 22, 1949, DOS: 845.C.00/2-2249; Douglas to Acheson, Feb. 23, 1949, DOS: 845C.00/2-2349; Henderson to Acheson, Feb. 26, 1949, DOS: 845C.00/2-2649; Memorandum of Conversation (Sparks), Feb. 15, 1949, Acheson Papers, Box 64.

23. Cady, *History of Modern Burma,* pp. 597-607; Fifield, *Americans in Southeast Asia,* pp. 52-55; Johnstone, *Burma's Foreign Policy,* pp. 55-58; Huddle to Acheson, April 29, 1949, DOS: 845C.00/4-2949; Memorandum by Collins, Sept. 14, 1949, DOS: 845C.00/9-1449; McGhee to Acheson, Oct. 21 1949, DOS: 845C.00/10-2149; Clifford to Usher, Nov. 25, 1949, DOS: 845C.00/11-2549; Acheson to Huddle, Dec. 7, 1949, DOS: 845C.00/12-749.

24. Johnstone, *Burma's Foreign Policy,* pp. 58-61; Memorandum of Conversation (Jessup), Feb. 8, 1950, *FRUS 1950* 6:229-32; Acheson to Rangoon Embassy, Feb. 17, 1950, *FRUS 1950* 6:232-33; Policy Statement prepared by State Dept., June 16, 1950, *FRUS 1950* 6:233-44; Rangon Embassy to Acheson, Dec. 31, 1949, DOS: 845C.00/12-3149; Lawton to Truman, May 22, 1950 HST Papers, WHCF-Box 25.

25. Reed to Butterworth, Nov. 30, 1948, DOS: 892.00/11-3048.

26. Wilson, "Thailand," in Kahin, ed., *Governments and Politics of Southeast Asia,* pp. 23-25.

27. Stanton to Landon, Feb. 18, 1949, DOS: 892.00/2-1849; Butterworth to

Acheson, Jan. 26, 1949, DOS: PSEA, Box 17; Stanton to Acheson March 8, 1949, DOS: 892.00/3-849; Reed to Butterworth, March 29, 1949, DOS: 892 00/3-2949; Stanton to Acheson, Aug. 2, 1949, DOS: 892.00/8-249; Butterworth, Berkner, and Rusk to Acheson, Aug. 5, 1949, DOS: 892.00/8-249.

28. Acheson to Cochran, Dec. 27, 1949, *FRUS 1949* 7:588; Beam to Acheson, Dec. 29, 1948, DOS: 856D.01/12-2949.

29. Taylor, *Indonesian Independence and the United Nations,* pp. 388-89; Andrew Roth, "Indonesia: Republic with Strings," *Nation,* Dec. 31, 1949, pp. 640-43; McVey, *Soviet View of the Indonesian Revolution,* p. 83.

30. Kahin, *Nationalism and Revolution in Indonesia,* pp. 438-44; Feith, *Decline of Constitutional Democracy in Indonesia, pp. 13-15;* Memorandum of Conversation (Lacy), Sept. 14, *1949, FRUS 1949* 7:483-85; Steere to Acheson, Oct. 8, 9, 11, 19 and 23, 1949, *FRUS 1949* 7:505-9, 512-15, 522-24, 541-43, 546-47; Stikker to Acheson, Sept 16, 1949, *FRUS 1949* 7:489-92; Acheson to Chapin, Oct. 14, 1949, *FRUS 1949* 7:528-29; Chapin to Acheson, Nov. 1 and 2, 1949, *FRUS 1949* 7:558-61.

31. Memorandum by Thompson, Oct. 18, 1949, DOS: 856D.01/10-1849.

32. Acheson to Chapin, Oct. 18, 1949, *FRUS 1949* 7:535-36; Nolting to Acheson, Oct. 20, 1949, *FRUS 1949* 7:543-44; Chapin to Acheson, Oct. 30-31, 1949, *FRUS 1949* 7:550-58; Memorandum of Conversation (Rusk), Nov. 4, 1949, *FRUS 1949* 7:564-65; Rusk to Burns, March 22, 1950,*FRUS 1950* 6:985-87.

33. Acheson to Hague Embassy, Nov. 2 and 4, 1949, *FRUS 1949* 7:562-64; Memorandum of Conversation (Lacy), Nov. 7, 1949 *FRUS 1949* 7:567-70; Acheson to Cochran, Dec. 15 and 20, 1949, *FRUS 1949* 7:582-84; Acheson to Truman, Jan. 9, 1950, *FRUS 1950* 6:1964-66; Cochran to Acheson, Jan. 19, 24, 29, April 3, and May 18, 1950, *FRUS 1950* 6:967-71, 973-75, 1000-5, 1023-25; Memorandum of Conversation (Scott), March 21, 1950, Acheson Papers, Box 21. On Indonesian domestic developments and their relationship to foreign policy at this time, see Feith, *Decline of Constitutional Democracy in Indonesia,* pp.23-88.

34. Memorandum of Conversation (Acheson), Feb. 16, 1950, *FRUS 1950* 6:730-33; Bruce to Acheson, Feb. 23, Arpil 8, and June 17, 1950, *FRUS 1950* 6:743-44, 772-73, 822-23; Gullion to Acheson, March 18, May 6, June 16 and 18, 1950, *FRUS 1950* 6:764-65, 802-09, 820-21, 823-27; Ogburn to Butterworth, March 21, 1950, *FRUS 1950* 6:766-67; Acheson to Truman, April 17, 1950, *FRUS 1950* 6:785-86; Lemnitzer to Bruce, April 19, 1950, *FRUS 1950* 6:787-89; Bissel to ECA Mission in France, *FRUS 1950* 6:801-02; Irving, *First Indochina War,* p. 100 Rotter, "The Big Canvas," pp. 341-52.

35. Fifield, *Americans in Southeast Asia,* pp. 142-43; Stanton to Acheson Feb. 17, 18, and 27, 1950, *FRUS 1950* 6:18-20, 27-30; Memorandum of Conversation (Jessup), Feb. 6, 1950, *FRUS 1950* 6:11-18; Record of Conversation, March 11, 1950, *FRUS 1950* 6:46-51.

36. Memorandum of Conversation (Ogburn), April 3, 1950, *FRUS 1950* 6:68-76.

37. Memorandum of Conversation (Jessup), Feb. 3, 1950, *FRUS 1950* 6:975-78; Acheson to Cochran, Feb. 7, 1950 *ibid.,* p. 978.

38. Samuel P. Hayes, ed., *The Beginning of American Aid to Southeast Asia;* Fifield, *Americans in Southeast Asia,* pp. 143-45; Stanton to Acheson, April 12, 1950, *FRUS 1950,* 6:79-81; Poole to Acheson, March 21, 1950, *FRUS 1950* 6:64-65; Lacy to Rusk, June 30, 1950, *FRUS 1950* 6:106; Griffin to Acheson, April 22, 1950, *FRUS 1950* 6:1011-16.

39. Webb to Gullion, May 15, 1950, *FRUS 1950* 6:93-94.

40. Record of Interdeparmental Meeting on Far East, May 11, 1950, *FRUS 1950* 6:87-92.

41. Acheson to Marshall, Feb. 1, 1950, *FRUS 1950* 6:5-8; Webb to Acheson, Feb. 3, 1950, *ibid.*, pp. 8-11; NSC Report (Webb), Feb. 27, 1950, *ibid.*, pp. 30-35; Acheson to Truman, March 9, 1950, *ibid.* pp. 40-44; Ohly to Rusk, March 11, 1950, *ibid.*, pp. 52-53; Memorandum of Conversation (Robertson), March 14, 1950, *ibid.*, pp. 55-57; Parelman to Merchant, April 12, 1950, *ibid.*, pp. 76-79; Rusk to Webb, April 25, 1950, *ibid.*, pp. 83-84; Lacy to Rusk, May 22, 1950, *ibid.*, pp. 94-96; Memorandum by Ohly, June 1, 1950, *ibid.*, pp. 98-100; Minutes, Foreign Military Assistance Coordinating Committee, June 30, 1950, *ibid.* pp. 107-13.

42. Acheson to Saigon legation, July 1, 1950, *FRUS 1950* 6:113-14; Acheson to Truman, July 10, 1950, *ibid.*, pp. 115-16; Minutes, Southeast Asia Aid Policy Committee July 13, 1950, *ibid.*, pp. 117-19; Acheson to Rangoon Embassy, July 21 and Aug. 20, 1950, *ibid.*, pp. 120, 252; Minutes of Undersecretary's Meeting, Nov. 8, 1950, *ibid.*, pp. 155-57; Final Report, Joint Survey Mission, Dec. 6, 1950 *ibid.*, pp. 164-73; Cochran to Acheson, Sept. 30, 1950, *ibid.*, 1069-72; Joint Survey Mission to Foreign Military Assistance Coordinating Committee, Aug. 6, 1950, *ibid.*, pp. 840-44; Heath to Acheson, Aug. 7 and 9, 1950, *ibid.*, pp. 844-51; Melby to Lacy, Sept. 28, 1950, *ibid.*, pp. 1493-95.

43. David Wurfel, "The Bell Report and After," pp. 120-45; *Manila Chronicle,* July 10, Oct. 18, 30-31, 1950; Bell to Acheson and Snyder, Aug. 1, 1950, *FRUS 1950* 6:1468-72; Memorandum of Conversation (Bell-Marshall), Aug. 21, 1950, *FRUS 1950* 6:1474-80; Acheson to Truman, Aug. 31, 1950, *FRUS 1950* 6:1482-83; Memorandum of Conversation (Acheson), Sept. 11, 1950, *FRUS 1950* 6:1483; Report of Bell Mission, Oct. 9, 1950, *FRUS 1950* 6:1497-1502; Acheson to Cowens, Oct. 17, 1950, *FRUS 1950* 6:1503-4; Webb to Truman, Oct. 23, 1950, *FRUS 1950* 6:1505.

44. NSC 84/2, Nov. 9, 1950, *FRUS 1950* 6:1514-20; Memorandum of Philippine-American Agreement, Nov. 14, 1950, *ibid.*, pp. 1521-23.

45. Albert Ravenholt, "The Philippines: Where Did We Fail?" pp. 406-15; Fifield, *Americans in Southeast Asia,* p. 154.

46. *Ibid.*, pp. 98-99, 155; Fifield, *Diplomacy of Southeast Asia,* p. 250; Policy Statement, Oct. 15, 1950, *FRUS 1950* 6:1529-39.

47. Cady, *History of Modern Burma,* pp. 599-621; Trager "Burma's Foreign Policy," pp. 91-92; Hares to Rusk, July 1, 1950, *FRUS 1950* 6:244-45; Acheson to Taipei Embassy, July 28, 1950, *FRUS 1950* 6:246-47; Strong to Acheson, Aug. 11, 1950, *FRUS 1950* 6:249-50; Key to Acheson, Aug. 15 and Dec. 6, 1950, *FRUS 1950* 6:250-51, 254-55; Acheson to Key, Dec. 11, 1950, *FRUS 1950* 6:255.

48. Rotter, "The Big Canvas," pp. 260-313; Sodhy, "Passage of Empire," pp. 250-55.

49. Cochran to Acheson, July 15 and 26, Aug. 9, 16, and 26, Sept. 25, Oct. 10 and 26, and Dec. 8, 1950, *FRUS 1950* 6:1030-33, 1037-39, 1046-57, 1066-69, 1078-80, 1090-92, 1096-98; Acheson to Cochran, July 26, 1950, *FRUS 1950* 6:1039-40; Policy Statement on Indonesia, July 27, 1950, *FRUS 1950* 6:1041-43; Marshall to Acheson, Nov. 7, 1950, *FRUS 1950* 6:1092-93; Rusk to Acheson, Dec. 29, 1950, *FRUS 1950* 6:1100-5; Sumner to Griffin, March 10, 1950, John D. Sumner Papers, Truman Library. Feith, *Decline of Constitutional Democracy in Indonesia,* pp. 90-92, 155-157, 175.

50. Jacques Soustelle, "Indo-China and Korea: One Front," *Foreign Affairs* (October 1950) 29:56-66; Irving, *First Indochina War,* pp. 101-2; Acheson to Truman,

July 3, 1950, *FRUS 1950* 6:835-36; Acheson to Saigon Legation, July 1, 1950, *FRUS 1950* 6:833-34; Guillion To Acheson, June 29, 1950, *FRUS 1950* 6:831-33.

51. PPS Memorandum, Aug. 16, 1950, *FRUS 1950* 6:857-58; Memorandum of Conversation (O'Sullivan), July 31, 1950, *ibid,* pp. 839-40.

52. Bruce to Acheson, Aug. 17 and Sept. 15, 1950, *FRUS 1950* 6:859-60, 875-76; Heath to Acheson, Aug. 23, Sept. 4 and 19, Oct. 23, 1950, *FRUS 1950* 6:864-67, 873-75, 882-84, 902-05; Ogburn to Rusk, *FRUS 1950* 6:862-64; Acheson to Saigon Legation, Sept. 1, 1950, *FRUS 1950* 6:868-70; Rusk to Acheson, Sept. 11, 1950, *FRUS 1950* 6:878-80; Webb to Saigon Legation, Sept. 16, 1950, *FRUS 1950* 6:880-81; U.S. House, CAS, *United States-Vietnam Relations, 1945-1967* (Book 1), IV, A-2 to A-14.

53. Irving, *First Indochina War,* pp. 81-101; Memorandum by Lay, Dec. 21, 1950, *FRUS 1950* 6:945-53; CIA Memorandum, Dec. 29, 1950, *FRUS 1950* 6:958-6:63; Southeast Asia Policy Committee to Acheson and Marshall, *FRUS 1950* 6:886-890; Matthews to Acheson, Oct. 19, 1950, *FRUS 1950* 6:900-1; Merchant to Rusk, Oct. 19, 1950, *FRUS 1950* 6:901-2; Acheson to Saigon Legation, Oct 30, 1950, *FRUS 1950* 6:913-14; Ohly to Rusk, Nov. 20, 1950, *FRUS 1950* 6:924-30.

# Bibliography

## Manuscript and Archival Collections

Great Britain: Public Record Office, London
    Cabinet Conclusions
    Cabinet Memoranda
    Cabinet Minutes
    Chiefs of Staff Committee
    Colonial Office Files
    Foreign Office Files
    Prime Ministers Office Files
U.S.: National Archives, Washington, D.C.
    Dept. of Interior
      Records of the Office of the Secretary
      Records of Office of Territories
    Dept. of State
      Decimal Files
      Interdepartmental-Intradepartmental Committee File
      Harley Notter File
      Leo Pasvolsky File
      Philippine and Southeast Asian Division File
      State-War-Navy Coordinating Committee File
      Secretary of State Staff Committee File
    Chiefs of Staff Minutes
    Office of Strategic Services, Research and Analysis Reports
U.S.: Federal Archives, Suitland, Maryland
    China Theater, Wedemeyer Files
    Southeast Asia Command Files

Dean Acheson Papers, Harry S. Truman Library.
Adolph A. Berle Papers, Franklin D. Roosevelt Library.
Myron M. Cowen Papers, Harry S. Truman Library.
James Forrestal Papers, Seeley C. Mudd Manuscript Library, Princeton, N.J.
Warren W. Gardner Papers, Harry S. Truman Library.

Stanley K. Hornbeck Papers, Hoover Institution Archives, Stanford University Palo Alto, Calif.

Cordell Hull Papers, Library of Congress, Washington, D.C.

Louis Johnson Papers, Alderman Library, University of Virginia, Charlottesville.

J. Weldon Jones Papers, Harry S. Truman Library.

Douglas MacArthur Papers, MacArthur Memorial Library and Archives, Norfolk, Va.

George C. Marshall Papers, George C. Marshall Library, Lexington, Va.

Paul V. McNutt Papers, Lilly Library, Indiana University, Bloomington.

Willys Peck Papers, Hoover Institution Archives, Stanford University, Palo Alto, Calif.

Eleanor Roosevelt Papers, Franklin D. Roosevelt Library.

Franklin D. Roosevelt Papers, Franklin D. Roosevelt Library, Hyde Park, N.Y.

Samuel I. Rosenman Papers, Harry S. Truman Library.

Edward Stettinius Papers, Alderman Library, University of Virginia, Charlottesville.

John D. Sumner Papers, Harry S. Truman Library.

Charles W. Taussig Papers, Franklin D. Roosevelt Library.

Harry S. Truman Papers, Harry S. Truman Library, Independence, Mo.

Louis Wehle Papers, Franklin D. Roosevelt Library.


## Books, Articles, Dissertations, and Papers

Abaya, Hernanda J. *Betrayal in the Philippines.* New York: Wyn, 1946.

Agoncillo, Teodoro A. *The Fateful Years: Japan's Adventure in the Philippines, 1941-1945.* 2 vols. Quezon City: Garcia, 1965.

Aidit, D.N. *Problems of the Indonesian Revolution.* Bandung: Demos, 1963.

Aidit, S.N. *A Short History of the Communist Party of Indonesia.* New Delhi: People's Publishing House, 1955.

Anderson, Benedict R. O'G. "Japan: The Light of Asia." In Josef Silverstein, ed., *Southeast Asia in World War II,* pp. 13-50. New Haven: Yale University Press, 1966.

Anderson, Benedict R. O'G. *Some Aspects of Indonesian Politics Under the Japanese Occupation, 1944-1945.* Ithaca: Cornell University Southeast Asian Program, Modern Indonesia Project, 1961.

Anderson, Benedict R. O'G. *Java in a Time of Revolution: Occupation and Resistance, 1944-1946.* Ithaca: Cornell University Press, 1972.

Anderson, Irvine H. *The Standard-Vacuum Oil Company and United States East Asian Policy, 1933-1941.* Princeton: Princeton University Press, 1974.

Anderson, Irvine H., Jr. "The 1941 De Facto Embargo on Oil to Japan; A Bureaucratic Reflex." *Pacific Historical Review* (1975), 44:201-231.

Baliga, Bantval Mohandas. "The American Approach to Imperialism in Southeast Asia--The Attitude of the United States Government in the Philippines, Indo-China, and Indonesia, 1945-1958." Ph.D. dissertation, Southern Illinois University, 1961.

Batson, Benjamin A. "American Diplomats in Southeast Asia in the 19th Century: The Case of Siam." *Journal of Siam Society* (1976), 64:39-111.

Benda, Harry J. *The Crescent and the Rising Sun.* The Hague: W. van Hoeve, 1958.

Bernstein, David. *The Philippine Story.* New York: Farrar, Strauss, 1947.

Blake, I. George. *Paul V. McNutt: Portrait of a Hoosier Statesman.* Indianapolis: Central, 1966.

Blum, Robert M. *Drawing the Line: The Origins of the American Containment Policy in East Asia.* New York: Norton, 1982.

Bodard, Lucien. *The Quicksand War: Prelude to Vietnam.* Patrick O'Brien, tr. Boston: Little Brown, 1967.

Borden, William S. *The Pacific Alliance: The United States Foreign Economic Policy and Japanese Trade Recovery, 1947-1954.* Madison: University of Wisconsin Press, 1984.

Borg, Dorothy and Shumpei Okamoto, eds. *Pearl Harbor as History: Japanese-American Relations, 1931-1941.* New York: Columbia University Press, 1973.

*Breaking Our Chains: Documents on the Vietnamese Revolution of August 1945.* Hanoi: Foreign Languages Publishing House, 1960.

Buhite, Russell. *Soviet-American Relations in Asia, 1945-1954.* Norman: University of Oklahoma Press, 1981.

Burns, James MacGregor. *Roosevelt: The Soldier of Freedom.* New York: Harcourt Brace, Jovanovich, 1970.

Butow, Robert J.C. *Tojo and the Coming of the War.* Stanford: Stanford University Press, 1961.

Buttinger, Joseph. *Vietnam: A Dragon Embattled.* 2 vols. New York: Praeger, 1967.

Cady, John F. *History of Modern Burma.* Ithaca, N.Y.: Cornell University Press, 1958.

Cady, John F. *History of Postwar Southeast Asia.* Athens: Ohio University Press, 1974.

Cady, John F. *The United States and Burma.* Cambridge: Harvard University Press, 1976.

Cameron, Allen W., ed. *Viet-nam Crisis; A Documentary History.* 2 vols. Ithaca: Cornell University Press, 1971.

Campbell, Thomas N. and George C. Herring, eds. *The Diaries of Edward R. Stettinius, 1943-1946.* New York: New Viewpoints, 1975.

Chen, King. *Vietnam and China, 1938-1954.* Princeton: Princeton University Press, 1969.

Chesneaux, Jean. *The Vietnamese Nation.* Malcolm Salmon, tr. Sydney, Australia: Current Books Distributors, 1966.

Chowdhry, Carol. "Dusk of Empire: Roosevelt and Asian Colonialism, 1941-1945." Ph.D. dissertation, University of Virginia, 1973.

Cohen, Warren I. "Acheson, His Advisers, and China, 1949-1950." In Dorothy Borg and Waldo Heinrichs, eds. *Uncertain Years: Chinese-American Relations, 1947-1950,* pp. 13-52. New York: Columbia University Press, 1980.

Colbert, Evelyn. "The Road Not Taken: Decolonization and Independence in Indonesia and Indochina." *Foreign Affairs* (1973), 51:608-628.

Collins, J. Foster. "The United Nations and Indonesia." *International Conciliation* (1950), 115-120.

*Complete Presidential Press Conferences of Franklin D. Roosevelt.* New York: DaCapo Press, 1972.

Cooper, Bert, John Killigrew, and Norman LaCharite. *Case Studies in Insurgency and Revolutionary Warfare: Vietnam 1941-1954.* Washington, D.C.: Special Operations Research Office, 1964.

Cooper, Chester. *The Lost Crusade: America in Vietnam.* New York: Dodd, Mead, and Co., 1970.

Cortes, Teodoro V. "Interaction Patterns in a Big Power-Small Power Relationship: The United States-Philippine Experience, 1946 to 1971." Ph.D. dissertation, University of Illinois, 1972.

Coyle, Joanne Marie. "Indochina Administration and Education: French Policy and Practice, 1917-1945." Ph.D. dissertation: Fletcher School, Tufts University, 1963.

Dahm, Bernard. *Sukarno and the Struggle for Indonesia Independence.* Mary F. Somers Heidhues, tr. Ithaca: Cornell University Press, 1969.

Dallek, Robert. *Franklin D. Roosevelt and American Foreign Policy, 1932-1945.* New York: Oxford University Press, 1979.

Darkow, Warren W. "American Relations with Burma, 1800-1950." M.S. thesis, University of Wisconsin, 1951.

Davies, John P. *Dragon by the Tail.* New York: Norton, 1972.

Decoux, Jean. *A la Barre de l'Indochine: Histoire de mon Government Général.* Paris: Librarie Plan, 1949.

de Gaulle, Charles. *The War Memoirs of Charles de Gaulle: Salvation, 1944-1946.* Richard Howard, tr. New York: Simon and Schuster, 1960.

Devèze, Michel. *La France d'Outre-Mer: de l'Empire colonial a l'Union Francaise, 1938-1947.* Paris: Librairie Hachette, 1948.

Devillers, Philippe. *Histoire de Viêt-Nam de 1940 a 1952.* Paris: Editions du Seuil, 1952.

Djajadiningrat, Idrus Nasir. *The Beginnings of the Indonesian-Dutch Negotiations and the Hoge Veluve Talks.* Ithaca: Cornell University Southeast Asia Program, Modern Indonesia Project, 1958.

Donnison, F.S.V. *British Military Administration in the Far East, 1943-1946.* London: HMSO, 1956.

Drachman, Edward R. *United States Policy Toward Vietnam, 1940-1945.* Rutherford, N.J.: Farleigh Dickinson University Press, 1970.

DuFault, David V. "Francis B. Sayre and the Commonwealth of the Philippines, 1936-1942." Ph.D. dissertation, University of Oregon, 1972.

Duiker, William J. *The Rise of Nationalism in Vietnam, 1900-1941.* Ithaca: Cornell University Press, 1976.

Dulles, Foster Rhea and Gerald Ridinger. "The Anti-Colonial Policies of Franklin D. Roosevelt." *Political Science Quarterly,* (1955), 70:1-18.

Eden, Anthony. *The Memoirs of Anthony Eden, Earl of Avon: The Reckoning.* Boston: Houghton Mifflin, 1965.

Eggleston, Noel. "The Roots of Commitment: United States Policy Toward Vietnam, 1945-1950." Ph.D. dissertation, University of Georgia, 1977.

Elsbree, William H. *Japan's Role in Southeast Asian Nationalist Movements, 1940 to 1945.* Cambridge: Harvard University Press, 1953.

Etzold, Thomas H. "The Far East in American Strategy, 1948-1951." In Thomas H. Etzold, ed., *Aspects of Sino-American Relations since 1784,* pp. 102-126. New York: New Viewpoints, 1978.

Fall, Bernard B. *Last Reflections on a War.* Garden City, N.Y.: Doubleday, 1967.

Fall, Bernard B. "The Political Development of Viet-Nam, V-J Day to the Geneva Cease-Fire." Ph.D. dissertation, Syracuse University, 1955.

Feis, Herbert. *Churchill, Roosevelt, Stalin: The War They Fought and The Peace They Sought.* Princeton: Princeton University Press, 1967.

Feis, Herbert. *The Road to Pearl Harbor: The Coming of the War Between the United States and Japan.* Princeton: Princeton University Press, 1950.

Feith, Herbert. *The Decline of Constitutional Democracy in Indonesia.* Ithaca: Cornell University Press, 1962.

Fenn, Charles. *Ho Chi Minh: A Biographical Introduction.* New York: Scribner, 1973.

Fifield, Russell. *Americans in Southeast Asia: The Roots of Commitment.* New York: Crowell, 1973.

Fifield, Russell. *The Diplomacy of Southeast Asia, 1945-1958.* New York: Harper, 1958.

Fine, Herbert A. "The Liquidation of World War II in Thailand." *Pacific Historical Review* (1965), 34:65-82.

Fischer, Louis. *The Story of Indonesia.* New York: Harper, 1959.

Flood, Edward T. "Japan's Relations with Thailand, 1928-1941." Ph.D. dissertation, University of Washington, 1967.

Flood, E. Thadeus. "The 1940 Franco-Thai Border Dispute and Phibun Sonkhraam's Commitment to Japan." *Journal of Southeast Asian History* (1969), 10:304-325.

Friend, Theodore. *Between Two Empires: The Ordeal of the Philippines, 1929-1946.* New Haven: Yale University Press, 1965.

Gaddis, John Lewis. "The Strategic Perspective: The Rise and Fall of the

'Defensive Perimeter' Concept, 1947-1951," In Dorothy Borg    and Waldo Heinrichs, eds., *Uncertain Years: Chinese-American Relations, 1947-1950*, pp. 61-118. New York: Columbia University Press, 1980.

Gaddis, John Lewis. *Strategies of Containment; A Critical Appraisal of Postwar American National Security Policy*. New York: Oxford University Press, 1982.

Garfield, Gene J. "The Genesis of Involvement: The Truman Decision to Assist the French in Indo-China." Ph.D. dissertation, Southern Illinois University, 1972.

Garrett, Clark W. "In Search of Grandeur: France and Vietnam, 1940-1946," *Review of Politics* (1967), 29:303-323.

Gerig, Benjamin. *Open Door and the Mandates System; A Study of Economic Equality Before and Since the Establishment of the Mandates System*. London: Allen and Unwin, 1930.

Golay, Frank H., ed. *The United States and the Philippines*. Englewood Cliffs, N.J.: Prentice-Hall 1966.

Grunder, Garel and William Livezey. *The Philippines and the United States*. Norman: University of Oklahoma Press, 1951.

Guyot, Dorothy. "The Burma Independence Army: A Political Movement in Military Garb." In Josef Silverstein, ed., *Southeast Asia in World War II*, pp. 51-65. New Haven: Yale University Press, 1966.

Guyot, Dorothy. "The Political Impact of the Japanese Occupation of Burma." Ph.D. dissertation, Yale University, 1966.

Hammer, Ellen J. *The Emergence of Viet Nam*. New York: Institute of Pacific Relations, 1947.

Hammer, Ellen J. *The Struggle for Indochina, 1940-1955*. Stanford: Stanford University Press, 1966.

Hartendorp, A.V.H. *The Japanese Occupation of the Philippines*. 2 vols. Manila: Bookmark, 1967.

Hayes, Samuel P., ed. *The Beginning of American Aid to Southeast Asia: The Griffin Mission of 1950*. Lexington, Mass.: Heath Lexington Books, 1971.

Heinrichs, Waldo H., Jr. *American Ambassador: Joseph C. Grew and the Development of the United States Diplomatic Tradition*. Boston: Little, Brown, 1966.

Heinrichs, Waldo H., Jr. "The Role of the United States Navy." In Dorothy Borg and Shumpei Okamoto, eds., *Pearl Harbor as History; Japanese-American Relations, 1931-1941*, pp. 197-224. New York: Columbia University Press, 1973.

Herring, George C. "The Truman Administration and the Restoration of French Sovereignty in Indochina." *Diplomatic History* (1977), 1:97-117.

Herring, George C. *America's Longest War: The United States and Vietnam, 1950-1975*. New York: Wiley, 1979.

Hess, Gary R. *America Encounters India, 1941-1947.* Baltimore: Johns Hopkins University Press, 1971.

Hess, Gary R. "Franklin Roosevelt and Indochina." *Jounal of American History* (1972), 59:353-368.

Hess, Gary R. "United States Policy and the Origins of the French-Viet Minh War, 1945-46." *Peace and Change* (1975), 3:21-33.

Hess, Gary R. "The First American Commitment in Indochina: The Acceptance of the 'Bao Dai Solution' 1950." *Diplomatic History,* (1978), 2:331-350.

Hudson, W. J. "Australia and Indonesian Independence." *Journal of Southeast Asian History,* (1967), 8:226-239.

Hull, Cordell. *The Memoirs of Cordell Hull.* 2 vols. New York: Macmillan, 1948.

Ickes, Harold L. *The Secret Diary of Harold L. Ickes: The Lowering Clouds, 1939-1941.* New York: Simon and Schuster, 1954.

Ike, Nobutaka, ed. and tr. *Japan's Decision for War: Records of the 1941 Policy Conferences.* Stanford: Stanford University Press, 1967.

Iriye, Akira. "Japanese Imperialism and Aggression: Reconsiderations." *Journal of Asian Studies* (1963), 23:103-113.

Iriye, Akira. *Across the Pacific: an Inner History of American-East Asian Relations.* New York: Harcourt, Brace, Jovanovich, 1967.

Iriye, Akira. *The Cold War in Asia: A Historical Introduction.* Englewood Cliffs, N.J.: Prentice Hall, 1973.

Iriye, Akira. *Power and Culture; The Japanese-American War, 1941-1945.* Cambridge: Harvard University Press, 1981.

Irving, R. E. M. *The First Indochina War; French and American Policy, 1945-1954.* London: Croom Helm, 1975.

Isaacs, Harold. *No Peace for Asia.* New York: Macmillan, 1947.

Isoart, Paul. *Le Phénomène national vietnamien: De l'indépendance unitaire à l'indépendance fractionée.* Paris: Librairie General de Drooit and Jurisprudence, 1961.

James, D. Clayton. *The Years of MacArthur.* 3 vols. Boston: Houghton Mifflin, 1970-1985.

Jessup, Philip C. *The Birth of Nations.* New York: Columbia University Press, 1973.

Johnstone, William C. *Burma's Foreign Policy; A Study in Neutralism.* Cambridge: Harvard University Press, 1963.

Jones, F. C. *Japan's New Order in East Asia: Its Rise and Fall, 1937-1945.* London: Oxford University Press, 1954.

Kahin, George McT. *Governments and Politics of Southeast Asia.* Ithaca: Cornell University Press, 1964.

Kahin, George McT. *Nationalism and Revolution in Indonesia.* Ithaca: Cornell University Press, 1952.

Kahin, George McT. "The United States and the Anticolonial Revolutions in Southeast Asia, 1945-50." In Yonosuke Nagai and Akira Iriye, eds., *The Origins of the Cold War in Asia,* pp. 338-361. New York: Columbia University Press, 1977.

Kanahele, George S. "The Japanese Occupation of Indonesia: Prelude to Independence." Ph.D. dissertation, Cornell University, 1967.

Kaplan, Lawrence S. *A Community of Interests: NATO and the Military Assistance Program, 1948-1951.* Washington, D.C.: Department of Defense, 1980.

Kattenburg, Paul M. *The Vietnam Trauma in American Foreign Policy, 1945-75.* New Brunswick, N.J.: Transaction Books, 1980.

Khanh, Huynh Kim. "The Vietnamese August Revolution Reinterpreted." *Journal of Asian Studies* (1971), 30:761-82.

Kim, Sung Yong. *United States-Philippine Relations, 1946-1956.* Washington: Public Affairs Press, 1968.

Kimball, Warren F., ed. *Churchill and Roosevelt: The Complete Correspondence.* 3 vols. Princeton: Princeton University Press, 1984.

Kirk, Grayson. *Philippine Independence: Motives, Problems, and Prospects.* New York: Farrar and Rinehart, 1936.

Kolko, Gabriel. *The Politics of War: The World and United States Foreign Policy, 1943-1945.* New York: Random House, 1969.

Lacouture, Jean. *Ho Chi Minh: A Political Biography.* Peter Wiles, tr. New York: Random House, 1968.

Lach, Donald F. and Edmund S. Wehrle. *International Politics in East Asia Since World War II.* New York: Praeger, 1975.

LaFeber, Walter. "Roosevelt, Churchill, and Indochina." *American Historical Review* (1975), 80:1277-1295.

Lancaster, Donald. *The Emancipation of French Indochina.* New York: Oxford University Press, 1961.

Landon, Kenneth. "Southeast Asia and U.S. Foreign Policy." *United Asia* (Bombay) (1965), 17:267-277.

Langer, William L. *Our Vichy Gamble.* New York: Knopf, 1947.

Lear, Elmer. *The Japanese Occupation of the Philippines: Leyte, 1941-1945.* Ithaca: Cornell University Southeast Asian Program, 1961.

Lee, Bradford. *Britain and the Sino-Japanese War, 1937-1939; A Study in the Dilemmas of British Decline.* Stanford: Stanford University Press, 1973.

Legardia, Benito and Robert Y. Garcia. "Economic Collaboration: The Trading Relationship." In Frank H. Golay, ed., *The United States and the Philippines,* pp. 125-148. Englewood Cliffs, N.J.; Prentice-Hall, 1966.

Leupold, Robert J. "The United States and Indonesian Independence, 1944-1947: An American Response to Revolution." Ph.D. dissertation, University of Kentucky, 1976.

Leutze, James R. *Bargaining for Supremacy: Anglo-American Naval Collaboration, 1937-1941.* Chapel Hill: University of North Carolina Press, 1977.

Lord, Donald G. "Missionaries, Thai, and Diplomats." *Pacific Historical Review* (1966), 35:413-431.

Louis, William Roger. *British Strategy in the Far East 1919-1939.* New York: Oxford University Press, 1971.

Louis, William Roger. *Imperialism at Bay: The United States and the Decolonization of the British Empire, 1941-1945.* New York: Oxford University Press, 1978.

Lowe, Peter. *Great Britain and the Origins of the Pacific War: A Study of British Policy in East Asia, 1937-1941.* London: Oxford University Press, 1977.

Lowenheim, Francis L., Harold D. Langley, and Manfred Jonas, eds. *Roosevelt and Churchill: Their Secret Wartime Correspondence.* New York: Dutton, 1975.

McAlister, John T. *Vietnam: The Origins of Revolution.* New York: Knopf, 1969.

McHale, Thomas R. "The Philippines in Transition." *Journal of Asian Studies* (1961), 20:331-342.

McLane, Charles B. *Soviet Strategies in Southeast Asia: An Exploration of Eastern Policy Under Lenin and Stalin.* Princeton: Princeton University Press, 1966.

McMahon, Robert J. "Anglo-American Diplomacy and the Reoccupation of the Netherlands Indies," *Diplomatic History* (1978), 2:1-24.

McMahon, Robert J. *Colonialism and Cold War: The United States and the Struggle for Indonesian Independence, 1945-1949.* Ithaca: Cornell University Press, 1981.

McVey, Ruth. *The Calcutta Conference and the Southeast Asian Uprisings.* Ithaca: Cornell University Southeast Asia Program, Modern Indonesia Project, 1958.

McVey, Ruth. *The Rise of Indonesian Communism.* Ithaca: Cornell University Press, 1965.

McVey, Ruth. *The Soviet View of the Indonesian Revolution: A Study in the Russian Attitude toward Asian Nationalism.* Ithaca: Cornell University Southeast Asia Program, Modern Indonesia Project, 1957.

*Manila Chronicle,* 1946-1950. *Manila Daily Bulletin,* 1946-1950.

Marr, David G. *Vietnamese Anti-Colonialism.* Berkeley: University of California Press, 1982.

Marr, David G. *Vietnamese Tradition on Trial.* Berkeley: University of California Press, 1982.

Martin, James V., Jr. "Thai-American Relations in World War II," *Journal of Asian Studies* (1963), 22:451-467.

Melby, John. "Vietnam-1950." *Diplomatic History* (1982), 6:97-109

Meyer, Milton W. *A Diplomatic History of the Philippine Republic.* Honolulu: University of Hawaii Press, 1965.

Millis, Walter, ed. *The Forrestal Diaries.* New York: Viking Press, 1951.

Minot, Patricio R. "Paul V. McNutt: His Role in the Birth of Philippine Independence." Ph.D. dissertation, Ball State University, 1974.

Mountbatten, Louis, Earl. *Post-Surrender Tasks: Section of the Report to the Combined Chiefs of Staff by the Supreme Allied Commander, Southeast Asia, 1943-1945.* London: HMSO, 1969.

Mountbatten, Louis, Earl. *Report to the Combined Chiefs of Staff by the Supreme Allied Commander, Southeast Asia, 1943-1945.* London: HMSO, 1951.

Mus, Paul. *Viet-Nam: Sociologie d'une Guerre.* Paris: Les Editions du Seuil, 1952.

Neuchterlein, Donald E. *Thailand and the Struggle for Southeast Asia.* Ithaca: Cornell University Press, 1965.

Neumann, William. *After Victory: Churchill, Roosevelt, Stalin, and the Making of the Peace.* New York: Harper and Row, 1967.

Neumann, William. *America Encounters Japan from Perry to MacArthur.* Baltimore: Johns Hopkins University Press, 1967

*New York Times,* 1940-1950.

Notter, Harley. *Postwar Foreign Policy Preparation, 1939-1945.* Washington, D.C.: GPO, 1950.

"NSC 68: A Report to the National Security Council by the Executive Secretary on United States Objectives and Programs for National Security, April 4, 1950." *Naval War College Review,* May-June 1975.

O'Ballance, Edgar. *The Indo-China War, 1945-1954: A Study in Guerrilla Warfare.* London: Faber and Faber, 1964.

Offner, Arnold A. *The Origins of the Second World War: American Foreign Policy and World Politics, 1917-1941.* New York: Praeger, 1975.

Ohn, Byunghoon. "United States and Southeast Asia, 1945-1954: The Evolution of American Policy in Southeast Asia." Ph.D. dissertation, University of Kentucky, 1966.

Paterson, Thomas G. *On Every Front: The Making of the Cold War.* New York: Norton, 1979.

Patti, Archimedes L. A. *Why Viet Nam? Prelude to America's Albatross.* Berkeley: University of California Press, 1980.

Paxton, Robert O. *Vichy France: Old Guard and New Order 1940-1944.* New York: Knopf, 1972.

Penders, C. L. M. *The Life and Times of Sukarno.* London: Sidgwick and Jackson, 1974.

Petillo, Carol Morris. *Douglas MacArthur: The Philippine Years.* Bloomington: Indiana University Press, 1981.

Pike, Douglas. *History of Vietnamese Communism.* Stanford: Stanford University Press, 1978.

Pluvier, Jan. *South-East Asia from Colonialism to Independence.* London: Oxford University Press, 1974.

Poole, Peter A. *The United States and Indochina from FDR to Nixon.* Hinsdale, Ill.: Dryden Press, 1973.

Ravenholt, Albert. "The Philippines: Where Did We Fail?" *Foreign Affairs* (1951), 29:406-415.

Reynolds, David. *The Creation of the Anglo-American Alliance, 1937-1941; A Study in Competitive Co-operation.* Chapel Hill: University of North Carolina Press, 1981.

Roth, Andrew. "Jokja Journal," *Nation,* June 26, 1948, pp. 715-717.

Roth, Andrew. "American Flipflop in Indonesia," *Nation,* July 10, 1948, pp. 39-41.

Romanus, Charles F. and Riley Sunderland. *Time Runs Out in CBI.* Washington, D.C.: Office of Chief of Military History, Department of Army, 1959.

Romanus, Charles F. and Riley Sunderland. *United States Army in World War II: China-Burma-India Theater--Stilwell's Command Problems.* Washington, D.C.: Office of Chief of Military History, Department of Army, 1956.

Roosevelt, Elliot. *As He Saw It.* New York: Duell, Sloan, and Pearce, 1946.

Rosenman, Samuel I. *The Public Papers and Addresses of Franklin D. Roosevelt.* 13 vols. New York: Harper, 1950.

Rotter, Andrew J. "The Big Canvas: The United States, Southeast Asia and the World." Ph.D. dissertation, Stanford University, 1981.

Rotter, Andrew J. "The Trianguar Route to Vietnam: The United States, Great Britain, and Southeast Asia, 1945-1950." *International History Review* (1984), 6:404-423.

Russell, Ruth B. *A History of the United Nations Charter; The Role of the United States.* Washington, D.C.: The Brookings Institution, 1958.

Sabattier, Gen. G. *Le Destin De L'Indochine, Souvenirs et Documents, 1941-1951.* Paris: Librairie Plan, 1952.

Sainteny, Jean. *Histoire d'une Paix Manquée: Indochine 1945-1947.* Paris: Amoit, Dumont, 1953.

Sainteny, Jean. *Ho Chi Minh and His Vietnam; A Personal Memoir.* Herman Briffault, tr. Chicago: Cowles, 1972.

Schaller, Michael. "Securing the Great Crescent: Occupied Japan and the Origins of Containment in Southeast Asia." *Journal of American History* (1982), 69:392-414.

Schaller, Michael. *The U.S. Crusade in China, 1938-1945.* New York: Columbia University Press, 1979.

Schlesinger, Arthur M., Jr. *The Bitter Heritage: Vietnam and American*

*Democracy, 1941-1968.* Greenwich, Conn: Fawcett, 1968.

Sellen, Robert W. "Comparative Perspectives on Indochina During World War II: The French Viewpoint, 1940-1945." Presented at American Historical Association Meeting, San Francisco, 1978.

Service, John S. *The Amerasia Papers.* Berkeley: University of California Press, 1971.

Sethachuay, Vivat. "United States-Thailand Diplomatic Relations during World War II." Ph.D. dissertation, Brigham Young University, 1977.

Shaplen, Robert. *The Lost Revolution: The U.S. in Vietnam, 1946-1966.* New York: Harper and Row, 1966.

Sherwood, Robert E. *Roosevelt and Hopkins: An Intimate History.* New York: Grosset and Dunlap, 1950.

Short, Anthony. *The Communist Insurrection in Malaya, 1948-1960.* London: Unwin, 1975.

Silverstein, Josef. "Burma." In George McT. Kahin, ed., *Governments and Politics of Southeast Asia,* pp. 75-181. Ithaca: Cornell University Press, 1964.

Silverstein, Josef. "Political Thought in Burma, 1945-1948," *Asia* (1966), 5:78-90.

Silverstein, Josef. "The Importance of the Japanese Occupation of Southeast Asia to the Political Scientist." In Josef Silverstein ed., *Southeast Asia in World War II,* pp. 1-12. New Haven: Yale University Press, 1966.

Singh, Rajendra. *Post-War Occupation Forces: Japan and Southeast Asia.* New Delhi: Combined Inter-Services Historical Section, India and Pakistan, 1958.

Siracusa, Joseph M. "The United States, Viet-Nam, and the Cold War: A Reappraisal," *Journal of Southeast Asian Studies* (1974), 5:82-101.

Siracusa, Joseph W. "NSC 68: A Reappraisal." Presented at Organization of American Historians Meeting, San Francisco, 1980.

Smith, Gaddis. *American Diplomacy During the Second World War, 1941-1945.* New York: Wiley, 1965.

Smith, Robert A. *Philippine Freedom, 1946-1958.* New York: Columbia University Press, 1958.

Sodhy, Pamela. "Passage of Empire: United States-Malayan Relations to 1966." Ph.D. dissertation, Cornell University, 1982.

Spector, Ronald H. *Advice and Support: The Early Years of the U.S. Army in Vietnam, 1941-1960.* New York: Free Press, 1985.

Spector, Ronald H. *Eagle Against the Sun; The American War with Japan.* New York: Free Press, 1985.

Spector, Ronald H. "What the Local Annamites are Thinking: American Views of Vietnamese in China, 1942-1945." *Southeast Asia* (1974), 3:741-751.

Stanley, Peter W. *A Nation in the Making; the Philippines and the United States, 1899-1921.* Cambridge: Harvard University Press, 1974.

Stannard, Raymond E. "The Role of American Aid in Indonesian-American Relations." M.A. thesis, Cornell University, 1957.

Stanton, Edwin F. *Brief Authority: Excursions of a Common Man in an Uncommon World.* New York: Harper, 1956.

Steinberg, David. "The Philippine 'Collaborators': Survival of an Oligarchy." In Josef Silverstein, ed., *Southeast Asia in World War II,* pp. 67-78. New Haven: Yale University Press, 1966.

Steinberg, David. *Philippine Collaboration in World War II.* Ann Arbor: University of Michigan Press, 1966.

Stettinius, Edward. *Roosevelt and the Russians.* Garden City, N.Y.: Doubleday, 1949.

Taylor, Alastair M. *Indonesian Independence and the United Nations.* Ithaca: Cornell University press, 1960.

Taylor, George E. *The Philippines and the United States.* New York: Praeger, 1964.

Thompson, James C., Jr. "The Role of the Department of State." In Dorothy Borg and Shumpei Okamoto, eds., *Pearl Harbor as History: Japanese-American Relations, 1931-1941.* New York: Columbia University Press, 1973.

Thompson, James C., Jr., Peter W. Stanley, and John Curtis Perry. *Sentimental Imerialists; The American Experience in East Asia.* New York: Harper and Row, 1981.

Thorne, Christopher. "Indo-China and Anglo-American Relations, 1942-1945." *Pacific Historical Review* (1976), 45:73-96.

Thorne, Christopher. *Allies of a Kind: The United States, Britain, and the War Against Japan, 1941-1945.* New York: Oxford University Press, 1978.

Tongdhummachart, Kramol. "American Policy in Southeast Asia, with Special Reference to Burma, Thailand, and Indochina, 1945-1960." Ph.D. dissertation, University of Virginia, 1962.

Toru, Yano. "Who Set the Stage for the Cold War in Southeast Asia?" In Yonosuka Nagai and Akira Iriye, eds., *The Origins of the Cold War in Asia,* pp.321-337. New York: Columbia University Press, 1977.

Trager, Frank N. *Building a Welfare State in Burma: Reconstruction and Development, 1948-1956.* New York: Institute of Pacific Relations 1955.

Trager, Frank. "Burma's Foreign Policy, 1948-1956: Neutralism, Third Force, and Rice." *Journal of Asian Studies* (1956), 16:90-102.

Trager, Frank. "Historical Perspectives on Independent Burma." *Asia* (1968), 13:71-91.

Trager, Frank N., ed. *Burma: Japanese Military Administration; Selected Documents, 1941-1945.* Philadelphia: University of Pennsylvania Press, 1971.

Troung Chinh. *Primer For Revolt: The Communist Takeover in Viet-Nam.* New York: Praeger, 1963.

Turner, Robert F. *Vietnamese Communism: Its Origins and Development.*

Stanford: Stanford University Press, 1978.

U Nu. *Saturday's Son.* U Law Yone, tr.; U Kyaw Win, ed. New Haven: Yale University Press, 1975.

U.S. Congress. *Congressional Record,* 1943-1947.

U.S. Department of Commerce. *Commerce Yearbook 1931.* Washington, D.C.: GPO, 1931.

    *Foreign Commerce Yearbook 1933.* Washington, D.C.: GPO, 1933.

    *Foreign Commerce Yearbook 1935.* Washington, D.C.: GPO, 1935.

    *Foreign Commerce Yearbook 1938.* Washington, D.C.: GPO, 1939.

    *Foreign Commerce Yearbook 1939.* Washington, D.C.: GPO, 1942.

    *Foreign Commerce Yearbook 1948.* Washington, D.C.: GPO, 1950.

U.S. Department of State. *American Foreign Policy, 1950-1955: Basic Documents.* 2 vols. Washington, D.C.: GPO, 1957.

____*Department of State Bulletin,* 1940-1950.

____*FRUS (Foreign Relations of the United States) 1939.* Vol. 3: *The Far East.* Washington, D.C.: GPO, 1955.

____*FRUS 1940.* Vol. 4: *The Far East.* Washington, D.C.: GPO, 1956.

____*FRUS 1941.* Vol. 5: *The Far East.* Washington, D.C.: GPO, 1956.

____*FRUS: The Conferences at Washington, 1941-1942 and Casablanca, 1943.* Washington, D.C.: GPO, 1968.

____*FRUS 1942.* Vol. 1: *General: The British Commonwealth; The Far East.* Washington, D.C.: GPO, 1960.

    Vol. 2: *Europe.* Washington, D.C.: GPO, 1960.

    Vol. 3: *Europe.* Washington, D.C.: GPO, 1961.

    *China.* Washington, D.C.: GPO, 1956.

____*FRUS: The Conferences at Cairo and Teheran, 1943.* Washington, D.C.: GPO, 1961.

____*FRUS 1943.* Vol. 3: *The British Commonwealth; Eastern Europe; The Far East.* Washington, D.C.: GPO, 1953.

    *China.* Washington, D.C.: GPO, 1957.

____*FRUS: Conference at Quebec, 1944.* Washington, D.C.: GPO, 1972.

____*FRUS 1944.* Vol. 3: *The British Commonwealth; Europe.* Washington, D.C.: GPO, 1965.

    Vol. 5: *The Near East; South Asia and Africa; The Far East.* Washington, D.C.: GPO, 1965.

    Vol. 6: *China.* Washington, D.C.: GPO, 1967.

____*FRUS: The Conferences At Malta and Yalta.* Washington, D.C.: GPO, 1955.

____*FRUS: The Conference of Berlin (The Potsdam Conference), 1945.* Washington, D.C.: GPO, 1960.

____*FRUS 1945.* Vol. 1: *General: The United Nations.* Washington, D.C.: GPO, 1967.

    Vol. 4: *Europe.* Washington, D.C.: GPO, 1968.

    Vol. 6: *The British Commonwealth; The Far East.* Washington, D.C.: GPO, 1969.

Vol. 7: *The Far East; China.* Washington, D.C.: GPO, 1969.

___*FRUS 1946.* Vol 5: *The British Commonwealth; Western and Central Europe.* Washington, D.C.: GPO, 1969.

Vol 8: *The Far East.* Washington, D.C.: GPO, 1971.

Vols 9 and 10. *The Far East: China.* Washington, D.C.: GPO, 1972.

___*FRUS 1947.* Vol. 6: *The Far East.* Washington, D.C.: GPO, 1972.

Vol 7: *The Far East: China.* Washington, D.C.: GPO, 1972.

___*FRUS 1948.* Vol. 6: *The Far East and Australia.* Washington, D.C.: GPO, 1974.

___*FRUS 1949.* Vol. 7: *The Far East and Australia.* Washington, D.C.: GPO, 1975.

___*FRUS 1950.* Vol. 6: *East Asia and the Pacific.* Washington, D.C.: GPO, 1976.

___*Papers Relating to the Foreign Relations of the United States: Japan, 1931-1941.* 2 vols. Washington, D.C.: GPO, 1943.

U.S. House. CAS (Committee on Armed Services), *United States–Vietnam Relations, 1945-1967* (U.S. Dept. of Defense Study). 12 vols. Washington, D.C.: GPO, 1971.

U.S. Senate CFR (Committee on Foreign Relations). *Hearings on the Causes, Origins, and Lessons of the Vietnam War.* 92d Cong., 2d Sess., May 9-12, 1972. Washington, D.C.: GPO, 1973.

___*The United States and Vietnam, 1944-1947.* Washington, D.C.: GPO, 1972.

Viorst, Milton. *Hostile Allies: FDR and Charles de Gaulle.* New York: Macmillan, 1965.

*Washington Post,* 1940-1950.

Watt, D.C. "Britain and the Cold War in the Far East, 1945-58." In Yonosuka Nagai and Akira Iriye, eds,. *The Origins of the Cold War in Asia,* pp. 89-122. New York: Columbia University Press, 1977.

Wehl, David. *The Birth of Indonesia.* London: Allen and Unwin, 1948.

Weigley, Russell F. "The Role of the War Department and the Army." In Dorothy Borg and Shumpei Okamoto, eds., *Pearl Harbor as History; Japanese-American Relations, 1931-1941,* pp. 165-188. New York: Columbia University Press, 1973.

Welles, Sumner. *The Time for Decision.* New York: Harper, 1944.

Wheeler, Gerald E. "Manual Quezon and the American Presidents." *Asian Studies* (1964), 2:231-246.

White, David H. "The United States and Indochina, 1942-1945." Ph.D. dissertation, Tulane University, 1974.

White, David H. "The American Perspective on Indochina: The Department of State, 1942-1945." Presented at American Historical Association Meeting, San Francisco, 1978.

White, Theodore. *The Stilwell Papers.* New York: Duell, Sloan and Pearce, 1947.

Wilkins, Mira. *The Making of Multinational Enterprise: American Business*

*Abroad from 1914 to 1970.* Cambridge: Harvard University Press, 1974.

Wilson, David A. "Thailand." In George McT. Kahin, ed., *Governments and Politics of Southeast Asia,* pp. 3-72. Ithaca: Cornell University Press, 1964.

Wilson, Theodore A. *The First Summit: Roosevelt and Churchill at Placentia Bay 1941.* Boston: Houghton Mifflin, 1969.

Wolf, Charles, Jr. *The Indonesian Story: The Birth, Growth, and Structure of the Indonesion Republic.* New York: Day, 1948.

Wolthuis, Robert K. "United States Foreign Policy towards the Netherlands Indies, 1937-1945." Ph.D. dissertation, Johns Hopkins University, 1968.

Woodward, Sir Ernest Llewelyn. *British Foreign Policy in the Second World War.* London: HMSO, 1971.

Wurfel, David. "The Bell Report and After: A Study of the Political Problems of Social Reform Stimulated by Foreign Aid." Ph.D. dissertation, Cornell University, 1960.

Wurfel, David. "Philippines." In George McT. Kahin, ed., *Governments and Politics of Southeast Asia,* pp. 679-762. Ithica: Cornell University Press, 1964.

Wurfel, David. "Problems of Decolonization." In Frank H. Golay, ed., *The United States and the Philippines.* Englewood Cliffs, N.J.: Prentice-Hall, 1966.

Wurfel, Violet. "American Implementation of Philippine Independence." M.A. thesis, University of Virginia, 1951.

Yoshihiko, Tanigawa. "The Cominform and Southeast Asia." In Yonosuka Nagai and Akira Iriye, eds., *The Origins of the Cold War in Asia,* pp. 362-377. New York: Columbia University Press, 1977.

Young, Kenneth. "The Special Role of American Advisers in Thailand, 1902-1949," *Asia,* (1969), 14:1-31.

Young, Lowell. "Franklin D. Roosevelt and Imperialism." Ph.D. dissertation, University of Virginia, 1970.

# Index

**441**